Believed-In Imaginings

Believed-In Imaginings

The Narrative Construction of Reality

Edited by
Joseph de Rivera and Theodore R. Sarbin

American Psychological Association
Washington, DC

Copyright © 1998 by the American Psychological Association. All rights reserved.
Except as permitted under the United States Copyright Act of 1976, no part of this
publication may be reproduced or distributed in any form or by any means, or stored
in a database or retrieval system, without the prior written permission of the
publisher.

Published by
American Psychological Association
750 First Street, NE
Washington, DC 20002

Copies may be ordered from
APA Order Department
P.O. Box 92984
Washington, DC 20090-2984

In the U.K., Europe, Africa, and the Middle East, copies may be ordered from
American Psychological Association
3 Henrietta Street
Covent Garden, London
WC2E 8LU England

Typeset in Goudy by EPS Group Inc., Easton, MD

Printer: Data Reproductions Corporation, Auburn Hills, MI
Cover Designer: Minker Design, Bethesda, MD
Technical/Production Editor: Catherine R. W. Hudson

Library of Congress Cataloging-in-Publication Data
Believed-in imaginings : the narrative construction of reality / edited by
    Joseph de Rivera, Theodore R. Sarbin. — 1st ed.
        p. cm.
    Papers presented at a conference held at Clark University, Worcester, Mass.,
May 24–25, 1997.
    Includes bibliographical references and index.
    ISBN 1-55798-521-9 (hardcover; acid-free paper)
    1. Imagination. 2. Imagination—Social aspects. 3. Memory.
4. Memory–Social aspects. 5. Delusions. 6. Delusions—Social aspects.
I. de Rivera, Joseph. II. Sarbin, Theodore R.
BF408.B39   1998
153.3—dc21   98-17312
                                                                   CIP

British Library Cataloguing-in-Publication Data
A CIP record is available from the British Library.

Printed in the United States of America
First Edition

CONTENTS

CONTRIBUTORS

Cindy Dell Clark is visiting scholar in the Psychology Department of the University of Pennsylvania. She is the author of *Flights of Fancy, Leaps of Faith*.

Joseph de Rivera is professor of psychology at Clark University and the author of *A Structural Theory of Emotion* and many articles on emotions and the influence of emotion. He is also the editor of *Field Theory as Human Science* and other books and journal articles dealing with the nature of human experience.

Richard J. Gerrig is associate professor of psychology at State University of New York, Stonybrook and is the author of *Experiencing Narrative Worlds*.

Janice Haaken is professor of psychology at Portland State University and is a clinical psychologist in private practice in Portland, OR. She is the author of the forthcoming *Pillar of Salt: Gender, Memory, and the Perils of Looking Back*.

Michael Kenny is professor of anthropology at Simon Fraser University and is the author of *The Passion of Ansel Bourne*.

Irving Kirsch is professor of psychology at the University of Connecticut and is the author of *Changing Expectations: A Key to Effective Psychotherapy*.

Timothy Lock is a graduate student in clinical psychology at Binghamton University, State University of New York. He has published and presented papers in the areas of hypnosis, memory, and sexual assault.

Elizabeth F. Loftus is professor of psychology at the University of Washington and is currently president of the American Psychological Society. She is the author of *The Myth of Repressed Memory*.

Steven Jay Lynn is professor of psychology at Binghamton University, State University of New York and has nearly 200 publications in the areas of hypnosis, memory, child abuse, and psychopathology. He is a former president of the American Psychological Association Division of Psychological Hypnosis and serves on the editorial board of numerous scientific journals.

Lisa Marmelstein is a graduate student in clinical psychology at Binghamton University, State University of New York. She has published and presented papers in the areas of hypnosis, psychological interviewing, and sexual assault.

Giuliana A. L. Mazzoni is a professor at the University of Florence, Italy and is visiting scholar at the University of Washington, Seattle.

Jill G. Morawski is professor of psychology and women's studies at Wesleyan University and is the author of *Practicing Feminisms, Reconstituting Psychology: Notes on a Liminal Science.*

Bradford H. Pillow is assistant professor of psychology at Northern Illinois University. His research focuses on the development of metacognition and social cognition during childhood.

Judith Pintar is a PhD candidate at the University of Illinois at Urbana-Champaign. She is the author of *The Halved Soul: Retelling the Myths of Romantic Love.*

Theodore R. Sarbin is emeritus professor of psychology and criminology at the University of California, Santa Cruz. He is the author of *Narrative Psychology: The Storied Nature of Human Conduct,* coauthor of *Hypnosis: The Social Psychology of Influence Communication,* and author of many publications dealing with emotional life, metaphor, and identity.

Karl E. Scheibe is professor of psychology at Wesleyan University and is the author of *Mirrors, Masks, Lies, and Secrets.*

Donald P. Spence is clinical professor of psychiatry at the Robert Wood Johnson School of Medicine. He is best known for his ground breaking book *Narrative Truth and Historical Truth.*

Jane Stafford is a graduate student in clinical psychology at Binghamton University, State University of New York. She has published and presented papers in the areas of posttraumatic stress disorder, hypnosis, and sexual assault.

Jeffrey S. Victor is associate professor of sociology at State University of New York, Jamestown and is the author of *Satanic Panic: The Creation of a Contemporary Legend.*

Penelope G. Vinden is assistant professor of psychology at Clark University and has published a number of articles on children's understanding of mind in a variety of cultures in Cameroon, Papua, New Guinea, and Peru.

Morton Wiener is emeritus professor of clinical psychology, Clark University and is the author of many papers dealing with epistemological and ontological aspects of clinical issues. He is the coeditor of *What Is Schizophrenia?*

PREFACE

The seed of this book was planted some 6 years ago. One of us (JdR) had experienced the pain of a family member constructing a belief (later relinquished) on the basis of a "recovered memory" of child abuse. This occurred at a time when hundreds of bewildered families were reporting similar experiences in which beliefs that were based on recovered memories were central to transforming the identity of the person claiming the abuse. Such transformations of identity were instrumental in disrupting family relationships. Troubled by the experience and alarmed by the increasing numbers of reports, he consulted Dr. Sarbin because of his work on the construction of identity.

Immediately interested, Sarbin grasped the tragic dimension of the problem and hypothesized that the genesis of erroneous memories could be understood by applying the narrative approach that he had employed in interpreting the counterfactual accounts often rendered by hypnosis patients. Going beyond the scientific and jurisprudential issues surrounding the recovered memory controversy, we formulated the problem in more general terms: What are the social and psychological processes that facilitate (a) the construction of beliefs and (b) the repudiation of previously held beliefs?

Both of us have had a long-standing interest in the various manifestations of the "believed-in imaginings" that are the subject of this book. My interest has grown out of my immersion in the work of Kurt Lewin and his students. Particularly relevant is Lewin's postulation that irrational behavior occurs when tension weakens the boundary that ordinarily separates fantasy from reality. Sarbin's work in hypnosis and role theory has frequently noted that people often engage in action on the basis of imaginings to which they assign the same degree of credibility as they do to perceptions of the "real" world.

Convinced of the importance of the topic, and eager to open up the discussion to our colleagues, we approached the Hiatt School of Psychology at Clark University for funds to support a 2-day conference on the broad topic of believed-in imaginings. Held in May 1997, the conference provided the basis for the current volume.

We are grateful for the generous support tendered by the Frances L. Hiatt School of Psychology for this conference and for a related conference held in 1993 on trauma and memory. We acknowledge with gratitude the readiness of the contributors to rewrite their conference papers for inclusion in this book. We also make note of the invaluable support of Joyce Lee, able secretary of the Hiatt School, as well as of the encouragement and wise counsel of Deborah de Rivera and the late Genevieve Sarbin.

Believed-In Imaginings

INTRODUCTION

JOSEPH DE RIVERA AND THEODORE R. SARBIN

When we study other cultures or "fringe" groups in contemporary society, or even our own history, we find beliefs that seem implausible to us. The Aztec's offering of thousands of human hearts to feed the sun, the burning of witches during the middle ages, the hundreds of recent reports of abductions by extraterrestrial aliens are but a few examples of behavior that is based on beliefs that seem strange to us and to demand some sort of psychological explanation. The ability to imagine is a fact of life. On occasion we can playfully behave "as if" an imagining were true. What excites our interest is a master question: What are the conditions that influence a person to assign credibility to imagining? The answer seems crucial, not only for clinical and social psychology, but also for the dialogue between clinical and scientific psychologists, for the legal system, and for the judgments required by citizens in a democracy.

"Believed-in imaginings" is a challenging phrase. The very concept is a battle cry of scholars wielding the weapon of social constructionism against those psychiatric and psychological theorists and clinicians who, together with a large segment of the public, believe in the reality of auras, dissociation, facilitated communication, past-life regression, retrieving repressed memories, and other controversial concepts and practices. The construction "believed-in imaginings" departs from the romanticism of feelings and beckons us to return to our pragmatic senses.

It is an important psychological observation that people can assign unconditional credibility to what is, in fact, only imagined. In this book, Lynn, Pintar, Stafford, Marmelstein, and Lock; Kirsch; and Mazzoni and Loftus all explore this theme from an experimental perspective, whereas de Rivera and Victor detail some of the interpersonal and societal conditions that foster the personally destructive consequences of believing in what is imagined from their respective empirically grounded work. However, this book goes far beyond a skeptical inquiry into the foibles of human nature. It inquires into the conditions under which we human beings are led astray, it examines when believed-in imaginings may be important for humans to encourage, how some may be more authentic than others, whether it is or is not possible to distinguish believed-in imaginings from other narratives, whether we are doomed to a nihilistic relativism or may legitimately search for some Reality. Hence, we hope this book will not only appeal to social scientists and skeptical inquirers, but also will be of use to practicing clinicians and intriguing to both social theorists and the educated public.

An important strength of this work is that its authors manage to bridge the gaps that often exist between the theoretical and the empirical, and between "scientific" and "clinical" psychology. This bridge makes it difficult to find appropriate labels for the sections around which the book is organized. Somewhat arbitrarily, we have sorted the chapters into four groups: (a) defining believed-in imaginings, (b) developmental issues, (c) creating interpersonal narratives, and (d) the social significance of believed-in imaginings. The defining chapters focus on the *concept* of believed-in imagining and whether the concept is viable in the sense that one can distinguish between narratives based on "facts" and narratives that are patently fictional. Chapters in the developmental section examine the concept from the perspective of social scientists who are familiar with the literature on how children and societies develop distinctions between "fantasy" and "reality." These more theoretical sections are followed by a set of four empirical chapters that focus on the interpersonal processes that lead individuals to give credence to what is only imagined. The fourth section contains chapters that focus on the social significance and the social and historical conditions that promoted specific imaginings that came to be believed. Two final chapters articulate the central conceptual argument and the agreements and disagreements with that argument.

DEFINING BELIEVED-IN IMAGININGS

In chapter 1, Sarbin argues that what we imagine is not a "mental picture" but a story—an "as if" narrative—that can be used to organize our experience. He argues that *believing* such a narrative is simply assigning it a high value, and that the "reality" of a narrative corresponds to the degree to which one is involved. At the highest level of involvement the actor interprets imaginings as being equivalent to perceptions and drops "as if" qualifiers to speak in terms of truth and reality. As examples, he considers cases of false memory, hallucination, mediumism, and religious experience, showing how the accounts of such experiences can be comprehended in terms of people placing high value on their self-involving narratives.

Although Sarbin explicitly states there is no way to distinguish the contents of believings from the contents of an imagining, and dismisses "reality" as a rhetorical construction, he operates from the postulate that we begin our inquiries from an actual world of occurrences. Thus, narratives may contain "facts" that are not largely imaginings. By contrast, in chapter 2, Wiener argues that there is no way to distinguish between narratives that are "believed-in imaginings" and narratives that are "true" accounts. Of course, as actors in this world, we are continually forced to make distinctions and to accept some narratives as credible and others as imaginings. We try to defend these decisions in terms of logical consistency, consensuality, pragmatism, authority, and so on. However, we can never be sure we are not simply involved in our own personal or cultural imagining. Moreover, when we hear another person's narrative—when we are in the role of a third person—as all practicing clinicians are, Wiener argues that we *should* simply accept narratives as narratives without in any way declaring a judgment on the "reality" or "truth value" of the narrative. Wiener argues that the clients' believed-in imaginings—whether labeled by others as hallucinations, delusions, or false memories should be accepted at face value.

Taking yet another perspective, Scheibe argues in chapter 3 that there *is* such a thing as an *authentic* work of art, dramatic production, narrative, but that such authenticity is becoming increasingly difficult to recognize when we live in a world of imitations and replicas. He points out that believed-in imaginings appear authoritative within their particular dramatic frame and that it is only when we step outside that dramatic frame that we can recognize the phenomena of believed-in imagining. Thus, the authenticity of narrative depends on the wider frame in which the imagining is constructed. Our contemporary world is becoming increasingly dominated by replicas and imitations that blunt living memory, making it more difficult to resolve questions of authenticity. While granting the importance of pragmatic tests, Scheibe argues that they are limited and overrated. His arguments suggest that human beings are simply better at believing than seeing.

THE DEVELOPMENTAL ISSUES

Although Western children soon develop distinctions between pretending, appearances, and reality, Vinden (chapter 4) questions whether this is universal. In many cultures, a distinction is *not* drawn between a "believed-in" spiritual world and an empirical world of fact. How then are we to navigate between the nihilism of postmodern deconstructionism and the fanaticism of true believers? Vinden argues that the very idea of different perspectives still assumes a real world that people are interpreting from different perspectives and that narrative *can* be objective and about that world. Furthermore, she argues that we humans need a world view, a meta-narrative, in order to give meaning to our lives. Such a narrative must transcend the split between spiritual and empirical reality that currently besets us.

Clark (chapter 5) also views imaginings with anthropologically trained eyes, focusing on the important role they play in children's lives. She builds on Winnicott's ideas of transitional objects and spaces to argue that imaginings have a definite type of reality. Clark shows how children gain security by using their imagination to create magical beings and charms that transform medical procedures. She asserts that the empirically oriented medical establishment might do well to encourage, or at least respect, how believed-in imaginings help children cope with chronic illness.

Do we have to suspend disbelief in order to enter the world of a narrative? Gerrig and Pillow argue that, to the contrary, we have a set to believe stories unless we make an effort to disbelieve. In chapter 5, they review the literature on how children learn to distinguish between imagination and reality. They present evidence that suggests that adults are just as susceptible to believing in the reality of events that are imagined. They postulate that in *both* children and adults imagination exerts its power because the emotional *products* of imagination affect judgments of reality. These consequences occur unless special circumstances inhibit our inclination to be transported into the world of imagined narratives.

CREATING INTERPERSONAL NARRATIVES

That humans assign credibility to imaginings is most clearly demonstrated in the experimental chapters in this section of the book. The chapter by Lynn, Pintar, Stafford, Marmelstein, and Lock (chapter 7) is a tour de force. Lynn and his colleagues give illustrative clinical cases and then provide data to show that "normal" participants in experiments are so familiar with narratives of UFO abductions, satanic abuse, and dissociative disorder that they know how to enact these roles without being instructed. When asked to pretend mental illness their participants "de-repressed memories" of traumatic experiences and filled in memory gaps with imaginative constructions. The investigators review the data showing that hypnosis results in pseudomemories and they then show that other suggestive techniques also result in pseudomemories. Even subtle suggestions (e.g.,

"Tell me when you get an earlier memory") appear to double the amount of pseudomemories and demonstrate that by encouraging participants to "let themselves go" and reinforcing their report, 78% of their participants could be led to report memories that occurred well below the age of infant amnesia. The chapter concludes with a theoretical discussion of the genesis of dissociative identity disorder. They argue that the narrative of a split identity is more likely to occur when people have suffered an abusive childhood but is not grounded in defensive dissociative processes. Rather, there has been a disruption in social roles and relationships so that the person cannot create a shared social narrative. People who are fantasy prone have more dissociative symptoms, and if such people also have an abuse history and a therapist who suggests that alters may emerge, it is easy to see how a person could enact "multiple" identities.

Chapter 8, by Mazzoni and Loftus is an answer to those who believe that the experimental findings from the laboratory cannot really be applied to what happens in the clinician's office. The authors report a series of studies that focused on investigating how dream interpretation may be used to influence memories. The first studies simply show how people can believe that the experimenters had shown them words that were, in fact, taken from reports of their own dreams. The latter studies mimic clinical engagements. Participants in one study bring a dream to a "clinician" who interprets the dream (regardless of content) as suggesting a forgotten experience. The investigators are able to show that many of the participants believe that the "forgotten" experiences actually occurred. In other words, a short (30-minute) dream interpretation session changed participants' beliefs about their own past.

Kirsch (chapter 9) argues that the experience of willing an action is highly problematic. Those who work with hypnosis are often intrigued by how participants experience their own behavior as being unintentional. Thus, participants who are asked to imagine a balloon that is tugging the arm upward "find" the arm raising under the imagined balloon's pull. Investigators of "facilitated communication" have suggested a variant on this phenomenon that has had disturbing consequences. Many people have been led to believe that autistic children have an inner life that they can communicate if their communication is facilitated by someone who is trained to give them emotional support by gently holding their arms as they type messages. Facilitators "find" that the autistic child communicates meaningful messages in spite of the fact that investigators have shown that the messages are actually coming from the facilitator. The autistic child is perceived as "willing" a message that is actually coming from the self of the facilitator. Kirsch shows that *all* of the participants in his studies (college students) came to believe that another person is communicating messages that are actually coming from themselves! That is, under the conditions he establishes, *all* of his participants are successfully led to a believed-in imagining. He goes on to argue that our perception of having willed any behavior is a believed-in imagining.

In chapter 10, de Rivera examines how 56 persons attempt to explain why they developed what has been termed "false memory syndrome." About a third of the participants endorsed what might be termed a "self-narrative" account. These people now believe that they used their imagination to create stories that were believed because they helped explain behavioral problems, gained sympathy, and provided relief from demands for perfection. Participants who endorsed a "role-enactment" account were likely to have participated in groups of survivors and been aware of receiving *attention* (rather than sympathy) for the role they were enacting. At least some experienced themselves as choosing to try on the survivor role and then becoming overinvolved in that role. However, a majority of the participants endorsed a "mind-control" account. They reported that their therapists undermined their self-confidence and *insisted* that they had been abused. That is, they now believe that the story they had believed was actually imagined by their therapists rather than themselves. They state that they were "trapped" in therapy, with many reporting they were told that they would become insane if they left. Their descriptions make it clear how intelligent, normal people can be led into believing contrafactual imaginings. During the course of therapy, 29 of the participants were diagnosed with multiple personality disorder, and many came to believe they were the victims of satanic abuse and, hence, provide concrete examples of what Victor (below) calls "ostension" of that contemporary legend.

THE SOCIAL SIGNIFICANCE OF BELIEVED-IN IMAGININGS

The witch hunts that disturbed medieval Europe (and are still occurring today in Africa) and the "Red Scare" of the 1950s are examples of collective beliefs in imagined dangers. In chapter 11, Victor analyzes the conditions and processes that lead to such believing in imagined dangers. He delineates the characteristics of such "moral panics" and relates them to "contemporary legends." He then demonstrates that the collective belief in satanic ritual abuse (SRA) is a typical moral panic that began with the publication of *Michelle Remembers* in 1980. Victor shows that the spread of the SRA panic can best be accounted for by an interest group model. He argues that the social authority to interpret deviant behavior has shifted from religious and political to medical and mental health authorities, and he shows how the latter group was inevitably drawn into the forefront of detecting child sexual abuse. These specialists functioned as an interest group that struggled to gain greater recongition and respect within their larger community of professionals. Their claims to have recovered memories of SRA lent credibility to the imaginings. *Ostension*, the process of appropriating a role from a contemporary legend, may have contributed to many patients coming to believe that they were victims, and the mass media publicized these accounts. Finally, Victor argues that moral panics always involve a "demonology" that functions as a master frame for interpreting possible threats to moral values. In the case at hand, he shows how SRA resonated with the demonologies of two particular groups (Christian traditionalists and feminists) and spread most rapidly through their social networks.

In chapter 12, Spence discusses "treatment narratives" and the practices that accompany them. He points out that the professional is often confronted with telling a story that strikes a balance between capturing facts and meeting a client's expectations. Professional practices such as bleeding, the hyperoxygenation of premature infants, and prescriptions of rest for those with stomach ulcers were all based on fashionable treatment stories that normalized complaints, removed uncertainty, and satisfied the need for explanation. Yet how are we to account for the preposterous "grassroots" stories that so many people believe in the absence of confirming evidence, believed-in imaginings that become part of everyday reality in dictating treatment reimbursement, training in techniques, and grant support? Spence argues that human beings do not tolerate the absence of explanation, and they construct irrational accounts when compelling explanations are not available. Furthermore, constructed accounts meet a number of other important psychological needs They provide excitement and a distraction from the unbearable complexity of modern existence, and, Spence conjectures, we may need a certain level of mystery that defies scientific explanation. They provide a new identity for the victims of circumstance, an identity that allows victims to become authorities—because the truth of the story relies solely on the narrator's personal experience— and permits them to escape from the aloneness and insignificance of contemporary life. This chapter is an excellent psychological companion piece to Victor's sociological account.

Morawski (chapter 13) shows how physicians encouraged couples to believe that an infertile husband was the biological father of a child conceived from the sperm of a donor. Our understanding of men's and women's parallel contributions to reproduction is a surprisingly modern one: Not until the mid-19th century did scientists discover that both sperm and egg contribute equally to creating an embryo and, ultimately, an offspring. Prior to this discovery, cultural imaginings about parentage were all that sustained knowledge of shared paternity. This chapter examines a residue of such imaginings about reproduction by tracing the beliefs and practices of artificial insemination by donor sperm. Morawski proposes that believing the "natural" parentage of an offspring was a marital partnership—rather than a donor—was sustained not only by the earnest role taking of the parents, but also through professional influence and scientific ritual. The production and maintenance of this imagining required ongoing practices of collective suppression and deception by physicians, parents, and psychological experts alike. In doing so, medical and psychological experts encouraged couples to engage in an imagining of—an imagining that contradicted scientific fact. The extent to which these imaginings constituted true belief or social collusion is considered, as are the reasons for the sudden abandonment of these practices in the 1970s.

In chapter 14, Haaken examines the believed-in imagining of multiple personalities. In contrast to Lynn et al., who examine the conditions that may lead individual clients to enact multiple personalities, Haaken examines the sociocultural conditions that support such enactments. On the one hand, she argues that the hidden selves of the dissociated patient are analogous to, and represent, the private selves of women that have no other public voice. The narrative of multiple personalities permits an unleashing of the feminine imagination, a rebellious expression of prohibited aggression and sexuality, a perfect metaphor for the conflicts between Madonna and whore, entitlement and helplessness, opportunity and captivity. On the other hand, Haaken argues that the resolution of these actual conflicts is betrayed by a therapeutic construction of multiplicity that itself reflects conflicts within the field of psychiatry and within individual therapists. Within psychiatry, the narrative of trauma-based dissociation provided a scientific rationale for therapeutic procedures that were not based on drugs. Haaken describes the relationship between Sybil and her mother-like therapist and suggests that the sadistic memories retrieved by many patients may be fantasies that symbolize their therapist's aggressive treatment procedures.

Kenny (chapter 15) examines the concept of catharsis and traces its history from Aristotle's initial observations through Freud's beliefs and into contemporary clinical thought. Central to Kenny's inquiry is the role of emotional expression. As an anthropologist, he is sensitive to the crucial role emotional expression plays in ritual processes that help people to identity transformations. However, as a cultural historian, he is skeptical of social constructions that pose as realities when they appear, in fact, to be believed-in imaginings. The display of emotion is taken to be evidence that a traumatic memory has surfaced; the absence of emotional display may be used as an argument for alexithymia and the repression of a traumatic memory. Placed in historical perspective, the concept of passion as a guardian of the authenticity of a remembering is an example of therapists assigning credibility to their imaginings.

CONTRASTING AGREEMENTS

The final section consists of two chapters. In the first, Sarbin reviews the preceding chapters by commenting on three constructs that are repeatedly used: truth, emotion, and reality. He argues that all three are fundamentally poetic in their very nature. They are believed-in imaginings. Although in many respects de Rivera agrees with Sarbin's position, in the last chapter he argues that the concept is necessary but not sufficient. It is necessary because we do construct reality; it is never given to us. It is not sufficient because we cannot simply construct Reality but must also behave within reality. The various religions attempt to grasp this Reality, and de Rivera argues further that we must have some way of evaluating the poetic constructions they offer because we cannot simply tell stories about Reality but must act in relationship to Reality.

I

DEFINING BELIEVED-IN IMAGININGS

1

BELIEVED-IN IMAGININGS:
A NARRATIVE APPROACH

THEODORE R. SARBIN

This chapter is written from the perspective that the narrative is an organizing principle for contemporary psychology. I have made the claim for a narrative principle previously (Sarbin, 1986, 1989, 1990, 1993, 1997)—the readiness of human beings both to organize their experience and to interpret their social lives according to narrative plots. The grounds for my claims are common experiences. Our fantasies and daydreams are storied. Our night dreams are experienced as stories, often with mythic undertones. Rituals of daily life are organized to tell stories. The pageants of special occasions are fashioned along story lines. The plans we make, our rememberings, even our loving and hating, are all guided by narrative plots. Survival in a world of meanings would be problematic in the absence of skill to make up and to interpret stories about interweaving lives.

From this perspective, I examine the terms *imagination* and *belief*, terms that appear to have an assured place in the lexicon of psychology.

Prepared for the Conference on Believed-In Imaginings held at Clark University, Worcester, MA, May 24 and 25, 1997. The formulations are revised and updated from an earlier set of papers (Sarbin, 1967, 1972; Sarbin and Juhasz, 1967, 1970, 1975). I am grateful to Ralph M. Carney, Gerald P. Ginsburg, Joseph B. Juhasz, John I. Kitsuse, and Karl E. Scheibe for stimulating discussions that helped me round out the text.

To the unreflective user, the referents for these words are those that denote happenings in the mental apparatus. To understand how and why people assign credibility to imaginings, and to more completely understand the phenomenon of believed-in imaginings, it is helpful to undertake a historical and linguistic analysis that unpacks the meanings of these terms. I begin by sketching several reference narratives that exemplify the concept of believed-in imaginings.

Mrs. Jones, a 38-year-old office worker, distraught and concerned about her inability to control her weight and also her inability to cope with an indifferent husband, a tyrannical employer, and two problem teen-agers, consulted a psychotherapist. After she was diagnosed as anxious, depressed, and having an eating disorder, the therapist inquired if she had been the victim of child abuse. When she replied that she had no such memories, the therapist told her that her particular symptoms were indicative of the repression of memories of abuse. He outlined a simplistic account of the repression concept and urged Mrs. Jones to try to recover childhood memories of abuse. He also recommended a book on recovered memory therapy. Subsequently, Mrs. Jones reported memories of being abused by her father when she was 3 or 4 years of age. At first the reported memories were vague, but, as the therapy continued, she recounted her victimization in great detail. When Mrs. Jones confronted her father, he vehemently denied the accusation. She broke off all relations with him and also with her mother and sisters who declared that the accusation against the father was false. After almost 2 years of therapy, Mrs. Jones's adjustment problems were more acute than before. On the advice of a close friend, she discontinued her relationship with the therapist and sought help from a second therapist who was not an advocate of the repression doctrine. In the course of working with the second therapist, she realized that she had had no clear-cut memories of abuse, but on the prompting of the first therapist she had been able to imagine what it would be like to be a victim of abuse.

A second reference case is one that belongs to a large class of stories that mental health professionals identify as hallucinations. A typical story is that of an aging, retired postal worker, disabled by severe arthritis, who claimed to have frequent visits from St. Margaret and St. Theresa and to engage in conversations with them. His claim was made with great conviction. He was a widower, and his grown children lived in other parts of the country. He had been a devout Catholic and had attended worship services regularly. To imagine conversations with long-dead religious figures is one thing; to act as if the imaginings had the warrant of veridical perception is another.

A third reference case is the much-discussed story of the 39 men and women who took their lives as part of the Heaven's Gate religious movement. The information provided by former members of the group, by the coroner, and by police investigators makes clear that the members shared an imaginatively constructed cosmological story in which they would rid themselves of their mortal coils and advance to a higher stage of development on a distant planet. As in the other reference cases, the members apparently transfigured their constructed imaginings to indubitable believings. There exist numerous other similarly illustrative narrative accounts, including those of young children's imaginary companions, people who claim to have been abducted by aliens, people who assign credibility to the millenium of Christian prophecy, individuals who participate in imaginary social worlds, and certain self-reports of hypnosis subjects who deny agency for their actions.

My avoidance of using the nouns *belief* and *imagination*, serves an important rhetorical purpose. Being substantive words, they lend themselves to reification. In the absence of critical analysis, they can connote mental objects, quasi-organs, or regions in a hypothetical mind-space. Such concrete construal reflects an adherence to a discredited mentalistic psychology that regarded the metaphorical mind as composed of discrete faculties with special powers. From a contemporary constructionist position, imaginings and believings are actions that serve human intentions and purposes. They refer to the *doings* of people rather than happenings in the mind. For this reason, I prefer the gerunds, *imagining* and *believing*, for denoting these active, constructive features of human conduct.

With this introduction, I turn first to a historico-linguistic analysis of the concept of imagination, showing how the concept was deformed to be consistent with mentalistic psychology. Second, I offer an alternative metaphor, *hypothetical instantiation*. Third, I discuss the concept of belief and make the case that the contents of those human actions we call believings have no independent status outside of imaginings. I also make the claim that assigning credibility to an imagining is an action in the service of sense-making to meet the demand for a consistent self-narrative. I conclude with a discussion of the contexts that promote the assignment of credibility to imaginings.

A LINGUISTIC ANALYSIS OF IMAGININGS

The commonly held view of imaginings as pictures-in-the-mind is a premise developed from Cartesian dualism. Such a construction was supportable when the requirements of logic and science were less stringent than they are today. To regard imagining as a process taking place on the shadowy stage of the mind or in the photographic laboratory of the psyche is to affirm a demonstrably futile model of human conduct. My review of theories and research that were designed to clarify the concept of imagining has made one fact abundantly clear: The model of pictures-in-the-mind has produced virtually nothing in the way of pragmatically useful or heuristically exciting propositions.

According to the *Oxford English Dictionary*, the etymological root of *imagining, imago*, was derived from *imitari*, a form that gave rise to our current word, *imitate*. The root form *imago*, as well as *imitari* and other cognates, denoted imitating, that is, copying, through fashioning three-dimensional forms such as a carved likeness, a sculptured statue, or a graven image. On the basis of partial similarity between events ordinarily denoted by *imitari* and the copying activities of artisans, the root form of imitate, *imago*, was borrowed to denote the latter. Until the 16-century use of *imago* and its cognates denoted the active construction of three-dimensional imitations. That is to say, the pre-Renaissance imaginer was regarded as a fashioner, an image maker, a fabricator, a doer. The implication that the imaginer was a passive registrant of a mysterious process happening in an equally mysterious mind evolved only when the Cartesian "mind" become the concept of choice to give philosophical credibility to the theological conception of "soul." Imagining, believing, and other private and silent actions not easily explained by concurrent rule-following theories were assigned to the mysterious domain of mind.

Of special interest to linguistic historians is the question, how did the metaphor of constructing three-dimensional images become transformed into pictures in the mind? Three-dimensional icons and optical images are similar in the sense that both are copies: One is obviously constructed through human action; the other appears just to happen. When the mind was conceptualized as being an internal organ, it was assigned the job formerly given to its more active predecessor, "minding," which included imagining along with thinking and remembering.

We can only speculate about the nature of the bridge between imagining as three-dimensional copying and imagining as mental pictures. In the distant past, a curious person looked into the eyes of a companion and beheld there a little child, a miniature, a pupil. (The locus of the reflection was later designated by the same word.) Unlike ordinary mirror images, the copy was miniaturized. In the absence of optical science, the tiny copy was assumed to lie somewhere behind the eye. Since the mind stuff could be anywhere within the body, the interiorized image could logically be located behind the eyeball, "in the mind." If a person reported "seeing" an absent object, and there was no reflection from the body's eye, then the "seen" copy had to be in the "mind's eye."

Although these speculations may not be confirmable, it is undeniable that a shift in metaphor occurred. After assigning images to the mind, the next step was the assimilation of imagining as active three-dimensional copying to an interiorized form of seeing. Our language is full of instances of this assimilation: "seeing in the mind's eye," "visualizing," "seeing mental pictures," "having a visual image," and so on. These everyday expressions are witness to the fact that we have been captivated by the unlabeled metaphor—we now talk (a) as if there are pictures (sometimes called impressions or representations) and (b) as if there are minds that, like art galleries, provide a place for displaying these pictures.

This assimilation of imagining to seeing is confounded by the different meanings of the verb *to see*. An equivalence is assumed when *to see* is used to denote ordinary seeing of objects in space and when it is employed in the special sense of "seeing in the mind's eye." The uncritical acceptance of this particular transformation has produced no fruitful suggestions for the psychological study of imaginings.

Before proceeding further, I point to an important distinction. Because of lack of precision in the use of vocabulary, the words *imagery* and *imaginings* are often used interchangeably. For my purposes, these terms have different referents. The study of imagery is the study of images, experiences that usually focus on optical and ocular phenomena, such as, for example, negative after-images. The typical study of imagery is about the responses of research participants to instructions of this kind: "visualize a three-inch cube." The verbalized introspections of the participants are the raw data for such a study. Imaginings, on the other hand, are narratives. The contents are sequences of actions in which self and others are involved—narratives with beginnings, middles, and endings. They are fashioned from concurrent perceptions of proximal and distal stimulus events, rememberings, bedtime stories, folktales, cultural myths, articulated theories, and experiences with art forms. In short, imaginings are storied constructions. (I have suggested resurrecting *poetics* as a replacement for *constructions*. *Poetics* more neatly reflects the making of stories, avoiding the architectural flavor of *constructions*.)

To recapitulate before presenting arguments to support the alternative notion that imaginings are poetical constructions: In the linguistic history of imagining as pictures in the mind, metaphysical developments brought about the construction of imagining as a mental activity, performed by a mythical organ, and resembling the seeing of spatial objects.

IMAGINING AS HYPOTHETICAL INSTANTIATION

Mentalism is not the only thought model available to students of silent and invisible processes. An alternate way of conceptualizing begins with guiding postulates quite different from those that influenced the conclusions of, among others, John Locke (1690/1924), who wrote "For in bare naked perception, the mind is, for the most part, only passive; and what it perceives, it cannot avoid perceiving" (p. 73). An alternative view construes human beings as active, exploring, manipulating, inventing, doing creatures. Within limits, human beings construct their worlds instead of being merely the envelopes of a passive mind and at the mercy of a capricious world.

Human beings demonstrate complex systems for acquiring and processing information and, most significantly, the skill to function at various levels of hypotheticalness. This skill makes it possible to distinguish between sentences of the form "I heard the voice" (ordinary perception), "It is as if I heard the voice" (imagining), and "I heard the voice of conscience" (metaphor). That is to say, a hierarchy of hypothesis-making, *as if* skills liberates human beings from the constraints of the immediate environment. With this skill the actor can interact with events that are spatially distant and temporally remote. By entertaining hypotheses, a person can relocate self in different times and places.

The pictures-in-the-mind metaphor collapses when somesthetic experience rather than distal events are imagined. The absurdity of the metaphor becomes apparent when we phrase the question: "What faculty of the mind would have to be activated in order to imagine the taste of French onion soup, the fragrance of a freshly cut gardenia, or the feel of cracker crumbs in bed?" The concept that I want to propose and defend is that of "hypothetical instantiation" (synonyms: suppositional instantiation, imitated perception, quasi-perception, pretend instantiation, *as if* or metaphorical instantiation). Broadly speaking, *instantiation* means to represent an abstraction by a concrete instance. In my view, the process by which this occurs is one in which people sort inputs as instances of epistemic classes. For example, a person registers visual inputs that might be identified as four rigid legs supporting a flat top, and interprets the inputs as an instance of the class of objects called tables. Thus, through instantiation human beings assume as concrete not only objects and events that are present in the world, but also those that are not. Hypothetical instantiation refers specifically to the act of instantiating *absent* objects and events. Such an act can occur only when the person has achieved skill in using fictions, a skill that follows from the acquisition of sign and symbol competences. These linguistic competences have been described by Vaihinger (1925) and by others as skill in using the *as if* grammatical form. As is outlined in the following paragraphs, the *as if* form leads to the formation of narrative plot structures.

A three-stage sequence of child development accounts for the achievement of the *as if* skill. As we know, the child acquires knowledge in a number of ways, one of which is imitation. In the developmental sequence, the first stage is the outright copying of performances of another person. This is the paradigm of imitation. That is to say, to imitate is to copy the actions of a model that can be seen and heard. In the second stage, a complexity is introduced. The child imitates the actions of another, but that other is absent. The child imitates the motions and the talk of the absent model. This is the paradigm of role-taking. It is a high-order achievement to pretend to be Daddy when Daddy is out of sight. A child may set up a tea table with limited stage props; she may pour fictional tea into ephemeral cups, and talk to an unoccupied chair holding an imaginary companion. The child's role-taking is integral to her current self-narrative. She is following a script with a beginning, a middle, and an end.

The third stage is concurrent with another achievement of early childhood: the muting of speech. To talk to oneself rather than aloud at first requires only the skill to control the volume of air that passes over the vocal cords. With practice, the child learns to inhibit most of the obvious muscular characteristics of speech. At the same time that the child acquires the skill in muting speech, he or she learns to attenuate the role-taking performance, to reduce the amplitude of the overt responses that comprise the "let's-pretend" roles. This third stage—muted and storied role-taking—is a referent for imagining. But, although I am using the pre-Renaissance version of the word to denote the active, constructive copying of absent models, in this case the products of such constructional activity are narratives rather than statues or carvings.

The parallel between the semiotic analysis sketched before and the three-stage development of skill in imagining is indeed striking. This three-stage development brings the construction of imagining back to its definition as active three-dimensional imitating, and displaces the Cartesian reification connoted by "seeing in the mind's eye." The words *skill* and *competence* are used intentionally to connote that *as if* behavior is subject to variation among individuals, and that it is acquired through commerce with people, things, and events. Skill in the present context takes on the same meaning as when employed with such modifiers as mechanical, verbal, or social. Competence is used here in similar fashion: It is not a mental state word, but a word that signifies ability or readiness to perform certain acts.

BELIEVINGS DEFINED

The challenges to Cartesian psychology have turned contemporary theorists away from the position that beliefs are quasi-objects residing in one's mind. It is now more common to refer to those constructions that serve as guides to action as expectancies, or, alternatively, believings. A continuing task for psychologists and philosophers is to determine what a person means when he or she prefaces a sentence with "I believe . . .". Two questions are frequently raised: (1) Can the act of believing be assigned to the same family of behaviors as seeing, hearing, and tasting? and (2) How does one determine the truth value of a particular believing? To the first query, phenomenological inquiry provides a ready answer: Believing is not in the same class of behaviors as seeing, hearing, and so on. These behaviors presuppose specific sense organs, and it would be absurd to postulate a sense organ for believing. The second query takes us deeply into the formidable and confusing task of trying to define Truth. The multireferentiality of truth is an almost insurmountable obstacle to a useful analysis. If there is merit to my claim that the contents of believings are the same as the contents of imaginings, then asking about the truth value of a particular believing is problematic.

Any linguistic study must take into account the historical contexts that enter into the process of forming meanings of words. A significant context has been the Judeo-Christian tradition in which the notion of belief was infused with the idea of religious faith. This particular conception of faith is complex and includes such notions as trust (a reciprocal relationship between the person and his or her God), fear (a response to the Uncertain and Unknowable), and obedience (follow God's rules or those of his or her earthly surrogates). Imaginings that are the sources of religious beliefs are most often stimulated by sacred stories, parables, sermons, and catechisms that have the imprimatur of authority.

If we can discover the defining attributes of belief by analyzing its use in religious contexts, then we may come closer to comprehending the conduct of our reference cases. That is to say, a person's reliance on religious faith in place of a pragmatic test of knowledge provides a model for the certainty that the people described in the reference narratives at the beginning of the chapter assigned to their believings, some of which may have been contrary to empirical fact. To supplement the concept of faith, theologians have for centuries put forth ontological and cosmological arguments to support the belief in the existence of God. Notwithstanding, men and women who ordinarily apply the laws of logic to everyday affairs are not likely to accept such arguments as *sufficient* to warrant their believings. The concept of faith removes any grounds for contradiction by a nonbeliever and makes impossible the use of traditional logic. The philosopher Alisdair MacIntyre offered a similar argument: "There is no logical transition which will take one from unbelief to belief. The transition is not in objective considerations at all, but in the person who comes to believe. There are no logical principles which will make the transition" (1957, p. 209).

To this point I have tried to make the case that the content of experiences identified as believings cannot be differentiated from the content of experiences identified as imaginings. It now remains to show how some imaginings become believings, that is, serve as guides to conduct. The following story will serve as a prologue to a discussion of how some poetic imaginings become identified as believings.

Two men were given copies of a book that recounted the adventures and espionage exploits of secret agents. For both readers, the contents of the book stimulated storied imaginings centered around the clandestine practice of transmitting government secrets. The first reader construed the book as a curious and entertaining thriller but irrelevant to his times or to his purposes. After reading the book, he put aside the imaginings stimulated by the prose and returned to his daily routines. The second reader became deeply engrossed in the imaginings generated by the text and transported himself into the world of espionage with its cover stories, dramatic escapes, clandestine meetings, and so on. He made contact with men who had identified themselves as Soviet agents. He asked that he be assigned a code name, Scorpio, and also that a still-to-be-recruited woman be assigned as his partner. The imaginings generated by the spy story had evolved into believings in the sense of providing narrative guidance for risky actions in the world of military secrets (Sarbin, Carney, & Eoyang, 1994).

What conditions are responsible for warranting some poetic imaginings and not others? I preface an answer to this question with a brief etymological tracing of our modern word *believe*. The tracing provides some clues to help establish what differentiates believing from imagining, even though they cannot be differentiated in terms of content.

An etymological tracing of *believe* takes us from an Indo-European form *leubh* translated as "strongly desires" through Latin forms that gave us *libido*, also translated as desire, through Germanic forms that include the Gothic *liufs* meaning "dear" and *gelaubjen* meaning "to believe." Especially pertinent to my argument are the Germanic derivatives: *lieb*, meaning dear; *Liebe*, meaning love; *lieben*, to love or to cherish; *glauben*, to believe; *Glaube*, meaning faith; *loben*, meaning to praise (Needham, 1973). It should be noted that the evolution of the words retained the meaning of being "highly valued," a meaning that could be assigned to abstractions as well as to objects.

This brief sketch points to the utility of etymological analysis for identifying the potential meanings of the English word *believe*. The etymological connection between *belief* and the various words for valuing is central to my thesis: that *believings are highly valued imaginings*. Thus, within the cognitive term *belief* reside variants of a concept associated with emotional life. In this context, I am interpreting the concept not in the narrow sense of "desire" but in the more general sense of "being highly valued." One may assign positive or negative value to particular imaginings. For many children, the belief in Santa Claus is a highly valued imagining of the positive kind, whereas the belief in Satan is a highly valued imagining of the negative kind.

To account for the differential responses of the two readers of the spy story one must look into their self-narratives. We can infer that for the first reader, the imaginings engendered by stories of espionage made no connection with his self-narrative. For the second reader, however, the imaginings provided opportunities to enhance a fading self-narrative. He placed such a high value on his poetic constructions that he committed acts of treason against his country.

DEGREE OF INVOLVEMENT AND THE REALITY OF IMAGININGS

The problem of truth or falsity of imaginings-cum-believings is often rendered in discourses on reality. In earlier times, the reports of religious figures have been used to ratify the claim that, under some conditions, what appeared as imagining was taken to be a veridical perception that was identified with the descriptor "real." The problem of what is real turns out to be a pseudo-problem. The words *real* and *reality* are excluder words. They tell only what something is not, and then only if the context is known. J. L. Austin (1962), a linguistic philosopher, and Morris Cohen (1964), a philosopher of science, made a convincing case that *real* and *reality* have no function in an argument. Cohen put it cogently. After demonstrating that the word *reality* be condemned as devoid of significance, he continued:

> I am not unmindful of the many attempts to define the unreal. But the question is: What corresponds to these definitions? The Hindoo mystic is deeply irritated when the wise Chinese suggests that the realm of Maya or illusion does not really exist. . . . The reality of illusion is the emphatic center of the Hindoo's philosophy, and similarly, of all those who sharply contrast reality and appearance. The difficulty here is classic. What I am more especially concerned about, however, is to call attention to the fact that the word reality maintains itself as a term of praise rather than of description. To be "in touch with reality" is our way of expressing what our less sophisticated brothers and sisters do by the phrase "in tune with the infinite. . . ." ["Real" is an expression that carries] an agreeable afflatus without dependence on any definite meaning. Such edification is pleasing and would be harmless if it did not also cause intellectual confusion. (pp. 455–456)

The problem contained in those self-reports that declare that the imagining has the appearance of reality cannot be dismissed merely by informing the reporter that his or her choice of language is questionable. It is important to recognize that *real* is employed as a term to convince one's self or another that the credibility assigned to an imagining is warranted.

The more general question is now open: What are the antecedent and concurrent conditions that account for the credibility a person assigns to propositions arising from poetic imaginings, some of which are in those areas of dim knowledge that are sometimes labeled intuitive, unsystematic, phenomenal, and feeling? Of the many efforts to deal with the problem of belief, the formulations of David Hume (1740/1888) are worthy of study, particularly Hume's selection of the metaphors *lively* and *vivid* (among others) to describe that bit of dim knowledge to which he had assigned the words *impressions* and *ideas*. He was of course writing in the historical period when mentalism was an unquestioned doctrine. The everyday language of vision and spatial relations was available as a framework for a theory of mind. To be consistent with the language of vision he could have employed such descriptive terms as *degrees of clarity*, *brightness*, and *distinctiveness* when referring to imaginings. Such words were currently available. Instead, he used adjectives more appropriate to a language of action: *lively*, *vivid*, *vivacious*, and *forceful*.

This inconsistency poses a problem: Why did he employ adjectives with a transparent relationship to bodily effort rather than descriptors of visual phenomena? Hume selected them not because they were appropriate to fictive mental contents but rather because such words denoted high degrees of organismic involvement in constructional activity. That is to say, in doing a phenomenological examination, Hume was engaged in a form of action, rather than in the passive reception of sensory stimuli or in the observation of impressions and ideas flitting hither and yon in mental space according to the laws of association. He was struggling to generate new knowledge and expanding effort in the process. So when he examined his own conduct (not his own mind), he responded to the bodily signs of effort, of organismic involvement in the intellectual role. Adjectives such as lively, forceful, and active were more appropriate to the conclusions drawn from his self-examination than the attributes of spatial stimuli.

In speculating about Hume's phenomenology, I am suggesting that the action concept "degrees of involvement" is applicable to silent, attenuated, *as if* behavior. To prepare the way for incorporating this concept into the present argument, I refer to a concept that has already demonstrated its usefulness: degree of involvement in role enactment. The referent here is a quantitative one: In overtly enacting a role, the actor may participate with varying amounts of force and vigor. For routine roles, few organismic systems are activated, and we speak of minimal involvement in the role. For other roles, more organismic systems are activated, the role engages the self, so to speak, and we refer to moderate involvement. Take, for example a professional actor who is portraying a role on stage. His actions must be convincing; he must be alert to cues from other actors and from the audience. High involvement in role behavior is illustrated in conditions such as ecstasy, mystical experience, religious conversion, and sexual union (Sarbin & Allen, 1968).

Just as we may fruitfully talk of degree of involvement in overt role-enactment, so may we talk of degree of involvement in muted role-taking, that is, in storied imaginings. An example of minimal level of involvement is the college sophomore who participates in a required laboratory exercise. He imagines tasting salt when a few drops of tasteless distilled water are put on his tongue. He is probably not highly involved in the *as if* behavior of tasting salt. An example of moderate involvement in imagining is a novelist struggling to construct a character or a scene—especially if he or she were facing a deadline. The degree of involvement could be noted in the motoric accompaniment of the creative process such as nervous pacing, speed of writing on the note pad or vigorous striking of the keyboard, inattention to extraneous stimuli, and so on. A similar level of involvement in imagining is illustrated by the reader of a novel who weeps upon reading the tragic death of the hero.

An unusually high degree of involvement in *as if* behavior was shown by 10 pre-teenage neighborhood boys who had been invited to a Halloween party. The house was completely dark except for one room that was dimly illuminated by a jack-o-lantern. The host asked the children to form a circle and tell ghost stories. At the beginning of the storytelling the diameter of the circle was about 11 feet. By the time of the final ghost story, the circle had been spontaneously reduced to approximately 3 feet (Feshbach & Feshbach, 1963).

I have given what may seem like an inordinate amount of space to developing the concept "degree of involvement." The tactic is justified if the description is helpful in understanding why some individuals claim their imaginings are real and why some imaginings are believed to be of the same character as literal happenings in the distal world. The arguments are intended to convey the proposition that when people claim that their imaginings are real, they are probably deeply involved in *as if* behavior, behavior that may be described as being lively, forceful, and vivid—words that connote the bodily effects of emotional life.

The higher the degree of involvement, the more likely the actor will interpret imaginings as being equivalent to veridical perceptions. In formulating them for relevant audiences, the actor will use identity terms rather than *as if* terms. After a conversion experience, a Pentacostal churchgoer testified: " I actually felt the Holy Spirit entering my body" rather than "It was *as if* the Holy Spirit entered my body." Even under conditions of moderate involvement people drop *as if* qualifiers when they reproduce stories (Chun & Sarbin, 1970). Under conditions of high involvement, more organismic systems are engaged, and imaginings are accompanied by interoceptive and proprioceptive sensory inputs (Stepper & Strack, 1993).

The following autobiographical excerpt, written by George Trosse, a 17th-century clergyman, is instructive. Note how he shifts back and forth from *as if* statements to statements of certainty.

> While I was thus walking up and down, hurried with these worldly disquieting thoughts, I perceiv'd a Voice (I heard it plainly), saying unto me, Who art thou? Which, knowing it could be the Voice of no Mortal, I concluded, was the Voice of God, and with Tears, as I re-

member, reply'd, I am a very great Sinner, LORD! Hereupon, I withdrew again into the inner-Room, securing and barring the Door upon me, I betook myself to a very proper and seasonable Duty, namely, Secret Prayer. . . . For while I was praying upon my Knees, I heard a Voice, as I fancy'd, as it were just behind me, saying, Yet more humble; Yet more humble; with some Continuance. And not knowing the Meaning of the Voice, but undoubtedly concluding it came from GOD, I endeavour'd to comply with it. . . . (cited in Hunter & MacAlpine, 1963, p. 154)

From the text, we can assume that the Reverend Trosse was struggling to maintain his moral identity. In the course of his meditation, some input (not necessarily generated externally) was instantiated as a voice. Most logically, because there was no one else in the room and God was everywhere, he concluded that the voice came from God.

One does not entertain lightly an experience that concerns one's relationship to the transcendental world. As William James wrote: ". . . 'religion,' whatever more special meanings it may have, signifies always a serious state of mind. . . . It [religion] favors gravity, not pertness; it says 'hush' to all vain chatter and smart wit" (James, 1902, p. 56). When engaging in conduct of a religious character, then, a person's imaginings are likely to be influenced by a high degree of organismic involvement.

The autobiographical statement of the late Bishop James A. Pike lends itself to an interpretation in the present idiom (Pike, 1968). He died in 1972, but his story is pertinent to my inquiry. A theological scholar of many accomplishments, he reported having communications with his dead son through psychic mediums. The account may be briefly summarized as follows. His son, Jim, age 20, killed himself in a New York hotel room. The tragic event occurred at the end of a period during which father and son had shared a sabbatical in England and had become close friends. Shortly after the suicide, a series of unexplained events occurred in the apartment that he and his son had shared. For example, objects that had belonged to the younger Pike, or were related to his interests, mysteriously appeared in a geometrical pattern. The bangs of the hair style of Bishop Pike's secretary were mysteriously removed by an undiscovered burning instrument. Some time before, the younger Pike had expressed disapproval of her hair style. These events, among others, led Bishop Pike and his two staff members to the conclusion that a poltergeist was at work.

To make sense of these events, Bishop Pike consulted psychic mediums. Communication was established with the spiritually alive (although physically dead) son. A few excerpts establish the basis for regarding Pike's imaginings as being characterized by a high degree of involvement. For example, commenting on his thoughts when his son's ashes were scattered at sea, he wrote: "I felt the deep sorrow of having lost not only a son, but my closest friend" (1968, p. 73). A number of passages reveal the expectation of occult events. He described his contact with Jim through the medium:

> I then made bold to address Jim directly, feeling somewhat strange in doing so since he was of course nowhere to be seen. 'Did you know that was going to happen when you left me at the airport?' He seemed to reply, "I had a fear of it because I dreaded your leaving me this last time." (p. 123)

That Pike was deeply affected by his son's death is easily documented. Like most men with deep parental feelings, in this case reinforced by a period of intense comradeship, the "grief work" was intense and pervasive. That he had feelings of guilt over his son's suicide is an inference that a reader might safely draw. These conditions set the stage for high involvement, for "hearing" and "feeling" in the absence of distal input.

Subsequent to the publication of the book, Bishop Pike was interviewed on a television program. The interviewer asked: "Do you *know* that you communicated with Jim?" After a moment's thought, Pike replied, "I don't *know*, but I *believe*" (KRON Channel 4, 1968). The response epitomizes my arguments. Knowing implies that a proposition has passed pragmatic tests. No pragmatic tests have been developed to allow one to equate knowing and believing. Believing requires no test, only high degrees of organismic involvement—a condition of emotional life produced by placing a high value, either positive or negative, on storied imaginings.

CONCLUSION

Recall the reference narratives described at the beginning of the chapter: Mrs. Jones, under instructions from an authority figure, tried to remember events for which she had no memory. Remembering is a constructive process, a principle demonstrated by Bartlett (1932) and repeatedly reaffirmed. Rememberings are constructed from bits and pieces of experience, perceptions, imaginings, even events that occurred after the purported remembering. It is a common observation that rememberings and imaginings are often conflated. Given that Mrs. Jones was trying to repair a failing self-narrative, she placed a high value on imaginings that provided a new identity, that of survivor. Her conduct was guided by these highly valued imaginings, that is, believings stimulated by the first therapist.

The so-called hallucinations cited in the narrative of the postal worker fit neatly into the formulations of imaginings becoming believings. For many years, he had prayed in church before icons of various saints. Now the icons were absent—so he used his hypothetical skills to construct them. He placed a high value on such imaginings-cum-believings. They served to maintain his self-narrative as a pious man.

The Heaven's Gate affair is a transparent illustration of imaginings becoming believings, believings that provided the reasons for ultimately engaging in irreversible action. The 39 participants in the suicide pact acted on believings that could come only from a set of highly evolved imaginings that, in their case, included the rhetoric of science fiction. The participants were enthralled by the story of eternal life on a special planet.

To summarize, then, from a constructionist and narrative perspective, I have tried to justify the claim that imaginings are storied constructions. Imagining may be fruitfully construed as a form of hypothetical or "as if" behavior, namely, muted, storied, role-taking. I also claimed that the contents of imagining and the contents of the phenomena usually identified as believings cannot be differentiated. The two constructions can be differentiated, however, in terms of the value that the imaginer places on particular imaginings. A clue to the connection between value and belief is provided by an etymological tracing that shows the linkage between "belief," a cognitive term, and value terms associated with emotional life. Individual differences in the readiness to assign value to some imaginings can be accounted for by reference to the imaginer's self-narrative. Assigning a high value, positive or negative, leads to increased organismic involvement (focused attention and physiological arousal) in a particular narrative sequence, a condition that helps authenticate hypothetical instantiations as credible. No logical support for a person's claims accrues to describing an imagining as "real." A person's claims that begin with "I believe . . ." do no more than demonstrate that a high degree of value has been placed on a particular hypothetical instantiation.

REFERENCES

Austin, J. L. (1962). *Sense and sensibilia.* London: Oxford University Press.

Bartlett, Sir F. C. (1932). *Remembering: A study in experimental and social psychology.* Cambridge, England: Cambridge University Press.

Chun, K., & Sarbin, T. R. (1970). An empirical demonstration of metaphor to myth transformation. *Philosophical Psychology, 4,* 16–21.

Cohen, M. R. (1964). *Reason and nature.* New York: Free Press.

Feshbach, S., & Feshbach, N. (1963). Influence of the stimulus object upon the complementary and supplementary projection of fear. *Journal of Abnormal and Social Psychology, 66,* 498–502.

Hume, D. (1888). *A treatise of human nature* (L. A. Selby-Bigge, Ed.). Oxford, England: Clarendon Press. (Original work published 1740)

Hunter, I., & MacAlpine, A. (Eds.). (1963). *Three hundred years of psychiatry.* London: Oxford University Press.

James, W. (1902). *Varieties of religious experience.* New York: Longmans, Green.

Locke, J. (1924). *An essay concerning human understanding.* London: Oxford University Press. (Original work published 1690)

MacIntyre, A. (1957). The logical status of religious belief. In S. Toulmin, R. W. Hepburn, & A. MacIntyre (Eds.), *Metaphysical beliefs* (pp. 167–206). London: SCM Press.

Needham, R. (1973). *Belief, language, and experience.* Chicago: University of Chicago Press.

Pike, J. A. (with Diane Kennedy). (1968). *The other side: An account of my experiences with psychic phenomena.* Garden City, NY: Doubleday.

Sarbin, T. R. (1967). The concept of hallucination. *Journal of Personality, 35,* 359–380.

Sarbin, T. R. (1972). Imaging as muted role-taking: A historico-linguistic analysis. In P. Sheehan (Ed.), *The function and nature of imagery.* New York: Academic Press.

Sarbin, T. R. (1986). *Narrative psychology: The storied nature of human conduct.* New York: Praeger.

Sarbin, T. R. (1989). Emotions as narrative emplotments. In M. J. Packer & R. M. Addison (Eds.), *Entering the circle: Hermeneutic investigation in psychology.* Albany: State University of New York Press.

Sarbin, T. R. (1990). The narrative quality of action. *Philosophical and Theoretical Psychology, 10,* 49–65.

Sarbin, T. R. (1993). The narrative as a root metaphor for contextualism. In S. Hayes, L. Hayes, H. Reese, & T. R. Sarbin (Eds.), *Varieties of scientific contextualism.* Reno, NV: Context Press.

Sarbin, T. R. (1997). The poetics of identity. *Theory and Psychology, 6,* 67–82.

Sarbin, T. R., & Allen, V. L. (1968). Role theory. In G. Lindzey & E. Aronson (Eds.), *Handbook of social psychology* (Vol. I, pp. 488–567). Reading, MA: Addison-Wesley.

Sarbin, T. R., Carney, R. M., & Eoyang, C. (1994). *Citizen espionage: Studies in trust and betrayal.* Westport, CT: Praeger.

Sarbin, T. R., & Juhasz, J. B. (1967). The historical background of the concept of hallucination. *Journal of the History of Behavioral Sciences, 3,* 339–358.

Sarbin, T. R., & Juhasz, J. B. (1970). Toward a theory of imagination. *Journal of Personality, 38,* 52–76.

Sarbin, T. R., & Juhasz, J. B. (1975). The social psychology of hallucination. In R. Siegel & L. J. West (Eds.), *Hallucination: Theory and research* (pp. 247–256). New York: Wiley.

Stepper, S., & Strack, F. (1993). Proprioceptive determinants of emotional and nonemotional feelings. *Journal of Social and Personality Psychology, 64,* 211–220.

Vaihinger, H. (1925). *The philosophy of as if.* London: Harcourt.

2

BELIEVED-IN IMAGININGS: WHOSE WORDS, BELIEFS, IMAGININGS, AND METAPHORS?

MORTON WIENER

My interest in this re-analysis of Professor Sarbin's thoughtful and evocative exegesis of *believed-in imagining*, and of his representations of his reference cases is to demonstrate once again how subtly *psychopathology* may be introduced, whenever unconventional or atypical acts and doings are represented. The method is a hermeneutic analysis of the sense of the connotations in the word usages and in the hidden metaphors that have become entrenched in our representations and explications of uncommon, unusual, unorthodox, or different acts or doings. By exploring similar nontypical doings that seemed to have escaped the stigma of psychopathology, it will also be possible to argue against the prevailing view that a different kind of explanation is required for doings that are now designated as psychopathological. The creation of a new category, *believed-in imaginings*, the subject matter of this volume, would seem to be uniquely useful for this kind of enterprise.

In chapter 1, Sarbin states:

This chapter is written from the perspective that the narrative is an organizing principle for contemporary psychology. . . . From this perspective, I examine the terms *imagination* and *belief*. . . . To understand how and why people assign credibility to imaginings, and to more completely understand the phenomenon of believed-in imaginings, it is helpful to undertake a historical and linguistic analysis that unpacks the meanings of these terms.

In that citation there is a conjoining of several terms, *narrative* (story, fable), *imagination*, *belief* as precursors to "understand how and why people assign *credibility* to *imaginings*." Each alone can be said to include a connotation of implausibility. Does not this conjoining already entail that any representation labeled by any of the terms connotes doubtful credibility? Given that possibility, I would argue that the prior problem is what kinds of tacit or explicit criteria are invoked when individuals, including professionals, assign credibility to their own versus to others' representations. When I use the term *criteria*, my meaning includes circumstances and contexts as the more significant concern, rather than the ostensible psychological status in traditional approaches.

A caveat is in order here. Over the years I have understood, admired, and agreed with many of Sarbin's other ideas and proposals (e.g., the importance of language usages as a vehicle to infer differences in doings and explication; a questioning of allusions to inner agencies as causes of public doings). That apparently I will be questioning the thesis and arguments that he has posed in this book necessitates a disclaimer. I am concerned that other readers may take my interpretations of Sarbin's offerings as if they were his understandings. This concern seems particularly cogent because Sarbin's reference narratives seem to connote, allude to, or intimate psychopathological doings. In any case, as noted above, my reanalysis of believed-in imagining will offer yet another opportunity to identify a proclivity by investigators and clinicians in traditional frameworks to classify infrequent, atypical, and unusual doings as being abnormal or psychopathological.

NARRATIVES AND THE POTENTIAL FOR BIAS

The well-known historical episode of Joan of Arc may not adequately represent Sarbin's or other writers' sense of believed-in imaginings, but this historical event, story, allegory, fable, morality tale, or parable is a remarkably transparent illustration of the omnipotence and omnipresence of our tacit biases when affirming, doubting, or questioning reported occurrences. I will attempt to be as neutral as possible in the description of that historical happening, although *neutral* seems to be an oxymoron when united with *historical*. That is, one could argue that selection and emphasis in representation (sic) are biases of the historian and that there are no historical facts per se.

It has been said that there was a prophecy in Lorraine that the kingdom lost by a woman—Queen Isabella—would be saved by a virgin. In that context, Joan of Arc, a very devout Catholic, came forward and announced that God came to her, which she understood as a mission to lead the French troops against the English who had laid siege to Orleans. (I could have used the words *saw* or *heard* instead of the more ambiguous *came* and *understood*, but those alternatives, in the current era, might too easily be transposed to *hallucination*,[1] which can connote psychopathology.) She was armed and commissioned to lead the under-manned French troops to relieve that siege. Although Joan was successful, in later fighting, she was captured by the English, tried as a witch, and burned at the stake. Still later, she was canonized as a saint by the Catholic Church.

There are a number of questions that may be posed about this "historical" report. The most obvious, in the context of believed-in imaginings, is what label (category) is to be assigned to this atypical and unusual narrative of a direct encounter with God; one that has apparently become associated with a series of significant social consequences. Was Joan of Arc carrying out God's will, or was she imagining, hallucinating, misinterpreting, deceived, or dissembling in her re-presentations? Were the French and the Church duped? Were the English sacriligious? What facts would help any decision? What particular additional information was Saint Joan provided? What evidence, justification, explanation, or rationalization could be offered to affirm, question, or doubt her reporting? Whatever our classification—belief, doubt, or rejection as an hallucination or misinterpretation—each would seem to be a correlate of our beliefs (tacit biases) about God and what shall be taken as evidence.

Some might claim that Joan of Arc's story ("history") is only a controversy about religious ontology, rather than about the omnipresent biased decisions educed by it. Three related rejoinders seem appropriate in this context. The first is, the very choice of terms to label the re-presentation can be used to identify a bias about acceptable ontologies or metaphysical presumptions. Another is that the first rejoinder is an example of the kinds of analyses I will use in re-presenting Sarbin's referent examples cases. The third, in my ontology, is that all epistomological theories and claims entail opaque and unexamined ontologies, in metaphoric forms, in every disciple and discourse. As far as I can discern there is no way to escape that state of affairs, except to accept one or another, and function in our world *as if* our ontology is the ontology. As I will argue, credibility is in the eye of the observer, focussed by societal conventions and traditions.

In more general terms, is not every theory, concept, construct, or model a believed-in imagining, or are the labels "imaginings" or "mistake"

---

[1]Sarbin has written several articles where this very concept seemed to have been interpreted somewhat differently—or as I may be misinterpreting his representation here.

to be appended only to those avowals that are incongruent with our believings? Do not our concepts, particularly those of nonpublic doings that are posited to account for public happenings, entail tacit believed-in imaginings? Are our categories, identified examples, and event-specifications self-evident, or are these posited and unquestioned givens that change as our believings change? Incidently, even were we to identify some criterion (sign) that correlates highly with our beliefs of truth, lie, or mistake, a predication for a particular instance is only a probability claim.

One could argue that most of our believings (biases) are opaque or masked in our traditional, conventionalized language use, suppositions, and *disciplinary matrix* imperatives. Were the case otherwise, we would not so readily find explications in which infrequently occurring events or less traditional or novel representations are considered as flawed actions and are paired all too often with less than subtle attributions of past or concurrent psychological dysfunction. I will speak more on this particular issue when I later explore the narrative examples Sarbin described in chapter 1.

I do not know any way to escape bias. I readily acknowledge that I am no less constrained by mine. I have rationalized this quandary by claiming that my describing, categorizing, interpretations, and explications of things can be contrasted with those who have observed the same happenings and doings in the same time and space. The use in my interpretations, analyses, and critique of believed-in imaginings may be better understood were my own identifiable biases outlined. I usually describe my biases as an amalgam, constellation, juxtaposition or patchwork of assumptions and premises probably misinterpreted and misappropriated from several philosophical or conceptual approaches, which I list here.

- ordinary language philosophy (see, e.g., Wittgenstein, (1958), in which "sense" and "meaning" are usages ("doings") in contexts, not references to, or signs or symbols for, other "things" or "doings"
- Ryle's (1949) *Concept of Mind*, particularly the arguments and concerns about usages of terms mistakenly transported from one discourse type (e.g., person doings) to another (e.g., mind doings)
- Turbayne's (1970) *The Myth of the Metaphor*, in which the concerns are about how metaphors become myths, with continued, frequent usages
- Sapir's (1921) and Whorf's (1956) hypotheses of the inseparability of language and reality, or language determinism
- my interpretation and extension of Kuhn's sense of disciplinary matrix, to a notion of the tacit imperatives of language usages in all theories

From my interpretations of these perspectives, I have come to believe that all describing, categorizing, understandings, and interpreting incorporate both egocentric (individual) and ethnocentric (community or societal) biases. In earlier eras this approach might have been labeled as "perspectivism;" currently it might be considered a kind of postmodernism.

Any one familiar with the approaches I have cited will not be surprised that my critique of believed-in imaginings focuses, to a considerable extent, on the connotations, metaphors, and tacit believings that are inferable from the words used in describing a representation. It seems important to acknowledge one additional correlate of my biases explicitly. In contrast to those who understand meaning as if its definition were inferable from a word—and a specific denotation—in this perspective the "sense" of a "word" is in its usages—in its linguistic, social, and situational contexts—that is, by their connotations. With my biases now known, I will try to deconstruct the narratives below, or to use Sarbin's (this volume) most intriguing metaphor "social poetics," in my re-presentations (sic) of Sarbin's descriptions of the exemplar cases of "believed-in imaginings." Poetics is an ideal characterization of language in this framework, because the word connotes the metaphorical use of language more explicitly than does its use as if uniform, fixed, and immutable denotations.

A DECONSTRUCTION OF NARRATIVES

In this section I reprint the three narratives that Sarbin presented in chapter 1; he offered these narratives to exemplify the concept of believed-in imaginings. In these reprints, I have put in brackets any words that seem to me to be a justification for identifying elements of the narratives as being doubtful or noncredible acts or doings. After each reprint, I offer an alternative narrative for each account in which I emend all terms that connote non-normative ways of doings. The two versions of narratives are followed by specific, and then general, commentary.

The Mrs. Jones Exemplar

Original Version

Mrs. Jones, a 38-year-old office worker, [distraught and concerned] about her [inability to control] her weight and also her [inability to cope] with an [indifferent] husband, a [tyrannical] employer, and two [problem] teenagers, [consulted a psychotherapist]. After she was [diagnosed] as [anxious, depressed,] and [having an eating disorder], the therapist inquired if she had been the [victim] of [child abuse]. When she replied that she had no such memories, the therapist [told] her that her [particular symptoms] were indicative of the [repression] of memories of [abuse]. He outlined a [simplistic] account of the [repression] concept and [urged] Mrs. Jones [to try] to [recover childhood memories of abuse]. He also recommended a book on recovered memory therapy. Subsequently, Mrs. Jones reported memories of being abused by her father when she was 3 or 4 years of age. At first the reported memories were vague, but, as the therapy continued, she recounted her [victimization] in [great] detail. When Mrs. Jones [confronted] her father, he vehemently denied the accusation. She broke off all relations with him and also with her mother and sisters who declared that the accusation against the father was false. After almost two years of therapy, Mrs. Jones's [adjustment problems] were [more acute] than before. On the [advice] of a close friend, she [discontinued] her relationship with the therapist and [sought help] from a second therapist who was [not an advocate] of the repression [doctrine]. In the course of [working] with the second therapist, she [realized] that she had no clear-cut memories of abuse, but on [the prompting] of the first therapist she [had been able to imagine] what it would be like to be a [victim] of abuse. (Sarbin, chapter 1, this volume)

Alternate Version

Mrs. Jones, a 38-year-old, married mother of two teenagers, employed full-time in a business office, had a list of things in her current life situation that she thought needed changing: her indifferent husband, learning how to better control her weight, and what things could be done to try to deal more effectively with her now difficult teenaged daughters. Mrs. Jones also reported not knowing how to deal with her tyrannical boss and her now more defiant teenagers. After exploring Mrs. Jones's descriptions of current situations, and of her sense of powerlessness with her tyrannical boss, her therapist, who operated within a rather traditional neo-Freudian dynamic perspective, hypothesized that Mrs. Jones's current unhappiness may have had its origins in earlier childhood difficulties—that is, it might be a repetition of some earlier childhood sense of powerlessness. To explore this possibility, he asked Mrs. Jones whether she had had similar feelings earlier. When she claimed that she did not remember any, the therapist apparently concluded that her failure to come up with any memory at all suggested that her difficulty in thinking of any early distressful events was characteristic of patients who are repressing anxiety-producing memories. This Freudian-oriented therapist described the concept of repression in layperson's terminology, and to make that concept more concrete, as well as to reassure Mrs. Jones that it is not unusual for people to repress thoughts of distressing events, the therapist suggested that she read a popular book on recovered memories. After reading it, she reported vague memories of something happening with her father when she was 3 or 4. As the therapist explored for more details, she recounted her memory of an abuse in greater and greater detail. After dealing with her distress at this remembering, the therapist believed that it would be cathartic and liberating for the patient, now an adult, to talk to her father about these long-repressed feelings. The therapist suggested that she do so. Her father denied that anything like her memories ever occurred. Mrs. Jones broke off all relations with him and with her mother and her sister, who believed her father's denials. Two years later, when her friend heard Mrs. Jones still talking about many of the same everyday frustrating problems, she urged Mrs. Jones to change therapists. This second therapist had a more behavioral orientation. He told Mrs. Jones that current difficulties are the only things that matter in psychotherapy and that he did not believe in the notion of repression. Working with this therapist, she gradually came to feel less certain about her memory of the abuse. Over time, she became more and more convinced that the memories were not real. She then recanted her earlier story and attributed the story of abuse to the promptings of the first therapist.

Commentary

There are several differences in the two re-presentations. One is the way in which the two therapists are described. A second is the attempt in the alternate version to describe Mrs. Jones in more normative terms. There is also an unstated presumption in the second re-presentation: Neither the two therapists, the mother, the sister, the friend, Sarbin, nor I would have any apparent bases for assigning either credibility or doubt to Mrs. Jones's claims. As was noted earlier about Joan of Arc, any decision made by me or by any of the others about the credibility of Mrs. Jones's reporting can be said to be predicated on each of our particular biases. Even were we to agree that there may be some indeterminate probability that the "abuse" did occur as Mrs. Jones described in the original exemplar, I can predict with some confidence that if the same so-called facts were given to a large sample of individuals, some would find Mrs. Jones's claim of abuse credible; others would not. One has only to recall the nonagreement in the notorious O. J. Simpson trial or the Sacco-Vanzetti case to appreciate this problem.

Sarbin's presentation of the first therapist can be read (incorrectly perhaps) as if that the therapist was naive, simple-minded, and manipulative in urging Mrs. Jones to imagine an abuse memory. In the alternative presentation, an attempt was made to describe both therapists as competent and dedicated and as advocating their individual theoretical perspectives. Furthermore, the statement in Sarbin's presentation that the second therapist, "was not an advocate of the repression doctrine" could be (mis)interpreted that this therapist was more objective, or that therapists who believe in Freud's concept of repression are more doctrinaire than therapists with other perspectives. My readings of the therapy literature is hardly consistent with either of these propositions. There have been any number of claims (e.g., Brody, 1980; Frank & Frank, 1991) that persuasion and placebo are a most potent explanation for change and healing in much of medicine and in psychotherapy.

Is Mrs. Jones's subsequent recanting of abuse the convincing criterion? Given my stance on the omnipotence of bias, how shall we debate a conversion of an atheist to any religion? Would that recanting convince other atheists about the reality of religion? Would a renunciation by a believer convince other believers? Are not conversions and renunciations often attributed to brainwashing by malevolent "thems" or to that ubiquitous, tautological term *suggestibility*? How might we assess the same exemplification were the ostensible recovered memory were not recanted? There exist numerous claims of childhood abuse—claims that have not been recanted, as well as instances in which the alleged abuser acknowledged the acts and thus substantiated the claims. Would we give more credence to Mrs. Jones's remembering had her family members sided with her but the father still denied the happenings? Nothing in these questionings is an argument for either decision, that is, for believing or not believing the claim. The question remains, what criteria are to be used to represent Mrs. Jones's remembering as either a believed-in imagining or as a tenable, credible report?

Is it reasonable to infer that the core criterion for believing or doubting in the Jones exemplar, and in the contentious disagreements about recovered memories, is the Freudian concept *repression*? Not being a dyed-in-the-wool Freudian, I have sometimes considered that term *as if* it were invoked sometimes to account for a failure of an analysand (client, patient) to report doings or happenings that are expected, given some of the premises in that theoretical framework. Allow me to extend the same sort of questionings to a less contentious example. When long-separated friends reminisce or grandparents tell stories from their childhoods, are the events reported to be considered recovered memories—as if they had been buried away somewhere? (A discussion of an alternative conception of memory would take us too far afield here.) Would we come to the conclusion that, were the friends or grandparents to disagree about the rememberings ("no, that never happened") but then recant ("oh yes, I remember that now"), a new psychological term—*believed-in imaging*—might be required?

If the Mrs. Jones' exemplar is presumed to be different than those we consider socially normative (i.e., frequent or common occurrences), what are the criteria that one might invoke for accepting Mrs. Jones believings, in either version of that exemplar? Are they such criteria as the contents of the "memory," a characterization of the person as one needing psychotherapy, a (psychologically) distressed person, the contexts in which the memory arises (therapy), the orientation or kind of therapist, a belief that someone would not make up that kind of story, and so forth? Are not all of these also predicated on *our* beliefs as well?

The Retired Postal Worker Exemplar

Original Version

"A second reference case is one that belongs to a large class of [stories] that [mental health professionals] identify as [hallucinations]. A typical [story] is that of an aging, retired postal work ... who claimed to have frequent [visits] from St. Margaret and St. Theresa and to engage in [conversations] with them. His [claim] was made with [great conviction]. . . . To [imagine] conversations with long-dead religious figures is one thing; to act as if the [imaginings] had the [warrant] of [verdical] perception is another" (Sarbin, chapter 1, this volume).

Alternate Version

A retired postal worker, a devoutly religious believer in a literal interpretation of the words of God as represented in the Scriptures, reported having frequent conversations with St. Margaret and St. Theresa. When doubted, he was adamant and insistent that these were most helpful spiritual happenings; he dismissed the doubters as nonbelievers.

Commentary

There are several directional biases in the original re-presentation. The first is that the case is categorized as a mental health care, which then justifies use of the label *hallucination,* or is it the other way around—the label *hallucination* justifies classifying the case as a mental health case? Characterizing the postal worker's claims being made with "great conviction" seems to connote that this is somehow evidence to justify disbelief. Sarbin's statement about the veridicality of a perception also warrants some comment. Certainly if we identify a report that is considered by some to be an hallucination, it is redundant to say that it is not a veridical perception. However, deciding which perceptions are veridical is a different problem. Are veridical perceptions those that are consensual? As was noted elsewhere, are reports of mirages or illusions to be considered veridical, if we have consensual classification? If witnesses give different reports of a happening, which is veridical, and how shall we classify the others?

Would we classify devout people who say daily personal prayers aloud after kneeling, genuflecting, and lighting candles because they believe in sin, redemption, and resurrection as having believed-in imaginings or being a mental health case? What about people who pray for "heavenly direction," "the safe passage of a loved one," or "strength to resist temptation"? If we ask these people if they are really communicating with God or God really hears them, would we not expect a devout believer to say "yes" with great conviction? Would we not be surprised to hear the person say, "Well, it's only as if . . ."?

Are people who make ritual sacrifices to their deities mental health cases? How shall we categorize reports of near-death experiences," that were given without promptings from others? Would we consider a statement such as, "My life flashed in front of my eyes when I was drowning (or in a terrible accident)" as a believed-in imaginings? Would the label *believed-in imaginings* be assigned to those who believe the "official" explanation versus those holding "with great conviction" to a "conspiracy explanation" of the assassinations of Presidents Lincoln and Kennedy? How do we classify Albert Einstein's assertion that, "God does not play dice"? "Imagine" the doubting and incredulity that once accompanied claims such as "I saw the microbes and they caused your illness," or "the world is round." Many of my students seem to react as if something is amiss when I claim that "if you are on the moon and you look down, you cannot see the earth."

The Heaven's Gate Exemplar

Original Version

A third reference case is the much-discussed [story] of the 39 men and women who [took their lives] as part of the Heaven's Gate religious movement. The information provided by former members of the group, by the coroner, and by police investigators makes clear that the members shared an [imaginatively constructed cosmological story] in which they would [rid] themselves of their mortal coils [and] advance to a higher stage of development on a distant planet. As in the other reference cases, the members apparently [transfigured their constructed imaginings to indubitable believings]" (Sarbin, chapter 1, this volume).

Alternative Version

Taking the arrival of the comet Hale-Bopp as a sign of the availability of a cosmic vehicle that could transport their cosmic essence to a higher plane of being, 39 members of the Heaven's Gate religious order initiated the essential rituals for that transmutation. These rituals included the wearing of particular clothing, the use of particular coverings over their bodies, and the ingestion of a substance that would make that transmutation possible. A short time after those rituals were completed, the comet moved into a different spatial orbit. Some of the members of this religious order who were not participants in that ritual reported later that they were regretful that they had not felt ready to accompany the other members of their congregation on their journey.

Commentary

My concerns about Sarbin's characterization of the doings and believings in the Heaven's Gate exemplar are analogous to those I identified for Joan of Arc, and for the religious postman. With word usages and connotations such as, *story; imaginatively constructed cosmological story; transfigured their constructed imaginings to indubitable believings*; Sarbin seems to be representing those unusual doings as evidence of mistaken believings, which require explanations that are different than those we invoke for our more typical or traditional believings. Furthermore, labeling one aspect of their ritual as *took their lives* (connoting suicide), is unlikely to be their representation—they were going to another place. Sarbin does apparently offer a more ambiguous characterization of one aspect of the ritual with the phrase, *they would rid themselves of their mortal coil*. Again, my arguments here are not whether we agree with, or reject the believings of that community, but to make the case again that the conventional believings that we take as the only rational believings also incorporate the biased metaphors and myths embedded in our everyday language. (See Turbayne, 1970, for a detailed explication of this last assertion.) Furthermore, are those individuals who did not participate, but stated that they wished that they could have, also exemplars of believed-in imaginings? Are these kinds of imaginings any different than those entailed in the rituals that are performed to attain redemption and heaven? What about the Islamic concept of martyrdom, whereby believers are assured a place in heaven if they die while killing infidels? Is not the sense of a different existence after leaving this life and the rituals (e.g., sacraments) necessary to attain that state of being, analogous believed-in imaginings? Are believings in reincarnations a lesser form of believed-in imaginings? What of the prevalent belief by people in many parts of the world in Obeah, voodoo, spirits, angels, and devils? Are the awaiting of the coming of a Messiah by Hasidic Jews or the belief in immediacy of the Apocalypse by Seventh Day Adventists different? The only difference seems to be the atypicality of the believings relative to one's own believings. Are reports of UFOs and aliens "hallucinations," "believed-in imaginings," or "sightings"? In this same vein, what shall we say to scientists who insist that if we search the universe with electromagnetic or optical devices we will eventually contact, and be able to communicate with, intelligent beings in other universes? Are these scientists to be considered mental health cases?

OTHER ISSUES AND CONCERNS

The focus of the analyses thus far has been to question the tenability of traditional ethnocentric criteria for determining which believings are to be considered counterfactual and taken as signs of a psychopathological condition by identifying communities where the same sort of believings are apparently consensual believings. Here, the same kinds of doings, but labeled differently *within* the same community are examined.

Instances that are labeled as *eidetic imagery* are choice examples to demonstrate differences in connotations and valuative status of the different labelings of doings that seems to be similar, but where contents, context, or kinds of doers differ. The term *eidetic imagery* was first used in psychology as an explanation for an atypical doing; namely, when an individual can reproduce a text, line by line, after a quick scanning of the page. The same kind of doings with other contents of sensory inputs have also been noted. That is, there are some individuals who can "visualize," and afterwards reproduce the sequence of the moves by each participant, and the positions of all of the chess pieces following each move in a chess match. There are other individuals who can play a piece of music after one hearing; and some who claim they can play the music in their heads after hearing a performance.

When a musician can play a piece after one hearing, it seems to be noteworthy, but not considered an unexpected competence. When an untrained individual can reproduce a musical rendering after one hearing, it is considered a rather unique and valued competence. However, when someone who seems to be limited in other normative doings (e.g., "social awareness," difficulty in mastering many common everyday tasks), the label, *idiot savant* is assigned, as if that achievement by that doer was *peculiar*, with a connotation of *bizarre*.

Synesthesia or cross modal sensory responses (e.g., hearing music when viewing colors; reporting a vivid sense of odors in particular locations; experiencing bodily sensations and overt sexual responses when dreaming, when imagining a past episode, or while fantasizing a sexual encounter, etc.) are not typically labeled as psychopathological doings. Although these kinds of events are unusual, they do not seem to be significantly different kinds of doings than those ordinary instances where one can produce tones when reading or writing musical symbols (notes). In fact these seem no different than the transformations of graphic texts to auditory sounds (reading), or *visa versa*, transcribing sounds to writing.

Within this context, we can compare those kinds of doings with those that are labeled as hallucinations. For example, it is unclear what differentiates "I actually *heard* my father's voice telling me to take the job" (memory or hallucination?), from some one who reports that he or she hears music while writing or reading notes. Similarly, those who can reproduce a visual text after reading or scanning it previously (sometimes called *photographic memory*), and those reporting flashbacks can be said to be involved in similar doings, only the kinds of contents are different. What then warrants a connotation probable psychopathological doing for *flashback* rather than the more conventional label *memory*?

Still further, we apparently do not consider descriptions of dreams, day dreams, fantasies (private doings) any differently than descriptions of past events, also private doings, nor is the question raised about their credibility. Is it the particular contents or the context of the report that warrants the label of *believed-in imagining*? As Turbayne (1970) and Whorf (1954) have claimed, language communities delineated events within the beliefs and metaphors of their particular historical languages; what is believable or strange are our tacit biases. When we classify atypical, nonveridical perceptions or unverifiable reportings (*cross modal effects* or *synesthesia*; *déjà vu* experience; or a perception as an *illusion* or a *mirage*) it would seem that the assignment to a conventional believing shelters these peculiar doings from that special category of *believed-in imaginings* that would also require a different sort of explanation.

The kinds of concerns and issues introduced here for *believed-in imaginings*, are analogous to those considered in some of my other writings (e.g., Kellner, Butters, & Wiener, 1961; Marcus & Wiener, 1989; Wiener, 1989, 1991; Wiener & Cromer, 1967; Wiener & Devoe, 1974; Wiener, Devoe, Rubinow, & Geller, 1972; Wiener & Marcus, 1994; Wiener & Schiller, 1960). All of these reflect a long held belief in the diversity of believings and doings for individuals and peoples with different personal and socio-cultural histories, and in the variability of doings by the same individual in different contexts and situations. With these presumptions, it seems more reasonable, and pragmatically more helpful to understand doings and happenings as *different*, rather than as defective, deficient, disrupted, disorganized, or with other attributions of impairment as is the traditional dogma. A second demand in this alternative perspective is that we focus on the sense of *differences in doings in contexts and situations*, rather than on whether they are traditional, typical, normative, frequent, unusual, or who is doing them.

If one begins to consider doings in contexts and situations as different, ineffectual, intrusive, unpredictable, socially inappropriate, logically unlikely, strange—or their antonyms—when imposing tacit conventional criteria, none of these designations would seem to require positing of a defective, deficient, disrupted, or disorganized "mind." As Ryle (1949) noted, one does something *poorly*, *well*, or *expertly*, these are assessments of the doing, not of invisible processes posited to cause them.

Turning again to the issue of consensus being a determinant of the credibility of believed-in imaginings, how different or unusual do doings or their particular contents and contexts have to be before we can arrive at a consensus that these doings are dysfunctional? Were we to use the term *different*, with whatever sets of qualitative differentiations, we would have the same information, could make as many predictions, would be less pejorative and could more readily subsume positive instances of atypical doings (e.g., genius, creative). With my self-appointed mission to focus on the forms of conduct in situations and contexts, and a requirement of a common explication for typical, frequent, and atypical or infrequent events, the ostensible presumptions and claims inferable as believed-in imaginings are too enticing to ignore.

The correlation between the atypical or unusual and the psychopathological also seems to involve a sort of word game. One starts with *unusual*, which becomes *atypical* and then *non-normative*, each a statistical frequency term. When these are paraphrased as *abnormal*, *anomalous*, or *deviant* (also statistical frequency terms), they also connote *peculiar* or even *bizarre*. It is then a minimal leap to transform them to *psychopathological*. Another argument against accepting word usages as if they were independent of context or situation is that words in themselves for the most part have no single meaning. For example, the attribution of the same descriptive term to different targets does not entail a conclusion that the same term denotes the same happening (e.g., "aggressive" football player vs. "aggressive" lawyer). Another example is the term *argue*, understood by some as connoting "discuss," by others, "fight." Asch (1946) and Larrow & Wiener (1989) made an analogous claim of a shift in the understanding of "personality" attributes when the same words occur in a different matrix of traits. One could also add that a different categorization in describing may be said to represent a difference in the perspective by the *labelers*, rather than two different denoted doings, events, or instances (e.g., *rebel* vs. *freedom fighter*, *religious zealot* vs. *religious fundamentalist*), with no one perspective granted privileged status. A thesaurus is a wonderful repository for such differences in usages.

The issue here is not whether categorization, classification, predictions, or empirical tests are reasonable or not for any sets of doings in contexts and situations, but rather that language usages and their connotations are contentious. As I alluded to previously, my biases in my understandings of ordinary language philosophies has been leavened by my observations, as a clinical psychologist, of the pervasive, omnipresent variability of individual, community, societal, and cultural narratives, despite common social histories and consensual understandings of language. For this reason, I have difficulty in imagining any clinical psychologist who would deny the innumerable observations of a) differences in narratives produced by individuals when each is required to "tell a story" about the same picture (e.g., Thematic Apperception Test); b) the variability of responses to the same ambiguous display (e.g., Rorschach ink blots); c) the differences in reporting by couples, family members, and collections of individuals of the same time–space happenings (i.e., who did what to whom, when, and where); d) the changes and qualifications added in repeated repetitions by one individual at later times, or to different audiences, or in different contextual situations. It is these kinds of differences that have convinced me that there is no conventional or normative way to describe a time–space doing or happening. My conviction remains that concerns about individual differences, variability, and diversity of individuals doing over times and contexts have more interesting possibilities for psychology than does the categorization of collectives, or of the averaging of population doings and patterning.

In the context of this critique of believed-in imaginings, it is important for me to assert that my acceptance, as a clinician, of an individual's imaginings is not predicated on a presumption that acceptance is essential for establishing a rapport with that individual (rapport is often claimed as being essential context for successful therapeutic outcome). To describe what I, as a clinician, might do were an individual, couple, or family unit to present the kinds of happenings and doings represented in Sarbin's exemplar cases is beyond the scope of this chapter. I can only say that neither I nor anyone else can claim to know what really happened, or who did what to whom, in which circumstances and contexts. These are the grist for the mill.

REFERENCES

Asch, S. E. (1946). Forming impressions of personality. *Journal of Abnormal and Social Psychology, 41*, 258–290.

Brody, H. (1980). *Placebos and the philosophy of medicine: Clinical, conceptual, and ethical issues.* Chicago: University of Chicago Press.

Frank, J. D., & Frank, J. B. (1991). *Persuasion and healing: A comparative study of psychotherapy.* Baltimore: Johns Hopkins University Press.

Kellner, H., Butters, N., & Wiener, M. (1964). Mechanisms of defense: An alternative response. *Journal of Personality, 32*, 57–74.

Larrow, M., & Wiener, M. (1989). Stereotypes and desirability rating for female and male roles. In J. C. Chrisler & D. Howard (Eds.), *New directions in feminist psychology* (pp. 239–249). New York: Springer.

Marcus, D., & Wiener, M. (1989). Anorexia Nervosa reconceptualized from a psychosocial transaction perspective. *American Journal of Psychopsychiatry, 59*, 346–354.

Ryle, G. (1949). *The concept of mind.* New York: Barnes & Noble Books.

Sapir, E. (1921). *Language: An introduction to the study of speech.* New York: Harcourt, Brace.

Sapir, E. (1964). *Cultures, language and personality.* Berkeley, CA: University of California Press.

Turbayne, C. M. (1970). *The myth of metaphor.* Columbia, SC: University of South Carolina Press.

Whorf, B. L. (1956). *Language, thought, and reality: Selected writings.* Cambridge: Technology Press of MIT.

Wiener, M. (1989). Psychopathology reconsidered: Depression interpreted as psychosocial transactions. *Clinical Psychology Review, 9*, 295–321.

Wiener, M. (1991). Schizophrenia: A defective, deficient, disrupted, disorganized construct. In W. F. Flack, Jr., D. R. Miller, & M. Wiener (Eds.), *What is schizophrenia?* (pp. 199–222). New York: Springer-Verlag.

Wiener, M., & Cromer, W. (1967). Reading and reading difficulty: A conceptual analysis. *Harvard Educational Review, 37,* 620–643.

Wiener, M., & Devoe, S. (1974). *Channels and regulators in communication disruption* (Grant No. MH 25775). Washington, DC: National Institute of Mental Health.

Wiener, M., Devoe, S., Rubinow, S., & Geller, J. (1972). Nonverbal behavior and nonverbal communication. *Psychological Review, 79,* 185–214.

Wiener, M., & Marcus, D. (1994). A sociocultural construction of "depressions." In T. Sarbin & J. I. Kitsuse (Eds.), *Constructing the social.* Newbury Park, CA: Sage.

Wiener, M., & Schiller, P. (1960). Subliminal perception and perception of partial cues. *Journal of Abnormal and Social Psychology, 61,* 124–137.

Wiener, M., Shilkret, R., & Devoe, S. (1980). "Acquisition" of communication competence: Is language enough? In M. R. Key (Ed.), *The relationship of verbal and nonverbal communication.* The Hague, Netherlands: Mouton Publishers.

Wittgenstein, L. (1958). *Philosophical investigations* (G. E. M. Anscombe, Trans.). New York: Macmillan.

3

REPLICAS, IMITATIONS, AND THE QUESTION OF AUTHENTICITY

KARL E. SCHEIBE

Believed-in imaginings, taken as real, can serve as the conditions for consequential conduct. Thus, the members of the Heaven's Gate community who committed collective suicide, in apparent anticipation of being picked up by a spacecraft, were merely enacting the logical consequences of their believed-in imaginings.[1] It is as if they entered into a dramatic frame and, having entered, could not escape its force. Within that frame, their imaginings seemed authentic; outside that frame, they seem ludicrous.

What are the consequences of living in a world that is increasingly dominated by replicated objects and events, so that we increasingly cannot be sure what is real? We need to examine the question of authenticity—how objects and experiences are taken as real or not real. What are we to make of apparently bizarre claims for authenticity—for UFOs, conversations with aliens, or out-of-body experiences? Believed-in imaginings are constructed within a synthetic dramatic frame. I argue that judgments of the authenticity of these imaginings depend upon the dramatic frame that is employed.

This chapter will appear in *The Dreams of Everyday Life* by Karl E. Scheibe (in preparation). Reprinted with permission of Harvard University Press. Copyright 1998.
[1]The bodies were discovered on March 26, 1997, in Rancho Sante Fe, CA.

THE PERVASIVENESS OF REPLICATION

The modern age is characterized, in part, by recognition of the value of the replicable event and object. Mass production, standardization of parts, photography, sound recording, facsimile transmission, electronic communication, and instant access to massive databases, as well as the cloning of living tissue, are all products of the 20th century. Most of us live in a world that is, in this sense, largely unoriginal. We spend our days in commerce with copies of things—photographs, recordings, reproduced art, cinema, television, and mass-produced objects, including computer screens and books.[2] If we are in a postmodern era, then that era must be characterized by a hypertrophied concern with easy and precise replication along with instant access to all of the recordings events, words, and people of the past. We also possess the capacity to record and replicate our own images, words, and activities completely and precisely for the benefit of the citizens of the future, and perhaps for the satisfaction to be derived from the apparent immortality of our replicated and preserved products. Cheap and efficient reproduction of things means ease of acquisition. Our imaginations and our acquisitive appetites seem to have no limits, even if our closets, bookshelves, and hard drives do.

The pervasiveness of loneliness, stress reactions, and depression in our time must be related to these observations. Unless we are masters of housecleaning and organization, we can easily be overwhelmed by vast quantities of replicated stuff and too much information. We live more and more in a world overfilled with replicas. Nature recedes, as do enduring relationships with living others. Boredom grows amidst the clutter, as our drama weakens.

Replication involves losses and raises questions, including some questions that are of the highest psychological significance. Everyone knows that some information is lost in copying anything from an original, and that increasing the generations of reproduction inevitably means the loss of information and detail. Restoration projects are conducted with great technical skill and precision, of course, and perhaps the restoration will seem an improvement on the original, as in the process of colorizing films originally printed in black and white. But time inevitably brings information decay, and even our language is not exempt from this effect. Witness the difficulty our ears have in understanding Shakespeare, as his ears must have strained to understand Chaucer.

---

[2] I do not wish to imply a sense of nostalgia or a desire to return to what Marx called the idiocy of village life. But I think something is out of whack when I am out for a run and encounter other walkers and runners who would rather listen to their portable stereos than to the chirping of the cardinals or the sound of the wind through the trees.

Problems of Veridicality and Nonduplicable Context

The more significant psychological problems with replication are of a different nature. The availability of precise copying techniques raises the possibility and likelihood of falsification—of the counterfeit, the ersatz, the shoddy, the manqué, the phony, the imitation. The question of authenticity is the inevitable sequel. Can we be sure that the bills in our wallet are truly legal tender? Can we be sure that the news reports we read and see in the media are true representations of reality, and not some concocted and tendentious story? What about scientific findings? Can we believe what they tell us about life forms in a Martian meteorite?[3] How about biography, history, and our own personal stories? Now we are told that Thomas Jefferson was a rogue, emancipation a charade, and avowed memories of personal history—such as those of sexual abuse—are of questionable validity.

In one form or another, these are all problems of veridicality—of matching the qualities of some reproduction with some original object or criterion of truth.[4] Another problem of veridicality must be raised, but it is not about information decay or changes intrinsic to memories or recordings of objects or events. This is the problem of dramatic context. Contexts cannot be replicated. It is impossible to reproduce the climate of circumstance and conventions of perception and understanding for any event. Who knows how Stuart's portrait of George Washington was seen and understood by its contemporaries? The reproductions are excellent, and the original is still in good shape, but the historical climate of the period, its modes of seeing and knowing and evaluating—these essential ingredients of understanding—are lost to us forever, for they cannot be captured and communicated in mere words and pictures. They have to be experienced. Our experience is, ineluctably, that of today, not of the 18th century, and no film or slide show or enthusiastic orator can take us back—not even a year, not to mention two centuries.

To be sure, the illusion of such historical transport is possible to attain, as when one is gripped by the power of an excellent historical narrator to convey a sense of remote times and places. But Kenneth Burns, the

---

[3]What are we to believe about the effect of estrogen replacement therapy on the prolongation of life for women? Research in this domain seems all the while to be the last word. But the last word seems regularly to contradict the penultimate word. The expectation is created that another last word will soon be pronounced, so that it is perhaps best to suspend belief and continue on with whatever half-blind beliefs and practices one has happened to acquire.
[4]Experimental psychologists studying the problem of false memory turn this into a rather easy matter through the simple expedient of controlling the truth. Thus, in Deese's (1959) original study, falsely remembered items are identified simply by comparing remembered lists with originally learned lists—the false intrusions are obvious. In the non-laboratory world, the criterion problem is not so easily solved, and is so intractable that the controversies about the false memory syndrome, its connections to sexual abuse and dissociative disorders will with difficulty be resolved by a simple appeal to fact, for in most cases the Ur-facts were nowhere recorded.

documentary producer, does not have the experience of the Civil War or of 19th-century baseball in his contemporary bones. He does have a considerable amount of experience with dusty archival material and lively old storytellers. From this, he applies his talent to make an era seem to come alive, but we lack the criteria to determine whether it is true, and my claim is that the recreation of climate and context is certainly false. To repeat, dramatic contexts cannot be replicated. We shall never know the Hamlet of the 17th century.[5] Hamlet, as a fictional creation, is with us still. But the winds and smells and conventions and climate of the time of his invention are irrevocably lost. Thus, it is senseless to strive for authenticity in the sense of matching the original.

Perpetual and pervasive doubt seems the only legitimate stance to take. Indeed, apologists for a postmodern mentality would say, "Forget about it! The whole question of authenticity is misplaced, for it smacks of essentialism, and we all know by now that nothing is essentially anything. Nothing is real, apart from our partial and idiosyncratic construction of the real. Plato is dead, thanks be, along with thousands of other quondam, white, male claimants to authority." However sustainable this position is from a logical point of view—and I admit it has merit—I submit that it is psychologically inadequate. Postmodernism, to be blunt, is a warmed-up version of nihilism, verging on solipsism, and such views have been around for centuries. The reason they have not generally been taken up has nothing to do with their logical inadequacy, but rather because they are psychologically insufficient, or, as I would prefer to say, postmodernism makes its believers dramatically impoverished. Moreover, the view that the entire world of our existence is socially constructed is pragmatically unsound. As Melville (1887/1984) has said, "The sea is, after all, the sea—and drowning men do drown"(p. 59) It is of little use or comfort to cancer victims to tell them that they are suffering from a fatal social construction.[6]

James (1890) told us that "Man needs a rule for his will, and will invent one if one be not given to him" (Vol. 2, p. 315). It will not do to say to Everyman and Everywoman that they must suspend belief on everything that cannot be personally and completely checked out. We take our aspirin from the bottle so marked and devoutly hope that we are not deceived. We marry and have children on the basis of vows not scientifically tested, and hope we will not be deceived, though here we often are. We pay large sums of money to educational institutions to educate our young, based on glossy catalogs, nostalgic memories, and a nervous hope that somehow our offspring might thus be prepared better to arrange themselves in an uncertain and chaotic future. We invest our money in what

---

[5] See Rosenberg (1992) for an exposition on the evolution of the fictional character over time.

[6] The reader can get a sense of how the strict constructionists can break all pragmatic tethers by perusing the essays in Sarbin and Kitsuse (1994).

are presented as legitimate companies, based on the quality of the story that can be told about those enterprises and their brokers.

Doubt is legitimate. But serious and pervasive doubt is also paralyzing, for it takes one out of play. We are urged to "Just do it." And, of course, we do—or at least we try—for we want to be in the drama of life. The question of authenticity, I propose, demands an address from the point of view of drama, for the dramaturgical perspective provides us with the keys to understanding why the problems of replication and the larger question of authenticity are so psychologically persistent and insistent.

THE QUESTION OF AUTHENTICITY

Commentators thought that the invention of motion pictures a century ago would produce a major change in the meaning of death, for now moving replicas of living forms could be maintained indefinitely. Technological advances now make possible the faithful reproduction of form and sound, as well as virtual realities, where one might have the experience of additional sensory dimensions in commerce with a replica of some remote or dead object. Recent advances in cloning living cells have produced additional questions about the finitude of life. The possibility of cloning indefinitely large numbers of precise genetic replicas of human beings certainly changes the ground rules of the ancient drama of life. Cloning and related feats of genetic engineering open up the possibility for developing human cultures that might be as efficient as a termite colony. We can finally envisage the elimination of sex, and with it an enormous source of worry and preoccupation. Freud can be shown to be quite wrong about sex as a drive: Its elimination will not remove the source of energy for all human activities, but rather will remove a noisome impediment to true psychological efficiency. (Of course, I am here imagining what a genetic engineer might be thinking, and I do not credit that engineer with the simple understanding that although sex might become superfluous technically, it will retain its dramatic interest. I recognize that my attitude here is ungenerous.)

Human cloning raises other questions of authenticity. Human clones are inevitable. The scientific knowledge to produce human clones is at hand, and although ethical strictures and pieties abound as to why this should not be attempted, no one can restrain the hand of curious science. Someone will perform the feat of reproducing a human being entirely from the genetic material of one parent before the century is over, although this may not become a matter of public knowledge for some time. The prospect is dramatically inviting, exciting. The question will arise, of course, as to whether a person so produced is an authentic human being, for, alternatively, such creatures might be regarded as a source of spare parts for human beings (especially their parent) or as robots. By the habits of millennia, we have developed the custom of judging the legitimacy of human material by its parentage. Can the charter of humanity be automatically extended to artificially produced clones, or are they to be regarded as a specially degraded form of bastard?[7] What role are they to play in the human drama?

Techniques of replication can be seen as attempts to defeat time, to create permanence, and thus to extend and expand away from the present moment and space and the confinements of finitude. But replication introduces the possibility of imitation. Replicated objects and experiences might not be identical to their originals, but might differ in some way—perhaps in detail, perhaps in essence. Some imitations present themselves as such—as copies of original objects—as prints and photographs and statues do not pretend to be the objects they represent.[8] Other imitations are fobbed off as the real thing: gold bricks meant to be taken for real gold, wooden nutmegs for real nutmegs, fake Rembrandts for real Rembrandts, and, yes, reported episodes of sexual abuse as representing genuine sexual abuse.

The worlds of Disney and other theme parks provide instructive cases illustrating the importance of successful replication in our times. A Disney park is a completely artificial construction and is original only in the consummate care devoted to imitative accuracy. They are places for pleasure, diversion, and amusement for the whole family. They are, quite obviously, successful, comprising the most attractive tourist destinations in the entire nation—perhaps in the world. They are clean and efficient and affordable. Now in touring Walt Disney World, one can have the experience of seeing real historical figures as well as real ghosts. One can experience real adventures, all the while knowing that nothing there is really real. Someone in the Disney corporation is doubtless thinking about combining their technology with a kind of psychic manipulation, perhaps by means of a variant of hypnosis, in order to create the illusion of an altered identity. In this way, it should be possible to participate convincingly in replications of Lincoln's assassination, or the Battle of Hastings, or the Crucifixion.

The most important products of the imagination of the late 20th century, after theme parks copying Disneyland, are the malls and the Internet—both conspicuous examples of the wild success of replication.

---

[7] If asexual reproduction had been the rule rather than the exception, then evolution could not have occurred, for the variation necessary for natural selection is a product of sexual reproduction. If not for moral reasons, asexually produced humans might be biologically reprehensible.

[8] Morgan le Fay fashioned a sword and scabbard in the exact likeness of Excalibur. The real sword was given to Accolar and the false to Arthur. As a consequence, Arthur was almost killed. The appearance was identical, but the functional characteristics were quite different— only the authentic object carried magical qualities. Quite obviously, Sir Thomas Malory, the teller of the Arthurian legend, was a Platonist and not a Pragmatist.

Malls are ruled by the principle of good function and allow easy access to a world of mass-produced objects, marketed in an attractive and effective way by chains of stores, many with branches worldwide (Ann Taylor, the Banana Republic, H. Stern, etc.). This makes malls quite similar throughout the developed world; they differ only in size and in the dominant language. The same credit cards are taken everywhere.

Sherry Turkle's (1995) book, *Life on the Screen*, provides an excellent description of the possibilities and consequences of living in a world of replicas. The book concerns the use of MUDs (Multiple User Domains) on the Internet, as a focus of interaction for a substantial number of individuals. One can draw the conclusion that for this group of avid participants, RL (Real Life) is not nearly as interesting or involving as life within a MUD. Virtual sex is but one of the many forms of imaginative involvement with others, others of an indeterminate RL gender, for there are cases of men pretending to be women pretending to be men, straight people pretending to be gay, and other interesting constructions. Such a life has its moments of wistful consummation, for as the author points out, virtual sex games are played "sometimes with both hands on the keyboard, sometimes with one." Relationships on a MUD must be infinitely more satisfying than the non-reciprocated fantasies of off-line people. On-line, one can share fantasies with utter strangers and develop relationships that must never be acted upon in the messy flesh. A MUD releases one from the confines of physicality. One can be perfect or at least more interesting if one never need be seen in the flesh.

Human life did not start off being a movie, but it is fast becoming one. My Wesleyan colleague, Joseph Reed (1989), in *American Scenarios*, provided an intense yet breezy journey through major genres of American film (the Costume Picture, the Inventor Movie, the Horror Movie, the High School Picture, Epic, Empire, Westerns, and so on). The theme is developed that we take our attitudes, gestures, ways of thinking, dressing, conversing, loving, hating, and fighting from the movies. Marilyn Monroe's open-mouthed smile soon begins to appear in high school yearbooks. Jimmy Stewart becomes a role model for good guys, and John Belushi a type for the fraternity animal. Yes, of course.

> In a way ... it is all a movie: We continually live one movie or another, or a scene, or a genre fragment as we move through anything from mundane encounter to major transition, from a chance meeting to those moments when we enter a room to discover that all the parts have been handed out before we arrived and we must take the one that's left. (p. 3)

A number of scholars and critics of contemporary American culture base their analyses in large part on their viewing of films from the archives. An example is another Wesleyan colleague, Richard Slotkin, whose books and essays on the American West and on our tradition of violence have become modern classics (Slotkin, 1973, 1985, 1992). I remember thinking, and perhaps even saying, "Richie, you've seen too many movies. You can't base an analysis of American attitudes about violence on your viewing of John Wayne. Real life is not a movie!" But I was wrong: He can and has based a convincing analysis of these and other issues on his viewing of John Wayne movies, along with countless other replicas of the past.

Even so, my reservations remain: In the rural world of my development, movies were not reality but an escape from reality. Reality was a corn crib full of corn, collecting eggs from the hens, the wonderful smell and feel of recently harvested wheat in a granary. Reality was the cold grease and streaking water on the block of an old engine that would not stay repaired. Reality was a runny nose and a chipped tooth. A broken scooter was reality, as were our cow and goat. I explored reality with my chemistry set, and although I could never make anything truly impressive happen with it, I did get a glimpse of the alchemical vision of the relation between magic and science. My father's hands were the most real things in the world to me—a working man's hands that could do anything, hung on the arms of a preacher. I was surer of his hands than I was of his head, which seemed to me full of unseen and unacknowledged things.

So I had a hard time learning to take movies seriously as sources of instruction and of modeling, for as a preacher's kid I was not allowed to see many. My context in living, let us say, was different from that of contemporary colleagues, Reed and Slotkin. It took me a while to recognize the truth in their position. James (1890, Vol. 2) has reminded us that "each world whilst it is attended to is real after its own fashion; only the reality lapses with the attention" (p. 293). Attention shifts as we enter the movie house and once again as we leave it. Reality is convincing as long as attention lasts and, as we continue attending to the movies, their reality becomes pervasive. For some of us, the movie continues to seem more real than ordinary Main Street as we come out of the theater blinking in the sunlight after a Saturday matinee.

Even so, there is a distinction to be made between the primary reality of cows and piles of grain and the derivative reality of Western movies, for the latter is based on replicas. The question of authenticity becomes paramount. A cow is, after all, a cow. Whitehead (1929) has said, "The second-handedness of the learned world is the secret of its mediocrity. It is tame because it has never been scared by facts" (p. 79). I think Whitehead had a point, and I doubt that there are many postmodernists or deconstructionists on farms or in factories. But farmers and factory workers are subject to their own forms of mediocrity, and I can assure you that they are commonly scared by the facts of primary experience. As it happens, any world view can defeat any other world view, if your world view happens to be at the immovable center of your existence. Tests for authenticity are perhaps easier on the farm than they are in the library, but difficult cases are to be found in both worlds.

TESTS FOR AUTHENTICITY: THE PRAGMATIC POSITION

James proposed that if a stick inserted in a glass of water looks bent and broken, then it is possible to draw it out of the water, there to inspect its linear quality, or to insert one's hand into the water to feel it, and gain thereby the advantage of another sensory dimension in determining the real nature of things. These are examples of pragmatic tests for determining authenticity.[9] An illusion is only an illusion if some pragmatic test exists to show by some comparative criterion that one version of perceived reality is more convincing than another. Thus, we can see that the apparent large size of the moon on the horizon is an illusion by devising a technique to measure the actual equal angles subtended by the moon at its zenith and on the horizon.

The difficulty is that many interesting questions and problems exist for which no pragmatic test exists to show whether an appearance or an assertion is illusory or not. The experimental psychologist always makes sure a comparative criterion is at hand for determining whether something is learned, perceived, or remembered correctly. The clinical psychologist can never be sure about the authenticity of what is reported, for the comparative criteria are usually not available. As a consequence, the clinician must make judgments about authenticity based upon the rather more shaky grounds of plausibility, consistency, coherence, and, perhaps, fit with what is generally thought to be true. Loftus (1975) has shown that eyewitness testimony is often wrong and, by extension, suggests that many cases of purported eyewitness identification might also be wrong. Lie detection studies (Lykken, 1974; Orne, Thackray, & Paskewitz, 1972) show the inaccuracy of these techniques for identification of truthful and false assertions and, by extension, the results of all lie detection studies are cast into doubt. One cannot just feel along the stick to determine what is true all the time. Sometimes pragmatic tests do not exist, or if they exist, they become indirect and problematic.

The discovery of the Dead Sea Scrolls half a century ago provided a new way of refining the general understanding of the authenticity of the Bible. A team of biblical scholars, called the Jesus Seminar, has been earnestly meeting over the past decade in order to determine which of the many words of Jesus Christ attributed to him in the Gospels might be regarded as authentic (see, e.g., Funk, Hoover, & the Jesus Seminar, 1993).

---

[9]See Barzun's (1983) chapter "The Test of Truth" in A Stroll with William James for an excellent discussion of the applications and misapplications of the principles of pragmatism as tests for truth.

To this day, major controversies abound over issues such as control of the Dead Sea Scrolls, the legitimacy of the Jesus Seminar's authority to designate certain sayings of Christ as authentic, and related questions such as who really wrote the biblical texts, when were they first written, who copied them out, and how ought they to be read. Not only deconstructionists but also ordinary skeptics assure us that all such questions are indeterminate, footless, and ultimately a waste of time. But such a verdict is naïve in that it ignores dramatic significance: These questions are among the manifold human efforts to find out God. Any news from this front—no matter how speculative or ultimately flawed—is fraught with deepest importance for those of us (uncountably many of us) who are caught in the drama of the question of origin. It matters not that there are no answers: The quest is the thing.

Suppose your drama is a different one: Suppose you are a psychoanalyst. Again, the question of authenticity is paramount. What did Freud really say, and have the Strachey translations betrayed him? More important, what did he really think? Did Freud truly believe in the universality of the Oedipus Complex, the generality of the seduction theory, the importance of the nose as a determinant of physical and psychological health? Was his early advocacy of cocaine as a panacea for human ills based on his own experimentation with this drug, and, if so, could the early formulations of psychoanalytic theory have been facilitated by drug-induced ecstasy—so that the composition of *The Interpretation of Dreams*, like Robert Lewis Stevenson's *Dr. Jekyll and Mr. Hyde*, might be a product of an imagination enflamed by cocaine? What really was the problem with Freud and Carl Jung? And speaking of Jung, what about this Toni Wolf business? Was she really his conduit to the Anima, and was he really in the habit of having sexual intercourse with his female clients and then transforming them into collaborators? And speaking of sexual infidelity and back to Freud, did the master have carnal knowledge of his own niece, and why did he seem so repressed about homosexuality?

Again, deconstructionists and ordinary skeptics might warn us away from such titillating but footless questions, arguing (pace Freud) that such matters are indeterminate. But some cracking good stories are to be found in this domain for those who are heirs to the psychoanalytic legacy and who, in their own way, are bent on finding out God. Serious scholarly work on these questions is guaranteed to continue and to be avidly read. The flap about Freud's seduction theory between Masson (1984) and Malcolm (1980) in the 1980s, involving intrigue, banishment from favor, secret papers, suppressed letters, Anna Freud's desire to protect her father, and sundry elements of loyalty and heresy—all of this elaborate drama was about the question of authenticity, was ultimately without a particle of importance for those of us (and that is most of us) outside its dramatic range, and was and is, as a factual matter, indeterminate. Even so, it is a fascinating story, full of dramatic appeal.

The problem of authenticity is of high importance if beliefs about the world and about ourselves are derived from some remote source, as most of our beliefs are. We do not, in general, speak with God or Jesus, nor even have commerce with Freud. Rather, virtually all of our contact with the *Ur*-sources in our lives is mediated by replicas, copies of materials. How do psychologists, in general, derive their knowledge? Like other scientists, we read books and journals, and therein we learn of experiments, surveys, clinical studies, and learned theories from respected authorities. We do not, in general, replicate first hand the studies we teach or regard as authoritative for our own understanding of the psychological world. The replication of knowledge is a tricky business and highly subject to distortion.

One of the first experiments I ever published was a study of the effect of demand characteristics in a psychological experiment that purported to be about sensory deprivation. This study was done under the direction of Martin Orne at Harvard Medical School in the summer of 1961, while I was still a graduate student at Berkeley. The study was published in 1964 (Orne & Scheibe, 1964), but became well known in certain quarters even before its publication, for it was one of the first studies to demonstrate the potentially confounding effects of subtle implicit instructions in common social psychological experimentation. When I returned to Berkeley in the fall of 1961, I had a conversation with a fellow graduate student who had heard about the study from a friend of his at Harvard, but he did not know that I had actually performed the experiment. His account of the experiment to me—an account I allowed him to give without giving away my own involvement–was a classic example of leveling and sharpening. The gist of his account was true, but the effects he reported to me were far more dramatic and stronger than what we actually found, and the experimental manipulations he described only vaguely resembled what we actually did. And yet he had full confidence in the authenticity of his report.

I should also note that whereas other studies have demonstrated the effects of demand characteristics on the outcomes of psychological experiments, the best and closest attempt to replicate our original study failed to produce findings similar to the original (Barabasz, 1991). Suffice it to say here that the effect we described was not terribly robust, at least not under the conditions of the replication experiment. But that has not stopped generations of psychologists from citing this study rather uncritically as demonstrating a general and authentic truth. It is quite difficult for me to imagine that our results would not replicate precisely, but this is an example of "identity politics", or of the invulnerability of my personal world view to an alien competitor.

The same can be said, of course, about a host of other psychological studies and reported truths. I remember trying to replicate Gibson's visual cliff phenomenon with kittens and with babies. Both crawled out on the glass, apparently over open space. I tried to demonstrate the consistency of Piaget's observations about conservation of mass with my own children. The results were far messier than the theory. Rosenthal's studies of experimenter bias proved to be, in some hands, rather hard to replicate (cf. Barber, 1969). I noticed another kind of replication problem recently in a study of how Skinner's views on cognitive processes were or were not correctly reported in common introductory texts (Jensen & Burgess, 1997). The study showed that virtually all of the 15 introductory texts missed what the authors of the study regarded as a fundamentally correct version of Skinner's account of cognition. They complained that the views of the 20th-century's most prominent experimental psychologist were not being represented in an authentic manner. In summary, some experiments that are thought to be of central importance to psychology do not replicate very well, and some conceptual approaches of major theoreticians are not necessarily represented or reproduced with accuracy. James (1890, Vol. 2) has said, "The empiricist says he believes only what he sees, but he is better at believing than at seeing" (p. 299). Claims of authenticity are often mere convictions masquerading as facts, supported more by bluff and bravado than by evidence.[10]

STATIC VERSUS DYNAMIC AUTHENTICITY: THE PATH TO THEATER

The Ambiguous Ephemeral

I know a professor of music who does not use recordings in his teaching and who does not even listen to recorded music. I know another professor who no longer writes for publication, although he is a brilliant thinker and lecturer and has much to say. Yet another professor of my acquaintance refuses to have his picture taken—not because he fears that his spirit will be captured thereby, but rather because he thinks that any recorded visual image of him is false the moment after it is taken, and he does not want to be falsely represented. These are tender and strange spirits, one might say, and yet they have in common a strong respect for the value of the ephemeral, verging on a reverence for it, coupled with an aversion to replicas.[11]

---

[10]Claims for the authenticity of the work of artistic masters rely ultimately on the authority of experts, as do claims about bloodlines for dogs and horses, the age and provenance of antiques, and the probative value of DNA evidence.

[11]I have my own aversion to replicas, it must be confessed. I own a 1952 MG-TD. I have several times restored this car in the 30-plus years I have owned it, and I know it exceedingly well. Having attended a number of rallies of MG owners, I also know what is called "the breed" quite well. Thus, I am offended by plastic-bodied cars slung over Volkswagen chassis that pretend to be MGs. In fact, as classic car buffs know, the concern with authenticity can become an obsession, so that some old car owners refuse to use nondetergent oil in their crankcases and insist on repainting their cars in original-only colors.

The ephemeral is defined is being "of the day," impermanent, transient. The anthropologist Edmund Carpenter (1978) described Alaskan Eskimo mask makers, who having created a mask out of some inner impulse, use it once and then burn it. Similarly, Japanese and Tibetan Buddhists create paintings and images that are not to be seen, and Navaho sand paintings are to be destroyed almost as soon as they are finished. Carpenter suggested that these examples are unified by a concern for the spirit of the act of artistic creation and that this is entirely different from a veneration for the material product of artistic creation. Eskimos would not create their own museums.

Ortega y Gassett (1973) has said, "To live fully is always to try to present a first performance" (p. 30). This is related to the theatrical maxim that "every night is opening night." The freshness of real theater is its enduring appeal, and no matter how successful and virtual the photographed and recorded replicas of theatrical performances become, there will always be audiences who prefer to take their theater live and actors who prefer to perform in that way.

The theatrical director, Mark Lamos, has said, "The performing arts actually benefit from their ephemeral nature. They live on most perfectly in memory. Their legacy is primarily verbal and requires transmittance from 'one who was there,' actually allowing a narrative condition to continue" (Lamos, 1996, p. 1). Dramatic authenticity, in this view, is of the moment, real, and powerful but evanescent. A presentation occurs in the unique context of a particular moment, with a particular cast in particular conditions to a particular audience. Memory, of course, is what gives the ephemeral event some lasting value, for what occurred can be described and talked about with others, including others who were not present for the original event. So it is with trips to foreign and exotic places, or sicknesses endured and overcome, or accidents, or conventions and meetings, or ceremonies—weddings and graduations and funerals and other dramatic rituals.

Averill (1988) and Sarbin (1986) have argued that emotions ought to be described as situated actions. Fear, happiness, and anger are not abstract states that can be described independently of the circumstances in which they are experienced. Here is an example: I am seated in a church, witnessing an initiation ceremony for ten adolescents who have just concluded a two-year initiation-into-adulthood program (see Roberts, 1982). A hymn is sung, and these are some of its words: "I was there to hear your borning cry, I'll be there when you grow old." Year after year, parents break down in tears while singing this song. They know it is coming. Their own children are no longer involved in the initiation program. But they cry despite themselves; they cannot help it. Yesterday, I cried. But as I repeat this story, I do not cry—nor do I feel a twinge of a tendency to cry. You had to be there. Emotions are authentic but ephemeral. We move on.

Events recede, even as the living memory of them is carried forward into the present, and occasionally events are revivified, *mutatis mutandis*, by sympathetic conversation. Emotions are dramatically embedded. They are no less real or authentic for this qualification.[12]

Although I am suggesting that one might have a certain reverence for the ephemeral, this posture does present some problems, particularly in a world where contexts and conditions change so rapidly as to obliterate memory, where the actual exercise of memory in verbal discourse disappears because of the ubiquity of useful replicas of events and facts, where a learned person may find no interested venue in which to display learning, but where stand-up comics find plenty of customers ready to enjoy the disconnected and ephemeral experience of laughing at the expense of others. Living memory is absolutely crucial to the existence of a sense of historical continuity, and this, I am not the first to argue, is central to civilization. When memory breaks down—and the plethora of replicas encourages its breakdown—we have problems.

Arthur Miller (1996) has described his writing of *The Crucible*, meant as an allegorical treatment of the evils of McCarthyism, for which he used the Salem witch trials as allegorical vehicle. He remarked that it is hard to convey now (in 1996) the sense of fear that pervaded the 1950s:

> I remember those years—they formed The Crucible's skeleton—but I have lost the dead weight of the fear I had then. Fear doesn't travel well; just as it can warp judgment, its absence can diminish memory's truth. What terrified one generation is likely to bring only a puzzled smile to the next. (p. 158)

Miller then described an audience reaction to an old film of Hitler at the Nuremberg rallies. They giggled at Hitler's absurd posturing and his overacting.

Not something to giggle at, surely. But taken away from the spirit of the times, reframed on a screen in a darkened room many years later, with Hitler dead and the Nazi movement discredited, and with savvy friends, it all seems faintly amusing. One wonders how he did it. How did this comical little man with the Charlie Chaplin mustache and the slicked black hair inspire a great nation to perform massive atrocities and inspire fear in the entire world? Apparently, you had to be there. The chilling thought occurs that the recording of history is a literal impossibility—that even with the most sophisticated and wide-angle recording devices, it is not possible to capture and preserve the ephemeral historical circumstances

---

[12]But this does not mean that the events or experiences associated with emotions are themselves real or authentic. When Little Nell dies in Dickens' *Old Curiousity Shop*, the readers tears are real even though the death is not. And the memories forming the basis of presently reported anguish over sexual abuse often do not refer to events that actually took place, forming the grounds for what is called the false memory syndrome (see Ofshe & Watters, 1994).

surrounding events. Because the meaning and consequences of actions cannot be understood outside of their dramatic context, and because that context cannot be captured, we can only achieve an approximate understanding of what the contemporary reaction was to important events. Not that our present reaction to historical events is necessarily weakened by the passage of time. I conjecture that those who witnessed the execution of Jesus or of Joan of Arc or who saw Lincoln give the Gettysburg Address might have been less filled with awe and wonder than were those of us who came after them and see things through the mythology created around the larger historical context. Many stories become wonderful only upon their retelling. Historical authenticity, it turns out, differs from the ephemeral authenticity of the moment, and there are merits and demerits to each.

In a splendid book called *Within the Context of No Context*, George Trow (1997) developed the argument that America has become a culture without context, and that television is the major vehicle for bringing about this state of affairs. Television has overwhelmed formerly important events such as political conventions, converting them into nonevents whereby the commentary by experts (now more famous than the politicians they talk about) becomes the main feature as the convention itself becomes utterly devoid of interest or importance. Television has shortened our attention span and obliterated our sense of historical continuity. Trow argued that it has tickled and titillated us into a state of vulnerable and supine stupidity. If one grows up watching 35 hours of television a week, the norm for American children, then surely replicas become the prime reality, and it becomes faintly absurd to try to disentangle what is meant by authenticity, for there are no pragmatic reality checks on television.

MTV videos represent a simple extension of the television medium. The cuts are rapid and as incongruous as a dream. No attempt is made to maintain a consistent story line or to make sense. A music video is a visual representation of total fantasy, and because it is made with great skill, with arresting images and carefully coordinated sound, it can be captivating— more likely to be much more developed and interesting that any internally produced fantasy the viewer might produce.[13] Robert Bly (1996) provided a complementary vision:

> When a young man in our culture arrives at the end of adolescence, the river of secularity typically carries him over the waterfall and he's out in the big world. The speakers at his high school graduation will

[13]Sut Jhally (1995) has produced an analysis of the portrayal of women on MTV in a video called "Dreamworlds." Jhally made the point that MTV is dominated by male producers, and that the collective image of women is that they are sex-starved, aggressively after the male stars, and without independent interests or abilities. It is truly a self-serving male fantasy. The women portrayed on MTV really appear to be after the bodies of the male singers. Young viewers of MTV might be excused for mistaking this appearance for reality—a synthesis of apparent authenticity out of fantasy.

say, "The future belongs to you." But the speaker does not mention to whom the student belongs. He belongs to nothing; he belongs to the river; he belongs to the trash at the bottom of the waterfall. He belongs to light beer, and sitcoms about bars, and forgetting. In ten years his muscles will be looser then they were at graduation, and high school will be very nearly his last experience of form. . . . He will find around him a group centered on the acquisitive instinct, by which I mean that impulse toward taking and consuming. (p. 79)

The obliteration of memory and reason can be so great as to bring about the acceptance at face value the fake altruism of talk show hosts, as they invite strange people onto their stages for the stated purpose of displaying for the first time the hidden reality of sexual deviates, criminals, and assorted weirdos—but with the authentic purpose of drawing large audiences, who seem able to yawn and be titillated simultaneously. A sociological content analysis of several of the most popular talk shows concluded as follows:

> Television shows offer us an anomic world of blurred boundaries and at best normative ambiguity. Cultural distinctions between public and private, credible and incredible witnesses, truth and falseness, good and evil, sickness and irresponsibility, normal and abnormal, therapy and exploitation, intimate and stranger, fragmentation and community are manipulated and erased for our distraction and entertainment. Nothing makes conventional sense in this deconstructed society. (Abt & Seeholtz, 1992, p. 174)

The ephemeral is potentially both wonderful and horrible. Those who can bring their memory, their reason, and their the emotional capacity to an event are prepared to be transported by the singularity of the moment, perhaps to achieve an indescribable ecstasy. These peak experiences can then become the basis for waves of narrative extension, and they might become even more wonderful through the retelling. Those who come to the same event with dulled memory, lazy reason, and emotional indifference are merely subjects for manipulation—not sentient human beings, but dead to the authentic significance of the moment. Termites live in the moment, without sentiment, without a sense of history, without moral sensitivities. It is, unfortunately, easier for human beings to become like termites than it is for termites to become like human beings.[14]

---

[14]The problem with the human sciences is that human beings are reactive to historical context. Science is predicated on the principle of uniformity of nature and the correlative principle that matter is not reactive to the cultural or historical context surrounding it. Virology is one of the more difficult and problematic areas of biological inquiry, precisely because viruses seem to mutate in reaction to environmental pressures. They do not just hold still as proper scientific material is supposed to. Human beings are even worse at holding still. Not just the stock market, but history itself is a random walk.

From Boredom to Restlessness to Theater

Infants are born with an interest in novelty. As neonates, they turn their eyes in the direction of novel stimuli. As a stimulus becomes familiar, young babies will no longer turn their eyes in its direction. They become habituated or, to use different term, they become bored with that particular stimulus. But young children maintain interest in repeated stimulus patterns, such as repeated viewings of a video of Barney. Their curiosity seems insatiable. But for adults, boredom is the final consequence of repetition.[15]

As ours is the era of the replicated event and the replicated object, ours is also the era of boredom. Boredom, not sex, may be the major motivational base of our times. G. K. Chesterton has said that a bore is someone who takes away our solitude without giving us conversation. Conversation requires that people who are together have something to talk about—perhaps an exciting, if ephemeral, experience that one or the other of them has had. But if they have been watching MTV, it may not be possible to have much of a conversation about what they have seen, or if there is a conversation, it will probably be on the Beavis and Butthead level—composed mostly of the word *like* and grunts and giggles. Parents are boring to their children. Children are boring to their parents. Sex can become just one way of relieving boredom, joining cable or satellite television, with their options of hundreds of channels, and the Internet, with its information highway to nowhere, and escapist literature—by far the largest-selling category of books. Or, perhaps a trip to the mall would be fun, or perhaps the Indian casino down the road.

Solitary confinement is the most intense punishment human beings have been able to design for each other. Those who have studied penology (Sykes, 1958), brainwashing, or thought reform (Lifton, 1956) agree that the consequences of prolonged isolation are profound psychological and physical deterioration. The boredom produced by isolation produces disconnected thoughts and images and renders one incapable of maintaining one's bearings in relation to people, places, things, events, or time. Creeds remain, for they can be more or less cultivated in one's head. Lifton reported that prisoners of war with strong religious convictions did better than their skeptical colleagues at resisting the destructive consequences of brainwashing during the Korean war.

Restlessness is a product of the urge to avoid boredom, and restlessness produces, among other things, theater. The essence of drama is

---

[15]The relation between affective response and repetition is a progression. Repetition initially produces familiarity and positive pleasure (cf. Zajonc, 1968). If affective response is plotted against number of repetitions, then the curve will have a positive inflection at first, will peak at some point, and will then decay into negative territory. Anyone might confirm this general effect by looking at one's record collection and thinking about the records that are chosen for current replaying.

transformation—the transformation of the quotidian world into something that commands interest and stimulates conversation, the rippling out of novelty away from its time and place or origin. The Russian master of theater, Nikolas Evreinoff (1927) has described the instinct to theater as a protest against mechanical repetition. But Evreinoff observed also that professional theater can turn toward this evil rather than against it, and that the repetitive acting and sure-fire speech patterns and gestures of the professional actor can lack all spontaneity and can become stale and a torture to behold.

By extension, the drama of an entire culture can become excruciatingly boring, when manners become so standardized as to permit no variation, roles so standardized as to admit no cadenzas, beliefs so conventional as to permit no dissent. Enter Ibsen, Brecht, Artaud, Beckett, Albee, Mamet, Tennessee Williams, Pinter, commedia dell'arte—enter all those playwrights and dramatic traditions that would challenge the established order. Drama becomes the instrument of salvation from sameness, and when the drama itself becomes stale, it becomes necessary to produce something like a political revolution, even if the revolution amounts to no more than turning over the sick and sore body politic in its bed.

This characterization of drama introduces a twist into my developing argument about replicas and authenticity. Replicas depart from authenticity and produce boredom in their train. Boredom is a negative motivation that produces restlessness. And restlessness can produce theater—and theater is authentic only if it is novel, spontaneous, and fresh, and becomes inauthentic as it comes to match exactly some preexisting model. Thus, the criterion for authenticity is transformed away from the matching-to-criterion standard that has been articulated earlier. Instead, authenticity in the drama of everyday life has to do with our capacity to improvise with creativity and originality on the materials and themes we have been given to play on, and with the companions who adventitiously form our company. The play is uninteresting as a mere rerun. Dynamic authenticity is a matter of being alive to the moment.

Both criteria for authenticity have utility. I think of static authenticity as that of matching an example to some standard, as when a substance is examined to determine whether it is a diamond. These are pragmatic tests. The authenticity of historical events becomes finally indeterminate, because of their context dependence, the reactivity of human beings to the context of the moment, and because contexts are ephemeral. Dynamic authenticity is the more difficult case but the more delightful. Great and original performances can take place around us at any moment, if we are but alert to them and are ourselves, on occasion, willing to depart from common and safe pathways.

LOOPS AND CYCLES AND THE AUTHENTICATION OF SELF

Clinical psychologists are often troubled by the problem of the authenticity of the self. A common problem is that of individuals who seem to have lost track of who they really are. They experience genuine doubt about their identities. Other people seem to have problems engaging their lives in a meaningful way. Their lives seem empty, devoid of authenticity or significance.

In this last section, I would like to turn the problem of authenticity toward the self. In so doing, I would like also to illustrate the utility of two metaphors—the loop and the cycle. A *loop* for human identity is provided by the invention of a social category, the taking on by an individual of the category label, and the continuation of the person's life drama under the conditions implied by the label. The role of student is invented, taken on, and then lived out.

Cycle is shorthand for "cycle of meaning." A student studying for an exam, taking an exam, and receiving a grade for an exam has completed a cycle of meaning—including the essential ingredient of some kind of response from the social or physical environment that provides sense or meaning for one's activities.

The application of these metaphors to the problem of personal authenticity can be illustrated by some familiar clinical types. Here is an example of a loop. I had a client some time ago who took to writing me letters between her appointment times. The letters consisted of commentary on the content of therapeutic sessions—critical, approving, or interpretive. The letters were always beautifully written, meticulously typed, and correct to the last detail of grammar and spelling. They were signed, "The Observer." I had seen this client over a period of about three years, and after about two and one-half years, she became comfortable enough to tell me that she was really three different people. Later however, I met another, "The Keeper," who was also not among the three who appeared in my office.

This client had been a foster child and complained of a long history of sexual and physical abuse in her childhood. Her first marriage was also reported to be highly abusive, leading her at one point to attempt suicide. She came to me initially presenting symptoms of major depression, following recovery from alcohol and drug abuse. Only much later was I gradually introduced into her more authentic complaints, which as you have seen, fit exactly the contemporary paradigm for dissociative identity disorder (DID). This is how she thought of herself—as a case of DID.

Now, I asked myself, what kind of a drama is this? I am not a believer in DID. I had the impression that such patients were likely to appear before therapists who had a stake in reinforcing the legitimacy of this diagnostic category—and I, most assuredly, had none. Even so, I learned to play my complementary role in a satisfactory way. The first time I received a letter from The Observer, I casually showed it to my client on her next visit. She was utterly bewildered. She said it must have come from her, but that she had absolutely no memory of having written it. Later, her husband called me to say that she was frantically looking about the house to find the computer disk on which the letter had been composed, only to find that the disk had been erased. The next letter I received from The Observer reproved me for having shown the letter to my client, for it was not meant for her eyes. She was not gentle with me. Thereafter, I made no such mistakes and the course of therapy went along smoothly.

I did not supply my client with a script for the part she was to play, but the concept of DID is out there in the culture, defined and illustrated. My client certainly had a troubled and fragmenting history—a history that she was able to interpret, probably without even trying, in terms of the categories proffered to her by the popular dissemination of stories from people diagnosed as having DID. Perhaps if she had seen that I would be more cordial to the possibility of entertaining multiple personalities in my office, she would have "outed" sooner. Once she had defined herself in that way, there was little that I could do in a constructive way other than accept the legitimacy of the story she was presenting to me, and in a pragmatic way, I did accept that story—as an authentic story, not as an ontological truth. I could see no point in trying to convince her that she was imbedded in an artificial social construction. "The sea is, after all, the sea." And if you think you are in some psychological sea, who am I to tell you that you are dry?

This client examplified what Ian Hacking (1995) referred to as the "looping effect in human kinds." My client was self-classified as having DID, and she came to behave in accord with the requirements of this category of people, with her own authentic variations and cadenzas. Many human beings loop into their identities in something like this fashion—Christians, homosexuals, Republicans, Freemasons, hippies, new agers, and schizophrenics are other examples that come to mind. Thus are created social categories, and once created are real, just as president of the United States is real. Once you are defined in the category, you become an authentic case of the type. It is regressive and contrafactual to argue that the category itself was or is a mistake.

Here is an example of a cycle. I have a client who is a 72-year-old man. He is married, retired, and financially comfortable. He is commonly bored and sometimes irritated at his wife, who tends to be controlling and overbearing. He has two means of escape. One is to read books. He consumes thick novels, one after the other. Occasionally, to break the monotony, he will buy a half-pint of vodka and drink it down in his garage or cellar, for his wife will not permit him to drink and he has to sneak his libations. This cycle is unsatisfactory in several respects: The alcohol use is harmful and potentially fatal. Already my client has had several bad falls because of alcohol use, one of which resulted in a severe head trauma. Second, the reading habit is not part of a complete cycle of meaning. He reads novels as if he were pouring water into the desert sand. The material goes nowhere. He does not talk about what he reads—not to his wife, not to his therapist, not to his few friends—it just pours in and disappears. He is bored with his life, and the only things he can think to do to break the boredom are either self-destructive or else boring in themselves. As his therapist, I struggle to create an authentic completion of a cycle for him. I listen to his stories, and I respond to them with as much vitality and interest as I can muster.

What does a complete and satisfactory cycle look like? A colleague once described to me the ideal connections between teaching, research, and publication as being phases or parts of a cycle or a series of cycles. One is first and always a student. As a student one learns, and in order to demonstrate and make fast the learning, one recites what one has learned. But one is stimulated by what one has learned to inquire beyond what is initially given as the product of the past. This is research or scholarship, and, like theater, is a product of restlessness and a lack of satisfaction with mere repetition. This scholarship, if blessed by success, leads to the class-room as well as to reading books and journals, because both provide a means for performing and then being corrected on what you think you have learned as a result of your research. Always there are new questions. Always there are new fields to explore. Always there are new audiences, before whom one might lay out the provisional results of one's inquiry. And those audiences, by their reactions of indifference, hostility, or cordial appreciation, are informative about the authenticity of one's work. This is a satisfactory cycle. It is a dramatic cycle.

REFERENCES

Abt, V., & Seeholtz, M. (1992). The shameless world of Phil, Sally, and Oprah: Television talk shows and the deconstruction of society. *Journal of Popular Culture, 28*, 160–182.

Averill, J. (1988). Disorders of emotion. *Journal of Social and Clinical Psychology, 6*, 247–268.

Barabasz, M. (1991). Effects of experimental context, demand characteristics, and situational cues: New data. *Perceptual and Motor Skills, 73*, 83–92.

Barber, T. X. (1969). Five attempts to replicate the experimenter bias effect. *Journal of Consulting and Clinical Psychology, 33*, 1–6.

Barzun, J. (1983). *A stroll with William James*. New York: Harper & Row.

Bly, R. (1996). *The sibling society*. Reading, MA: Addison-Wesley.

Carpenter, E. (1978). Silent music and invisible art. *Natural History*, *87*, 90–99.

Deese, J. (1959). On the predition of occurrences of particular verbal intrusions in immediate recall. *Journal of Experimental Psychology*, *58*, 17–22.

Evreinoff, N. (1927). *The theatre in life*. London: Harrup & Co.

Funk, R. W., Hoover, R. W., & the Jesus Seminar. (1993). *The five gospels: The search for the authentic words of Jesus*. New York: Scribner.

Hacking, I. (1995). *Rewriting the soul*. Princeton, NJ: Princeton University Press.

James, W. (1890). *Principles of psychology* (Vols. 1–2). New York: Holt.

Jensen, R., & Burgess, H. (1997). Mythmaking: How introductory psychology texts present B. F. Skinner's analysis of cognition. *Psychological Record*, *47*, 221–232.

Jhally, S. (Writer, editor, and narrator). (1995). *Dreamworlds II: Desire/Sex/Power in Music Video*. [Video]. Northampton, MA: Media Education Foundation.

Lamos, M. (1996). Reflections. In Program for *The servant of two masters*, performed by Hartford Stages Company, September 28–November 2, 1996.

Lifton, R. J. (1956). "Thought reform" of Western civilians in Chinese Communist prisons. *Psychiatry*, *19*, 173–195.

Loftus, E. F. (1975). Leading questions and the eyewitness report. *Cognitive Psychology*, *7*, 560–572.

Lykken, D. T. (1974). Psychology and the lie detector industry. *American Psychologist*, *29*, 725–739.

Malcolm, J. (1980, November 24). Profiles: The impossible profession. *The New Yorker*, 85–133.

Masson, J. M. (1984, February 3). Freud and the seduction theory. *The Atlantic*, 33–60.

Melville, H. (1984). Vol. 10 of *The writings of Herman Melville*. Chicago: Northwestern University Press and Newberry Library. (Original work published 1887)

Miller, A. (1996, October 21 & 28). Why I wrote "The crucible." *The New Yorker*, 158–165.

Ofshe, R., & Watters, E. (1994). *Making monsters: False memories, psychotherapy, and sexual hysteria*. New York: Scribner.

Orne, M. T., & Scheibe, K. E. (1964). The contribution of nondeprivation factors in the production of sensory deprivations effects: The psychology of the panic button. *Journal of Abnormal and Social Psychology*, *68*, 3–12.

Orne, M. T., Thackray, R. I., & Pasketitz, D. A. (1972). On the detection of deception. In N. S. Greenfield & R. A. Sternbach (Eds.), *Handbook of psychophysiology*. New York: Holt, Rinehart & Winston.

Ortega y Gassett, J. (1973). *An interpretation of universal history*. New York: Norton.

Reed, J. (1989). *American scenarios*. Middletown, CT: Wesleyan University Press.

Roberts, W. O. (1982). *Initiation to adulthood*. New York: Pilgrim Press.

Rosenberg, M. (1992). *The masks of Hamlet*. Newark: The University of Delaware Press.

Sarbin, T. R. (1986). Emotions and acts: Roles and rhetoric. In R. Harré (Ed.), *The social construction of emotions* (pp. 83–97). Oxford, England: Basil Blackwell.

Sarbin, T. R., & Kitsuse, J. I. (1994). *Constructing the social*. London: Sage.

Slotkin, R. (1973). *Regeneration through violence*. Middletown, CT: Wesleyan University Press.

Slotkin, R. (1985). *The fatal environment*. New York: Atheneum.

Slotkin, R. (1992). *Gunfighter nation*. New York: Atheneum.

Sykes, G. (1958). *The society of captives*. Princeton, NJ: Princeton University Press.

Trow, G. (1997). *Within the context of no context*. New York: Atlantic Monthly Press.

Turkle, S. (1995). *Life on the screen: Identity in the age of the Internet*. New York: Simon & Schuster.

Whitehead, A. N. (1929). *The aims of education*. New York: Macmillan.

Zajonc, R. B. (1968). The attitudinal effects of mere exposure. *Journal of Personality and Social Psychology, 9*, 2–11.

II

DEVELOPMENTAL ISSUES

4

IMAGINATION AND TRUE BELIEF: A CROSS-CULTURAL PERSPECTIVE

PENELOPE G. VINDEN

In order to explore why some people believe in things that are imaginary, one has to ask on what basis one can claim that some beliefs are only imaginings, whereas others are not. For in calling some beliefs "imaginings"—Santa Claus, or false memories, or spaceships behind meteors—one implies that some beliefs are true beliefs and that one is able to distinguish between beliefs that are true and those that are not. But on what basis do we make such a distinction? Can we really talk about believed-in imaginings at all?

What led me to question the validity of talking about believed-in imaginings was my own experience in doing research in children's understanding of mind in a variety of non-Western cultures. Children's theory of mind is a fascinating area of research that has blossomed in the last decade. It has to do with when and how children come to understand that people are intentional agents whose thoughts affect their actions. Researchers within the field of theory of mind have tended to be universalists, assuming that all people everywhere develop the same theory of mind as do Westerners. My research has led me to question this assumption. Living for various lengths of time in a number of cultures quite different from my own, and struggling both to understand others and to be understood, helped me to see in a hands-on way that people come at things from very different perspectives, and that most are convinced that their beliefs are indeed true.

My experiences have also given me a dislike of the term "Westerners," and I use it advisedly. What I mean by the term is something like "the white middle-class set of attitudes, beliefs, and behaviors that in some sense dominates North America and Europe." I do not intend to imply by my use of the term "Western" either that there is some single undifferentiated homogeneous cultural grouping in North America and Europe that includes all people, nor that all people everywhere can be neatly divided into a dichotomy. At present, however, I find no other way to talk about the kind of distinction that I wish to make and that has some utility in the present discussion.

In this chapter I raise some questions about what I take to be the assumptions that underlie a topic such as believed-in imaginings. I do this in several ways: First, by talking about the kinds of beliefs held by young children that we take to be imaginings; second, by looking at examples of beliefs in non-Western cultures that Westerners think of as imaginings and discussing why those beliefs could be seen to be every bit as valid as ours; and, third, by exploring whether or not it is possible, or even necessary, to salvage true belief from the deconstructionist rubble of our postmodern age.

THE REAL VERSUS THE IMAGINED FOR YOUNG CHILDREN

What do I mean by an imagining? In the first place, it is a mental event (or brain activity, if you insist) that differs from true belief in that, unlike true belief, it does not have real-world correlates. A real-world correlate is that which exists outside of the brain and provides a kind of physical substrate for what happens inside the brain. I realize that the way in which mental events correspond to what is outside the brain is a matter of much debate and is a complicated issue. But in order to talk about imaginings we must think of them as in some way distinguishable from the real world, that is, that which might be said to truly exist outside our heads.

An imagining might be considered a pretense. In pretense we create a world in our imagination, whereby what is imagined is only believed in within the pretend world. What is the relation of the pretend world to the real world? Can we really separate the two? Children as young as 2 begin to realize that the pretend is not the same as the real—a pretend ice cream cone cannot be really eaten, for example. But you can pretend to eat a pretend ice cream cone. So the pretend world is like a parallel world, which has some overlap with the real world, which is based on the real world, but is quite distinct from the real world. It is a world created by our minds, which can be laid aside at will and taken up again.

But this distinction between fantasy and reality is by no means clear among young children—even 4- to 6-year-olds, who claim that monsters are not real, in some situations act as if they are. This inability to entirely divorce oneself from the nonreal fantasy world persists into adulthood. After watching the movie *Psycho*, many adults report that they feel ill at ease in the shower for the next few days, even though they are very clear that the events in the movie did not really happen. Thus it would seem that our emotions somehow make us lose on grip on, if only temporarily, what are intellects are telling us is the case.

Even when our emotions are not initially involved in a situation, we can still become confused about what is real. A study by Rozin, Millman, and Nemeroff (1986) demonstrated how for adults, what we clearly know to be true concerning something does not necessarily dictate how we behave toward it. Subjects were shown two empty bottles, and sugar was poured into each. Then they were asked to place a label, "sugar," on one bottle and a label, "cyanide," on the other bottle. Despite the fact that they had arbitrarily chosen which bottle to label as what, subjects were reluctant to sample from the bottle labeled "cyanide." This phenomenon points to a rather mysterious aspect of the naming process: In a situation fraught with emotion, it seems as if the naming, like the imagining, is actually calling something into being—making the nonreal become real. Whatever is going on in these cases, it seems as if emotional arousal appears to throw off our judgment somewhat, so that we lose the distinction between what is real and what is not, or the distinction blurs somewhat. So emotional involvement might offer us a clue to what moves us to believe in an imagining.

But pretending something is the case is clearly not always the same as imagining something. One of the characteristics of pretense, both in the child and adult worlds, is that the pretender really does know that the pretense is not real, even if he or she is not always able to act that way. But a believed-in imagining is something that is clearly thought (by the one believing it) to be true or real. In fact, it is not thought of as an imagining at all, but as knowledge, as true belief. In that sense, a believed-in imagining has more in common with deception. In most cases we do not want to be the holders of false beliefs. When we are deceived, whether by ourselves or by others, we unwittingly hold false beliefs to be true.

Of course there are various ways in which we can be deceived. One way is to take appearance for reality. Again, in normal development, a child is able to clearly distinguish appearance from reality in a broad sense at a young age—the actor on television is not a real policeman, the toy firetruck is not a real fire truck, and so on. However, at times we become deceived, or allow ourselves to be deceived. Actors who play unpleasant characters have been attacked, verbally or physically, by adults who have forgotten that the actor is just an actor, and does not necessarily share the characteristics of the person he or she portrays. Again, emotions seem to be part of the picture here (anger with the way the character treats other people, for example). But another factor may be repetition through time: Seeing a character day after day may wear down the fantasy–reality barrier and allow us to become confused or deceived about what is real.

By about age 4, children in Western cultures are able to understand a narrower set of appearance–reality phenomena that focus on genuinely deceptive appearances. Consider, for example, the sponge rock—it looks like a rock, but careful inspection reveals that it is in fact a sponge painted to look like a rock. In this case the appearance actually conflicts with the reality, but both are equally true: It truly looks like a rock, but it also truly is a sponge. In order to understand this distinction between appearances and reality, the young child must have some notion, among other things, that objects have some sort of essence that defines what is truly real, and that this essence can contrast with the object's somewhat more ephemeral properties, such as color, smell, and so on.

The sponge rock is an example of an object about which we might be deceived but that is accessible. We can hold it, squeeze it, and come to understand it better—we can move from our false belief about its identity to a true belief without much trouble. Other objects, events, or situations may not be so readily accessible for examination, and they may challenge other beliefs we have about the way things are. In such cases preschool children in our culture often appear to engage in a type of believed-in imagining that we call magical thinking. Magical thinking is used primarily as a means of explaining things that do not fit in with their view of the world, explaining things that they do not yet understand. So, for example, when confronted with a situation in which they are deceived into thinking that a solid object fell through another solid object, they are surprised, because this violates their fledgling beliefs about the laws of nature (Chandler & Lalonde, 1994). So children are often inclined to explain evidence that contradicts their beliefs in terms of magic. The second solid object was magically made to disappear, for example.

THE REAL AND THE IMAGINED ACROSS CULTURES

Similarly, we often view magical thinking among people in other cultures as a means to explain things they do not understand or things that violate other cherished beliefs. We may also tend to view them in a somewhat paternalistic or maternalistic fashion as children who do not yet fully understand the world (as "enlightened" Westerners do) and therefore need to fall back on magical thinking. Let us look more closely, then, at some examples from other cultures in which people believe in things that West-erners would classify as imaginings, such as magic and witchcraft, to see to what extent these beliefs serve as explanatory devices, and whether or not that is their only function.

One such example of magical thinking is witchcraft. Witchcraft concerns "the powers that individuals or agencies have to harm others or disrupt social relationships" (Heelas, 1981, p. 11). Lévy-Bruhl (1927/1966) reported that in many cultures "it is neither unprecedented nor absurd that an animal should appear in human shape, just as it is neither surprising nor terrifying to see a man assuming the outward appearance of an animal" (p. 42). Arnot described the reaction of Zambesi youths to a wily leopard that had attacked them but consistently avoided capture: "This leopard is not an animal; it is a person" (cited in Lévy-Bruhl, 1927/1966, p. 47). While I was conducting research among the Tainae speakers of the Papua New Guinea lowlands, a woman was pointed out to me, and I was told that she was a witch who had recently turned into a pig and gored a young boy. Interestingly, the children in this culture did not respond as expected when confronted with the appearance–reality items such as a sponge rock that are used to test Western children. In fact, no clear way was found to ask the children the reality question: What is this really? This should not surprise us. For people to whom a witch can be a pig one minute and a woman the next, what is an appearance, and what is a reality?

The interesting thing about witchcraft, however, is that it is not really necessary as an explanatory device in the physical realm. Tainae people know that wild pigs are fierce and that they sometimes attack people. Zambesi youths surely expect some variation in the wiliness of leopards. So . . . why witchcraft? Why is this, to us, a seemingly wild believed-in imagining? Many explanations have been given. Some say that witchcraft is a means of channeling anxiety that results from random misfortunes that could not have been prevented by ordinary means. Some say it is a means of social control. Whatever the explanation given (by us) for the use (by them) of witchcraft, it all seems to center around crossing some barrier between the tangible material world and some unseen less tangible world—the world of morality or relationships or emotions.

The entanglement of the material world with moral and emotional issues can be seen in terms of the need people have to explain suffering, illness, and emotional disturbance. Harris (cited in Heelas, 1981) reported that for the Taita of Kenya, angry hearts cause misfortune and suffering. Whereas Western culture also retains the use of body language to describe some emotions (e.g., "my heart aches," "that makes my blood boil"), it is not really thought that these emotions are directly manipulatable through some sort of bodily activity. For the Taita, however, ritual purifications can be performed in order to deal with misfortune and distressful emotions. In this way, antisocial anger is replaced with peace, thus ensuring that social relationships run smoothly.

For the Oriya of India (Shweder & Miller, 1991), physical suffering is caused by prior sins—not remaining secluded during menstruation, looking lustfully at a widow, and so on. A man kicks his father; later his leg becomes crippled. A relative unwittingly eats beef; later he dies a long and painful death. Sometimes we do not even know the exact cause of our suffering. It does not matter. Life is still seen in terms of simple logic: If you sin, bad things will happen to you; if bad things happen to you, you must have sinned. A widow recounted, "I was born a woman. I gave birth to a daughter. My daughter died. My husband died before I did . . . Now I am a widow and blind . . . I cannot say which sin I have committed in which life, but I am suffering now because I have done something wrong in one of my births. All sins are gathered near me" (Shweder & Miller, 1991, p. 159).

So violations of a moral code lead to physical consequences. In our culture we might make similar kinds of statements. We might say that someone's back problems, for example, are caused by his having an extramarital affair. But we would also elaborate and say it was because he felt so guilty and that caused stress, which in turn caused tension in the back muscles, and so on. We would want to elaborate a whole sequence of causes, highlighting one or other of the causes according to our goals. If we think he has a good marriage and acted foolishly by getting involved with someone else, we might highlight the moral and emotional causes, but if we think the affair is inconsequential, we might highlight the direct physical causes.

But with the Oriya there is no sense of there being some causal chain between the sin and the consequence—they seem to be saying that the sin directly causes the suffering. Could we say then that the Oriya have just observed cases where there *is* some actual physical connection between a believed violation of a moral code and some physical problem, and then generalized to all violations of the moral code? I think not. The Oriya and others like them share more in common at this point with the person who declares that AIDS is a punishment from God for homosexual sin. Both are assuming—indeed, their entire lives are based on the assumption—that there is an immaterial world that interacts with the material world.

The crux of the matter, from my perspective, is that other cultures and, in fact, a large number of people within this culture, start from certain presuppositions that are radically different from the presuppositions of the majority of Western academics. The starting point for people of many other cultures is that reality consists both of the natural and the supernatural. Exactly how the two interact is not an issue, because the supernatural, although it shares many characteristics with and is instantiated in the material, natural world, is at its core immaterial. And, of course, the immaterial is not open either to empirical verification or falsification.

The belief in the supernatural that is also prevalent in the West is, I think, in many cases of a more dichotomous kind than it is in other cultures. I think in the West many people who claim to believe in the supernatural do so in a way that keeps it as a separate, different world—in the way children have a pretend world and a real world. We go to church, or we believe in channeling, but it has very little to do with our everyday life. Or we may have a good luck charm that we always take with us in competitive sports. We have odds and ends of beliefs that involve the supernatural, which we tuck in various corners of our basically materialistic world view, often with a bit of embarrassment. Sometimes we simply divide the world into separate realities: There is my religious life and my academic life, and never the twain shall meet.

But for some other cultures, and some individuals, the supernatural is every bit as real as the natural world and every bit as important. Not only that, but the very division of life into natural and supernatural would seem odd to these people, because they are so inextricably intertwined and interrelated. For the Nuer, for example, there is simply no way to ask whether or not God exists. Of course God exists! You may trust him or not, but it does not occur to them to question his existence.

This is not to say that the interactions of the immaterial world and the material world are not seen as unusual, or noteworthy, or extraordinary. On the contrary, they are of great interest. For the Fang of Cameroon (Boyer, 1994), witches are people with an additional organ, that leaves the body at night and has all sorts of bizarre skills—it can fly on banana leaves, turn someone's blood thick, kill fetuses, and so on. The Fang find these stories both fascinating and terrifying, precisely because they violate their notions about the everyday material world. They are not taken as *ordinary* real events, but they are nevertheless perceived as *real* events. This does not imply that the Fang have the same view of nature as we do. It does mean, however, that we may share some of the same intuitive expectations about the everyday behavior of physical objects in space, biological processes, and so on. And they have the same cognitive means to sort out which events violate these expectations and which do not. The difference between "them" and "us" lies in the fact that we assume that explanations for all events, extraordinary or ordinary, must be found in the material world—that is our starting point. They assume that the very real immaterial interacts with the very real material, so they expect their intuitions to be violated from time to time.

So where does this leave us? Are we left with merely saying that there is no such thing as a believed-in imagining, that any belief is as good (valid, true) as any other? The fact that we still conduct tests of understanding of the appearance–reality distinction with young children, which assumes that objects do in fact have some sort of reality to which we are all privy, would also indicate that we do not want to go in that direction. But to say that objects have some sort of existence apart from our knowledge of them, that they are in fact knowable, is to say something that is certainly not in vogue these days. Rather, it smacks a kind of traditional or common-sense view of the world—the good old or bad old days, depending on your perspective—when people thought that you could actually know things, that a reality external to ourselves really existed. Let me pause here for a minute and give a quick overview of some of the philosophical territory that I think we Westerners have traversed during this century. I do not pretend to be a philosopher and am leaning heavily on the work of others, so I hope you will bear with me as I paint with rather broad strokes.

THE DEMISE OF REALITY

The common-sense view of the world to which I just referred is the view on which many of us were raised—namely, that our beliefs, when well-founded, are objective. Our beliefs were thought to be objective in two senses. First, they did not depend on what was specific to some of us as opposed to the rest. Rather, they were things that, at least in principle, any properly functioning group of people who were careful thinkers could agree on. Second, our beliefs were about objects, things-in-themselves that existed independently of us but could be known by us. So if I believed that a certain object was a bird, that belief was well founded if the properties I took to be of a bird really were properties that the things we call birds actually have. The assumption is that there are birds, and they have certain properties, such as wings and feathers (Plantiuga, 1995).

There was an assumption, at some points in the past, that we could truly know things because we had been designed to know, so that our cognitive faculties are in a sense aimed at the production of true beliefs. But gradually the focus shifted from the knower to the known—the universe was seen as being governed by mechanical laws and, as such, was measurable and predictable. Armed with the scientific method and our physical senses, we could really get to know the way things were. But it soon became clear that scientists just were not agreeing on everything, that we really were not just getting to know the way things were out there. Not only physicists, but also philosophers, got on the bandwagon, questioning whether or not there was any view of the world that could be free from our interpretation. Even reading theorists started to question whether or not we could really access an author's intention by a close reading of the text. The conclusion was that all our investigations have been theory-laden, and there is no neutral quest for truth.

Thus dawned the postmodern age. Objectivity, in the sense of ultimate reality, was long-since dead and gone. Now objectivity as a means of impersonal inquiry is also under fire (cf. Daston, 1992). No longer is it enough to acknowledge that there exists a multiplicity of perspectives on any single issue, event, or object. Rather, it is assumed that there are no objective things-in-themselves that are at the center of the perspectives. There is in fact no center at all, no overarching "reality" to be known.

As Smith (1995) has pointed out, there are three main reactions to the death of the big picture. Some postmodern thinkers only go so far as to say that there exists no accepted worldview at this point. Others go farther and argue that this condition is permanent and irreversible. Still others say that worldviews only marginalize minorities anyway. Some emphasize a naturalist or materialist perspective—there is nothing beyond nature, so human beings must be understood in terms of their commonalities with the rest of nonhuman nature. Others emphasize what makes us different from other animals, the fact that we are responsible for the basic structure of the world, that we impose upon the world categories that do not really characterize the world at all—that we ourselves form or structure the world in which we live. Of course the next step is that we all live in different worlds, that there simply is not any such thing as the way the world is, in the sense of being the same for each of us. And of course there is no such thing as truth—but only what is true from my perspective, and what is true from yours. Or as Rorty said, "truth is what our peers will let us get away with saying" (1979, p. 176).

So do we let young children get away with believing in Santa Claus or the Tooth Fairy because they are fairly innocuous imaginings and because these beliefs play some role in our society that the majority of us deems to be useful? But what of the Chinese authorities who compounded the murders at Tiananmen Square with lies? From a postmodern point of view, in denying it ever happened they were merely trying to bring it about that their peers would let them get away with saying they did not do it. They no doubt felt that it was really better for their country if people believe that the whole Tiananmen Square affair was simply a misunderstanding and that their credibility and authority remains intact. To bring it home to one's personal life, if you have done something that most people would consider wrong, perhaps the best thing to do is to lie about it, to try to get your peers to let you get away with saying you did not do it. After all, according to a functionalist view of truth, is it not really better that people think well of you?

I think many of us recoil from this perhaps overdrawn view of postmodernist thought. But is this an overdrawn view? Consider the following quotations from prominent postmodern thinkers: "Postmodern thought focuses on the *surface*, with a refined sensibility to what appears, a differentiation of what is perceived. The relation of sign and signified is breaking down ... A dichotomy between fantasy and reality breaks down or loses interest" (Kvale, 1995, p. 21). "Why the truth rather than lies? Why the truth rather than myth? Why the truth rather than an illusion?" (Foucault, 1995, p. 45). Jean Baudrillard (1995) described the four historical stages through which our understanding of an image had progressed. First we see it as "a reflection of basic reality," then something that "masks and perverts a basic reality," then something that "masks the *absence* of a basic reality, and finally that it bears no relation to reality whatsoever, it is its own simulacrum," its own image, a mere shadow or pretense (p. 81).

Earlier, I said that the pretend world is a creation of our minds, but if the real world is also simply a creation of our minds, how do we separate the two? If there is no reality, then whatever one believes to be true is true.

BEYOND BELIEVED-IN IMAGININGS

But can we really live this way? We want to say that there is a world of difference between the lives of Mother Teresa and Saddam Hussein, both in the acts that they have committed but, more importantly, in the meaning of those acts. We want to be able to say that there really were deliberate killings at Tiananmen Square, and that the holocaust really did happen, and that there can be no explaining away of the facts. However we also want to go further than that. We want to say that these acts were horrendous, terrible, wrong. But can we? Can we believe that all that exists is the material world, and that each of us views the world through person-specific lenses, that how we see the world is a unique construction of who we are. Can we be postmodernists and still believe in morality, truth, reality? Can we say with confidence that some beliefs are true beliefs, whereas others are only imaginings?

I do not believe that we can. Not if we are consistent postmodernists. But perhaps postmodernism is not the only alternative. So, although I have been doing a little deconstruction myself in the previous few paragraphs, let me now see if I can find some foundational stones among the rubble. Because, as Smith (1995) said, "When there is no *via* (way, truth) to deviate from, mistakes have no meaning" (p. 212).

First, we do need worldviews, or metanarratives, as some like to call them. We cannot live without them. Even deconstruction is a kind of metanarrative, which some maintain with almost a religious zeal, that maintains that differences, fragmentation, and sensitivity to others' views are good and helpful. I like the image Smith (1995) gave of replaying the video of this century's social and conceptual earthquakes, where we see the deconstructionists "scurrying around like madmen trying to spot places where a little more demolition and destabilization might prove useful" (p. 209). We crave being useful to others, making sense of things, and making sense of the whole of things, and even deconstruction is a kind of crazed attempt to make sense of a world in which there is no center, in which there is no ultimate truth, in which there is no sense.

Second, not all worldviews are created equal. Postmodernism takes something obvious—the fact that we all see things from different perspectives—and runs amok with it, transforming that fact into an epistemological dogma. That is, we cannot know things as they really are; in fact there is no reality at all. What this overlooks, however, is that in order to know that we are seeing something only from a certain perspective, we must have some sense of the whole. Otherwise we would assume that the other's perspective was the thing in itself. To recognize that other people look at the world differently than we do, we have to have some sense of the world that we are looking at. And we must be able to in some way step into other people's shoes. Postmodernists insist that we cannot, that we are hopeless, tied to our own space and time. They are right in one sense, that we can never entirely escape ourselves.

However, we do share something in common with all the diverse cultures that I have spoken of in this chapter. We do seem to share common intuitive expectations about things like the behavior of physical objects under ordinary circumstances. If we back off slightly from rabid postmodernism, we can see that most of us seem to take as a starting point that there really is something out there, at least a physical world that we are prone to view, ordinarily, in the same way. But that does not get us very far. It does not get us to truth, or morality, or any kind of basis, utilitarian or otherwise, for deciding among beliefs when beliefs conflict. It gives us no standard for saying "My belief is true, but yours is an imagining."

I do not think we can get to that kind of standard by looking within ourselves. Now some would maintain that this idea smacks of absolutism, and that absolutism results in closed minds, and that absolute values lead to a kind of fanatical fundamentalism that is hateful and destructive. The fact that people have used their belief in absolutes to justify horrible things does not, however, mean that it is absolute values per se that are the problem. To believe in truth does not mean you have to rid the world of all who disagree with you. The problem is not that truth leads to intolerance, but rather that, to paraphrase Jonathan Swift, we have just enough of it to make us hate, but not enough of it to make us love. The dark side of belief in absolutes is fanaticism and hatred, but the dark side of relativism is nihilism and meaninglessness: "Wandering through a forest late at night I have only a faint light to guide me. A traveler appears and says to me, 'My friend, you should blow out your candle in order to find your way more clearly.' The traveler is a deconstructionist."

So what are we left with? If we are to be true to the spirit of our age, then it seems we cannot declare that some beliefs are credible and others are not. We can do nothing more than hold up the diversities of beliefs, giving them all equal status. The title of this chapter would then become something like "Listening to the Multivocalities of Others as a Means to Learning About the Biases That Mediate Our Identities" (cf. Katz, 1995). We would not only be wandering in the dark without a light, but we would have lost any sense of where it was we were wandering to, or even if it was important to find our way.

I may be spoofing postmodern-speak for a moment, and radical deconstructionism is not something I can embrace. That does not mean, however, that I am not wholehearted in favor of some aspects of the enterprise. We do need to be shaken to our very roots and forced to examine the presuppositions on which our academic enterprise rests—the biases and unspoken assumptions, the marginalizing of others, the cultural egocentrism, and so on. But I also believe that we need to pay attention to what our hearts are saying: Perhaps nihilism is not liberating, perhaps the fact that it takes such energy and determination to give up notions such as truth and knowledge is not an indication that we are cultural and historically hog-tied, but rather points to the fact that we need to look for a worldview that provides a foundation for truth and knowledge. A fear that believing in truth will lead to fanaticism and intolerance should not deter us. It is when we give in to that fear that we are bound by our culture and history. Certainly it is a mistake to cram truth down other people's throats, but that does not mean we should abandon truth. Unless there is truth, there are no imaginings to be falsely believed in.

REFERENCES

Baudrillard, J. (1995). The map precedes the territory. In W. T. Anderson (Ed.), *The truth about the truth: De-confusing and re-constructing the postmodern world* (pp. 79–81). New York: Putnam.

Boyer, P. (1994). Cognitive constraints on cultural representations: Natural ontologies and religious ideas. In L. A. Hirschfeld & S. Gelman (Eds.), *Mapping the mind: Domain specificity, cognition and culture* (pp. 391–411). Cambridge, MA: Cambridge University Press.

Chandler, M. J., & Lalonds, C. E. (1994). Surprising, magical and miraculous turns of events: Children's reactions to violation of their early theories of mind and matter. *British Journal of Developmental Psychology, 12,* 1–83.

Daston, L. (1992). Objectivity and the escape from perspective. In *Social studies of science* (Vol. 22, pp. 597–618). Newbury Park, CA: Sage.

Foucault, M. (1995). Strategies of power. In W. T. Anderson (Ed.), *The truth about* the truth: De-confusing and re-constructing the postmodern world (pp. 40–45). New York: Putnam.

Heelas, P. (1981). Introduction: Indigenous psychologies. In P. Heelas & A. Lock (Eds.), *Indigenous psychologies: The anthropology of the self* (pp. 4–18). London: Academic Press.

Katz, S. (1995). How to speak and write postmodern. In W. T. Anderson (Ed.), *The truth about the truth: De-confusing and re-constructing the postmodern world* (pp. 92–95). New York: Putnam.

Kvale, S. (1995). Themes of postmodernity. In W. T. Anderson (Ed.), *The truth about the truth: De-confusing and re-constructing the postmodern world* (pp. 18–25). New York: Putnam.

Lévy-Bruhl, L. (1966). *The "soul" of the primitive.* (L. A. Clare, Trans.). New York: Praeger. (Original work published in 1927)

Plantiuga, A. (1995). Christian philosophy at the end of the 20th century. In S. Griffioen & B. Balle (Eds.), *Christian philosophy at the close of the twentieth century* (pp. 29–53). Kampen, Germany: Kok.

Rorty, R. (1979). *Philosophy and the mirror of nature.* Princeton, NJ: Princeton University Press.

Rozin, P., Millman, L., & Nemeroff, C. (1986). Operation of the laws of sympathetic magic in disgust and other domains. *Journal of Personality and Social Psychology, 50,* 703–712.

Shweder, R., & Miller, J. (1991). The social construction of the person: How is it possible? In R. Shweder (Ed.), *Thinking through cultures: Expeditions in cultural psychology* (pp. 156–185). Cambridge, MA: Harvard University Press.

Smith, H. (1995). Postmodernism and the world's religions. In W. T. Anderson (Ed.), *The truth about the truth: De-confusing and re-constructing the postmodern world* (pp. 204–214). New York: Putnam.

5

CHILDHOOD IMAGINATION IN THE FACE OF CHRONIC ILLNESS

CINDY DELL CLARK

In American childhood, a routine cycle of festivals is drawn largely from imaginal practices: the cult of Santa (at Christmas), the Easter Bunny (at Easter), and ghosts and goblins (at Hallowe'en). As investigations of the cycle of American children's festivals have shown (Clark, 1995), children learn how to invest credibility (or better put, faith) in mythic entities through their transactions with Santa and the Easter Bunny. The propensity for investing faith has value for children because it allows them (through placing trust in unseen, culturally shared entities) to find sanctuary and meaning. Moreover, parents encourage the process of assigning credibility to imaginings (Santa and the Easter Bunny) and typically give leeway to children to invest faith, so that children gain an appreciation of spiritual belief.

In this chapter I look at the routine use of the imagination in another context: How American children employ imaginative strategies to cope

This investigation was supported by grants from the Kellstadt Center for Social Marketing at DePaul University, and the Rainbow Foundation for Children's Research. Holly Blackford, Melissa Gerdes, and Kathy Sullivan aided in the research as participant–observers at camps for chronically ill children. For purposes of privacy, the names of informants have been disguised.

with chronic illness. This observation is based partly on research (e.g., Chan, 1980) in hospitals, where play therapists sometimes explicitly use play as a means of helping children cope with the emotional traumas of hospitalization and treatments. Evidence that children cope imaginally with chronic illness comes also from my own ethnographic research conducted over time in the homes of 46 Chicago-area families, as well as in 3 Midwestern summer camps for chronically ill children. Home-based ethnographic research reveals that children with severe asthma and diabetes use imaginative means to cope on their own initiative, without necessarily having explicit suggestions from the adults around them. In exploring the mechanism of imaginal coping as it applies to chronic illness, I also draw from Winnicott's (1971) theory of transitional space as a key theoretical guidepost.

IMAGINAL COPING DEFINED

Even on a historical basis, children's experiences when confronting illness have been known to take forms that go beyond strict literal reality or stern seriousness. Consider the origin of the children's game, ring-around-a-rosey. The game was once called "ring, a ring, a rosey" and was first played during the Black Plague of the Middle Ages, when the lyrics sung for the game went like this: "Ring, A Ring, A Rosey; A pocketful of posies; Achoo, Achoo. We all fall down." According to O'Connor (1991, p. 9), the game refers to "the round red blotches that first appeared on those stricken with the plague" and "the practice of stuffing the victim's pockets with flowers to cover the smell of both the illness and death because quick burial was not possible." In other words, children surrounded by deadly disease used this rhythmic game to reenact (reframed in play) the sequence of events in the all-too-familiar course of the Plague. The game, according to O'Connor, "in some bizarre way helped to make death less frightening" (p. 9). Children reflected and reflected upon the deadly atmosphere of the time in their play, and in the process displayed resilience in the face of fearful suffering.

Ring-around-a-rosey exemplies the capacity for human actors to mutually suspend disbelief, and to interpersonally share an intermediate sphere in which exists "a neutral area of experience which will not be challenged" (p. 2, Winnicott, 1951/1958; see also Winnicott, 1971). This shared imaginal experience is what Winnicott called "transitional space," the realm of experience in which artistic and religious experience also occur. Reality claims are suspended in transitional space, which provides a "resting place" that relieves the strain of relating inner (personal) and outer (shared) reality.

Winnicott derived the notion of transitional space from his allied notion of the transitional object, Winnicott's term for that blanket, teddy bear, or other security-giving item that a child treats with special trust and attachment. The participation of the subject or perceiver is so decisive in making contact with the transitional object that the paradox of whether the item is subjective or objective in status is left unresolved. Faith is involved with the transitional object (and with transitional space) in that trust provides the affective milieu that suspends the question about what is objectively real. Winnicott (1971) further theorized that cultural experience is an extension of the child's (and adult's) capacity for maintaining transitional space. Transitional space is where the child puts (mentally) the cultural constructs that are meaningful by virtue of the child's active, creative reaching out to shared or inherited tradition (including family rituals).

Winnicott viewed transitional phenomena not as perceptions, but as particular forms of reality inherently meant to be drawn from, played with, and shared. Imaginal phenomena are creative, maneuverable, unstereotypical, interactive, variable, and derived from nonliteral, multivocal sources of meaning, such as symbols, metaphor, and narrative. They are not rephrased perceptions of an outer reality but belong to a domain of meaning with malleable validity of its own.

Winnicott's theory of transitional experience allows for social and family contexts. Indeed, in Winnicott's conception, the child's attachment to a blanket or soft toy derives from social experience—the early parent–child relationship. To quote Winnicott (1971), "The use of an object symbolizes the union of two now separate things, baby and mother, at the point in time and space of the initiation of their state of separateness" (pp. 96–97). It is this paradox of union yet separateness, a domain felt to be simultaneously inside the child yet outside, both subjective and objective, out of which transitional space arises (Winnicott 1951/1958, 1971).

The child's use of transitional space can be embedded within family ritual, such that the rest of the family serves to support the child's imaginal experience. An example from my own research on American family rituals is the Tooth Fairy ritual (Clark, 1995), by which contemporary North American families mark the loss of the child's primary (or baby) teeth. In this ritual, parents serve as witnesses and co-participants in encouraging the child's imaginative capacity to participate in an unseen, nonempirical reality (that is, the Fairy who exchanges the child's lost tooth for money). Child informants suggest that this imaginal process helps them to cope with the physical distress of losing a tooth and their feelings about the loss (bleeding, fear of being toothless, etc.).

Even in the absence of direct family support or shared ritual, children use nonliteral means to cope with illness, as was revealed by this recent research. During interviews, it was not unusual for children to wrap themselves in their security blanket as they described to me their fears and troubles associated with chronic illness. At times, children seemed to treat their medical paraphernalia (such as a diabetes ID bracelet or a Band-Aid with a character on it) as a source of security and trust as well. (For example, one boy hung a crucifix on the same chain as his diabetes ID necklace, which he never took off, and which he felt safe wearing.) Medications sometimes took the role of security-giving, trusted entities—such as a particular asthma inhaler, that a child was deeply upset about surrendering to the medical staff upon attending camp.

The child's regard of treatment devices and medicine as sources of trust is consistent with prior hypotheses by anthropologist Van der Geest and colleagues (Van der Geest, 1996; Van der Geest & Whyte, 1989). Van der Geest hypothesized that the concreteness of medicines allowed medications to take hold of an inchoate sense and turn this vague feeling into something graspable, sometimes transforming the meaning of medicine into a magic-like charm. Survey research by Erkolahti (1991) has shown that rheumatic and diabetic children keep their transitional objects longer than do children without chronic illness. This suggests that the soothing brought by the transitional possession indeed has prolonged value in the lives of chronically ill children, which is consistent with my ethnographic research.

EXAMPLES OF IMAGINAL COPING

A case from my research that illustrates the use of transitional objects by chronically ill children concerns a 5-year-old boy, Randy S. Randy, who had severe asthma, had developed a special regard for (and dependence on) toy race cars. When I sat down with Randy S. to interview him about having asthma, he chose to begin our time together by running out of the room to retrieve his race car to show me. This conversation followed:

Randy: I'll show you my [car], that I like to play with.

CDC: Oh, you [seem to] love that. Now do you play with that when you're sick? That car?

Randy: [Nodding] Mm hm. [Zooming car around] Vroom! Vroom!

CDC: Let's say you're sick and you're pretending with that. What would you pretend with that big race car?

Randy: The ride in it!

CDC: And ride where? Where would you ride to?

Randy: Chicago!

CDC: To Chicago? Uh huh.

Randy: Mm hm. And every time we needed gas.

Through his transitional object, Randy was empowered to mentally tranform the present reality, transporting himself metaphorically to another place—albeit on a trip when "gas," like his supply of oxygen, was in short supply. His mother's field notes kept over a course of months (as part of the study) confirmed that Randy relied on his car as a means of coping in times of suffering or fear. She documented this, for example, during a bout of breathing difficulty for Randy:

> It is very cold and damp, and Randy's breathing is not good. He was very restless and breathing hard when he was sleeping. He is still very pale and not looking himself ... When his breathing problems come and he is having an asthma attack he sometimes looks up to me with his big blue eyes with the dark rings around them, and asks me for his green race car. And I get it for him. He hugs it closely and falls asleep. (Maternal Field Notes, 1994)

Randy had several race cars, all special to him. During interviews, he imputed magical qualities to each car as an object that, he insisted, "worked wonders." He claimed not to even feel a shot when his race car was with him. He volunteered that his race car could make bad medicine taste better. Randy's mother confirmed that when Randy was allowed to hold his race car at the hospital emergency room, it calmed him, acting (to use her term) as a "Godsend." She kept a race car on hand at all times, sending one to school in Randy's backpack and keeping one in her car. She was sensitive to, and grateful for, Randy's reliance on the race car so that he could find calmness when he needed it. "The cars have gone through it all with him," she observed, in a voice that showed her willingness to assign credibility to Randy's transitional object. She expected Randy to continue to have a race car "tucked away in the closet" even when he was old enough to marry.

For children with severe asthma, illness means a life interrupted by the need for medication, often taken during a lengthy and boring session using the nebulizer (a machine used to inhale medication). Some children used imaginal coping during nebulizer treatments. For example, one boy drove a toy airplane through the smoke of the nebulizer, imagining himself to fly away to other places in the process. The face mask he wore, attached to the nebulizer tube, reminded him of a pilot's mask in the movie *Top Gun*.

Asthma also involves repeated terror when an attack interferes with a child's breathing. Fear of death in some form was an almost universal concern shared during interviews by children with severe asthma. A lack of breath is not experienced by children without a sense of its life-threatening consequences. Again, imaginal coping seems to be a mental process that can reassure children during such a frightful time. For example, one boy had sheets on his bed depicting the Teenage Mutant Ninja Turtles. He imagined that, should a nighttime emergency with his breathing occur, one of the Turtles would fly off his sheets and go to get the doctor. This calmed him during bouts of bronchitis.

For children with diabetes, their life is a steady intrusion of dietary restrictions and schedules, blood tests, and shots. Imaginal coping provides an outlet for distraction and acceptance. For instance, Sherry C. (a 5-year-old diabetic girl) loved to play the game Candyland over and over—delighting in the sugar-laden fantasy of the game. (While I played with her, she imagined aloud to me her expectation that she "could get to eat lots of candy" and "would eat it up in two whole days.") The game Candyland was also said by another mother to be well liked by other children as child-directed entertainment at diabetes support group meetings. In general, daydreaming about indulging in denied activities, such as when fantasizing about an imagined cure for diabetes, was commonplace.

Also widely reported was role-reversal play, when a child pretends to administer a treatment rather than receive it as usual. A common game for a diabetic child was to give a pretend shot to a playmate or toy, or even me, the interviewer. Giving disliked treatments to others, in play, has been a form of imaginal coping reported in other studies of hospitalized children (Bluebond-Langner, 1978, p. 118; Slade & Wolf, 1994, p. 35; Wilson, 1985, p. 116). This kind of play is thought to project mastery, control, and empowerment, in the context of a pretend interaction.

Children sometimes did not reveal (to parents or familiar adults) their thought process involving a transitional object or routine. Roger P. (a 6-year-old diabetic boy) showed me a photo of himself during a doctor's visit (taken as part of study procedures). He pointed out about the photo, "There's me with my White Ranger" (a toy white-outfitted Power Ranger character). He brought the toy to his appointment "because I had nothing to play with" and "I wanted to play with it." But moments later he added that the toy also made him feel better about his diabetes. As he put it, "I have nobody to count on ... I can always count on him." Further probing revealed that the White Ranger "has diabetes too" and received the same regimen of blood tests and insulin shots as Roger. Yet neither Roger's mother nor doctor were at all aware of the illness-related aspect of Roger's toy. Imaginal coping is sometimes held private by children, outside the awareness of adults who care for them. In turn, as Leffler (1988) has pointed out about children experiencing the process of divorce, parents unwittingly can mistake a transitional object for an ordinary casual toy.

HINDERED IMAGINAL COPING

In not a few instances among these American midwestern families, transitional objects were disregarded in importance by adults, including both parents and medical personnel. Children diagnosed with asthma were often subject to medical restrictions (in order to remove suspected allergens from their environment) that included the medically ordered removal of all plush animals or special blankets (as well as pets). Many parents carried out these restrictions out of respect to biomedicine, sometimes oblivious to a child's attachment to and reassurance derived from the object being discarded.

Confiscation of a transitional object comprised the narrative of Rick K., 8 years old upon being interviewed, who recalled the "yellow giraffe blanket" (a blanket depicting yellow giraffes) that he used to comfort himself prior to his diagnosis with asthma at age 9 months. Under a physician's instructions, the blanket was taken away from Rick (as a potential allergic trigger); Rick proceeded to wake up at night with severe panic attacks (interpreted by his doctor as "just airway obstruction"). Later, when Rick's mother decided to return the blanket to him (because its removal had not improved his asthma symptoms), his panic attacks subsided completely, an improvement that she attributed (in retrospect) to the returned blanket.

Grace W., a 7-year-old diabetic girl, told a tearful narrative about her own stuffed tiger, a gift given to her by her uncle when she was hospitalized upon diagnosis with diabetes at age 22 months. Her remembered hospitalization was retold sadly, with tears. The hospital scared her, with its jail-like crib bars and hurtful procedures. The huge stuffed tiger, her uncle's gift, made her feel safe amidst that danger. To quote from her narrative of events:

> I hated lying in that bed ... and I had a tiger. My uncle ... got it. It's like a huge tiger ... The nurses used to take it away because they thought it would scare me. But it didn't. And I was only two years old. (CDC: How did the tiger make you feel?) It made me feel safe. (CDC: Really? How come?) It kept me company. (Girl, Age 7)

The mother of Randy S. (described earlier) had repeatedly encountered opposition to Randy's race car from the medical establishment. One nurse, she reported, had looked at her with disbelief when she brought the toy car to the hospital, asking "What kind of parent are you? Normal kids have blankets or pillows or stuffed animals. You bring this kid to the hospital with a car?" Randy's mother lost her temper in reaction to this comment, defending the car as an allergen-free toy that "makes him feel safe." On another occasion, an X-ray technician refused to let the car (or for that matter, Randy's mother) go into the X-ray room with Randy, even though the car was entirely plastic (not metal). His mother was concerned about Randy's fears of, first, the "big machine" that would be taking his X-ray and, second, the restraints that held him still. "It's very scary, a big ordeal for the child," she asserted. "Everybody familiar to him is gone." She had many other memories as well, she said, "of crying my eyes out because of seeing him cry" because the hospital denied Randy access to his toy cars or his parents.

Sherman and her colleagues (Sherman, Hertzig, Austrian, & Shapiro, 1981) have described the usual gradual process of emotional detachment from a transitional object (as a child grows older) among healthy children. When the detachment process is under a child's own control, the child eventually sets aside the transitional object but may occasionally retrieve it (during stressful occasions, such as leaving for summer camp), therefore keeping it accessible even when it is put away. For the chronically ill child, occasions of illness or hospitalization might be times when a child would experience severe stress—yet, lacking accessibility, the abrupt removal of the transitional object would be detrimental to the usual detachment process. In contrast to ordinary childhood ritual (such as the Tooth Fairy) in which adults conspire in the suspension of disbelief, imaginal coping during chronic illness is prone to be undermined by adults, albeit unwittingly.

IMAGINAL COPING AMONG CHRONICALLY ILL PEERS

Researchers studying illness camps around the globe have consistently found such camps to be effective in raising the level of control children have over childhood illness symptoms (e.g., Fitzpatrick, Coughlin, Chamberlin, & the Pediatric Lung Committee, 1992; Mimura, 1994; Misuraca, Di Gennaro, Lioniello, Duval, & Aloi, 1996; Punnett & Thurber, 1993; Silvers et al., 1992; Sorrells, Chung, & Schlumpberger, 1995). When children with a particular illness are brought together in a camp setting, they are often exposed to adult-guided biomedical education about their illness, which, according to past studies, is presumed to be a pathway for the improvement in symptoms. In ethnographic studies of summer camps attended by chronically ill children (Clark, 1997), however, it was found that biomedical education was often ignored by very young campers. That is, despite adults' attempts to instill campers with the biomedical model of their disease, the attempts were paid little heed by many young children, based on direct observation.

Yet summer camp does provide an opportunity to be with other children experiencing the same illness, such that the disease is "woven into the fabric of everyday life" at camp (see Bluebond-Langner, Perkel, Goertzel, Nelson, & McGeary, 1991, p. 211). Children at camp shared a particular medical condition and common treatments, which led to shared interactions about the illness experience. Children participated in joint play-like activities that served to reconstruct reality not through knowledge alone, but largely through play. At diabetes camp, visual art was created using syringes and paint, recontextualizing the syringe as a fun expressive device. At asthma camp, nebulizer machines were used to inflate balloons, and asthma inhaler devices were used as noisemakers (by inhaling overly fast) and as devices for blowing chewing gum bubbles. Campers taught each other how to cheat at breathing tests (peak flows), by holding their thumb on the back of the device. That is, shared play conveyed a common means of control over the breathing test, a test about which children normally felt vulnerable when performing poorly.

Shared rituals at camp included celebrations and performances, which provided another context for shared play-like activities. At diabetes camp, there was a pig-kissing contest on the final day of camp, honoring pigs as a source of insulin. The shared humor of kissing the pig provoked joint laughter, and presumably cathartic relief:

> The main event this morning was "Kiss A Pig." All the campers and staff had raised money as pledges before they came. For each dollar they had raised, they could cast a vote for someone else to kiss the pig. The idea was to raise as much money as possible in order to vote the kissing privileges away from yourself. . . . Jenny was runner-up so she got to hold the pig. Bruce [a drug rep who came to camp as a counselor] won . . . He applied lipstick and kissed the pig on the mouth for five full seconds, which left the whole camp in tears, they were laughing so hard." (Diabetes overnight camp field notes, 1995)

A climactic ritual at asthma camp involved a performance of skits written by campers from each cabin. One cabin's campers wrote a skit that parodied the "Three Pigs" story, but in which the wolf character was said to have asthma.

Wolf's mother: Wolf junior!

Wolf: Yes?

Wolf's mother: Would you go out and catch us some nice plump sheep, or some nice plump pigs, for dinner tonight?
[Wolf visits homes of three pigs, unable to blow down the house due to asthmatic coughing. Wolf is taken to the hospital, after peak flow was found to be very low—50—a number too low to sustain life, which evoked deep laughter as an audience response. Wolf then receives a lung transplant.]

Wolf: The doctors are so good here, that I feel I can huff and puff and blow any house down.
(Asthma overnight camp field notes, 1995)

By forming an interpersonal environment in which all members had the same chronic illness, the camp set up a ripe frame for transformative imaginal coping. Campers began to play at, and make light of, their treatments and symptoms. Anxieties and irritations gave way to jointly constructed fun. Behavior at camp shows how shared play among children can serve as a coping device, in a setting that provides a ready context. Peers mutually framed illness in nonliteral terms, empowered to do so within a social setting that made their illnesses a social norm.

In the biomedical model, disease is an explanatory system deemed to be universally applicable as a biological entity that transcends social or cultural context (Good, 1994). Yet illness is experienced in a social environment (Kleinman, 1988). Conventional medical models of coping with illness have emphasized cognitive coping that occurs on an individual basis. Cognitive coping is viewed as a matter of perception, a matter of readjusting the perceived life world amidst an empirically given outer world (Behr & Murphy, 1993). This study of summer camp (Clark, 1997) suggests that coping can be socially interactive, in a manner that uses the plane of transitional (rather than empirical) space, a more paradoxical process than cognitive coping.

BIOMEDICINE MEETS IMAGINAL COPING

The written field notes that were kept by mothers in this study, often showed a focus of concern that was largely biomedically phrased. The following passage illustrates. In this passage, the child is represented in terms of posing a constellation of symptoms and measurements.

> Peak flows are still up to 175–190. Normal is 200–225 but this is still okay. Cough is better. Congestion is still there in the nose. He is off all medication except maintenance inhalers. (Maternal Field Notes, 1995)

When mothers and other adults attempted to educate very young children about an illness, they commonly used a didactic approach derived directly from the biomedical model. Brochures, books, or videotapes showed the internal bodily organs involved in the disease process and explained the unseen (or microscopic) mechanisms. The biomedical approach to disease typically was not internalized by children. But biomedicine was often the mainstay of the adult belief system about illness. It seemed to offer adults reassurance and security, such as when Mrs. A. discussed the knowledge of her doctor in an interview.

> I've got a great doctor. This guy is fabulous … He just got back from a seminar in California on asthma. He updates himself constantly … I like him so much because he is up on all the latest research. (Maternal Interview)

Given that mothers had a propensity to concentrate their attention and trust on biomedical constructions of illness, some mothers were not inclined to conspire in the playful activities that children used to deal with their illness, unless it was in the service of biomedical treatment. Mothers might reward a child (perhaps by buying a toy) after a tiresome medical visit or procedure. A parent might keep a child company and read to him or her during a lengthy nebulizer treatment. A few mothers devised playful ways to entertain children while they were taking medication, by counting and clapping along with inhalations. One parent (for a diabetes blood test) allowed the child to wager in advance what the numerical reading would be. Overall, however, these family-based behaviors were not (in adult eyes) instances of shared imaginal reality so much as simple distractions or rewards that accommodated the biomedical treatment.

This is not to say that adults are incapable of imaginal thought or playful coping. Indeed, research emerging from cognitive developmental investigations reinforces that adults and children both have continuous capacities for imaginal as well as rational thought (Wooley, 1997). Adults who become sick or stressed themselves are likely to use prayer or spirituality (Potts, 1996), family ritual (Johnson & Suedfelt, 1996), and even stuffed toys or transitional objects (Ahluvalia & Schaefer, 1994) to cope. Rather, the point is that the so-called objective approach of biomedicine has a narrowing impact on the parental caregiver's world view, just as it does for physicians (Good, 1994). From the rationalist stance of biomedicine, imaginal activity can be taken more as a means to gain compliance with biomedical treatment than as a full-fledged, socially condoned way of being.

CONCLUSION

Much of chronically ill children's imaginal coping (outside of interaction with trained play therapists or interviewers) occurs either in solitude or in conjunction with other children. Occasionally, parents may provide tools for such play (such as play syringes or toy doctor's kits), but they do not enter into playful coping interactions to the same degree as do children. Among adult caretakers, the shared cultural explanation for the child's plight comes from biomedicine, which does not accommodate the emotional or interpersonal impact of the illness experience. There is no culturally shared equivalent to the Tooth Fairy, in which parents and child both participate imaginally to ease the child's plight.

Biomedical treatment does provide the child with some symbolic content, such as inhalers, nebulizer tubes, and syringes. But the vantage point of biomedical treatment is oblivious to the multivocal meanings that can be attached to such devices. To the medical care team and, to some extent, the parent, the tools of medical treatment are functional at a sterile, controlled, physical level. Yet for children, the same tools can serve as symbolic material from which they can derive imaginal content. The stripes on a syringe can be likened to zebra stripes. The nebulizer mask can be a pilot's mask. Children may be reluctant to volunteer such meanings in the contrived setting of a doctor's office (cf. Potts, 1996) as opposed to in the settings of home and camp, but such meanings occur.

The medical literature contains examples of situations in which imaginal coping has been used as an intrinsic part of medical interventions, such as using puppet therapy during cardiac catheterization (Cassell, 1965), or a dinosaur toy that administers sedation (Cohen et al., 1995). The Child Life movement in pediatric hospitals has espoused imaginal coping as well (Association for the Care of Children's Health, 1986; Chan, 1980). Across such experience, imaginal approaches have been seen to augment biomedical treatments in a manner that relieves children's distress.

The research reported in this chapter reveals that the use of imaginal coping by chronically ill children living at home can go unrecognized or even be hindered by adults in many instances. When children turn hardship into fantasia, imagination potentially becomes a helpful balm. The imaginal process can be therapeutic (as Winnicott foresaw) and holds potential we can only imagine.

REFERENCES

Ahluvalia, T., & Schaefer, C. (1994). Implications of transitional object use: A review of empirical findings. *Psychology: A Journal of Human Behavior, 31,* 45–57.

Association for the Care of Children's Health. (1986). Child life: An overview. New York: Author.

Behr, S., & Murphy, D. (1993). Research progress and promise: The role of perceptions in cognitive adaptation to disability. In A. Turnbull, J. Patterson, S. Behr, D. Murphy, J. Marquis, & M. Blue-Banning (Eds.), *Cognitive coping, families, and disability* (pp. 151–163). Baltimore: Brookes Publishing.

Bluebond-Langner, M. (1978). *The private worlds of dying children.* Princeton: Princeton University Press.

Bluebond-Langner, M., Perkel, D., & Goertzel, T. (1991). Pediatric cancer patients' peer relationships: The impact of an oncology camp experience. *Journal of Psychosocial Oncology, 9,* 67–80.

Cassell, S. (1965). Effect of brief puppet therapy upon the emotional responses of children undergoing cardiac catheterization. *Journal of Consulting Psychology, 29,* 1–8.

Chan, J. (1980). Preparation for procedures and surgery through play. *Paediatrician, 9,* 210–219.

Clark, C. D. (1995). *Flights of fancy, leaps of faith: Children's myths in contemporary America.* Chicago: University of Chicago Press.

Clark, C. D. (1997). *Camp and Chronic Illness: An Interpretive Study.* Poster Session presented at the Society for Research in Child Development, Washington, DC.

Cohen, M., Gur, E., Wertherym, S., Eddy, W., & Shafir, R. (1995). Intranasal administration of midazolam with a dinosaur toy. *Plastic and Reconstructive Surgery, 95,* 421–422.

Erkolahti, R. (1991). Transitional objects and children with chronic disease. *Psychotherapy and Psychosomatics, 56,* 94–97.

Fitzpatrick, S., Coughlin, S., Chamberlin, J., & the Pediatric Lung Committee of the American Lung Association. (1992). A novel asthma camp intervention for childhood asthma among urban blacks. *Journal of the National Medical Association, 84*(3), 233–237.

Good, B. (1994). *Medicine, rationality, and experience: An anthropological perspective.* Cambridge, England: Cambridge University Press.

Johnson, P., & Suedfelt, P. (1996). Coping with stress through the microcosms of home and family among arctic whalers and explorers. *The History of the Family, 1,* 41–62.

Kleinman, A. (1988). *The illness narratives: Suffering, healing and the human condition.* New York: Basic Books.

Leffler, B. (1988). Transitional relatedness through the eyes of school-aged children: A qualitative study of children of divorce and intact families. In P. Horton (Ed.), *The solace paradigm: An eclectic search for psychological immunity* (pp. 251–270). Madison, CT: International Universities Press.

Mimura, G. (1994). Summer camp. *Diabetes Research and Clinical Practice, 24,* S287–S290.

Misuraca, A., Di Gennaro, M., Lioniello, M., Duval, M., & Aloi, G. (1996). Summer camps for diabetic children: An experience in Campania, Italy. *Diabetes Research and Clinical Practice, 32,* 91–96.

O'Connor, K. J. (1991). *The play therapy primer.* New York: Wiley.

Potts, R. (1996). Spirituality and the experience of cancer in an African-American community: Implications for psychosocial oncology. *Journal of Psychosocial Oncology, 14,* 1–19.

Punnett, A., & Thurber, S. (1993). Evaluation of asthma camp experience for children. *Journal of Asthma, 30*(3), 195–198.

Sherman, M., Hertzig, M., Austrian, R., & Shapiro, T. (1981). Treasured objects in school-aged children. *Pediatrics, 68,* 379–386.

Silvers, W., Holbreich, M., Go, S., Morrison, M., Dennis, W., Marostica, T., & Buckley, J. (1992). Champ camp: The Colorado children's asthma camp experience. *Journal of Asthma, 29*(2), 121–135.

Slade, A., & Wolf, D. (1994). *Children at play: Clinical and developmental approaches to meaning and representation.* New York: Oxford University Press.

Sorrells, L., Chung, W., & Schlumpberger, J. (1995). The impact of a summer asthma camp experience on asthma education and morbidity in children. *Journal of Family Practice, 41*(5), 465–468.

Van der Geest, S. (1996). Grasping the children's point of view? An anthropological reflection. In P. D. Bush, D. Trakas, E. Sanz, R. Wirsing, T. Vaskilampi, & A. Prout (Eds.), *Children, medicines and cultures* (pp. 337–346). New York: Haworth Press.

Van der Geest, S., & Whyte, S. (1989). The charm of medicines: Metaphors and metonyms. *Medical Anthropology Quarterly, 3*(4), 345–367.

Wilson, J. (1985). Play in the hospital. In C. C. Brown & A. W. Gottfried (Eds.), *Play interactions: The role of toys and parental involvement in children's development* (pp. 113–121). Skilman, NJ: Johnson & Johnson.

Winnicott, D. W. (1958). Transitional objects and transitional phenomena. In *Collected papers* (pp. 113–121). New York: Basic Books. (Original work published 1951)

Winnicott, D. W. (1971). *Playing and reality.* London: Tavistock.

Wooley, J. (1997). Thinking about fantasy: Are children fundamentally different thinkers and believers from adults? *Child Development, 68,* 208–216.

6

A DEVELOPMENTAL PERSPECTIVE ON THE CONSTRUCTION OF DISBELIEF

RICHARD J. GERRIG AND BRADFORD H. PILLOW

Consider this excerpt from two preschoolers' conversation (Garvey & Berndt, 1977, cited in Bretherton, 1984, p. 25):

A: Pretend there is a monster coming, OK?

B: No, let's don't pretend that.

A: OK, why?

B: 'Cause it's too scary, that's why.

This excerpt presents the phenomenon of believed-in imaginings in its most transparent form: The act of imagination is in plain view; the child anticipates that it will not be possible to control the products of that act of imagination. In this chapter, we seek resonances of this child's fears in the performance of adults. Research in cognitive development informs our discussion of what it means for adults to believe in their own imaginings. We begin by articulating a theoretical perspective against which we discuss the developmental literature.

THE WILLING CONSTRUCTION OF DISBELIEF

How might we interpret what child B fears? One way of characterizing the anticipated experience would be as a fear of becoming sufficiently *lost* in the imagining that the real world, in which the monster does not exist, becomes inaccessible. An important part of the phenomenology of imaginings is that readers, viewers, and so on, report *being transported* from their own real world to the world of the story (Gerrig, 1993). Consider this pair of literary instances in which the metaphor of being transported is used:

> I had to laugh out loud. Little Brother and Little Sister. That fairy tale transported us to unfathomable depths of sadness when we were children and yet we always felt compelled to come back to it. Off we set, into the wilderness, again and again, hand in hand, turned out by the wicked stepmother. (Wolf, 1989, p. 72)

> So anyway, he says, "Thrift, Horatio." His voice fills the theater, and the dust from his clothes falls off, his paunch recedes, and he is in another world. He transports everyone with that one word (Powers, 1988, p. 192).

The metaphor of being transported suggests how completely some narrative experiences engage thought, attention, and emotion, to the exclusion of real world constraints. Our theoretical considerations about believed-in imagining are proffered against this background that imagined worlds are often phenomenologically isolated from the everyday world. The capacity to be transported, on our view, is an early and important developmental acquisition.

Let us return to the more specific concern of child B's fear. It is not difficult to find an adult parallel to child B's reluctance to imagine a monster. Adults routinely refuse to attend horror movies, presumably because they are unwilling to let themselves experience the emotional upheaval they anticipate—they are unwilling to let themselves be transported to a world that will require that range of emotions. It is easy to imagine two adults discussing an evening's plans, having a conversation much like the one excerpted earlier (e.g., "I won't go see *Psycho*, 'cause it's too scary"). Much like their children, adults' refusals to go to horror movies represent, in a sense, predictions that they will not be able to engage in a willing construction of disbelief with respect to the movie. Let us specify that claim in more detail.

The phrase "willing construction of disbelief" is intended to contrast with Samuel Taylor Coleridge's classic phrase, the "willing suspension of disbelief." In the original context, Coleridge used the phrase while explaining how he came to write "Lyrical Ballads" (Coleridge 1817/1973):

> . . . it was agreed, that my endeavors [in the "Lyrical Ballads"] should be directed to persons and characters supernatural, or at least romantic;

yet so as to transfer from our inward nature a human interest and a semblance of truth sufficient to procure for these shadows of imagination that willing suspension of disbelief for the moment, which constitutes poetic faith. (p. 6)

In literary and philosophical analyses, Coleridge's phrase—whatever Coleridge's original intentions—has often served as a slogan to stand in for the whole cognitive psychology of the experience of literature (for critiques, see Carroll, 1990; Gerrig, 1993). But what exactly does it mean? The phrase implies that there is something that readers of literary works are turning off: Whatever mental voice would cry out "do not believe this!" is willingly being rendered mute. Consequently, if one is committed to glossing the experience of fiction as an instance of the willing suspension of disbelief, one is making a rather strong claim about how the cognitive psychology of belief normally works: What must be disabled is disbelief.

Could this be right? Virtually every analysis that makes reference to the willing suspension of disbelief has been flawed by an a priori assumption in a taxonomic distinction—with respect to mental processes—between fiction and nonfiction. That is, virtually every account has hypothesized some type of *toggle* that bears a family resemblance to the willing suspension of disbelief, whereby readers act on fictional information in a different way than they act on nonfictional information (Gerrig, 1993). Outside the discipline of psychology, this assumption has gone virtually unchallenged.

The theoretical underpinnings of the willing *construction* of disbelief has as a central component the tenet that "information is information"—or, somewhat more usefully, "comprehension is comprehension" (Gerrig, 1993). Rather than getting disbelief for free, readers comprehend, and then they must adjust their beliefs strategically (Gerrig & Prentice, 1991; Prentice, Gerrig, & Bailis, 1997). This point of view can be traced to the philosopher Baruch Spinoza (Gilbert, 1991), who suggested that an immediate and automatic product of comprehension is an *acceptance* of belief. Readers must create "unacceptance" by effortfully evaluating the information.

A number of types of evidence support this Spinozan view of belief (e.g., Gilbert, Krull, & Malone, 1990; Gilbert, Tafarodi, & Malone, 1993). For example, in one experiment participants were told that a piece of novel information (e.g., "A twyrin is a doctor") was "true" or "false," but then were quickly distracted with another experimental task. When the participants were later asked to verify the information, the distraction affected performance only with respect to the "false" statements (i.e., participants were more likely to label "false" statements as "true" but no more likely to label "true" statements as "false"). This result fits the Spinozan perspective because it suggests that the novel information was immediately labeled as "true" even when circumstances prevented participants from applying external labels; the experimental distraction disproportionately affected the process of unacceptance (Gilbert et al., 1990). Note, in addition, that, under circumstances in which readers have been transported, the real-world information that could lead to unacceptance may not be readily accessible (Gerrig, 1989).

Consider one study in which experimental participants read one of two versions of a story (Prentice et al., 1997). What made the two versions of the story distinct was their settings: One was set at Princeton University (i.e., the characters were Princeton students); the other was set at Yale University. The participants were also either students at Yale or Princeton. The researchers predicted that students' attitudes would be changed when the story was set at the *away* school more than when it was set at the *home* school. For example, consider the statement "Penicillin has had bad consequences for humankind," a proposition that was discussed (in an identical manner) in both versions of the story. If acceptance is the default, we would expect everyone who reads information in support of that view initially to believe the information. At that point, however, the setting can start to play a role in readers' behavior. Research in social psychology has suggested that individuals work harder to scrutinize information (i.e., to construct belief or disbelief) when the topic is of personal importance (for reviews, see Johnson & Eagly, 1989; Petty & Cacioppo, 1986). This research finding generates the prediction for the *away* school vis à vis the *home* school. Prentice et al. suggested that readers would only be motivated to construct disbelief when the setting made the story personally relevant—e.g., Princeton students would behave differently toward the same words if the story were set at Princeton rather than at Yale. Another way to couch this prediction would be to suggest that personal relevance undermines, in part, the experience of being transported to a distinct narrative world.

Readers were asked to rate their acceptance of statements such as "Penicillin has had bad consequences for humankind." Persuasion in the direction of the story (i.e., movement away from a control group's baseline ratings) was reliably larger for the *away* story than for the *home* story. Note that the words of the text were the same at both schools. That is, the "Yale" version was identical for both Yale and Princeton students. All that differed was the readers themselves. Only in the case when the information had personal relevance—even though the relevance was established by the superficial manipulation of setting—did readers substantially construct disbelief.

The research precedents provide strong evidence in favor of *cognitive* aspects of the construction of disbelief. The perspective, however, is silent on the emotional consequences of belief and disbelief. Let us return to the group of adults who eschew the pleasures of *Psycho*. How is it that events that viewers know not to be real can nonetheless have an impact on their emotions? Philosophers have dubbed this question a paradox—*the paradox of fiction*. Here is a clear statement of the paradox (Radford, 1975):

> Suppose then that you read an account of the terrible sufferings of a group of people. If you are at all humane, you are unlikely to be unmoved by what you read. The account is likely to awaken or reawaken feelings of anger, horror, dismay or outrage and, if you are tenderhearted, you may well be moved to tears. You may even grieve.
>
> But now suppose you discover that the account is false. If the account had caused you to grieve, you could not continue to grieve. If as the account sank in, you were told and believed that it was false this would make tears impossible, unless they were tears of rage. If you learned later that the account was false, you would feel that in being moved to tears you had been fooled, duped. (p. 68)
>
> What seems unintelligible is how we could have [an emotional] reaction to the fate of Anna Karenina, the plight of Madame Bovary or the death of Mercutio. Yet we do. We weep, we pity Anna Karenina, we blink hard when Mercutio is dying and absurdly wish that he had not been so impetuous. (p. 69)

There have been a large variety of attempts made to dissolve the paradox of fiction (see Walton, 1978, 1990, for the benchmark approach; see Dadlez, 1996; Neill, 1993; Säätelä, 1994; Yanal, 1994, for more recent discussions). Almost all these solutions have centered, in one way or another, on (a) what it is exactly that readers (or viewers) can be said to believe or disbelieve, (b) what readers (or viewers) are required to believe as a precursor to experiences of emotion, or both. (That is, there are many discussions relevant to the topic of believed-in imaginings.)

How does the willing construction of disbelief figure into this problem? Let us suppose that, along the lines of the Spinozan account, a viewer immediately accepts it as real that Marion (the heroine, briefly, of *Psycho*) is being stabbed. Presumably, this gives rise to negative emotions. Suppose, now, that the viewer recites the mantra, "This is not real! This is not real!" How does this change the emotional experience? Does the construction of disbelief have consequences for emotional responses? Under what circumstances does disbelief penetrate emotional responses? This, of course, is an empirical question (which we do not believe has received much attention—see Frijda, 1989, and Walters, 1989). In the absence of data we take recourse in the anecdotal evidence with which we began: Adults are sufficiently aware that they cannot control their emotions in response to fictions such that they sometimes opt out of experiencing them.

We need to add one more wrinkle to this analysis: Perhaps vivid emotional responses themselves undermine efforts to cancel those responses. Suppose Greg sees a movie in which someone is murdered with a poisoned can of Coca-Cola. The next time Greg goes to buy a soft drink, he avoids Coke—even though, let us suppose, he is aware that his reluctance has its origin in fiction. He is likely to think or say, "The Coke *could* be poisoned," and he is, of course, correct. When the feeling of danger remains active, even when disbelief has been constructed toward the situation that generated it, Greg can work from the feeling to generate or locate new beliefs that make the emotion sensible.

Social psychologists have confirmed this tendency in a variety of ways. One group of researchers demonstrated, for example, that experimental participants who were given false feedback about their performance—whether they succeeded or failed—were difficult to debrief: When told that the feedback had been false, the participants still made estimates about their actual (i.e., unfictionalized) performance that were consistent with the original false feedback (Ross, Lepper, & Hubbard, 1975; see also Wegner, Coulton, & Wenzlaff, 1985). In the same way, the emotions that arise from works of fiction may sustain the "truth" of the fiction. That is, believed-in imaginings may give rise to affective responses that transcend disbelief.

Let us summarize this perspective. Research evidence supports the notion that comprehension brings with it initial, obligatory acceptance. Within the bounds of being transported, readers may then strategically construct disbelief with respect to the propositions they have read. However, if initial comprehension gives rise to emotional responses, it may not be trivial to vitiate the effects of initial belief. The emotional responses, in fact, may prompt a search for new beliefs that are consistent with those emotions. With this framework in hand, we now turn our eye toward the developmental literature.

DEVELOPMENTAL PERSPECTIVES ON IMAGINATION AND BELIEF

We have opted to take a developmental perspective on the construction of disbelief because researchers in developmental psychology have taken a determined lead in studying phenomena in this area. As shall soon become clear, developmental researchers have produced a body of solid evidence on the subject of the relationship of imagination and belief. We believe this evidence has important implications for the types of theories and research that might be pursued with respect to adult cognition. At the same time, the parallels we illustrate between studies of cognitive development and those with adult participants suggest that developmental theorizing must be informed by consideration of adult performance, the endpoint of development.

What Do Children Know About Imagination and Reality?

Let us return to the conversational excerpt with which we began this paper. Child B's concern that the pretense would be too scary leads naturally to the question of how and when children develop the ability to discriminate between what is imaginary and what is real. As we now describe, research evidence suggests that children are able to keep track of what is only imaginary at a very early age.

Consider a pair of studies by Woolley (1995) in which children, of ages 3 and 4 years, were asked to reason about states that did not accord with reality. The studies required the participation of two experimenters. In one of the studies, the children had to evaluate circumstances in which one of the experimenters either had a *false belief* about reality or *imagined* a situation that was at odds with reality. For the false belief task, the two experimenters and a child initially looked into a covered box to see its contents, which might be, for example, a crayon or a penny. When one of the two experimenters left the room, the second experimenter suggested to the child that they play a trick on the first by either changing the object that was in the box (e.g., from a crayon to a sock) or emptying the box. For the imagination task, the experimenters and the child again noted the contents of the box. In this case, however, one of the experimenters announced that she was going to imagine that an object was in the box (if it was initially empty) or imagine that something different was in the box (if it was initially full). The question put to the children, in each of these cases, was what the critical experimenter (i.e., the one who left the room or the one who announced what she was imagining) either believed or imagined.

The data revealed that all of the children, but particularly the younger children, were relatively more able to give correct answers when they were queried about the experimenter's *imagination*. That is, they were more likely to answer correctly the question "what is [she] imagining is inside the box?" (when what she imagined was in conflict with reality) than "what does [she] think is inside the box?" (when what she believed was in conflict with reality). Why might it be easier for children to understand other people's acts of imagination versus other people's beliefs? Here is Woolley's speculation:

> Given that beliefs are supposed to represent reality and most often do so, it seems sensible and perhaps even adaptive for young children to have such a conception and to have difficulty at first understanding that sometimes beliefs do not represent reality accurately. As imagination is not supposed to represent reality, and in most cases does not, an understanding of imaginary mental representations that are distinct

from reality should be a conceptually easier type of understanding. (1995, pp. 1019–1020)

This explanation has great intuitive appeal. At the same time, however, it leaves unclear how what is imagined can come to be believed: How do we account for believed-in imaginings?

Let us consider another type of developmental research that ultimately leads to the same question. Harris and his colleagues (Harris & Kavanaugh, 1993; Harris, Kavanaugh, & Meredith, 1994; Walker-Andrews & Harris, 1993) have examined children's capacity to use props to generate appropriate actions and inferences with respect to acts of the imagination. Do children, for example, understand that a bear over whom imaginary milk has been poured should then be labeled wet? The answer to this sort of question is substantially yes, although, of course, performance improves with age. Consider an experiment (Harris & Kavanaugh, 1993, Experiment 3) in which 12 "older" 1-year-olds (mean age 21 months) and 12 "younger" 2-year-olds (mean age 28 months) were assessed for the flexibility with which they could conceive of props taking on imaginary roles. In the study, the same props were embedded in two scenarios. For example, a popsicle stick was featured in a breakfast script, as a potential implement to stir imaginary tea: "Show me how you stir Teddy's tea with the spoon." The stick also figured in a bedtime script as a pretend toothbrush: "Here's Teddy's toothbrush. Show me how you brush Teddy's teeth with the toothbrush." The older children outperformed the younger children: A majority of the 2-year-olds produced two distinct responses, with the same prop, for at least two (of three) props. However, even among the younger children, 5 of 12 produced dual responses with respect to at least one prop. Thus, at a very young age, children start to understand the way in which props function in games of make-believe.

However, if children show such great facility with pretend play, what limits the scope of the pretense? Why is it, for example, that children do not overextend the pretense so that, at their own bedtimes, they imagine that a popsicle stick could stand in for a toothbrush? Leslie (1987) defined this potential problem with respect to pretense as an issue of potential *representational abuse*: The child must understand the relationship between what things really are, and what the game of make-believe stipulates them to be so as to avoid the error of laying down inappropriate mental representations. Leslie argued that children possess a *decoupling* mechanism: Their representations of entities in the pretend situation are decoupled from their representations of the same entities in their real-world uses. Harris and Kavanaugh (1993) advanced a theory of *flagging* that represents a somewhat different approach to the problem of keeping the imaginary distinct from the real. According to their theory, children flag mental representations of the pretend episode in which they are engaged to record the relationships stipulated in the game (e.g., that a popsicle stick is a toothbrush). These flags, which become ineffectual once the episode is over (although they are still available in long-term memory) help limit the potential for representational abuse.

This issue of mechanisms to prevent representational abuse has direct implications for any discussion of believed-in imaginings. To the extent that people (children or adults) can come to believe their own imaginings, they have suffered the consequences of representational abuse. The whole framework of the willing construction of disbelief suggests, in fact, that even adults have to labor strategically to avoid representational abuse. That is, decoupling or flagging are almost certainly not automatic concomitants of make-believe. Although very young children have demonstrated an impressive understanding of pretense, we wonder what the developmental end point might be among adults, with respect to representational abuse.

We can, perhaps, throw some light on this question by looking to a small number of studies in which researchers have considered the extent to which information from works of fiction becomes incorporated into real-world representations. Potts and his colleagues (Potts & Peterson, 1985; Potts, St. John, & Kirson, 1989) invented a methodology that enabled them to assess the coherence of representations of story information. This methodology enabled them to study the question of whether fictional information is distributed into existing memory representations (i.e., *incorporated*) or held apart as a coherent representation (i.e., *compartmentalized*). In their studies, readers were required to verify story information in one of two contexts: In *story contexts*, the critical statements were included within a verification list composed of other statements chosen from the same story; in *nonstory contexts* the other statements on the verification list did not appear in the original story. Research on text processing reveals that, when information is compartmentalized in memory, a whole body of information—a coherent subset from a story—becomes more accessible to people when one element of that subset is presented for appraisal (e.g., McKoon, Gerrig, & Greene, 1996). Thus, if story information is highly compartmentalized with respect to other information in memory, there ought to be a performance advantage when the critical statement was verified in the story context as compared to the nonstory context. For compartmentalized representations, each statement in the story context should call to mind other story information that is likely to be offered for subsequent verification. If no story context advantage accrues, one can conclude that the information has been incorporated in memory (i.e., not compartmentalized), independent of its original story context.

Potts et al.'s most important prediction was that the degree of compartmentalization would be greater when participants believed they were reading artificial (i.e., fictional) materials. Comparisons of performance in the story and nonstory contexts bore out that prediction. Across two experiments, Potts et al. found that those readers who believed the materials were artificial obtained a reliable advantage in the story contexts over the nonstory contexts. When readers believed the materials were real, no such advantage emerged. The texts were identical: All that could explain the compartmentalization shift was the readers' strategic stance toward what they believed to be real or artificial information.

The research by Potts et al. considered representations of factual and fictional story information that was largely new to their readers. Gerrig and Prentice (1991) extended Potts et al.'s analysis to circumstances in which information presented fictionally had direct bearing on familiar topics. The experiment used two versions of a short story that introduced some information that was consistent and some that was inconsistent with the real world. The types of information that could be consistent or inconsistent were *context details* (e.g., the town in which the story took place) and *context-free assertions* (e.g., "eating chocolate makes you lose weight"). The purpose of the studies was to determine which types of information would affect real-world judgments. Gerrig and Prentice suggested that information about context-free assertions should be more likely to lead to incorporation. (That is, representational abuse should be less likely to occur with respect to context details because it is easier to clearly demarcate real circumstances from fictional circumstances.)

After participants read the story, they were asked to verify statements such as "Eating chocolate makes you lose weight," as swiftly and accurately as possible. To assess the relative effects of story information on context details and context-free assertions, these readers' judgment times were compared to those of participants who had read a control story that contained no information relevant to the experimental topics. What was the cost associated with reading information in the fictional world that was inconsistent with the real world? For context details this cost was roughly 78 msec. For context-free assertions, the cost was 302 msec. In fact, for the context-free assertions, the entire effect was carried by the responses to inconsistent test statements like "Eating chocolate makes you lose weight." Subjects took 600 msec longer to say "false" to this statement, whereas they took only 3 msec longer to say "true" to a statement consistent with the real world.

A possible conclusion from this study is that representational abuse is systematic. That is, it ought to be possible to define circumstances in which people regularly will represent information from the domain of the imagination in such a fashion that it becomes incorporated with real-world information. Of course, these studies on fictional texts do not have the same proximity to explicit experiences of make-believe as do the developmental studies. The developmental studies establish the great facility that children show for reasoning about the products of their imagination. The studies with adults, as restricted as they are, establish that the developmental endpoint can not be a wholesale avoidance of representational abuse.

DO PRODUCTS OF THE IMAGINATION AFFECT BEHAVIOR?

The experiments we have reviewed so far have considered cognitive aspects of the relationship between imagination and belief. The work suggests that, on the whole, even young children understand the distinction between pretense and reality. Do children, even so, sometimes act as if the products of their imagination might be real? We will refer to this possibility as *transmigration*, the idea that entities can migrate from the imagination into reality (Harris, Brown, Marriott, Whittall, & Harmer, 1991). We now review studies in which researchers considered the extent to which products of the imagination can lead children (and adults) to change their behavior.

The central study we consider was carried out, once again, by Harris and his colleagues (Harris et al., 1991). At the start of the experiment, 4- and 6-year-old children entered a laboratory furnished with some chairs and two large boxes. The children were asked to look into the boxes, to verify that they were empty. The children were told that they were going to play a game: "It doesn't matter that the boxes are empty because we are going to play a game of pretend. I expect you're good at pretend games, aren't you?" The experimenter pointed to one of the two boxes at random, and then requested that the children imagine something to be in that box. The experimenter asked one group to imagine that the box contained a "nice, white, friendly rabbit" who "wants to come out so you can stroke him." The second group was asked to imagine a "horrible, mean, black monster" who "wants to come out to chase you" (Harris et al., 1991, pp. 116–117).

The children were initially asked whether there really was a rabbit or monster, or if they were just pretending. Of the 24 four-year-olds, 22 correctly answered that they were only pretending; 21 of the 24 six-year-olds also answered correctly. However, when the experimenter attempted to leave the room, 4 of the younger children in the monster condition did not want her to leave because they were scared (only 1 of the 4 had answered incorrectly that the monster was real). Although the experimenter had the children look inside the boxes again to verify that they were empty, the children still asked that she remain (and she did so).

The purpose of having the experimenter leave the room (which she did, for the 44 remaining children) was to see how the children would act with respect to the two boxes in the presumed absence of an observer—in fact, the behavior of the children was recorded by a hidden camera. How might the children be expected to act? Harris et al. suggested that even momentary uncertainty in the unreality of the pretend rabbits or monsters could prompt the children to behave differently toward the two boxes. When the experimenter left the room (to "fetch some sweets" that she had forgotten), the children were sitting down, but they were told that they did not have to remain seated. In both age groups, about half of the children stood up and either touched or opened one or both boxes. These children interacted with the box that housed the "rabbit" or "monster" reliably more quickly than they interacted with the neutral box. If they touched only one box, they overwhelmingly chose the box that had been the object of their pretense.

When the experimenter returned after two minutes, she gave the children a sweet and then asked them what they had done while she was gone (e.g., "Did you look inside one of the boxes?"). The critical question addressed children's expectations about what was in the box: "And what did you think when you went to open the box? Did you think there was nothing inside or did you think to yourself: 'I wonder if there's a nice, white, bunny rabbit [horrible, mean, black monster] inside'?" About half the children confessed that they *had* wondered—even though the vast majority had asserted, quite recently, that the rabbit or monster was only pretend. Most of the children, in fact, once again denied that an act of imagination could generate a real creature (14 out of 20 four-year-olds and 19 out of 24 six-year-olds), although the rest now asserted that pretense *could* bring creatures into existence. Even some of those children (5 at each age) who thought that they could not transform pretend entities into real entities believed that others might be able to do so.

Note that their were no particular consequences to the children for exploring the box. As far as they knew they were not being observed. Woolley and Phelps (1994) were interested in cases in which the practical consequences of transmigration might limit the instances in which children would act as if imagined entities had become real. In this pair of studies, 3- to 5-year-old children were shown four boxes and were allowed to open three of them, while the fourth remained unopened. The first of these boxes contained a real object, such as a sock. The second was empty. The third box (the *imagination* box) also was empty, but children were asked to imagine that it contained the same type of object they had seen in the first box (e.g., a sock). The children were questioned about their beliefs in the reality of the imagined sock. As in earlier experiments, some of the children reported that what they had imagined had become real. What happened next, however, was that a stranger entered the experimental room. The stranger appeared without socks and, complaining of cold feet, asked the children if there were socks in any of the boxes. Only very rarely did a child give the stranger the box with the imaginary sock. Instead, children typically gave the stranger the box with the real sock. These experiments suggest a way in which, even for young children, the products of imaginings are subject to pragmatic constraints. Note, however, that it might be instructive to examine how children would respond along a continuum from relatively neutral stimuli such as socks to more affectively charged stimuli such as monsters.

Before we offer a theoretical analysis of these results, we wish to report our first tentative attempts at collecting data from adults on the question of transmigration of fantasy into reality. We read the Harris et al. article, in particular, with great certainty that—with appropriate framing—we could evoke the same types of performance from adults. Before staging an elaborate study, however, we chose to explore participants' self-reports with respect to a familiar scenario:

> Imagine that you are driving yourself to the airport. You will be taking a trip for the weekend to visit a friend in Chicago. You're not sure that you should go because you have a lot of studying to do. You're only taking one carry-on bag, which is on the passenger seat, next to you. You put your ticket in a zippered pouch on the side of the bag right after you got into the car.

Now, consider this question:

> How likely is it that sometime during the trip you would check to see if you still had your ticket?

Suppose you were asked to circle a number from 1 (not very likely) to 9 (very likely). What is an appropriate response? Presumably, if one takes the information in the paragraph to be accurate, there is no need to check for the ticket—the answer should be 1. If, however, readers allow their imaginations to play a role—they imagine scenarios in which the ticket may have gone missing, they might give responses far greater than 1. This is what we set out to determine.

In our first experiment we used four versions of the scenario. Along one dimension, we varied the importance of the trip, whether it was a visit to a friend (as in the example earlier) or a job visit: "You are taking a trip for a very important job interview. This will be your opportunity to get the job you want most." Our idea was that the importance of the trip might prompt readers to predict themselves more likely to check for their ticket. Along a second dimension, we varied the ease with which the driver could check for the ticket. In the example earlier, the ticket was in a bag right next to the driver. In the contrasting versions, the bag was in the trunk "You're only taking one carry-on bag, which you locked in the trunk of the car." We predicted that readers should judge themselves less likely to check for the ticket when it had a higher practical cost for them (e.g., they would have to pull the car over). (This second dimension was intended as an echo of Woolley and Phelps's findings.) Sixty-five college undergraduates read one of the four versions of the scenario and indicated their likelihood judgment on the 1 to 9 scale. Results are given in Table 1.

TABLE 1
Mean Ratings of Participants in the Airplane Ticket Experiment

Trip's Purpose	Location of ticket		Mean
	On the seat	In the trunk	
Visit to Friend	7.20	6.00	6.56
Job Interview	7.93	6.44	7.12
Mean	7.57	6.23	

Note. Ratings were made on a scale of 1 (not very likely) to 9 (very likely).

Our first observation is that the average ratings were all above the midpoint on the scale. That is, readers were not reluctant to admit that, at least in this thought experiment, they were likely to check to see if they still had their ticket. Next we see that readers reported the likelihood to be greater when the ticket was in a bag on the seat next to them ($F(1, 61) = 4.98$, $MSe = 5.86$, $p < .03$). This supports our prediction that there would be an interaction between imagination and practicality. Finally, there was a nonreliable trend for readers to estimate that they would be more likely to check for the ticket if they were on their way to a job interview, rather than just visiting a friend ($F < 1$).

In a second version of the experiment, we decided to ask readers to explain their behavior. They made their judgment, and then we asked them, "Why would or would not it be appropriate to check for the ticket?" Some of the readers rated themselves toward the "not very likely" end of the scale and gave appropriate explanations. Here are some examples:

Where would it go?

The windows are closed so the ticket will stay there.

I would check once right before leaving. I don't think the ticket would disappear if I've already checked to see that it is there.

However, the majority of the readers rated themselves toward the "very likely" end of the scale and gave explanations that suggested that they had not taken the information in the scenario very much to heart. Again, here are some examples:

To make sure nothing goes wrong. I don't want to drive all the way to the airport and realize I don't have my ticket!

Because I wouldn't like to feel like an idiot at the airport to find out I forgot my ticket [and] missed the plane because I had to go back for it.

It would be appropriate because I always lose things.

These explanations suggest to us that readers were making their judgments against a more general background than just the one scenario we provided (because, that is, in our scenario it was unambiguous that the ticket could not have disappeared). That is exactly the point of the exercise: Readers' evaluations of the scenario depended in large part on their ability to imagine circumstances at odds with the ones we described.

What our airplane ticket experiment was meant to have in common with Harris et al.'s studies was what we think of as a *mental itch*: The desire, under low-cost conditions, to verify that what was imagined was, in fact, only imagined. To explain their data, Harris et al. suggested that children's acts of imagination might have increased their estimates of the subjective likelihood that they could encounter the pretend creatures. How might this happen? Although Harris et al. considered other mechanisms, the most persuasive one (i.e., the one that appears to have the greatest resonance for adulthood) makes reference to the powerful effect that the availability of information in memory has on judgments of the probability of real-world occurrences (Tversky & Kahneman, 1973).

Researchers have demonstrated a variety of ways in which information that is easily available from memory influences people's judgments. Consider a study in which researchers manipulated the mood of their participants, so that some became happy and some unhappy (MacLeod & Campbell, 1992). Each group of participants was asked to think of past instances of happy or unhappy events—for example, a welcome invitation or a painful injury—and to estimate how likely it would be that events of this type would happen to them again in the next six months. Participants found it easier to recall memories consistent with their mood, and the availability of mood-congruent memories predicted judgments about the future. Participants foresaw happy or unhappy futures depending on their current mood. Thus, the availability of information can have quite robust effects on people's moment-by-moment experience of the world.

How does this apply to believed-in imaginings? Harris et al. (1991) suggested that the children's experience of having imagined a creature in the box would increase the availability of instances in which the box might really contain a creature: "Objectively rare events may be judged as quite common if appropriate examples of the event can be readily brought to mind" (p. 121). Against this background, Harris et al. suggested that a decline in fear of imaginary creatures over development could be explained by "an increasing resistance to such 'availability' effects" (p. 121).

This availability hypothesis has much in common with the types of explanations our participants gave in the airplane ticket experiment. That is, they acted as if what was relevant was not local circumstances as much as the larger set of instances that the scenario caused them to evoke from memory. To the extent that the scenario made available instances in which they had lost or forgotten something, participants seemed likely to predict that they would check for their ticket—whatever the surface content of the scenario. In this context, believing in one's own imaginings can be equated with allowing the full set of circumstances that can be imagined —subject to the effects of availability—be the judgment set for action, rather than the details of reality. Part of what we are arguing here is that it is a mistake to imagine that this tendency undergoes a developmental change, at least with respect to the underlying mechanism. That is, there might be developmental changes in the types of *contents* that people will allow to penetrate to real-world judgments (e.g., adults might be less likely to scare themselves by imagining a monster), but the underlying tendency to experience transmigration from the imaginary to the real realm remains in place.

Our discussion has not quite gotten to the affective aspects of the phenomenon. In our discussion of the construction of disbelief, we suggested that believed-in imaginings can give rise to emotional responses that then help to maintain beliefs, or to reinstate discredited beliefs. Let us see how this might work with respect to the airplane ticket scenario. Suppose Suzanne is driving to the airport and she begins to wonder whether she has forgotten her ticket. She may have a fairly specific memory of placing the ticket in her bag, but her anxiety about the ticket may prompt her to start questioning the validity of that memory. As availability comes into play, Suzanne may begin to have a flood of memories of circumstances in which she *thought* she had done something but had not; she begins to fear that the current situation may belong to that set. As Suzanne wages an internal battle to convince herself that she is only *imagining* that the ticket is absent, her anxiety will notch up, which will make it easier (again, by virtue of availability) to recall more negative memories. At some point, the competition will become vastly unfair—one veridical memory (i.e., that Suzanne *did* bring her ticket) must compete with all of the nonveridical imaginings (i.e., reconstructions of what might have transpired, based on past life episodes). Note that this account in terms of availability yields a natural explanation for individual differences. Those people who cannot call to mind instances in which they have left important documents behind may be far less likely to experience a mental itch on their way to the airport.

Ultimately, then, we propose that it is not necessary that people— children or adults—come to believe their own imaginings. Rather, they may come to believe the *products* of those imaginings—the rich representational structure engendered by those imaginings—with the same ultimate impact. When someone watches *Psycho*, the movie events might not be real, but the fear feels real, and many of the memories and images that the movie events, and the fear, evoke from memory also enjoy a type of reality (in the sense that they seem to be veridical recollections of past experiences). Thus, the challenge of constructing disbelief is that it is likely to be quite difficult, in practice, to construct disbelief with respect to the products of imaginings. One can disbelieve a specific act of imagination, but still see far-reaching consequences.

In the conversational excerpt with which we began, a child declined to imagine a monster coming, in anticipation of it being too scary. The situation that the child anticipates—that the products of imagination will be too difficult to control—fits nicely with the perspective we have articulated in this chapter. We have suggested, in particular, that what presents the greatest challenge to the construction of disbelief is the products of imaginings. The developmental literature has provided us with a number of empirical precedents to support this view. We have questioned, however, whether people really develop as far as developmental theorists imagine. Basic principles of memory representation and memory search may ensure that adults, alongside their children, will sometimes experience the force of make-believe in the real world.

REFERENCES

Bretheron, I. (1984). Representing the social world in symbolic play: Reality and fantasy. In I. Bretherton (Ed.), *Symbolic play: The development of symbolic understanding* (pp. 3–41). New York: Academic Press.

Carroll, N. (1990). *The philosophy of horror.* New York: Routledge.

Coleridge, S. T. (1973). *Biographia literaria* (Vol. 2). London: Oxford University Press. (Original work published 1817)

Dadlez, E. M. (1996). Fiction, emotion, and rationality. *The British Journal of Aesthetics, 36,* 290–304.

Frijda, N. H. (1989). Aesthetic emotions and reality. *American Psychologist, 44,* 1546–1547.

Garvey, C., & Berndt, R. (1977). Organization of pretend play. *JSAS Catalog of Selected Documents in Psychology, 7* (Ms. No. 1589).

Gerrig, R. J. (1989). Suspense in the absence of uncertainty. *Journal of Memory and Language, 28,* 633–648.

Gerrig, R. J. (1993). *Experiencing narrative worlds.* New Haven, CT: Yale University Press.

Gerrig, R. J., & Prentice, D. A. (1991). The representation of fictional information. *Psychological Science, 2,* 336–340.

Gilbert, D. T. (1991). How mental systems believe. *American Psychologist, 46,* 107–119.

Gilbert, D. T., Krull, D. S., & Malone, P. S. (1990). Unbelieving the unbelievable: Some problems in the rejection of false information. *Journal of Personality and Social Psychology, 59,* 601–613.

Gilbert, D. T., Tafarodi, R. W., & Malone, P. S. (1993). You can't not believe everything you read. *Journal of Personality and Social Psychology, 65,* 221–233.

Harris, P. L., Brown, E., Marriott, C., Whittall, S., & Harmer, S. (1991). Monsters, ghosts and witches: Testing the limits of the fantasy–reality distinction in young children. *British Journal of Developmental Psychology, 9,* 105–123.

Harris, P. L., & Kavanaugh, R. D. (1993). Young children's understanding of pretense. *Monographs of the Society for Research in Child Development, 58* (1, Serial No. 231).

Harris, P. L., Kavanaugh, R. D., & Meredith, M. C. (1994). Young children's comprehension of pretend episodes: The integration of successive actions. *Child Development, 65,* 16–30.

Johnson, B. T., & Eagly, A. H. (1989). Effects of involvement on persuasion: A meta-analysis. *Psychological Bulletin, 106,* 290–314.

Leslie, A. M. (1987). Pretense and representation: The origins of "of theory of mind." *Psychological Review, 94,* 412–426.

MacLeod, C., & Campbell, L. (1992). Memory accessibility and probability judgments: An experimental evaluation of the availability heuristic. *Journal of Personality and Social Psychology, 63,* 890–902.

McKoon, G., Gerrig, R. J., & Greene, S. B. (1996). Pronoun resolution without pronouns: Some consequences of memory-based text processing. *Journal of Experimental Psychology: Learning, Memory, and Cognition, 22,* 919–932.

Neill, A. (1993). Fiction and the emotions. *American Philosophical Quarterly, 30,* 1–13.

Petty, R. E., & Cacioppo, J. T. (1986). The elaboration likelihood model of persuasion. In L. Berkowitz (Ed.), *Advances in experimental social psychology* (Vol. 19, pp. 123–205). Orlando, FL: Academic Press.

Potts, G. R., & Peterson, S. B. (1985). Incorporation versus compartmentalization in memory for discourse. *Journal of Memory and Language, 24,* 107–118.

Potts, G. R., St. John, M. F., & Kirson, D. (1989). Incorporating new information into existing world knowledge. *Cognitive Psychology, 21,* 303–333.

Powers, R. (1988). *Prisoner's dilemma.* New York: Collier Books.

Prentice, D. A., Gerrig, R. J., & Bailis, D. S. (1997). What readers bring to the processing of fictional texts. *Psychonomic Bulletin and Review, 4,* 416–420.

Radford, C. (1975). How can we moved by the fate of Anna Karenina? *Proceedings of the Aristotelian Society, 49,* 67–80.

Ross, L., Lepper, M. R., & Hubbard, M. (1975). Perseverance in self-perception and social perception: Biased attributional processes in the debriefing paradigm. *Journal of Personality and Social Psychology, 32,* 880–892.

Säätelä, S. (1994). Fiction, make-believe and quasi emotions. *The British Journal of Aesthetics, 34,* 25–34.

Tversky, A., & Kahneman, D. (1973). Availability: A heuristic for judging frequency and probability. *Cognitive Psychology, 5,* 207–232.

Walker-Andrews, A. S., & Harris, P. L. (1993). Young children's comprehension of pretend causal sequences. *Developmental Psychology, 29,* 915–921.

Walters, K. S. (1989). The law of apparent reality and aesthetic emotions. *American Psychologist, 44,* 1545–1546.

Walton, K. L. (1978). Fearing fictions. *Journal of Philosophy, 75,* 5–27.

Walton, K. L. (1990). *Mimesis as make-believe.* Cambridge, MA: Harvard University Press.

Wegner, D. M., Coulton, G. F., & Wenzlaff, R. (1985). The transparency of denial: Briefing in the debriefing paradigm. *Journal of Personality and Social Psychology, 49,* 338–346.

Wolf, C. (1989). *Accident: A day's news.* New York: Farrar, Straus & Giroux.

Woolley, J. D. (1995). Young children's understanding of fictional versus epistemic mental representations: Imagination and belief. *Child Development, 66,* 1011–1021.

Woolley, J. D., & Phelps, K. E. (1994). Young children's practical reasoning about imagination. *British Journal of Developmental Psychology, 12,* 53–67.

Yanal, R. J. (1994). The paradox of emotion and fiction. *Pacific Philosophical Quarterly, 75,* 54–75.

III

CREATING INTERPERSONAL NARRATIVES

7

RENDERING THE IMPLAUSIBLE PLAUSIBLE: NARRATIVE CONSTRUCTION, SUGGESTION, AND MEMORY

STEVEN JAY LYNN, JUDITH PINTAR, JANE STAFFORD,
LISA MARMELSTEIN, AND TIMOTHY LOCK

If we pay any attention to the media at all these days, it might be easy for some of us to conclude that we are regularly visited by aliens who abduct innocent earthlings and perform repugnant medical procedures on them and harvest their sperm and eggs, that secret satanic rituals are being conducted in the basements of our neighbors' homes, and that some of us live our lives unaware that our bodies host a boggling array of personalities. Not much more than a decade or two ago, such beliefs would be viewed as implausible at best, embraced only by fringe elements of our society or the psychological community. Now, it seems, such beliefs are infused in mainstream culture and are reflected in the narratives that clients construct in psychotherapy. Such beliefs can no longer be dismissed as excesses of millenial thinking or as mere hokum, because therapists are finding increasingly that clients hold fast to imaginative narratives that contain this kind of content.

What makes imaginative narratives of this kind so fascinating and the subject of debate are not only the far-fetched or implausible content of the narratives and the fact that they seem to be etched into more encompassing personal narratives, but also that they seem to modify the dynamics of important social relationships. When social relationships are affected, concern, of course, arises, when significant harm to the individual and those around him or her issues from these narratives. In the following section, examples from Steven Jay Lynn's clinical practice (presented in the first-person for the sake of readability) illustrate the latter point.

CLINICAL EXAMPLES OF IMPLAUSIBLE NARRATIVES

Example # 1

About eight years ago, I was consulted by the local police to hypnotize a woman who purportedly witnessed events related to a crime in which several people were murdered and burned, along with their trailer, to cover-up a drug-related crime. My task was to enhance her recall of cars parked along a road around the time of the crime. Of course, given that hypnosis was involved, it was doubtful that the witness would be able to testify, and I was doubtful that anything of any value would come of my hypnosis with her, but the police were desperate for leads.

The witness's mother came along because the witness was nervous and the mother was curious. After hypnosis, when the witness went to the bathroom, the mother, who appeared to be a very calm and rational person, told me that she had formerly been hypnotized by a therapist who wanted to get at the roots of her feeling that she was visited at night by strange creatures who immobilized her. Following repeated hypnosis sessions, she came to believe that she had been repeatedly abducted by aliens since childhood, although she noted that she at first resisted the idea. She further informed me that the aliens had inserted something that was undetectable by earth technologies into her brain, which explained why she had very severe headaches dating to childhood. She said that the hypnosis made many things clear to her, which she did not want to talk about when her daughter was around, because the discussion would upset her, as it had her husband. In fact, she informed me that her marriage was on the brink of collapse, suffering from her involvement in the "UFO movement." At the end of our brief discussion, she gave me her business card and invited me to call her if I wanted to learn more about her experiences with aliens. Not surprisingly, when her daughter returned from the bathroom, all discussion about aliens ended.

Example # 2

About three years ago, I was consulted by a woman who informed me that she wanted to do "post-integration work" to better cope with daily life hassles after her recovery from multiple personality disorder or dissociative identity disorder (DID), as it is now officially termed. Two things soon became apparent. The first was that she had been misdiagnosed; the second was that it would be impossible for us to work together. The woman consulted me because she had recently moved to the area after she had been in therapy for three years in a different locale. She had received the DID diagnosis after her therapist referred her to a specialty hospital clinic. After a 2-week stay at this clinic, during which she participated in group therapy with people diagnosed with DID who claimed they had been ritually abused, she stated that she had recovered many memories of sexual abuse perpetrated by her mother, her father, several members of the clergy, and even a former psychologist, all of whom she claimed had participated in a satanic cult involved in the ritual murder and cannibalism of children in her neighborhood.

Prior to her hospitalization, she was seriously depressed following the death of her father, her mother's developing Alzheimer's disease, her son's paralysis in a skiing accident, and her divorce from her husband, all of which occurred within a 14-month period. At the height of her depression, she began to have morbid dreams, which featured people whom she loved hurting her. She also suffered from sleep paralysis, and she felt that there were hostile, malevolent presences near her bed. Her therapist told her that her dreams indicated that probable likelihood of abuse, and that her sleep-related experiences tended to confirm this impression. She was instructed to keep a dream journal and to make associations between what she dreamed and her current and past life. These ideas and techniques were reinforced during her treatment at the inpatient facility for DID. One amazing aspect of this case was that none of her therapists entertained the diagnosis of major depression, nor was she treated with antidepressant medication, because it was thought that antidepressants would inhibit her ability to abreact and recover memories.

We could not work together because she insisted that I believe and accept all of her memories, even those she recounted from her first year of life. Although I empathized with her pain and struggles, when confronted with a direct question about whether I believed all of her memories, I replied that I had some doubts about the historical accuracy of detailed memories from her first week of life, and I was not in a position to corroborate her memories. Whereas she granted that her first-week memories might be inaccurate, she was convinced that all of the horrible memories of abuse, from the first year on, were accurate, because she remembered them so vividly. She was very clear with me that she could not begin to see herself as anything but a survivor of horrific abuse. She had already severed her relationship with members of her mother's and father's family, refused to visit her mother, and viewed herself as part of a very select group of people who had made a reasonably decent recovery after enduring satanic abuse. She had many friends in what she termed the "sexual abuse recovery movement," and to revise her personal history was, in her own words, "unthinkable." She said if she did not believe in these memories, she could not believe in herself and she would "be nothing anymore." Despite my failure to accept all of her memories as real, we parted on good terms.

Example # 3

Unlike the woman in the preceeding example, some individuals come to disavow memories of implausible experiences that appear to be inculcated during therapy. These are the so-called "retractors" whose divergent profiles are described by de Rivera (this volume). Many readers may have some passing acquaintance with the exemplary case of Nadean Cool, which was recently featured on the television program "60 Minutes." I (SJL) was an expert in this case in which Nadean won a 2.4 million dollar settlement of her malpractice suit against her treating psychiatrist. My impression was that Nadean had mostly minor adjustment difficulties and problems prior to starting therapy. However, during five years of therapy, Nadine was exposed to repeated hypnotic age-regression sessions in which she was encouraged to recover memories of horrific abuse, to access more than 125 "multiple personalities" and fragments, including a duck personality, and to participate in lengthy therapy sessions, one of which was reportedly 15 hours long. Several of these sessions involved "exorcisms" of "Satan" in which many of her personalities were called out.

My impression was that as more memories and personalities surfaced, Nadean became increasingly isolated from those she loved. As her psychological status deteriorated, her gratification and attention correspondingly focused on her therapist and on her thoughts and feelings regarding her latest uncovered memories. With her family's support, Nadean began to seriously question what had transpired in therapy and eventually was able to gain a sense of perspective on her treatment and herself. She ultimately was able to regain the equilibrium she had attained in her life before therapy commenced.

Shared Features of Implausible Narratives

Whereas these examples illustrate seemingly implausible imaginative narratives that appear to be different, there are similarities.

- Each imaginative narrative emerged in the context of a treatment in which the narrative provided an explanation for current life difficulties that achieved plausibility following therapeutic interventions that were suggestive in nature.
- Neither the therapist nor the client actively considered alternative explanations, such as sleep paralysis or depression, for puzzling experiences or difficulties.
- The therapist sought only confirmatory data.
- In certain respects, the narrative matched or fit the client's views of self and the world.
- There was a period of increasing commitment to the narrative on the part of the client and therapist, increasing dependence on the therapist and reducing anxiety associated with ambiguity reduction.
- The clinician or supportive community encouraged a "conversion" or "coming out" experience, which solidified the performed role associated with the narrative (e.g., UFO abductee) and was accompanied by feelings of empowerment, which constituted an additional source of positive reinforcement.
- The imaginative narratives were constructed within social relationships through the mechanism of shared narratives (see Sarbin, 1997b) with family, friends, and people in positions of authority.

The narratives illustrated in these examples provided a measure of continuity for the client in the past and the future, and they provided a certain degree of comfort and a sense of belonging and identity, if only because they defined the individual's place in the world. But social relationships variously shape, reinforce, perpetuate, or challenge roles enacted. In the examples given, these social relationships include the psychotherapeutic and hypnotic relationship, which are, in turn, dependent on shared narratives of the therapist as healer and expert, if not savior. Furthermore, the imaginative narratives described catapult the person to a special social status, at once a pawn and a survivor of forces much larger than the self. And in each case described, the person, at least initially, resisted pressures to step into the role associated with the imaginative narrative, but ultimately, came to defend the role, thus increasing commitment to it.

In the remainder of the chapter, we further illustrate how imaginative narratives can achieve a high degree of credibility. We describe research on the availability of certain imaginative narratives in our culture, as well as research on the reconstructive nature of memory, hypnosis and suggestive procedures, and individual differences in vulnerability to imaginative narratives. Finally, we present Lynn and Pintar's (1997) theory of the social nature of narrative constructions in dissociative identity disorder.

HOW THE IMPLAUSIBLE BECOMES PLAUSIBLE: A RESEARCH REVIEW

UFO Abduction Narratives

It is unlikely that personal narratives of UFO abductees, satanic ritual abuse victims, or hosts of multiple personalities would be so prevalent today if such narratives were not accessible in our culture as explanations for current life problems (see Sarbin, 1997b). UFO narratives, for example, are readily available to the general public. A recent Time/Yankelovic (1997) poll indicated that 22% of the American public believes that the earth has been visited by space aliens. Based on the results of a Roper survey, Hopkins, Jacobs, and Westrum (1992) estimated that by 1992 nearly 4 million Americans reported having been abducted by aliens and that, according to the typical UFO narrative, they were tormented, humiliated, and subjected to physical examinations. Newman and Baumeister (in press) have theorized that such themes pervade UFO abduction accounts and are motivated by people's need for an escape from self-awareness and loss of identity. Interestingly, the frequency of alien abduction accounts increase closely on the heels of popular books or movies on the subject (Klass, 1988; Newman & Baumeister, in press).

Several researchers have examined the availability of imaginative narratives and the culturally derived beliefs associated with UFO narratives. Lawson (1977) hypnotized 16 volunteers and told participants to imagine an encounter with aliens in which they see a UFO, imagine they are aboard the craft, that they are given a physical examination, that they get a message from the aliens, and so forth. Although Lawson's hypothesis was that such reports could be easily distinguished from the reports of people who claimed they had genuine contact experiences without being hypnotized, he concluded that the hypnotically suggested reports were not, in fact, substantively different. Unfortunately, Lawson provided subjects with specific suggestions to report information pertinent to what abductees claim, such as to imagine that they were examined by the aliens, so it is not surprising that no differences between instructed and noninstructed reports emerged. This makes it difficult to conclude that subjects' fantasies stemmed from culturally derived beliefs.

In a study designed to give participants an opportunity to generate abduction scenarios around a mysterious or ambiguous event, Lynn and Pezzo (1994) used a simulation paradigm adapted from Orne (1971). Unlike Lawson's study in which participants were actually hypnotized, participants in the Lynn and Pezzo (1994) study were asked to role-play the performance of excellent hypnotic subjects. That is, participants were instructed to use whatever they knew about hypnosis and the experimental procedures to convince the hypnotist. Participants were divided into 3 experimental groups. All groups were instructed to "age regress" to the time of a puzzling event that involved (a) driving in the country, (b) leaving the car to witness mysterious moving lights in the sky, and (c) having no clear recall of being in the car for 2 hours afterward. All participants were asked to describe what they could see, hear, and feel.

After hypnosis, three other phases occurred, varying slightly for each of the 3 groups. All groups participated in a structured interview, which began with open-ended questions, followed by increasingly specific and direct questions. All groups were administered a questionnaire devised by OMNI Magazine with Budd Hopkins (Weintraub, 1987). This questionnaire was used to survey readers of the magazine about purported UFO experiences to test the hypothesis that many people have repressed their abduction experiences. The questionnaire included questions about respondents' beliefs in UFOs, if they had sighted what they believed to be a UFO, memory gaps associated with the sighting, and so on.

Participants in the control group were interviewed first and then were given the OMNI questionnaire. The OMNI questionnaire was administered to group 2 at the beginning of the experiment, prior to the interview, to cue them to construe the mysterious experience in terms of a UFO encounter. Participants in the third group also received the OMNI questionnaire at the beginning of the experiment, prior to the interview, but they were also instructed to role-play a "close encounter of the third kind" in which they had contact with aliens on a spacecraft—an additional cue. In response to an initial opened-ended question, in the structured interview, 19% of the 21 participants in the control group said they had identified a UFO. When asked direct questions, 52% identified lights as UFOs, 24% indicated that they had interacted with aliens, and 14% reported that they boarded the UFO. Of the 21 participants in group 2 who received the OMNI questionnaire before the interview, 62% reported that they had witnessed a UFO in response to open-ended questions and, in response to a direct question in the structured interview, all but one (95%) reported witnessing a UFO. In addition, 62% reported that they had interacted with aliens and 33% reported that they had boarded the spacecraft by the end of the interview. In contrast, 95% of the participants in the third group, who were specifically instructed to role-play an encounter with the aliens, identified lights as a UFO, and 91% of the subjects stated that they had interacted with the aliens and boarded the spacecraft by the end of the interview.

Furthermore, the participants' reports of alien encounters contained many of the same features (e.g., telepathic contact; small bodies, large eyes and heads of occupants; forced or compelled actions; sexual contact, operations) reported by individuals who claim that they have actually made contact with or were abducted by UFO occupants. In fact, 32% of the total sample reported stories with at least one element of a sadomasochistic theme, and all of these reports came from participants who were cued (i.e., groups 2 and 3). Relatedly, more than a quarter of the sample (27%) reported either that they felt a loss of control during the experience or that they were being pulled or directly controlled by the aliens.

In summary, stories consistent with alien encounters varied as a function of the accessibility of cues that legitimized the report of UFO narratives. Our findings imply that abduction or alien contact narratives do not necessarily reflect an escape from the self, as Newman and Baumeister (in press) implied, but, rather, reflect the fact that widely available and highly scripted cultural narratives are widely available. Such narratives may, in turn, may be prompted and shaped by leading questions and suggestions from therapists who are informed by UFO abduction narratives that serve as explanations for puzzling or inexplicable symptoms and behaviors.

Satanic Ritual Abuse Narratives

Like UFO abduction narratives, imaginative narratives of satanic ritual abuse are based on scripts that are widely available in our culture. As far as satanic ritual abuse goes, this script includes "bizarre, horrendous acts such as murder, torture, and sacrifice of humans and animals; cannibalism; and baby breeding to supply the sacrificial needs of satanic cults" (Qin, Goodman, Bottoms, & Shaver, in press). Since the early 1980s when the influential book *Michelle Remembers* (Smith & Pazder, 1980) was published, reports of ritual abuse have skyrocketed. In this book, written by a claimed survivor of satanic ritual abuse, in collaboration with her psychiatrist, Michelle reported the recovery of many improbable, if not outlandish, memories of events (cf. Qin et al., in press).

Despite the fact that Kenneth Lanning, a noted FBI expert has noted that, despite concerted investigation, "There is little or no evidence for the portion of the allegations that deals with large-scale baby breeding, human sacrifice, and organized satanic conspiracies" (Lanning, 1991, p. 173), reports of satanic ritual abuse are currently so widespread that approximately a quarter of local prosecutors reported in a recent survey by the American Bar Association that they have dealt with cases involving alleged ritualistic or satanic abuse (Smith, Elstein, Trost, & Bulkey, 1993).

In order to assess culturally available scripts regarding satanic ritual abuse and dissociative identity disorder (DID), Stafford and Lynn (1997) asked college students to role-play either a well-adjusted student, a student with major depression, or a student with DID in a clinical interview situation. Students were provided with the DSM–IV (American Psychiatric

Association, 1994) diagnostic criteria for the disorders and, in the role-play that followed, were asked a series of questions about their life history including any physical, sexual, and satanic abuse they may have suffered. Participants were hypnotized to determine whether they could recall additional pertinent information and again asked questions about abuse a third time after the hypnotic interview. As was predicted, the participants associated serious psychopathology with abuse, particularly sexual abuse. Fully 82% of the participants asked to role-play DID reported that they had been sexually abused, in comparison with 68% of participants in the depressed and 28% of subjects in the well-adjusted group. Furthermore, 36% of the DID role-players indicated that they had experienced satanic ritual abuse, compared with 13% of the seriously depressed persons and 3% of the well-adjusted role-players.

Reports of satanic abuse included a variety of activities including being forced to eat unidentifiable substances, witnessing people being burned, and being forced to participate in sexual rituals. Not only did many reports of abuse emerge after hypnosis, but also the frequency and severity of abuse incidents increased as well. The findings are consistent with the idea that people believe that hypnosis "de-represses" buried memories of traumatic experiences.

Clients consult therapists because there is much that is going on in their lives that they cannot understand, explain, or contend with. The presence of serious psychopathology that cannot be explained by organic or physiological accounts raises the question of what in the person's past is sufficient to account for it. The Stafford and Lynn (1997) findings imply that individuals invoke a representative heuristic such that they believe that serious psychopathology requires traumatic antecedents sufficient to explain the disordered behavior or puzzling experiences. In situations where individuals cannot recall specific aspects of their past that could explain or account for current problems, they might assume that they have repressed memories of abuse and trauma, and, therefore, they may be particularly amenable to suggestive procedures or explanations from authority figures that trauma can account for current difficulties.

A high suggestible or hypnotizable client with a history of maltreatment during childhood, depression, or other psychological problems, and with a propensity to believe in Satan and satanic evil, may be particularly vulnerable and more prone to create an imaginative satanic ritual abuse scenario with a therapist who uses highly suggestive memory recovery techniques, believes in repressed memories and the traumatic and long-term effects of child abuse, and mixes religion with therapy (see Qin et al., in press). The construction of imaginative scenarios can happen only if memory and identity are malleable. Our sense of self and of our personal history are not static, as any person who has been seriously depressed, fallen in love, or had a mystical experience can attest.

THE CONSTRUCTIVE NATURE OF MEMORY

If there has been any significant development in the field of psychology over the past decade or so, it has been the decline and fall of the metaphor of memory as a vast, permanent, and potentially accessible storehouse of information, and the replacement of this metaphor with the idea that memory is fallible, quirky, and reconstructive in nature. More than 200 years ago, Coleridge recognized that thought is the result of the endless permutations of memories, threaded together by emotion. The autobiographical record is rarely continuous; often our memories achieve a semblance of coherence because we edit, splice, and cut and paste them into a story. In a recent *New York Times* article, Anna Quindlen (1997) wrote:

> The details of my childhood come swimming up at me through some primordial ooze, unanchored by context or plot line: the Good Humor truck bell, a broken nose and the feel of blood in my mouth, my mother in a maternity smock, my father sleeping on the sofa. To stitch them together would require considerable embroidery. A chair without a room, a tree without a street: there is nowhere to go with these disconnected details but into the land of fiction, where it is permissible to construct a world around them. (p. 35)

Quindlen implies that narrative fictions are most likely to occur when memories are hazy, disjointed, or completely unavailable. Not surprisingly, research supports this hypothesis. For instance, studies in Hirt's (Hirt, McDonald, & Markman, in press) laboratory have demonstrated that when individuals lack memories for specific events, they engage in a process of hypothesis-testing that increases the likelihood that what will be recalled will be consistent with hypotheses regarding what occurred. Memory errors are often not random. They are consistent with our best guesses based on past learnings, experiences, projected future experiences, and views of the self and others.

The tendency to develop or accept plausible accounts for what occurred when memories are not readily available or accessible can make memory quite serviceable; however, it can also lead to considerable memory errors. Studies in our laboratory have shown that individuals are most prone to suggestive influences when they cannot recall events and what is suggested is in keeping with events that could plausibly have occurred in the situation. In fact, pseudo-memory rates are more than twice as high for events that are rated as having a high base rate of occurrence in the situation than they are for events that are rated as improbable or unlikely to occur in the situation (Weekes, Lynn, & Myers, 1997). Based on such findings, one could speculate that if a trusted authority figure like a therapist implies that a history of childhood abuse has a high base rate of occurrence and accounts for the clients' present symptoms, it could increase the likelihood that the client would come to believe that abuse has been repressed and render the client vulnerable to the suggestion this may have been the case for them.

Stereotypes, schema, and scripts about what could or might have occurred in the past can serve as powerful organizers of memory (see Hirt et al., in press). The distinction between fact and fantasy may be more difficult than one might imagine, for it is now well established that we can be as confident of events that never occurred as we can be of events that occurred in reality. Furthermore, there may be little or no relationship between the emotional intensity with which we experience a memory and the accuracy of the memory. Clients cannot merely "trust their feelings" to discriminate accurate and inaccurate memories. Unfortunately, some therapists instruct their clients to do just that with respect to the memories that emerge in treatment.

In summary, empirical studies support what has long been known or suspected: When memory is absent or impoverished, people fill in the gaps with imaginative constructions, with stories about what happened based on what could have plausibly occurred. In an effort to make meaning and sense out of our lives, we integrate information from a variety of sources, including family members, therapists, and stories that thrive in the culture, to stitch together our personal unknowns in a manner consistent with our present and what we know of our past. Memory, then, can be thought of as a decision-making process, vulnerable to all of the imperfections of other decisions we make, including overconfidence.

THE USE OF SUGGESTIVE TECHNIQUES IN MEMORY RECOVERY

In the cases discussed at the beginning of the chapter, hypnosis and other memory recovery techniques were applied. Survey research (see Lynn, Myers, & Malinoski, 1997) has indicated that between 20% and 34% of psychotherapists use hypnosis to reinstate forgotten traumatic experiences or to establish the historical basis of events. This is unfortunate. In a recent review of the literature, Lynn, Lock, Myers, and Payne (1997) argued that hypnosis should not be used in psychotherapy to recover historically accurate memories. Whereas memories elicited during hypnosis are not always inaccurate, and hypnosis can sometimes yield a greater number of memories, meta-analyses (Steblay & Bothwell, 1994) have indicated that hypnosis results in more recall errors, more uncued errors, and more false memories in response to leading questions. Moreover, hypnosis increases unwarranted confidence in remembered events, although the effect is not always evident and is not invariably strong (cf. Lynn, Lock, Myers, & Payne, 1997).

Even when Green, Lynn, and Malinoski (in press) warned participants about the deleterious effects of hypnosis on memory, those who responded to the target suggestion reported just as many pseudo-memories as did those who did not receive the warning about the effects of hypnosis on memory. Although defenders of the use of hypnosis for memory recovery have maintained that hypnosis increases memories of emotionally valenced events, a review of seven studies that addressed this issue contradicts this assumption (Lynn, Lock, Myers, & Payne, 1997).

If hypnosis is not a viable way of recovering memories of the recent past, then there is no reason to believe it would be any more effective in recovering memories of childhood events. In his review of more than 100 years of research on hypnotic age regression, Nash (1987) concluded that the behaviors and experiences of age-regressed adults were often different from that of actual children. No matter how compelling age-regressed experiences appear to observers, they reflect participants' fantasies and beliefs and assumptions about childhood, and rarely, if ever, represent literal reinstatements of childhood experiences, behaviors, and feelings.

In one illustrative study (Nash, Drake, Wiley, Khalsa, & Lynn, 1986) participants who age regressed to age 3 years reported the identity of their transitional objects (e.g., blankets and teddy bears). Parents of 14 hypnotized participants and 10 role-playing participants in a control group were asked to verify this information. The results showed that those hypnotized were less accurate than were those in the control group in identifying the specific transitional objects they had used. Hypnotic subjects' hypnotic recollections, for example, matched their parents' report only 21% of the time, whereas role-players' reports after hypnosis were corroborated by their parents 70% of the time. This research, like other studies reported in the age-regression literature (cf. Nash, 1987), indicates that age-regression experiences can be compelling yet inaccurate.

Researchers agree that memories before age 2 are not likely to be veridical descriptions of actual historical events (Usher & Neisser, 1993). Sivec and Lynn (1996) elicited 40 hypnotized and 40 nonhypnotized participants' earliest memories. The first time participants were asked to report their earliest memory, only 3% of those not hypnotized recalled a memory earlier than at age 2. However, 23% of those hypnotized reported a memory earlier than at age 2, 20% reported a memory earlier than at 18 months, 18% reported a memory earlier than at 1 year, and 8% reported a memory of earlier than at 6 months. The second time participants were asked for an early memory, only 8% of those not hypnotized reported a memory at earlier than 2 years, and only 3% reported memories at 6 months or earlier. In contrast, 35% of those hypnotized reported memories earlier than at 18 months, 30% reported memories earlier than at 1 year, and 13% reported a memory at 6 months or earlier.

It would be easy to scapegoat hypnosis because it is the memory recovery technique that has received the most experimental scrutiny. However, the literature (Lynn, Lock, Myers, & Payne, 1997) indicates that when suggestive, nonhypnotic techniques are used, the pseudo-memory rates are roughly comparable to the rates secured in hypnotic conditions. Furthermore, when uncertainty exists about past events, such as in the case with very early memories, it is easy to manipulate memory, even when nonhypnotic suggestive pressures are brought to bear on participants, as was illustrated by a program of research conducted by Malinoski and Lynn.

In one of their studies (Lynn & Malinoski, 1996), participants were repeatedly (4 times) asked to tell about their earliest memories under conditions analogous to different kinds of clinical interviews. In one condition (low demand), the questions were phrased in a very permissive manner, with statements such as, "If you don't remember, it's all right." In a second condition (high demand), the questions were worded to subtly suggest that participants should be able to recall earlier memories on each trial (i.e., "Tell me when you get an earlier memory"). This small change in wording resulted in a difference of average recall of nearly 1 year across groups (low demand earliest memory M = 3.45 years versus high demand M = 2.28 years). Furthermore, by the end of the interview, fully 43% of participants in the high demand condition reported a memory of an event that occurred at or before the age of 24 months, compared with 20% of participants in the low demand group.

In another study (Malinoski & Lynn, 1995), when participants could no longer provide additional recall regarding their earliest memories, they were asked to close their eyes, see themselves "in their mind's eye" as a toddler or infant, and "get in touch" with memories of long ago. Participants were also informed that most young adults can retrieve memories of very early events—including their second birthday—if they "let themselves go" and try hard to visualize, focus, and concentrate. Interviewers then asked for memories of the second birthday, after which they gave participants additional instructions to visualize, concentrate, and focus on even earlier memories. Participants were complimented and reinforced for reporting increasingly earlier memories.

The mean age at which the initial reported memory occurred was 3.70 years, with only 11% reporting initial earliest memories at or before age 24 months. However, after receiving the visualization instructions, 59% of the participants reported a memory of their second birthday. After the birthday memory was solicited, interviewers pressed participants for even earlier memories. The mean age at which the earliest memory reported was 1.60 years, fully 2 years less than their initial memory report.

One of the most interesting findings was that 78% of the sample reported remembering at least one event that occurred at 24 months of age or earlier. Furthermore, 56% reported an event that occurred between birth and 18 months of life, 33% reported an event that occurred at age

12 months or younger, and 18% reported at least one memory of an event that occurred at 6 months or younger, well outside the boundary of infantile amnesia. Finally, 4% of the sample provided memory reports from the first week of life. Neither of these studies used particularly invasive methods for eliciting implausible memories; however, it is clear that with increasing pressure, participants reported increasingly implausible memories.

Other studies indicate that suggestive procedures can result in rich and detailed false memories. In fact, in studies conducted in two different laboratories (Burgess, 1994; DuBreuil, Garry, & Loftus, in press; Spanos, 1996) when participants were told that tests revealed that they had a personality type consistent with being born in a hospital room with a particular type of mobile hanging from the ceiling, the majority of hypnotized and nonhypnotized participants reported that they could see the mobile after they were asked to age regress to the day after their birth. Moreover, about a third of the participants reported that they were confident that the mobile was not merely imagined but was actually present in their room at birth.

The degree to which laboratory findings can be generalized to the clinic is an important and worthwhile question. To be sure, gaps exist in our knowledge of the coherence, strength, and durability of memories manipulated by suggestive procedures. However, in our opinion, the weight of the accumulated evidence indicates that hypnosis and other potentially suggestive techniques should not be used in psychotherapy to recover clients' memories.

Whereas we have outlined a general framework for understanding imaginative narratives, it is probably not the case that all individuals are equally susceptible to such influences. For instance, some individuals may regard UFO abduction, satanic ritual abuse, and multiple personalities as so implausible or lacking in "fit" with their current narratives and life experiences that highly coercive procedures would be necessary to elicit conformity to the imaginative narrative. Such coercive procedures could, in turn, elicit considerable reactance and, hence, backfire. However, if individuals find such narratives credible, then they may be more likely to adopt them. Research on past-life hypnotic regression illustrates this nicely: Prehypnotic beliefs about the credibility of past-life experiences have been shown to predict which subjects report an experience of a past life during hypnosis rated as believed in versus only imagined (Spanos, Burgess, & Burgess, 1994).

It has been well documented (Lynn, Lock, Myers, & Payne, 1997) that hypnotizability is a significant risk factor for producing pseudo-memories in hypnotic as well an nonhypnotic situations. Some studies have shown that those who are highly hypnotizable produce more pseudo-memories than do people who are less hypnotizable, whereas other studies have shown indistinguishable differences between highly hypnotizable people and people not receptive to hypnotism. However, the research consistently shows that people who are highly hypnotizable or somewhat hypnotizable are at greater risk for producing pseudo-memories than are those who are not receptive to hypnotism (see Lynn & Nash, 1994). Research in our laboratory has also shown that compliance, hypnotizability, and fantasy proneness are associated with implausible memories before age 2 (see Malinoski, Lynn, & Sivec, in press). Taken together, these findings imply that therapists should consider administering tests that measure these constructs before therapy and should exercise caution regarding using suggestive procedures with individuals who appear to be at particular risk for forming false memories.

THE SOCIAL CONSTRUCTION OF PERSONAL NARRATIVES

Although the evidence clearly shows that suggestive techniques can influence recollection, we question whether a few leading questions, suggestive comments, or errant remarks during therapy are likely to be the sole explanation for leading a person to assume the role of a UFO abductee, a person with multiple identities, or a victim of satanic ritual abuse. The degree to which a person constructs an imaginative narrative in response to suggestive influences in treatment probably depends on a number of variables, including the extent to which the suggested narrative is consistent with a person's world view and sense of self and can be integrated into important social relationships that satisfy needs for security, belonging, mastery, and control. In this section we describe a recently advanced argument for the existence of a narrative model of dissociated selves (Lynn & Pintar, 1997), which takes into account the importance of these other variables.

For instance, consider the importance of narrative fit with subjective experience in cases where UFO abduction narratives are associated with people who have had sleep paralysis experiences (Spanos et al., 1994). If people experience repeated episodes of sleep paralysis in which they feel strangely immobilized and anxious and sense malevolent presences near their bed, they might be more likely to adopt a UFO abduction narrative as an explanation for the anomalous experiences, regardless of whether the narrative is spontaneously authored or co-constructed with a therapist. In contrast to mechanistic conceptualizations that locate the phenomenon as a symptom of a disorder or as a defense mechanism outliving its usefulness the narrative model of dissociated selves allows one to identify one possible origin of the narrative of the self as representing a split in the subjective experiences and social relations of the individual. The model pivots on the hypothesis that identity is constructed, role-governed, and performed (Sarbin, 1986, 1997b).

If there is one finding that pervades the literature on DID, it is that people who are diagnosed with DID report a history of traumatic physical or sexual abuse (see Horovitz, 1993). Although reports of sexual abuse may be exaggerated and embellished in therapy, as in the case of many, if not all, reports of transgenerational satanic ritual abuse, all reports of abuse are by no means necessarily created (although they may be in certain therapies) during the course of treatment and may reflect the historical reality of individuals who carry a DID diagnosis. But it may not be the abuse itself so much as the disruption in social roles and relationships that issues from abusive situations that is at the core of DID narratives.

Indeed, only a small number of individuals who are abused construct narratives of dissociated identities. Lynn and Pintar (1997) hypothesized that individual differences in the ability to construct imaginative narratives (i.e., fantasy proneness), suggestive and iatrogenic psychotherapeutic procedures, and disruptions, upheavals, and contradictions in important social relationships are associated with the construction of multiple self-narratives. Furthermore, although imaginatively elaborated, self-narratives are often grounded in the perceived and actual social circumstances of the individual.

In highlighting the role of social relationships, Lynn and Pintar (1994) distinguished dissociated multiple identities from the multiple identities that we all experience that are merely complex. A child who lives in separate households may develop a complex sense of self that encompasses two distinct narratives—"I am a responsible big sister" in one household, and "I am just a little kid" in the other. This is a multiple personal narrative, but it is occurring within a larger social narrative that may be stressful but is not traumatic. Consider a girl who has toys and clothes at Mom's and different toys and clothes at Dad's and can bring the toys from Dad's house to Mom's house if she wants to. But what if she is being abused at Dad's house? There are still two personal narratives, but something is different: What Dad is doing is no longer reflected in a shared social narrative. What does the child do now? Who is she when she's with her Dad? Not the same person she is when she is with her Mom, where personal and social narratives match. She may say that she "split" at that point, but the crucial thing to note is that the world split first.

The social narrative on and through which this child constructed her identity ruptured. It lost coherence and consistency. Rather than being a way to separate from reality, dissociation may well be, under some circumstances, a way to bring identity in line with those circumstances. Trapped between a broad social narrative that says "fathers care for their daughters and don't hurt them" and a personal narrative that is based on the experience of being repeatedly raped by her father, the child's construction of a multiple identity is a realistic reflection of her actual social condition, and her subjective experience of having many selves, which appears to be a distortion of reality, is, in a sense, an accurate reflection of lived experience.

Multiplicity is perhaps the only way that both narratives can be true at the same time. She can be both a 9-year-old school girl and her father's lover. It may be true, as many have postulated, that pathology arises because she cannot "integrate" the two identities within one coherent self. But the reason the identities cannot co-exist is that the social world does not acknowledge that they might both be true. It may be accurate to suggest that the world and she are mutually dissociated from one another.

The important point to note is that what the experience of trauma disrupts is not identity itself but the social process through which identity is constructed. Correspondingly, in this view, the phenomenon of multiplicity is a disorder of identity or narrative construction. The suggestion that multiplicity is in part or wholly iatrogenic becomes less surprising (although no less problematic) in this light. Multiple identity, like unitary identity, is performed—that is to say, it is dynamically constructed through social relationships.

The narrative of multiple identity that underlies DID may be comfortable to many survivors of traumatic abuse because it fits their subjective experience of their disrupted identities more closely than it does with the dominant cultural narrative of ordinary unitary identity, an identity that assumes nontraumatic social conditions and relations. However, evidence of multiplicity often emerges for the first time in psychotherapy, and in fact, may be an iatrogenic creation (see Sarbin, 1997a; Spanos, 1996), in whole or in part, in many, if not the majority of instances. Therapists treating DID clients share with their clients a narrative about identity that includes a belief in the existence of DID. They engage in discussions with alters, developing relationships with them within which the alters come alive. The therapist–client relationship may not be the only one in which the alters perform, but it is often the most important one.

The process in which multiple identities are constructed or maintained within the discourse of a therapeutic relationship will be even more powerful in a relationship between therapists and their highly suggestible and fantasy-prone clients. Research (Lynn, Rhue, & Green, 1988) has shown that there are many parallels between people who have a profound history of fantasy involvements that date to early childhood and individuals diagnosed with DID. Indeed, when we look at what measures of dissociation index, one prominent component is fantasy and imaginative proclivities. Fantasy-prone people report that they played with imaginary companions during childhood, often pretend to be other people during times of stress, report out-of-body experiences to deal with traumatic and nontraumatic experiences, and create absorbing imaginative narratives during which time stands in abeyance. In short, they dissociate.

Several recent studies support this hypothesis. In two studies, Rauschenberger and Lynn (1995, 1997) have shown that fantasy-prone people have many more dissociative symptoms not only on a self-report scale of dissociative experiences, but also on an interview specifically designed to assess dissociative symptoms. Other research (Lynn & Rhue, 1988) has shown that fantasy-prone individuals are also more suggestible, even in nonhypnotic situations, than are their less fantasy-prone counterparts, particularly people rated low in fantasy-proneness. To say that a client is suggestible is also to say that he or she is particularly sensitive to the immediate social relationship, so that the influence of a hypnotherapist can override other preexisting social beliefs. For instance, if the therapist suggests that a woman's arm is getting lighter and will rise on its own, that narrative suggestion replaces, at least for the moment, the shared social belief that arms do not ordinarily do that.

In ordinary conversations, many of us talk about ourselves as having different parts or as feeling as if one part of ourselves is in conflict with another part. So suggestions for one part to "come out" in the context of psychotherapy or hypnosis may, in fact, conform more closely to one's ordinary experience of oneself that to the feeling of nonvolition and involuntariness that often accompanies responses to hypnotic suggestions for one's arm to rise, for example.

It is not likely, however, that suggestibility or imaginative tendencies alone can explain why an individual would take on and participate in the ongoing construction of multiple identities. It may be necessary for the therapist and the relationship to provide incentives such as the feeling of being special, meeting important needs of the client and therapist, and so forth, in order for the client to construe the self in terms of multiple identities. It may be necessary for this conceptualization to be reinforced and legitimized by therapeutic procedures such as repeated suggestions for alters to emerge during hypnosis that give fiber and body to nascent aspects of the self. The bottom line is that identity is a malleable narrative construct, exquisitely sensitive to social conditions.

We think it is fair to say that the diagnosis of multiplicity—with its narrative of separation and integration, can be a useful therapeutic tool for a few patients, but that for most patients it opens a veritable Pandora's box and can lead to an exacerbation of symptoms, a breakdown of relationships and social networks, and a tangled conflation of fantasy images with actual memories. Multiplicity is a narrative of identity that is compelling for certain trauma survivors because it comes closer to reflecting their subjective experience of self than other shared social narratives. It becomes problematic when it ceases to be just a useful metaphor and becomes a category of identification. This is especially dangerous for those whose presenting symptoms have to do with disruptions in identity to begin with. It appears, in this light, that the "epidemic" of DID during the last 20 years is not the deliberate product of a conspiratorial movement of therapists to construct a chronic disorder in a highly-suggestible and fantasy-prone subpopulation, but the byproduct of a compelling metaphor run wild.

REFERENCES

American Psychiatric Association. (1994). *Diagnostic and statistical manual* (4th ed). Washington, DC: Author.

Burgess, M. F. (1994). *False memory reports in hypnotic and nonhypnotic subjects.* Unpublished master's thesis, Carleton University, Ottawa, Canada.

de Rivera, J. (1992). The construction of false memory syndrome. *Psychological Inquiry, 8,* 271–292.

Dubreuil, S. C., Garry, M., & Loftus, E. R. (in press). Tales from the crib: Age-regression and the creation of unlikely memories. In S. J. Lynn & K. McConkey (Eds.), *Truth in memory.* New York: Guilford Press.

Green, J. P., Lynn, S. J., & Malinoski, P. (in press). Hypnotic pseudomemories: The effects of warnings and hidden observer instructions. *Applied Cognitive Psychology.*

Hirt, E., McDonald, H. E., & Markman, K. D. (in press). Expectancies effects in reconstructive memory: When the past is just what we expected. In S. J. Lynn & K. McConkey (Eds.), *Truth in memory.* New York: Guilford Press.

Hopkins, B., Jacobs, D. M., & Westrum, R. (1992). *Unusual personal experiences: An analysis of the data from three national surveys.* Las Vegas: Bigelow Holding Corporation.

Horovitz, R. (1993). Hypnosis in the treatment of multiple personality disorder. In J. W. Rhue, S. J. Lynn, & I. Kirsch (Eds.), *Handbook of clinical hypnosis* (pp. 395–424). Washington, DC: American Psychological Association.

Klass, P. J. (1988). *UFO abductions: A dangerous game.* Buffalo, NY: Prometheus Books.

Lanning, K. V. (1991). Ritual abuse: A law enforcement view or perspective. *Child Abuse and Neglect, 15,* 171–173.

Lawson, A. H. (1977). What can we learn from hypnosis of imaginary abductees? In *MUFON UFO Symposium Proceedings* (pp. 107–135). Seguin, TX: Mutual UFO Network.

Lynn, S. J., Lock, T., Myers, B., & Payne, D. (1997). Should hypnosis be used to recover memories in psychotherapy? *Current Directions in Psychological Science, 6,* 79–83.

Lynn, S. J., & Malinoski, P. (1996). *Early memories and social influence.* Unpublished manuscript, Ohio University.

Lynn, S. J., Myers, B., & Malinoski, P. (1997). Hypnosis, pseudomemories, and clinical guidelines: A sociocognitive perspective. In D. Read & S. Lindsay

(Eds.), *Recollections of trauma: Scientific studies and clinical practice* (pp. 305–336). New York: Plenum Press.

Lynn, S. J., & Nash, M. R. (1994). Truth in memory: Ramifications for psychotherapy and hypnotherapy. *American Journal of Clinical Hypnosis, 36,* 194–208.

Lynn, S. J., & Pezzo, M. (1994, August). *Close encounters of a third kind: Simulated hypnotic interviews of alien contacts.* Paper presented at the meeting of the American Psychological Association, Los Angeles.

Lynn, S. J., & Pintar, J. (1997). A social narrative model of dissociative identity disorder. *Australian Journal of Clinical and Experimental Hypnosis, 25,* 1–7.

Lynn, S. J., & Rhue, J. (1988). Fantasy proneness: Hypnosis, developmental antecedents, and psychopathology. *American Psychologist, 43,* 35–44.

Lynn, S. J., Rhue, J., & Green, J. (1988). Multiple personality and fantasy proneness: Is there an association or dissociation? *British Journal of Experimental and Clinical Hypnosis, 5,* 138–142.

Lynn, S. J., Rhue, J. W., Myers, B., & Weekes, J. W. (1994). Pseudomemory and hypnosis: Read versus simulating subjects. *International Journal of Clinical and Experimental Hypnosis, 52,* 118–129.

Malinoski, P., & Lynn, S. J. (1995). *The pliability of early memory reports.* Unpublished manuscript, Ohio University.

Malinoski, P., Lynn, S. J., & Sivec, H. (in press). The assessment, validity, and determinants of early memory reports: A critical review. In S. J. Lynn, K. McConkey, & N. P. Spanos (Eds.), *Truth in memory.* New York: Guilford.

Nash, M. R. (1987). What, if anything, is regressed about hypnotic age regression? A review of the empirical literature. *Psychological Bulletin, 102,* 42–52.

Nash, M. R., Drake, M., Wiley, R., Khalsa, S., & Lynn, S. J. (1986). The accuracy of recall of hypnotically age regressed subjects. *Journal of Abnormal Psychology, 95,* 298–300.

Newman, L., & Baumeister, R. (in press). Abducted by aliens: Spurious memories of interplanatary masochism. In S. J. Lynn & K. M. McConkey (Eds.), *Truth in memory.* New York: Guilford Press.

Orne, M. T. (1971). The simulation of hypnosis: Why, how and what it means. *International Journal of Clinical and Experimental Hypnosis, 19,* 183–210.

Qin, J., Goodman, G. S., Bottoms, B., & Shaver, P. R. (in press). Repressed memories of ritualistic and religion-related child abuse. In S. J. Lynn & K. M. McConkey (Eds.), *Truth in memory.* New York: Guilford Press.

Quindlen, A. (1997). How dark? How stormy? I can't recall. *New York Times,* p. 35.

Rauschenberger, S., & Lynn, S. J. (1995). Fantasy proneness, *DSM-III-R* Axis I psychopathology, and dissociation. *Journal of Abnormal Psychology, 104,* 373–380.

Rauschenberger, S., & Lynn, S. J. (1997). *Fantasy proneness, dissociation, and negative affectivity.* Unpublished manuscript, Binghamton University, Binghamton, NY.

Sarbin, T. (1986). *Narrative psychology: The storied nature of human contact.* New York: Praeger.

Sarbin, T. (1997a). Multiple personality disorder: Fact or artifact? *Current Opinion in Psychiatry, 10,* 136–140.

Sarbin, T. (1997b). The poetics of identity. *Theory and Psychology, 7,* 67–82.

Sivec, H., & Lynn, S. J. (1996). *The effects of hypnotic and nonhypnotic age regression on early autobiographical memories.* Unpublished manuscript, Binghamton University, Binghamton, NY.

Smith, B., Elstein, S. G., Trost, T., & Bulkey, J. (1993). *The prosecution of child sexual and physical abuse cases.* Unpublished manuscript, American Bar Association, Washington, DC.

Smith, M., & Pazder, L. (1980). *Michelle remembers.* New York: Congdon & Lattes.

Spanos, N. P. (1996). *Multiple identities and false memories.* Washington, DC: American Psychological Association.

Spanos, N. P., Burgess, C. A., & Burgess, M. R. (1994). Past life identities, UFO abductions, and satanic ritual abuse: The social construction of "memories." *International Journal of Experimental and Clinical Hypnosis, 3,* 155–159.

Stafford, J., & Lynn, S. J. (1997). *Dissimulated dissociative identity disorder: Sexual, physical, and satanic ritual abuse narratives.* Unpublished manuscript, Binghamton University, Binghamton, NY.

Steblay, N. M., & Bothwell, R. K. (1994). Evidence for hypnotically refreshed testimony: The view from the laboratory. *Law and Human Behavior, 15,* 639, 653.

Usher, J. A., & Neisser, U. (1993). Childhood amnesia and the beginnings of memory for four early life events. *Journal of Experimental Psychology: General, 122,* 155–165.

Weekes, J. W., Lynn, S. J., & Myers, B. (1997). *Hypnosis and pseudomemory: The effects of event base rates and distinctiveness.* Manuscript submitted for publication.

Weintraub, P. (1987, December). Secret sharers. *Omni Magazine,* 53–58.

8

DREAMING, BELIEVING, AND REMEMBERING

GIULIANA A. L. MAZZONI AND ELIZABETH F. LOFTUS

In the last two decades an enormous body of literature on memory distortion and the creation of false memories has accumulated. And in the last decade numerous authors have commented on the power of mental health professionals to alter memories. Much of the latter is about potentially risky therapeutic techniques such as using hypnosis, guided imagery, and sexualized dream interpretation for dredging up allegedly buried memories of abuse. In thinking about the literature in these two areas, one cannot help but observe that the experimental techniques that have successfully led to the recovery of false memories look different on the surface from the psychotherapeutic activities that appear risky. Yet, although there are differences on the surface, there still might be fundamental similarities in the processes by which people are influenced in these two settings—the laboratory and the therapist's office.

Part of this study was supported by a MURST grant to the first author. We are grateful for the Fulbright Award that allowed us the opportunity to spend time together on this collaboration.

We took one therapeutic activity, namely dream interpretation, and explored the extent to which we could use dream material, or even dream interpretation, to influence subjects' recollections of the past. Our goal in this chapter is to simply present the findings of several years of empirical research involving the use of dreams. One of the first observations that guided this research was the fact that people are sometimes not certain whether they actually saw or did something or whether they only dreamed about it (Bernstein & Putnam, 1986). Given this initial state of uncertainty, it ought to be possible to suggest that something that was dreamed was actually experienced in the waking state. For the sake of experimental simplicity and elegance, we began in the venerable tradition of experimental psychologists by working with lists of words. In our initial studies we examined whether we could, with a gentle suggestion, get people to believe falsely that items that came from their dream reports were words they had seen on a list that had been shown to them earlier in the experiment. In later studies we examined whether we could, with a not-so-gentle suggestion, get people to believe falsely that items that came from their dream reports proved that they had had certain critical experiences early in their childhood.

DREAM EXPERIENCES AND FALSE MEMORIES

Our initial research effort involved working with the dream material of our participants (Mazzoni & Loftus, 1996). In three experiments, we showed that after a subtle suggestion, people could be led to remember falsely that they experienced certain items in a waking state, when actually those items were things that came from their dreams. The procedure used in these studies involved three phases. During the first session of the study, participants brought in a dream report, they engaged in a variety of cognitive filler tasks, and they also studied a list of words. On the next day, during the second session, they received a subtle and false suggestion that some words (actually taken from their dream report) had been presented in the original list. Participants were presented with a list of 14 words, 10 of which were taken from the original list, 2 taken from their dream, and 2 taken from another participant's dream.

The subtle suggestion was the following: The experimenter told participants that the original list was lost, and that he had tried to reconstruct the list with the help of other participants. He had come up with 14 possible words. Could the participant help him by telling which words were actually part of the original list? One day later, during the third session, participants were presented with a new list, containing both the 14 previous words and 4 additional dream words taken from the same two dreams used before, 2 words taken from the participant's own dream, and 2 words taken from another participant's dream. Participants then tried to recognize which words had been presented on the initial list.

We found that participants falsely recognized their dream items at a very high rate—sometimes as often as they accurately recognized true items from the list. In the last session, participants also assigned a "remember/know" judgment to all recognized words. We found that they consistently reported that they genuinely remembered the dream items, as opposed to simply knowing that they had been previously presented on the list. They used remember judgments at least as often for these falsely recognized dream items as they did for true items that had been presented earlier on the list. By contrast, the majority of false recognitions of items that had not come from a participant's own dream tended to be assigned the know response. These findings demonstrate that dream material can sometimes be mistakenly remembered as if it had occurred in a waking state. When this happened in our research, the participants did not simply indicate that they knew the item was on the list, but that they actually remembered it having been on the list. In other words, these dream false alarms had a special recollective quality.

SELF-GENERATED STORIES AND FALSE MEMORIES

Why were dream items so readily believed to have been presented earlier in a waking state? One possibility is that the dream items came from a dream report that was personally generated in order to construct the dream report document that the participant was required to give to the experimenter at the beginning of the study. Perhaps the self-generation of the dream report is partially responsible for the recollective quality of the false recognitions that we obtained. If we are correct about this argument, we might expect to see other kinds of self-generated material behaving in a similar fashion. To test this idea, we conducted a similar study using self-generated stories rather than self-generated dream reports (Mazzoni, Vannucci, & Loftus, in press).

In the story experiments, we showed that after a subtle suggestion, people could be led to remember falsely that they experienced certain items on a prior word list, when actually those items had come from stories they had written about themselves. During the first session of the study, participants brought in a story that they had been asked to write that contained self as a central character. After various filler activities, they studied a list of words. On the next day, during the second session, they received a subtle and false suggestion that some words (actually taken from their story) had been presented in the original list. On the third and final day, they were asked to recognize only the words that had occurred on the initial list.

So, for example, if a participant had written a story about walking in a park, past a beautiful tall tree and a pond with a duck, we might extract the words *Tree* and *Duck* from the story, and add them to the list that was provided during the second session. During the third session, participants would be tested and would try to recognize only items that they saw in the original session on the first day of the study. We found that they falsely recognized their story items at a rather low rate during the third session. However, when participants did make a false recognition of a story item, their false recognitions tended to be given the remember response. By contrast, false recognitions of items that had not come from the participant's own story tended to be given the know response.

Comparing the dream studies to the story studies, we can make a few simple statements. In both cases, the self-generated activity did lead to false alarms that had the special recollective quality. Participants not only recognized these items falsely, but when they did, they assigned them the special "remember" status. These self-generated items thus presented differently from the false alarms that had not followed self-generation. In the latter case, the items tended to be assigned the know response. But the dream studies differed from the story studies in one important way. The overall rate of false recognition of items taken from the participants' own dream reports was much higher than the overall rate of false recognition taken from the personal stories. Thus, in at least one sense the dreams were more than simply self-generated material; the dream items must have had some quality about them that rendered them even more vulnerable to the suggestion that they were part of the participant's waking past.

DREAM INTERPRETATION AND FALSE CHILDHOOD BELIEFS

Of course it is one thing to make people believe that their dream material occurred as part of a recently seen word list, but quite another thing to make people believe that they had childhood experiences that never actually occurred. We developed an effective method for doing exactly this, which is illustrated in Figure 1 (Mazzoni, Lombardo, Malvagia, & Loftus, 1997). First we asked participants to answer questions about their lives before the age of 3. They all filled out a Life Events Inventory (LEI) at the beginning of what they believed was a study on early memories. In the LEI, we presented a list of possible experiences, and they told whether they had those experiences, using a scale ranging from 1 = *definitely did not happen* to 8 = *definitely did happen*. Embedded in that list were three critical experiences: got lost in a public space, was abandoned by my parents, and found myself lonely and lost in an unfamiliar place. We chose participants who reported that it was unlikely that they had had these particular critical experiences before the age of 3 (i.e., those with ratings of less than 4). All of these selected individuals, 3–4 weeks later, again filled out the LEI,

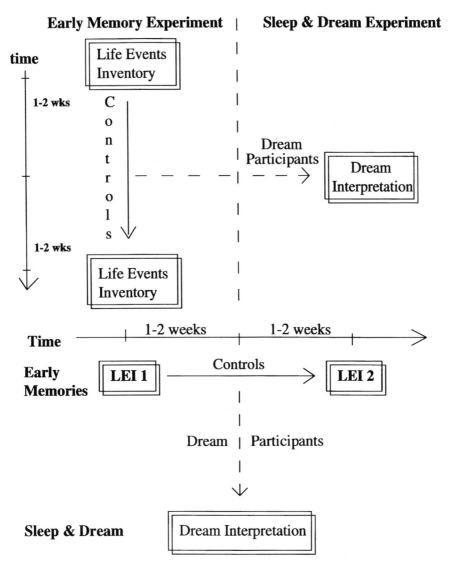

Early Memory Experiment | Sleep & Dream Experiment

time

1-2 wks

Life Events
Inventory

Controls

Dream
Participants

Dream
Interpretation

1-2 wks

Life Events
Inventory

Time — 1-2 weeks — 1-2 weeks ⟶

**Early
Memories**

LEI 1 — Controls ⟶ LEI 2

Dream | Participants

Sleep & Dream

Dream Interpretation

Figure 1. Design of an experiment on dream interpretation and the creation of
false beliefs. The dream participants thought they were participating in two
completely separate studies—one on early memories and one on sleep and
dreams.

which contained exactly the same list of possible childhood events presented in the same order as before.

Between the two testing sessions, some of the participants (dream
group) went through a 30-min mini-therapy simulation with a clinical psychologist who interpreted a dream that they presented. Regardless of the
dream content, the dream was interpreted as though it were indicative of
the person's having had the three specific critical experiences. This dream

session was presented as a completely different study. It involved a different investigator, and it was referred to by a completely different name (The Sleep and Dream Experiment).

The dream session was conducted by a well-known trained clinical psychologist who had a private practice in Florence, Italy. Participants brought a dream report to the session. The dream interpretation process began when the psychologist asked for comments about the dream. He behaved as if he would in a clinical interview, following a script but modifying that script in the light of responses. Early on, he explained that he had considerable experience in dream interpretation, and he explained that dreams are meaningful and symbolic expressions of human concern.

As a concrete example, suppose someone came in with a dream report about playing with friends, which included both positive and negative feelings. Suppose further that the person commented that the dream must mean that he finds his friends to be appealing. The psychologist might then discuss that part of the dream, mentioning the friends, and mentioning that the person also reported being uncomfortable. And, despite the person's verbal remark about liking the friends, perhaps the psychologist suggests that the discomfort experience might be a conflicting one for the person. In other words, the clinician tried to direct the interpretation of the dream.

At this point the clinician would try to induce the person to agree with the suggestion. The clinician would then move toward a "global interpretation," suggesting to the person that in his (the clinician's) vast experience with dream interpretation, a dream like this usually means that the person is not totally happy, needs challenge, resists being helped by others, and might have social or interpersonal difficulties. The clinician would then suggest that the dream content, and the feelings about the dream, were probably due to some past experience that the person might not even remember. The person would be further told that the specifics that he mentioned are commonly due to having had certain experiences before age 3, such as being lost in a public place, abandoned even temporarily by parents, or finding oneself lonely and lost in an unfamiliar place. Finally, the clinician would ask whether any of the critical events happened to the person before the age of 3. When people claimed not to remember these experiences, the clinician explained how childhood experiences are often buried in the unconscious but do get revealed in dreams.

From this example, some of the general steps that the clinician followed during dream interpretation become clear:

- He commented on specific items in the dream and tried to relate those items to possible feelings that the participant might have. In the example, the specific item about playing with friends, and discomfort, were related to the possible feelings about it being a conflicting experience.

- He tried to induce the participant to agree with and expand upon his interpretation.
- He provided a global interpretation of the dream meaning. In the example, the clinician suggested that possibly the participant was not totally happy with himself, needed challenge, resisted help, etc.
- He suggested the possibility that specific events of childhood are commonly associated with dream reports such as the one provided. In the example, the specific events were getting lost and feeling abandoned—in other words, the critical events used in this study for all participants.
- He suggested that in other individuals the dream material had suggested that particular critical events had happened in the past.
- He explicitly suggested that such events may have happened to the participant, and he asked for the participant's agreement.
- When the participant did not recall such an event, the clinician explained how unpleasant childhood experiences can be buried and remain unremembered but are often revealed in dreams.

Our results showed that the dream session caused participants to become more confident that the critical events had occurred. We calculated, for each of the three critical items, the percentage of participants whose responses increased, decreased, or did not change from the first to the second administration of the LEI. In Figure 2, we show only the percentage of those who increased their confidence that an event happened, shown

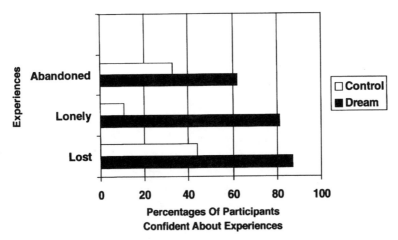

Figure 2. Percentage of participants increasing in confidence, after a dream session, that they experienced three critical events before age 3.

for each critical item, as a function of whether or not a dream session intervened. Notice that for each of the three items, many more participants increased in confidence after the dream session as compared to those in the control group. So, for example, 88% of participants became more confident that they had been lost in a public place before the age of 3 after the dream session, whereas only 43% became more confident in the control condition.

To analyze these data statistically, we assigned a numerical score to each participant depending on whether they increased (score of 3), decreased (score of 1), or gave the same score (score of 2) on the second administration of LEI relative to the first administration. We then performed a Mann–Whitney U test, comparing dream and control conditions. The two conditions differed significantly by Mann–Whitney U tests at $p < .01$ on the items "lost in a public place" and "lonely and lost." For the item "abandoned by parents," the difference was only marginally significant ($p = .09$).

To summarize the results, we found that a short, 30-min, dream session was sufficiently powerful to change participants' beliefs about their own past. In this study, the majority of the dream group became more confident in the belief that they had experienced critical events before the age of 3. This confidence expressed itself when assessed approximately one to two weeks after the dream session had occurred.

One might be tempted to argue that the dream session caused people to remember a genuine experience of being lost or abandoned. In assessing this argument, we remind readers that we deliberately referred to the age of 3 for the critical experiences. We did this so that any reports by our participants that they had had the experiences would be unlikely to be due to a genuine recovery. The research on childhood amnesia shows that adults rarely have complete episodic memories for events that happened to them before of age of 3.

REMEMBERING DANGER THAT NEVER HAPPENED

It has been argued that getting lost is a fairly common experience; therefore, getting people to believe that they were lost is not terribly impressive. To ascertain whether we could change beliefs about other events that might not be quite so common, we repeated the dream interpretation study with a new set of items. Moreover, in order to see whether the dream interpretation would last even longer than two weeks, we extended the time between the dream session and the final test to four weeks.

In this study we again asked participants to answer questions about their lives before the age of 3. They responded using the same scale, indicating whether certain events did or did not happen. Half of them received the three critical experiences used before (lost, abandoned, lonely). The other half received three different critical experiences: went through a very dangerous situation, my life was severely threatened, and was rescued from a dangerous situation. Those with a confidence score below 4 were tested again 5–6 weeks later, using the same list of possible childhood events.

Between the two testing sessions, half of the participants went through a 30-min mini-therapy simulation. As in the previous study, participants were led to believe that this was a completely separate experiment. The dream session, conducted by the same well-known clinical psychologist, occurred four weeks prior to the second occasion during which they answered questions about their childhood.

Our results showed that the dream session influenced participants to become more confident that each and every one of the critical events had occurred. We show in Figure 3 the percentage of participants whose confidence increased on each critical item. The data for the bottom three items replicate those of the previous study. After the dream session, participants became more confident that they had been lost in public place, lonely and lost in an unfamiliar place, and felt abandoned by their parents before the age of 3, as was confirmed by the significant results of the Mann–Whitney U tests for all three items (lost in a public place, $p < .01$; lonely and lost, $p < .01$, and abandoned by parents, $p < .05$).

The data for the new set of items are shown at the top of Figure 3. Again, participants who underwent the dream session were far more likely to increase their confidence that these events happened. For example, 66% of them became more confident that they had gone through a very dangerous situation before age 3 after the dream interpretation session; only 41% became more confident in the control condition. The results for

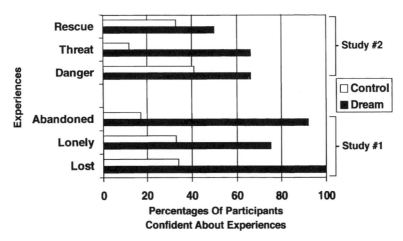

Figure 3. Percentage of participants increasing in confidence, after a dream session, that they experienced three additional critical events before age 3.

the threat item were even more impressive: 66% of participants became more confident after the dream session that their life had been severely threatened before the age of 3; only 12% became more confident in the control condition. The statistical analyses revealed that the dream and control conditions differed significantly for two of the three items by Mann–Whitney U tests: "faced a threat to life" ($p < .05$) and "rescued from a great danger" ($p = .01$). The difference between the dream and control conditions was not significant for the item "faced a great danger" ($p > .2$).

Another aspect of the data is worth mentioning. The dream interpretation was more successful in changing participants' beliefs about the "lost" set of items than in changing their beliefs in the "danger" set of items: For the lost set, the confidence of participants ranged from 75% to 100%; for the danger set, the corresponding percentages ranged from 50% to 66%. This suggests that even with a very powerful method for influencing beliefs about the past, there might still be differences in belief change depending upon the type of experience that is suggestively mentioned.

There is a final point about these results that we find particularly impressive. These participants underwent a 30-min dream interpretation that influenced the way they responded about their lives four full weeks later. More than any other of our results, this has convinced us of the potentially long-lasting influence that a simple therapy-like manipulation can have.

THE POWER OF DREAM INTERPRETATION

How important was the dream component to our ability to influence people's beliefs about their past? We believe that our mini-therapy manipulation might have influenced people even if we removed the dream component. This is because the manipulation would still contain other features that have been shown to increase the likelihood of illusory beliefs or memories. These features include a trusted authority who communicates a rationale for the plausibility of buried memories of childhood trauma (Lindsay & Read, 1995). The trusted authority offers repeated suggestions, giving anecdotes ostensibly from other "patients." These aspects of the mini-therapy might have led participants to have false beliefs even without the dream material.

Conversely, the dream aspects of the mini-therapy may have been an important ingredient in our ability to influence people. It might have enhanced the influence process, because many people already hold pre-experimental beliefs about the meaning of dreams in their lives and about how much dreams can reveal about the past. Evidence for the widespread faith that people have in the meaningfulness of dreams can be easily found.

For example, *Psychology Today* published an article containing extensive interview material from a well-known dream researcher, Rosalind Cartwright, reporting her strong belief that dreams provide direct access to key emotional issues in the dreamer's life. Cartwright was quoted as saying, "... People simply don't remember their dreams very well. The therapist's task is often like trying to reconstruct a 500-page novel from just the last page. But dreams collected from a single night in the sleep lab read like chapters in a book. They illuminate current concerns and the feelings attached to them" (cited in Lamberg, 1988, p. 36).

Other evidence for the faith that people have in the significance of dream material can be found in actual psychotherapy case histories. In one case, for example, two psychoanalysts seem to have become convinced that a woman was molested by her father after she reported repetitive dreams of assaults and penetrations of her by vicious men while no one offered to help (Person & Klar, 1994). Patients can easily be influenced by trusted authorities who draw on a priori beliefs and use them to alter autobiography.

FROM SUGGESTION TO BELIEF TO MEMORY

In thinking about the process by which people come to believe in things that never happened, several possible stages come to mind. To convince someone, it may first be necessary to make them believe that the suggested event is a plausible one. From this stage, it is possible to go forward and convince the person to believe that the suggested event did happen. From there, one can engage the person in various activities (e.g., visualization) that can convince them to actually "remember" the suggested experience. The notion that creating false memories occurs in a number of steps, with belief change preceding "memory" change has been advanced by others as well. In our dream interpretation studies, we would argue that the plausibility of and belief in the suggested event were created in part by the clinician's professed "knowledge" of a strong relationship between the participant's behavior and the high likelihood of the suggested event. We cannot say that the participants went on to "remember" the suggested event, as we had not included a specific memory measure in our experimental design. However, we have little doubt that with certain techniques such as guided visualization and imagery, some people would come to report a "memory" for the suggested event. How would we tell whether the reported memory was a subjectively real one to a person as opposed to mere agreement with the suggestion? One way is to see whether people will elaborate, express the memory with confidence, and tell others about the memory who are seemingly unconnected to the person who suggested it.

Given that suggestion can lead to false beliefs and even to false memories, what are the implications for individuals and their autobiographies? One immediate application that comes to mind is the world of therapy. Of course our simulation was different in some ways from actual therapy (one session versus many, students versus patients). However, our therapy simulation had similar features (e.g., strong authoritative suggestion), and this leads us to believe that similar kinds of influence occur in therapy.

CONCLUSION

To paraphrase Freud, dreams are the royal road to the unconscious. They reflect our "innermost thoughts unshackled from the confinement of our uptight, waking self." (Staff Report, 1995, p. 47). Freud may have been right about some aspects of dreams; however, he is also responsible in some measure for many of the cherished, but possibly mistaken, ideas that we as a society have about dreams. The lofty role he gave to dreams may be part of the reason why dream material is so effective as a weapon for changing peoples' beliefs about their past. Instead of calling dreams the royal road to the unconscious, we would argue that, in some cases, they might be called royal road to memory manipulation.

REFERENCES

Bernstein, E. M., & Putnam, F. W. (1986). Development, reliability, and validity of a dissociation scale. *The Journal of Nervous and Mental Disease, 174,* 727–735.

Lamberg, L. (1988, July/August). Night pilot. *Psychology Today,* 34–42.

Lindsay, D. S., & Read, J. D. (1995). "Memory work" and recovered memories of childhood sexual abuse: Scientific evidence and public, professional, and personal issues. *Psychology, Public Policy, and the Law, 1,* 846–908.

Mazzoni, G. A. L., & Loftus, E. F. (1996). When dreams become reality. *Consciousness and Cognition, 5,* 442–462.

Mazzoni, G. A. L., Lombardo, P., Malvagia, S., & Loftus, E. F. (1997). *Dream interpretation and false beliefs.* Unpublished manuscript.

Mazzoni, G. A. L., Vannucci, M., & Loftus, E. F. (in press). Misremembering story material. *Legal and Criminological Psychology.*

Person, E. S., & Klar, H. (1994). Establishing trauma: The difficulty distinguishing between memories and fantasies. *Journal of the American Psychoanalytic Association, 42,* 1055–1081.

Staff Report (1995, November/December). How to build a dream. *Psychology Today,* 47–62.

9

VOLITION AS A BELIEVED-IN IMAGINING

IRVING KIRSCH

The idea of believed-in imaginings comes from the work of Sarbin and Coe (1972), the focus of which is on responses to the kinds of suggestions typically given in context of hypnosis. These are usually referred to as "hypnotic suggestions," but the term is not entirely accurate. The same suggestions can be given without inducing hypnosis, and when they are, the responses are the same (although the frequency of their occurrence is slightly less). A more accurate label is "imaginative suggestion" (Kirsch, 1997), because the person is asked to generate experiences and behaviors that are consistent with imaginary states of affairs. The person may be told, for example, that his or her arm is getting lighter, as if it were being pulled up by helium-filled balloons, and that it is lifting of its own accord.

Responses to imaginative suggestions were interpreted by Sarbin and Coe (1972) as indices of believed-in imaginings. But are they? People report that in response to suggestion, they experience their arms as feeling lighter, or feel that they cannot bend their arms, or see a nonexistent cat sitting in their laps. Clearly, these are imaginings, but to what extent are they really believed in?

In a recent study (Comey & Kirsch, in press), a colleague and I sought

157

TABLE 1
Percentage of Responders to Suggestion Who Reported Particular Beliefs About the Suggestion

Suggestion	Belief during suggestion	% reporting belief
Arm levitation	My arm had actually become lighter.	60
	My arm rose by itself.	68
Arms moving apart on their own	A force was actually pushing my hands apart.	82
	My arms moved apart by themselves.	87
Arm too rigid to bend	My arm actually had become stiff and rigid.	64
	I could not have bent my arm even if I really wanted to.	37
Arm too heavy to lift	My arm actually had become heavy.	62
	I could not have lifted my arm even if I really wanted to.	45
Auditory hallucination	Music was actually playing.	32
Visual hallucination	A kitten actually was sitting in my lap.	46
Amnesia for the previous suggestions	I had actually forgotten the suggestions.	17
	I could not have remembered the suggestions even if I wanted to.	49

Note. Data are from Comey and Kirsch (in press).

to answer this question empirically. College students were given a hypnotic induction and the seven imaginative suggestions contained in the Carleton University Responsiveness to Suggestion Scale (CURSS; Spanos et al., 1983). As is typically done, participants were asked to rate their behavioral and subjective responses. That is, they were asked to indicate whether they had made the suggested movements (e.g., arm rising, cat petting, etc.) and whether they had experienced the suggested perceptual change (e.g., arm lightness, seeing the cat, etc.). We then asked them about their beliefs in the reality of the suggested experiences (e.g., did they believe at the time that their arms actually were lighter, that a cat was actually sitting in their laps, etc.).

The responses varied as a function of the type of suggestion and of the type of question asked. Table 1 displays the beliefs held by successful responders (i.e., those who passed the suggestion by displaying the suggested behavior) about the effects of each suggestion. Most people reported believing in the reality of the suggested ideomotor responses but their beliefs about challenge suggestions were more complex. They believed that their arms had become rigid and heavy in response to these suggestions, but most also believed that they could have resisted the challenge, had they really wanted to do so. Finally, even among those who pet an imagined cat, nodded their heads to suggested music, and displayed amnesia for the suggestions, very few thought a cat was really there, that music was really playing, or that they had really forgotten the suggestions. Perhaps there is less belief in the more difficult imaginings than is typically assumed.

The data in Table 1 suggest that ideomotor responses may be indications of believed-in imaginings for most people, but the term *believed-in imagining* suggests that the belief is false. For example, one would not call an accurate memory of something that really did happen a believed-in imagining. The question on which I wish to focus is: Are people's beliefs about the volitional status of their ideomotor responses accurate? Do people really lift their arms intentionally, as proposed by social psychological and neodissociation theorists (Kihlstrom, 1992; Spanos, 1986), or do their arms rise automatically, as proposed by dissociated control theorists (Woody & Bowers, 1994)?

An assumption common to all three theories is that mundane intentional behavior requires conscious initiation. Therefore, if responders to ideomotor suggestions think they did not raise their arms, they are mistaken, according to social psychological and neodissociation theorists. Either they are misattributing their actions (Spanos, 1986), or their conscious control is hidden behind an amnestic barrier (Hilgard, 1986). According to dissociated control theorists, ideomotor responding indicates the presence of an altered state that enables the automatic activation of behavior by suggestion (Woody & Bowers, 1994). Steven Jay Lynn and I have recently proposed an alternative to these formulations (Kirsch & Lynn, 1997). According to response set theory, automatic activation is a characteristic of all behavior, so that it is the reported volition of mundane behavior that is a misattribution, rather than the reported nonvolition of ideomotor responses. The remainder of this chapter is devoted to an exposition of this perspective.

VOLITION AS A JUDGMENT

There is a widespread assumption that the volitional status of a behavioral response is ascertainable through introspection. Ansfield and Wegner (1996), for example, stated: "We all know what it is like to do something . . . when we do it, we *feel* we are doing it. Some sort of sensation, an internal 'oomph,' goes with the effort of doing" (p. 482, emphasis in the original; also see James, 1890). Actually, the feeling of will is quite subtle, if there really is such a feeling. It is easy to identify introspectively where a pain is felt. But where exactly does one feel a volition? A century ago, psychologists attempting to examine volition through introspection failed miserably (e.g., Ogden, 1911), and current cognitive psychologists note that introspection fails in such a seemingly simple task as determining whether the simple lifting of an arm is intentional (Norman & Shallice, 1986). It is our contention that the so-called will is not really a sensation at all. Instead, it is interpretation or judgment about behavior (Kirsch & Lynn, 1997). It is an interpretation that can be made before, during, or after a response. When it is made before the response, it is called an expectancy; when it is made after the response, it is termed an attribution.

Typically, however, the judgment is not made at all. During the normal course of affairs, we do not often attend to the volitional quality of our behavior. It is only when we are asked or when something unexpected calls it into question that we think about whether our behavior is volitional, and, in these cases, our answers are not generally based on introspection, but rather on the consistency of the behavior with our goals. For example, consider the following thought experiment. Suppose that the beginning of the route from work to home is the same as the beginning of the route from work to a particular store at which you shop. The two routes diverge at a particular point, however, the route home requiring a right turn and the route to the store requiring a left turn. Suppose you decide one afternoon to go to the store rather than directly home. If you wind up at the store and are asked whether you intended to make the left turn that brought you there, you would most probably respond that you did. But suppose that, as happens all too often, you find yourself arriving at home (the more habitual destination) rather than at the store. In this case, you would probably report that your right turn was unintentional. But was your response based on some introspected sensation? Probably not! In these cases, the reported volitional and unvolitional quality of the act was a post hoc judgment, rather than an introspected sensation.

If the supposedly introspected feeling of will is really an interpretation based on consistency between the act and the goal, then ideomotor responding presents an apparent paradox. Successful responses to ideomotor suggestions are in fact consistent with goals. People who display automatic movements generally want to do so. What, then, accounts for their reports on nonvolition?

Nisbett and Wilson (1977) have argued that when people attempt to report on the cognitive processes eliciting their behavior, they do so on the basis of their implicit beliefs and of the stimuli that are salient in the situation. In the case of the hypothesized cognitive process of volition, goal consistency is one of the stimuli affecting the person's judgment, but it is not the only information by which volition is gauged. Other factors include the wording of instructions and people's expectancies and beliefs (i.e., their implicit causal theories). People understand the situation of hypnosis as one in which nonvolitional responding is to occur. This is reinforced by the wording of suggestions. Thus, Spanos and Gorassini (1984) have shown that people are more likely to judge their responses to be nonvolitional when the instruction is worded "your arm feels lighter ... and begins to rise" than when it is worded "raise your arm."

RESPONSE SETS AND THE AUTOMATIC ACTIVATION OF BEHAVIOR

From the perspective of response set theory, all behavior is activated automatically. Behavior is prepared for activation by the acquisition of response sets, which are preparatory sets for responding to environmental cues in particular ways. Response sets can be reported on introspectively as intentions or response expectancies, the only difference between the two being the person's subjective judgment about the volitional status of the behavior. Response sets are organized into schemas or scripts that guide behavior automatically.

Two or more conflicting response sets can be activated at any particular time. For example, one can intend one behavior but have a more habitual response set for another, as in the example given earlier of intending to drive to a store rather than home. Another way in which response sets can conflict is when a person intends one response but expects another. Examples of this include expecting to be unable to fall asleep, expecting a failure of sexual arousal, and expecting anxiety or panic (see Kirsch, 1990, for more examples and for data linking these reactions to expectancy). When two or more conflicting response sets are activated simultaneously, the resultant behavior will depend on the relative strength of activation.

Consider once again the situation in which one intends to follow the route to a less frequently traveled destination. In one case, the person correctly turns left; in the other, he or she incorrectly turns right. At the moment at which the response is made, it is likely that there is no difference in the volitional status of the response. So is the wrong turn voluntary, or is the right turn automatic? Because people do not generally make wrong turns intentionally, it seems most likely that making the right turn is automatic. Action slips and other parapraxes are quite common, but they are not instances of dissociation or evidence of unconscious motivation. Instead, they are events that reveal the high degree of automaticity that is characteristic of everyday life.

Normal behavior unfolds fluidly and rapidly in response to ever-changing environmental conditions. The cheetah, for example, judges the distance, velocity, and trajectory of a running gazelle and moves "instinctively" toward the anticipated location of its prey. In turn, the gazelle attempts to save itself by suddenly swerving and changing course. These behaviors are not simple routine habits, but they are performed too quickly to be the result of conscious deliberation. They are clearly guided by anticipations of the future, but it is unlikely that these anticipations are fully represented in awareness. Requiring willful initiation of each response would be both redundant and inefficient. It would quite literally leave the gazelle dead in its tracks.

EXPERIMENTAL EVIDENCE

The unconscious operation of response sets was first revealed at the beginning of the 20th century, during the course of introspective experiments on the thought process conducted under the direction of Oswald Külpe at Würzburg (described in Titchener, 1909). In these studies, introspective observers were given various tasks, such as that of mentally adding pairs of numbers. At first, participants reported being aware of the tasks they were to perform. During later trials, however, they reported that awareness of the task faded from consciousness. Nevertheless, their behavior was still guided by these response sets. If the task was addition, for example, participants continued to respond by reporting the sums of the pairs of stimulus numbers, despite their subsequent introspective report that they were no longer conscious of the instruction to add. Ach (as cited in Titchener, 1909) gave the names *determining tendency* and *mental set (Einstellung)* to these nonconscious response sets.

After the collapse of introspective experimental psychology, research on the automatic activation of responses by intentionally adopted response sets was largely abandoned. However, the recent work of Gollwitzer (1993) and his associates can be seen as a return to the topic. Gollwitzer has focused on the effects of *implementation intentions*, which he defined as commitments to take specific actions in response to specified situational cues. According to Gollwitzer (1993), explicit implementation intentions, taking the form "I intend to initiate behavior x whenever the situational conditions y are met" (p. 152), lead to automatic activation of the intended behavior by the specified cues.

Gollwitzer (1993) described a number of studies indicating that the formation of implementation intentions facilitates the initiation of intended behavior. One of these studies (by Malzacher, as cited in Gollwitzer, 1993) also provided a test of the hypothesis that this effect is automatic. In this study, students were exposed to a tape recording of an experimenter acting in an unfriendly and provocative manner. Half of the students were encouraged to adopt a goal of confronting the experimenter, without specifying exactly what they would say. The others were asked to form the specific implementation intention of telling her how unfriendly she was as soon as they saw her. All students were also shown photographs of the unfriendly experimenter and of other experimenters working in the laboratory.

In what was presented to them as a separate study, these same students were instructed to read as quickly as possible a series of positive and negative adjectives projected one at a time on a screen. Unbeknown to the students, pictures of either the unfriendly experimenter or a different experimenter were projected subliminally immediately prior to the presentation of each adjective. Subliminal presentation of the picture of the unfriendly experimenter decreased the reading latency for negative adjectives and increased the reading latency for positive adjectives, but only among students who had been primed to form a specific implementation intention. The automaticity of this effect was assured by presenting the pictures at speeds below each individual's perception threshold and then masking them with a pattern. According to Gollwitzer (1993), the results indicate that the formation of an implementation intention automatically facilitates initiation of an intended action and inhibits initiation of a contrary action.

The most impressive demonstrations of automaticity in intentional behavior are provided by the studies of Libet (1985) and Grey Walter (as cited in Dennett, 1991). Libet (1985) asked research participants to perform simple voluntary motor acts at will and to note the position of a spot on a revolving disk at the exact moment at which they formed the intention to execute the act. At the same time, readiness potentials (RPs) were recorded via electrodes placed on the scalp. Using electromyograms to determine the onset of the muscular response, Libet reported that RPs preceded the response by about 550 ms. Awareness of the intention to initiate the response occurred around 350 ms after the onset of the readiness potentials, indicating that cerebral initiation of these uncued voluntary acts began unconsciously. Accuracy of the person's assessment of the timing of the subjective event was ascertained by having participants use the same method to judge the timing of events for which the true onset could be determined objectively (e.g., the application of a stimulus to the skin). These data indicated that the subjectively judged time preceded the actual events, suggesting that the real onset of the conscious intention may have been even later than the time estimated by participants.

Grey Walter asked patients with electrodes implanted in the motor cortex to look at slides projected from a projector and to advance to the next slide whenever they liked. Unbeknown to the patients, the slides were actually advanced by an amplified signal from the implanted electrodes. The patients "reported that just as they were 'about to' push the button, but before they had actually decided to do so, the projector would advance the slide—and they would find themselves pressing the button with the worry that it was going to advance the slide twice" (cited in Dennett, 1991, p. 167).

What makes the Libet and Grey Walter studies so impressive is that they involve paradigmatic instances of volition. If doing something "whenever you like" is instigated automatically, then it seems likely that all behavior is instigated automatically. The onus should now be on researchers to find exceptions to this generalization.

CHANGING ATTRIBUTIONS OF AGENCY

If all behavior is automatic, and volition is a believed-in imagining based on prior beliefs and situational cues, then we ought to be able to convert voluntary behaviors into nonvolitional behaviors by altering those cues and beliefs. One situation in which this is routinely done is hypnosis. Some might object that hypnosis is a special state in which the normal rules of governing behavior are suspended (e.g., Woody & Bowers, 1994), but it seems more likely that the so-called hypnotic trance is itself a believed-in imagining. None of the responses to imaginative suggestions requires the induction of hypnosis (reviewed in Kirsch, 1997).

However, not everyone responds to suggestions, and some responses are relatively rare. Although ideomotor responses are the most common, even here there are some exceptions. Arm levitation, for example, is a moderately difficult response (Kirsch, Silva, Comey, & Reed, 1995), and automatic writing, which can be considered a complex ideomotor response, is considerably more rare (Hilgard, 1986). If the response set theory is correct, then we ought to be able to convert a complex behavior like writing into a nonvolitional response in virtually all people, and this is exactly what happens during the phenomena of facilitated communication.

Facilitated communication is a procedure intended to enable complex communication by people with autism and other developmental disabilities. This is done by the provision of physical support to a hand, wrist, or arm held over an alphabetic keyboard or facsimile. Subsequently, research (reviewed in Jacobson, Mulick, & Schwartz, 1995) revealed that the facilitator, rather than the participant, is responsible for the content of the communication. Facilitator access to information affects the manner and extent to which communication occurs, and when the information provided to the facilitator is different from that provided to the person being facilitated, the resulting communication is consistent with the information that was presented to the facilitator. However, facilitators do not appear to be aware that the communications are coming from them, rather than from the people whose communication they are attempting to facilitate. Thus, facilitated communication is a form of automatic writing.

To see the extent to which we could produce this phenomena, my colleagues and I taught 40 college students to "facilitate" via a commercially available training videotape (Burgess et al., 1998). The students were then asked to facilitate the communication of a confederate, who was described as developmentally disabled and unable to speak. Each was given different information about the confederate. Some were told that she had one brother; others were told that she had two. One was told that a brother's name was Bob, another that it was John, another that it was Fred, and so on. They were also given different information about her home town, favorite food, and what she enjoyed doing most. No two participants were given the same information, and except for the name "Jackie," the confederate was unaware of the information that was given to participants.

After watching the videotape and being given misinformation about the confederate, the participants were brought to another room. There they were introduced to Jackie, who sat silently in front of a computer staring at the wall behind the monitor. The participant was then instructed to support Jackie's hand and forearm over the computer keyboard as had been shown on the videotape, and Jackie was asked six questions about her brothers, her residence, and her preferences. Jackie continued to stare at the wall, not looking at either the monitor or the keyboard and not making eye contact with the research participant. This ensured that any coherent information that was typed would be due to the behavior of the participant and not to the behavior of the confederate.

All 40 participants produced responses to these questions. All but 2 of the participants attributed the responses to the confederate, and 89% of the responses corresponded to the information that had been provided to the participant. The attribution of the responses to the confederate was clearly an error. Just as clearly, participants were not aware of intentionally generating responses. Instead, the responses were automatic behaviors prepared by the intention to facilitate and their knowledge of the answers to the questions.

CONCLUSION

Hypnotic subjects are right when they say that their responses were activated without conscious volitional effort. Conversely, people are wrong when they say that their commonplace nonhypnotic behavior was initiated voluntarily. We should not be surprised by this conclusion. The concept of volition as anything more than an introspective judgment invokes the magic of free will (cf. Nash, 1997). It requires abandonment of the law of conservation of energy and of an explanatory science of behavior. Once one concludes that a behavior was genuinely chosen, one necessarily gives up the right to inquire into its determinants. It is for this reason that I defined nonvolitional responses in terms of subjective experience, writing that "nonvolitional responses are responses that are *experienced* as occurring automatically" (Kirsch, 1985, p. 1189, emphasis added).

It is at this point that some people object by pointing to the abandonment of absolute determinism in contemporary physics. They forget, however, that the assumption of determinism was held until data seemed to require the adoption of an uncertainty principle and that indeterminacy was proposed only for those data. The strategy of all science, including modern physics, can be described as methodological determinism. Determinism is assumed and determinants are sought until data indicate that further determination is, in principle, impossible.

Although there may be a high degree of automaticity in all behavior, I do not wish to leave the person buried without thought. That consciousness (or at least its physical substrate) evolved suggests that it has some function. In fact, conscious attention plays an important role in the selection and control of behavior. We contemplate possible future outcomes so as to choose between various courses of action, thereby biasing source schemas for activation (Norman & Shallice, 1986). We use attention to keep on track when we have selected a schema that overlaps a more frequently selected schema, so that the intended response will be activated at a critical choice point. For example, if the beginning of the route home (a more usual destination) is the same as the route to a nearby supermarket (a less usual destination), driving to the store may require attention at the point at which the two routes diverge. Counsciousness is also used to monitor the environment and our behavior when we engage in difficult achievment tasks and need to optimize performance. In these situations, consciousness may be used to detect discrepancies between outcomes and goals, so that behavior can be adjusted accordingly (cf. Carver & Scheier, 1982; Hyland, 1988). Attention is also engaged when stimuli are encountered that fall outside the range of schematic expectations.

What, then, is consciousness? Consciousness, in its most rudimentary form, is the monitoring and valuing by the brain of internal and external outcomes, so that behavior can be adjusted automatically to meet the organism's goals. In more complex organisms, in which advance planning occurs, there is also a reflective consciousness, which is the monitoring and valuing of anticipated outcomes of possible behavioral "choices," the end result of which is the automatic adoption of behavioral intentions. Thus, the functions of those brain activities on which we are able to report include monitoring actual and anticipated outcomes and comparing those outcomes with goals, but they do not include the activation of behavioral responses. Because complex acts need to be performed quickly and fluidly, requiring attention to activate movements would be redundant and disadvantageous. For this reason, conscious control over behavior is more adaptively relegated to advance planning and monitoring.

REFERENCES

Ansfield, M. E., & Wegner, D. M. (1996). The feeling of doing. In P. M. Gollwitzer & J. A. Bargh (Eds.), *The psychology of action: Linking cognition and motivation to behavior* (pp. 482–506). New York: Guilford Press.

Burgess, C. A., Kirsch, I., Shane, H., Niederauer, K. L., Graham, S. M., & Bacon, A. (1998). Facilitated communication as an ideomotor response. *Psychological Science, 9,* 71–94.

Carver, C. S., & Scheier, M. F. (1982). Control theory: A useful conceptual framework for personality–social, clinical, and health psychology. *Psychological Bulletin, 92,* 111–135.

Comey, G., & Kirsch, I. (in press). Intentional and spontaneous imagery in hypnosis: The phenomenology of hypnotic responding. *International Journal of Clinical and Experimental Hypnosis.*

Dennett, D. C. (1991). *Consciousness explained.* Boston: Little, Brown.

Gollwitzer, P. M. (1993). Goal achievement: The role of intentions. In W. Stroebe & M. Hewstone (Eds.), *European review of social psychology* (Vol. 4, pp. 141–185). Chichester, England: Wiley.

Hilgard, E. R. (1986). *Divided consciousness: Multiple controls in human thought and action* (expanded ed.). New York: Wiley.

Hyland, M. E. (1988). Motivational control theory: An integrative framework. *Journal of Personality and Social Psychology, 55,* 642–651.

Jacobson, J. W., Mulick, J. A., & Schwartz, A. A. (1995). A history of facilitated communication: Science, pseudoscience, and antiscience. *American Psychologist, 50,* 750–765.

James, W. (1890). *Principles of psychology* (Vols. 1–2). New York: Holt.

Kihlstrom, J. F. (1992). Hypnosis: A sesquicentennial essay. *International Journal of Clinical and Experimental Hypnosis, 50,* 301–314.

Kirsch, I. (1985). Response expectancy as a determinant of experience and behavior. *American Psychologist, 40,* 1189–1202.

Kirsch, I. (1990). *Changing expectations: A key to effective psychotherapy.* Pacific Grove, CA: Brooks/Cole.

Kirsch, I. (1997). Suggestibility or hypnosis: What do our scales really measure? *International Journal of Clinical and Experimental Hypnosis, 45,* 212–225.

Kirsch, I., & Lynn, S. J. (1997). Hypnotic involuntariness and the automaticity of everyday life. *American Journal of Clinical Hypnosis, 40,* 329–348.

Kirsch, I., Silva, C. E., Comey, G., & Reed, S. (1995). A spectral analysis of cognitive and personality variables in hypnosis: Empirical disconfirmation of the two-factor model of hypnotic responding. *Journal of Personality and Social Psychology, 69,* 167–175.

Libet, B. (1985). Unconscious cerebral initiative and the role of conscious will in voluntary action. *Behavioral and Brain Sciences, 8,* 529–566.

Nash, M. R. (1997). Why scientific hypnosis needs psychoanalysis (or something like it). *International Journal of Clinical and Experimental Hypnosis, 45,* 291–300.

Nisbett, R. E., & Wilson, T. D. (1977). Telling more than we can know: Verbal reports on mental processes. *Psychological Review, 84,* 231–259.

Norman, D. A., & Shallice, T. (1986). Attention to action: Willed and automatic control of behavior. In R. J. Davidson, G. E. Schwartz, & D. Shapiro (Eds.), *Consciousness and self-regulation* (Vol. 4, pp. 1–18). New York: Plenum Press.

Ogden, R. M. (1911). Imageless thought: Resume and critique. *Psychological Bulletin, 8,* 183–197.

Sarbin, T. R., & Coe, W. C. (1972). *Hypnosis: A social psychological analysis of influence communication.* New York: Holt, Rinehart & Winston.

Spanos, N. P. (1986). Hypnotic behavior: A social–psychological interpretation of amnesia, analgesia, and "trance logic." *The Behavioral and Brain Sciences, 9,* 449–502.

Spanos, N. P., & Gorassini, D. R. (1984). Structure of hypnotic test suggestions and attributions of responding involuntarily. *Journal of Personality and Social Psychology, 46,* 688–696.

Spanos, N. P., Radtke, H. L., Hodgins, D. C., Bertrand, L. D., Stam, H. J., & Dubreuil, D. L. (1983). The Carleton University Responsiveness to Suggestion Scale: Stability, reliability, and relationships with expectancy and "hypnotic experiences." *Psychological Reports, 53,* 555–563.

Titchener, E. B. (1909). *Lectures on the experimental psychology of the thought processes.* New York: Macmillan.

Woody, E. Z., & Bowers, K. S. (1994). A frontal assault on dissociated control. In S. J. Lynn & J. W. Rhue (Eds.), *Dissociation: Clinical, theoretical and research perspectives* (pp. 52–79). New York: Guilford Press.

10

RELINQUISHING BELIEVED-IN IMAGININGS: NARRATIVES OF PEOPLE WHO HAVE REPUDIATED FALSE ACCUSATIONS

JOSEPH DE RIVERA

Believed-in imaginings take a particularly destructive form when they result in false accusations against real people. Thousands of witches were killed in Europe during the Middle Ages, and hundreds of witches are being killed in Africa in contemporary time. In our own society, the providers of day care may find themselves in jail on unsubstantiated charges, and thousands of parents have been devastated when their children have entered therapy and emerged with memories that their parents sexually abused them, memories that later may be found to be false. This latter example of believed-in imagining has become known as false memory syndrome (FMS). FMS has not been proposed as a diagnostic entity. Rather, it refers to a pattern of behavior that has been characterized by Kihlstrom (in press) in the following way:

I would like to thank Christina Clarke for her assistance with the collation and analysis of the data presented in this chapter.

1. A belief that a behavioral problem—an eating disorder, a sexual inhibition or promiscuity, a depressive reaction, or any other behavior that *ought* not occur—is a reaction to a past event that was so traumatic that its experience was completely repressed or dissociated.
2. The development of pseudomemories that one was sexually abused as a child.
3. A centering of identity and relationships around these pseudomemories (so that the person becomes defined as a "survivor").
4. The development of an extreme dependence on the therapist and a distraction from the problems that initially precipitated therapy.
5. A defensive avoidance of any evidence that might challenge the belief system and a severing of contact with family members and friends who do not support the belief system and are considered to be in denial.

I realize that some psychologists seem to doubt the existence of this pattern of behavior, or believe that it is a rare phenomenon, or that it could only occur in extremely disturbed or suggestible people. However, Pendergrast's (1996) research establishes that the phenomenon is widespread and there is some evidence that suggests there are at least 66,000 instances of FMS in the United States (de Rivera, 1997b). Furthermore, if we are to trust the reports of families, people with FMS appear to be no different than most people who enter psychotherapy. Although some are skeptical of FMS as a phenomenon, others—familiar with the vicissitudes of alien abductions, false confessions, false memories, and witch hunts—may wonder why I regard FMS as at all puzzling. Let me contrast the belief that one repressed memories of abuse with the belief that one was abducted by an alien. Lynn and Kirsch (1996), each of whom has a chapter in this volume, have offered a convincing account of how a belief in alien abduction may occur. They postulated a person who is predisposed to accept the possibility that puzzling experiences might be signs of UFO abduction. The person sees a therapist who frames a puzzling personal experience in terms of an abduction narrative. The next steps in the account include a failure to explore possible alternative explanations of the personal experience, an increasing commitment to the abduction explanation as the person's anxiety is reduced along with ambiguity, and the legitimization of the explanation by the therapist. The account ends with the person's adoption of the role of abductee, and an integration of the role in the person's view of the self. That progression sounds straightforward enough, and because a substantial amount of child abuse actually occurs, it might seem even easier to use the same sort of explanation for the development of FMS. However, in the case of FMS, most people have three difficult hurdles to overcome: the love of one's parents, memories of a reasonably normal childhood, and the protests of other family members who indignantly deny that anything happened.

EXPLAINING THE DEVELOPMENT OF FALSE MEMORY SYNDROME

Three Accounts

How may one explain believing in an imagining that requires accusations against loved parents and contradictory evidence offered by one's own memories and family? I want to imagine how FMS might develop, present the beliefs of people who have recovered from FMS, and see if I can convince a skeptical audience to believe in the reality of several different narrative explanations. I have been able to imagine three accounts of how FMS might develop. Actually, my own imagining is largely second-hand in that I have simply reworked the ideas of others (Haney, Banks, & Zimbardo, 1973; Hassan, 1990; Sarbin, 1994). In the next three paragraphs I provide narrative accounts termed *mind-control*, *self-narrative*, and *role enactment*.

The Mind-Control Account

The essential underpinning of mind control is an undermining of our ability to make our own decisions. As a consequence, we eventually relinquish control and allow an authority whom we trust, such as a therapist, to provide us with a story that gives meaning to our lives. The undermining of confidence is accomplished by the authority figure who is controlling information, behavior, thoughts, and emotions. Information control is achieved by actively discouraging our contact with people who think differently and systematically distorting and disconfirming evidence. Behavior control is achieved by telling us what to do and requiring approval for personal decisions. Thought control is achieved by a particular use of language. On the one hand, the language that is used overly simplifies issues and makes us feel special and part of a group that is "good" and separate from the evil that is outside the group. On the other hand, the authority uses language that confuses us so much that we stop critical thinking. Emotion control involves reducing our sense of guilty responsibility and promoting the fear of what will happen if we leave. Once we have made the mistake of handing ourselves over to the therapist, he or she furnishes the story of our life, and although we may feel ashamed or guilty, it is important for others to realize that in a real sense we were not really responsible for the accusations the authority figure had us make.

The Self-Narrative Account

We all try to make sense of our lives by creating a story that will explain why we behave the way we do. When we are unhappy with the way we act, we may search for explanations from our childhood, trying to find an acceptable story. There are many books, and people who talk, about repressed memories, and, with a little help from isolated images and feelings, we may use our own imaginations to begin to create a story about how we were abused. Gradually, it may become clear that the best way to make sense of our problems is to assume that a horrible trauma must have occurred. Our therapist may believe an abuse story and try to help us develop it. She or he may assume that we must have repressed something, and they may even become co-authors of the story and help us discover what happened. However, in contrast with mind control, we must acknowledge that we were the first author of the story. In a sense, the therapist and well-meaning others led us to give credibility to our own imaginings.

The Role Enactment Account

We all enact roles that are furnished by our society. We may be fathers or mothers, teachers or students, prisoners or guards. Recently, our society has created a new role, that of the "survivor." Regardless of whether we choose that role or are cast in it, our behavior has to fit the expectancies of others who depend on us to behave in appropriate ways so that they can play *their* roles as therapists and sympathetic audience. Survivors are expected to search for traumatic memories and discover horrible things that happened. We are rewarded when we play our own roles correctly. And our roles are validated by others who play supporting roles. This role, like any other role, has certain advantages and disadvantages. One of the advantages is that survivors of sexual abuse are *not* expected to be perfect husbands, wives, or parents. However, they are expected to be justifiably afraid of, and angry at, those who abused them. We may be somewhat aware that we are enacting a role, or, like good method actors, we may almost completely forget that we have been cast into a role. In any case we were not so much authors of a story (as in the self-narrative account) or subjects of the therapist's story (as in the mind-control account), as we were actors in a drama that is being played out in our society.

ANALYSIS OF RESEARCH ON ENDORSERS OF ACCOUNTS

Endorsement of Accounts

There are good arguments for each of these models of how FMS may develop, and data suggest that different accounts may fit the experience of

TABLE 1
Model Accounts Endorsed by Respondents to Explain Development of False Memory Syndrome

Account endorsed	Number of 5–7 ratings
Mind control	23
Self-narrative	10
Role enactment	2
Mind control and self-narrative	1
Mind control and role enactment	7
Self-narrative and role enactment	3
Mind control, self-narrative, and role enactment	4
None	6
Total responses	56

Note. Respondents were 56 people who had retracted memories of sexual abuse. Models were rated on a 7-point scale, from 1 = has nothing to do with what happened to 7 = a perfect description of what happened. Ratings of 5 (captures a lot of my experience) and above indicate endorsement.

different people (de Rivera, 1997a). However, to be sure that the different narratives really captured the experience of persons who had experienced FMS, a much wider sample of people was needed. Accordingly, I asked the FMS Foundation to mail the above accounts to people who had contacted the Foundation to report retracted charges of sexual abuse that had been based on memories recovered in therapy. Of the 159 people who were contacted, 56 (36%) became research partners (RPs) who responded to a 14-page questionnaire. Eight of these 56 reported that they had been diagnosed with multiple personality disorder (MPD)—now termed dissociative identity disorder —17 with post traumatic stress disorder (PTSD), and 21 with both MPD and PTSD. On the questionnaire was the statement, "We are interested in the extent to which each of these accounts do or do not describe what happened to you." After reading all three accounts, the participants rated each on a 7-point scale ranging 1, *has nothing to do with what happened*, to 7, *a perfect description of what happened*. A rating of 5 (*captures a lot of my experience*) is a clear endorsement of a model account; the number of respondents endorsing the accounts, separately and in combination, is shown in Table 1.

As the table shows, 35 or 62% felt they could describe their experience by using one of the models, whereas 15 felt they needed more than one, and 6 felt that none of them did justice to their experience. Although mind control was the preferred model (endorsed by 35 respondents), 24 endorsed self-narrative and role enactment.

Descriptions of Therapy

Are these accounts simply different ways of construing the same set of events? *Before* rating them, respondents were asked to describe what happened in the course of their therapy by rating 51 statements (on a 5-point scale ranging from 1, *not true at all*, to 5, *completely true*). These statements were constructed on the basis of prior interviews (de Rivera, 1997a) and on autobiographical accounts given by retractors (Goldstein & Farmer, 1993). Table 2 shows items that significantly distinguished between

TABLE 2

Items Discriminating Between Endorsers and Nonendorsers of the Mind Control Account

	Questionnaire item	Endorsers ($\geq$5) $n = 35$	Nonendorsers ($\leq$3) $n = 17$
Q7	My therapist insisted that I must remember how I had been abused if I was to get well.	4.6	3.8
Q10	My therapist was not sure whether anything traumatic had happened to me that I could not remember.	1.1	1.8
Q49	I was supposed to search for childhood memories and find the trauma that had been repressed by writing journals, looking at pictures, fantasizing, etc.	4.7	3.9
Q35	When I presented information that I felt indicated that I had *not* been abused, my therapist interpreted the information in a way that indicated that I *had* been abused.	4.5	3.8
Q21	I was part of a group of survivors who expected that I would talk about how I had been abused.	4.1	2.9
Q27	My therapist led me to feel that I was part of a special group of good people in contrast to most people.	4.0	3.0
Q26	My therapist let me make my own decisions.	1.9	2.7
Q39	My therapist led me to believe that if I left therapy I might go crazy, commit suicide, or that something horrible would happen.	4.3	3.3
Q42	I always felt I had the freedom to leave therapy when I was ready.	1.7	2.6
Q51	The influences of the therapeutic relationship were so strong that I cannot imagine being able to change my beliefs as long as I remained with my therapist.	4.7	3.9
Q47	When I reflect on the history of my therapy, I can say that my therapist was really the main author of the story that I told as if it were my own.	4.0	2.8

Note. Items were significantly different at $p < .02$.

respondents who endorsed (≥5) or did not endorse (≤3) a mind-control account. Because 51 items were examined, a high level of significance was required ($p < .02$, two-tailed).

Whereas most of the therapists were described as believing in the power of repressed memories, it may be noted that the therapists of those who endorsed mind control appeared to be significantly more sure of themselves and insistent in the search for memories. They were more likely to reinterpret information and to have the client be part of a survivor group, and they were less likely to let the client make decisions. Furthermore, the clients who endorsed mind control were more likely to have reported that they felt trapped in therapy and that they could not imagine having been able to change their beliefs as long as they were in the therapeutic relationship. Finally, they experienced the *therapist* as the main author of the abuse story they told. It may be noted that the items themselves imply a consistent narrative. Statistically, they demonstrated a high internal consistency (alpha = .88).

Of course, all these ratings are retrospective, and it may be argued that even before answering the questionnaire, respondents tended to attribute responsibility to either the therapist or themselves, which led them to endorse therapist-blaming items to a greater or lesser degree. However, the questionnaire included 10 positive items (e.g., "my therapist taught me a way to think that allowed me to see my life issues more clearly") that were endorsed similarly by mind control and self-narrative endorsers. The means of these items were not significantly different. Hence, I am inclined to think that the therapists really believed in different ways; that some were, in fact, much more controlling; and that clients who had these therapists explained what happened in terms of a mind-control narrative.

Sixteen of the RPs, rated the mind-control account with a 7 (a perfect description) and accepted it without reservations:

"It is interesting reading this description—it truly is what happened in my therapy" (RP 46).

"Thank you for putting it into words" (RP 51).

Others, however, had partial reservations and endorsed the description but with a rating of less than a 7:

"I wasn't made to feel part of a 'special good' group. I was made to feel part of her 'special' really sick group. The word 'good' throws off the question" (RP 1).

"He felt I had been programmed to be evil and didn't even know it. I felt he thought I was 'special' but not in a way that was 'good' in my mind. I had always believed that I was good and the idea that I had done 'unspeakable acts' was more than I wanted to accept" (RP 4).

"Except for the last sentence—I feel very responsible for the 'beliefs' I accepted and the manner in which I relied on this therapist at a difficult time in my life" (RP 12).

In endorsing the mind-control model, many respondents noted how they had become dependent, confused, and lost their decision-making capacity. The following three examples illustrate.

"It was *gradual*—not overnight, I saw him and then was part of his support group for years. I couldn't make a decision without consulting him—I could no longer think for myself. What amazes me is how *relatively* fast this became obvious when I escaped from him. In four months I was able to work part-time and began to realize what he had done" (RP 48).

"Remember that many of us had had some serious troubles going into therapy (even if we weren't incest victims) so we were *vulnerable*. After a couple of years of therapy I was completely confused. I could no longer separate the truth from the fabrications" (RP 56).

"My so-called therapist demanded complete control of me. He was readily available and encouraged that I call frequently to discuss anything and everything. He gradually and increasingly conditioned me to separate from all family relationships and lean on him" (RP 51).

Sometimes control and dependency were based on fear, sometimes on the desire to please, as these respondents' statements show:

"At one point, when I wanted to go visit my family, my therapist threatened to 'do whatever was needed to hospitalize me ... until I gave up all the denial.' As a result of this threat, I both believed he truly cared for me and wanted to protect me from some horrible harm I was not aware of—and that I had to do things his way or risk losing my freedom" (RP 12).

"... told me on numerous occasions that if I left therapy I would die, commit suicide, or go to jail..." (RP 40).

"My therapist expected me to keep coming up with more and more memories and I think that on one level I wanted to please him so I felt it was important to tell him what he wanted to hear" (RP 15).

Many respondents noted how they used the authority of the therapist to overcome their doubts:

"I would quickly be also aware that it was something that was being made up as we went along. They said this was the normal response of an abused person, and I need to trust the emotions and visions as true" (RP 35).

"I always felt I was acting a role. I stated that frequently but my therapist was there with assurances that my feelings (my perceptions of *role* playing) were exactly like those of other MPD, incest victims. She even had articles in psych journals which reinforced what she was saying. Print has a lot of power" (RP 56).

"She had a very strong personality and although I would disagree with her sometimes she would eventually overcome any of my objections, mainly through the force of her personality. Anytime I would come up with an alternative explanation she would quickly dismiss it and accuse me of not wanting to get better. She led me to develop a story through hypnosis, EMDR, journaling, drawing, survivors groups, etc." (RP 32).

"... each time I requested that my therapist substantiate her accusations against my family or fiancee, she would tell me that my 'doubt' was part of the 'denial' process" (RP 7).

Let me contrast these descriptions of therapy with the descriptions provided by people who endorsed the self-narrative account. In addition to giving significantly *less* endorsement to the items in Table 2 that suggested an insistent and controlling therapist (such as items Q7, Q26, Q35, Q39), people who endorsed the self-narrative account showed significant differences on the items displayed in Table 3. We can see that these re-

TABLE 3
Items Discriminating Between Endorsers and Nonendorsers of the
Self-Narrative Account

	Questionnaire item	Endorsers (≥5) $n = 18$	Nonendorsers (≤3) $n = 32$
Q1	I felt pretty good about myself before I entered therapy with an issue that had nothing to do with my being abused as a child.	2.2	3.2
Q2	When I entered therapy I was unhappy with certain things about myself and wondered what might have happened when I was a child.	2.6	1.8
Q5	Even before I entered therapy I had some images, bodily sensations, or feelings that made me wonder if I'd been abused.	2.3	1.3
Q28	The belief that I was abused helped me understand why I could feel and behave in ways that I didn't like.	4.2	3.4
Q13	When I told others that I'd been abused, I was given attention and sympathy.	4.3	3.5
Q29	Although it was painful to be a "survivor," it was a relief to know why I was not a perfect spouse, parent, child, worker.	4.2	3.1
Q47	When I reflect on the history of my therapy, I can say that my therapist was really the main author of the story that I told as if it were my own.	2.9	4.0

Note. Items significantly different at $p < .02$.

spondents are more likely to have wondered about their childhood *before* they entered therapy (Q1, Q2, Q5). Furthermore, the abuse narrative seems to have been helpful in explaining behavioral patterns (Q28), gaining sympathy (Q13), and in providing relief from demands of perfection (Q29). The story seems to have been more functional. It *did* something for them the way a self-narrative should. And they experience the story as more authored by the self (Q47). These items yield an alpha of .70.

Respondents who endorsed the self-narrative account did not seem to feel their confidence was undermined by the therapist or that their therapist had *insisted* that they remember abuse. They saw themselves as the primary authors of the abuse narrative, but they often noted that their therapist suggested or supported the narrative:

"Provided an easy explanation for past difficulties" (RP 10).

"I was trying to explain why I had been diagnosed as a schizophrenic" (RP 28).

"My therapist believed the story I made up and tried to help me accept it and to let it go. I authored the story because I believed I needed to be sick to see him" (RP 52).

"My parents were divorced when I was 2 and I did not know my father very well. I went to therapy initially to deal with 'being away from home for the first time blues.' My therapist immediately capitalized on my estranged relationship with my Dad and encouraged me to 'remember' abuse" (RP 20).

"This is an accurate, well-balanced depiction of my descent into repressed memory. I was able to go back to her and ask her *why* on earth she was so *fixated* on repressed memory. Her response: 'I didn't know what else to do, you were so desperate for something to believe in'" (RP 49).

"My therapist felt that there had to be more to it than I was telling her because I was too upset for it to just be a babysitter and a relative's boyfriend—it must have been a family member. Since I was angry at my parents for 'allowing' me to be abused ... it seemed like it was probably that my parents had abused me since they had been so neglectful. ... A major aspect of my *real* problem was my low self-esteem, and so when my therapist gave me approval I felt like a void was being filled. In the role of survivor I had an excuse to not be perfect anymore, and that was what I needed—an excuse to take a break from it all. I was becoming overwhelmed with having to be the 'perfect daughter'" (RP 30).

Now let me examine the descriptions of therapy as recounted by those who endorsed a role-enactment account, as is shown in Table 4. Unlike those who endorsed self-narrative, these respondents *were not* more un-

TABLE 4
Items Discriminating Between Endorsers and Nonendorsers of the Role-Enactment Account

	Questionnaire item	Endorsers (≥5) n = 16	Nonendorsers (≤3) n = 35
Q3	*Before* I entered therapy I had heard that when children are sexually abused they might repress the trauma for years and wondered if perhaps that had happened to me.	2.4	1.5
Q21	I was part of a group of survivors who expected that I would talk about how I had been abused.	4.4	3.3
Q27	My therapist led me to feel that I was part of a special group of good people in contrast to most.	4.3	3.2
Q33	People expected me to be afraid of the perpetrator of my abuse, and that I would want to seek revenge so that justice would be restored.	4.4	3.1
Q34	My therapist encouraged me to confront my fears and speak openly with those who disagreed with me.	3.3	2.0
Q24	My therapist guided me so that I chose to search for memories.	4.5	3.6
Q25	I received more attention from my therapist when I described how I had been abused.	4.7	3.8

Note. Items significantly different at $p < .02$.

happy with their childhoods (there were no significant differences on items Q1, Q2, Q5) but *were* more familiar with the repression narrative (Q3). They were much more likely to have been in a group of survivors (Q21, Q27) and to report more awareness of the expectations of others and more encouragement to speak out (Q33, Q34). Their therapists were neither more nor less insistent but were more likely to be described as "… guiding me so that *I* chose to search for memories (Q24)." When compared with others who were placed in survivor groups, they were less likely to view the therapist as the main author of the story ($M = 3.2$ vs. 4.3, $p = .02$). Unlike those endorsing self-narrative, respondents did not report receiving more sympathy or feeling relief. Rather they were more aware of receiving *attention* from the therapist (Q25; Alpha is .65, rising to .71 if Q3 and Q34 are deleted).

Comments made by the respondents suggest that at least some of the respondents who endorsed role enactment experienced themselves as choosing to enter the survivor role to try it on and then becoming overly involved in that role:

> "I am a happy, well-adjusted person who probably would have never sought therapy until my sister's 'memories' of me being abused.... I do believe my therapist cast me in the role of survivor so she could be the helping therapist, performing guided imagery on me to 'help' me uncover my 'trauma'" (RP 34).

> "I was invited to attend a week long workshop at (a retreat center). My friend was there for a 28-day stay, and part of the therapy was *family week*; she considered me family and I attended. At (the center) they said I was sexually abused.... I didn't want to undermine my friend's confidence in the place, because she *was* abused. I however, became confused about myself ... they asked me to stay another week to go through 'survivor's week' ... if I had *no* memories, they said I was holding back or blocking memories ... I left thinking I was abused, and believed it for years after" (RP 35).

All but one of the people endorsing this account were members of survivor groups and noted the group influence:

> "... there was a lot of 'competition' involved as I was on a special inpatient unit for survivors. Somehow as a group of 'survivors' we fed off each other's information and imagination. It seemed we were constantly trying to 'top' each other as far as how extreme our memories got and how out of control we could act—all to get sympathy and attention I suppose" (RP 22).

One problem with the role-enactment account (or with communicating it) is that it suggests a degree of choice of role that is not experienced when people do not realize when they have been cast into a role. Although people endorsing role enactment reported that they chose to search for memories (under the therapist's guidance), they were more likely to report being unaware that they were playing a role during therapy (M = 4.6 vs 3.5, t = 3.5; p = .015). The following quote is from a person who endorsed the model as "half fits." She noted that she was never aware that she was playing a role at the time but that, if she was, she had been completely lost in it:

> "I am educated and intelligent and very embarrassed to have unwittingly 'lived' as a survivor. I hesitate to use 'acted' or 'played the role'—I wasn't acting or playing—I thought I was 'owning my truth'; living my life by integrating my past secrets with my present-day struggles. Realizing I traumatized my family by my false accusations has set back my efforts in building a sense of self-esteem and personal dignity (by) years" (RP 25).

Endorsement of More Than One Account

Mind-control and role-enactment accounts were endorsed in combination by 11 respondents, including 4 who endorsed all three accounts (see Table 1). One respondent commented on the relationship between mind control and role enactment:

"Once cast into the 'role' from the therapist and I believed the abuse was true though I often questioned it at times, it became a dance between therapist and myself. So these expected roles each played and fed off each other. However, the therapist is the one in charge, the one holding all the directions of the dance, what steps to take next and when to go. In this, it fits and overlaps 'mind control' as once one is under the control, one does the role (not knowing they are controlled nor in a role)" (RP 39).

Others noted how a story that was based on either mind control or self-narrative was extended by role enactments in the wider community. Two examples are provided.

"My entire life revolved around my identity as an abuse survivor. For a period of time I was even involved in training clinicians in how to work with SRA survivors. I am now going through a very difficult time as I try to make sense of who I really am" (RP 15).

"To the point that I became a regional expert on satanism in its many forms, involving TV appearances, police advisor, put on a 2-day professional seminar … etc." (RP 36).

The self-narrative model was often partially endorsed along with the mind-control model as fitting different periods of therapy:

"Therapy started this way, but soon developed into mind control theory. I was rewarded with more time, approval, a simple praise of 'good work' at the end of the session. With the deeper, more painful 'memories' I was given more time and attention and direction the 'harder' I worked at recovering memories. I was seen three times a week along with telephone conversations and letters written to therapist during the weekends. Therapy was no longer to help me with my life, it was *my life*. My therapist was the most important person in my life" (RP 8).

"Seems to fit the beginning of my therapy process. I knew something about me wasn't right, as I sought out therapy. I was put into a woman's group of other 'co-dependent' women. We were told *all* of our problems and how we handled them stemmed from our childhood. Because I couldn't remember much about my childhood (or yesterday for that matter, but no one seemed concerned about my short term memory lapses!) then the conclusion was that I must have been severely traumatized and 'repressed' the 'trauma'" (RP 3).

"Initially it was my therapist who insisted I must have been abused and indicated my only hope to get better was to uncover those hidden nightmares ... then from that point I was the main author trying to explain my weakness through memories, also fitting in other's described memories into my own experiences" (RP 22).

Nonendorsement

Those who did not endorse any of the accounts (i.e., those who did not rate any account or combination of accounts with at least a 5) tended to describe a mutual relationship in which they were misled by the authority of a therapist who did not appear to use undue power. They could not endorse the mind-control account, because their therapist suggested abuse without controlling, insisting, or undermining confidence. Yet they could not endorse the self-narrative account (as presented), because they did not really make much use of their own imagination. They rejected the role-enactment account because (perhaps mistakenly) they could not believe they were playing a role. Consider the following comments of nonendorsers:

"I went to counseling for marital help—nothing else. I did not go to justify my behavior, look into my childhood, or blame anybody. ... I was trying to survive and get better. Totally ashamed of my continual depression ... I believed the counselor when she told me God has people forget memories of abuse until they are older and can cope with the memories ... the rest is the story of remembering abuse that *never* occurred and the damage it did to myself, family, and parents" (RP 27).

"My therapist believed I was an abuse victim from the first session due to my high anxiety level (I did not know this until months later). Memories came after a very troubling nightmare followed by a 'snapshot' in my mind which my therapist brought to life through hypnosis. Through dreams, flashbacks, and sensory details I recalled an incidence of abuse which I was able to confirm to be true. When I began to recover from these memories, then my therapist began to suggest MPD, satanic cults, etc. ... He didn't know how to let go and he kept trying to create problems in me to fix. There was an undercurrent of control, and he definitely seemed to have an agenda. However, I did not feel he was creating the storyline until the last few months of therapy" (RP 31).

Other Findings

Ten of the 56 respondents reported that they had experienced some sort of real childhood abuse. They reported that, rather than helping them cope with the actual abuse, their therapists led them to create a false narrative:

> "I truly was abused as a child and that is why I started in therapy, but my therapist felt that there had to be more to it than I was telling her because I was too upset for it to just be abused by a babysitter and a relative's boyfriend—it must have been by a family member. Since I was angry at my parents for 'allowing' me to be abused (I was only 14 years old when I began therapy, I am 18 now), it seemed like it was probable that my parents had abused me since they had been so 'neglectful' and 'allowed' me to be abused" (RP 30).

> "I had real abuse memories but instead of working on that it led to having to find out/recover other memories such as satanic ritual abuse" (RP 55).

> "I knew I was molested as a child and that my father was an abusive man—but by the time I left therapy, my therapist had me believing I was abused by 20+ people, was a Satanic Ritual Abuse Victim and had Multiple Personalities. I am away from him now. My life is wonderful and I know the truth" (RP 17).

> "I am concerned that people who have had actual child abuse experiences are not getting the real help they deserve. Therapists are becoming obsessed with SRA and MPD and are not giving appropriate treatment for 'real' issues" (RP 15).

Finally, respondents' comments suggested several questions for future research.

1. What role does hospitalization play in the development of FMS?
2. To what extent do drugs dull the critical thinking needed to escape from FMS?
3. Is it the *conflict* between true memories and false memories (belief systems) that is responsible for much of the self-destructive behavior that is observed?
4. To what extent do people cling to the victim identity role until they have a clear alternative role?
5. How can people recover from the shame of having allowed themselves to develop a false belief system, recover their faith in their own ability to distinguish truth from fiction, and reestablish a firm sense of identity?

Common Themes in FMS Narratives

In one sense it may be argued that the three accounts presented in this chapter are simply variations on one essential theme. That is, regardless of which account they endorsed, respondents shared the belief that their problems were caused by a childhood sexual abuse that could be completely repressed. The belief in this imagining was developed in the course of a collaboration with a therapist, and it was usually supported by other therapists and groups of survivors who formed a subculture of believers. In fact, of 56 respondents, 48 reported that they were supposed to search for childhood memories to find repressed traumas, and 48 reported that another therapist or mental health worker confirmed or treated them as an abuse victim. By contrast, only 2 reported that their therapists were not sure whether anything traumatic had happened that they could not remember, and only 6 reported that they were encouraged to be objective in looking for information that could prove or disprove their abuse.

However, if we return to my initial query of how believed-in imaginings could be sustained in the face of contrary memories and the disbelief of family members, it seems we need to add three factors: Dependency on the therapist, the cutting off of contact with the disbelieving family, and the shame of having made a false accusation. These factors interlock together. In regards to dependency, 40 of the 56 respondents reported (by endorsing items with at least a 4, *very true*) that they were afraid of what would happen if they left therapy, and 37 reported that they knew their therapist felt they were very special because of what they had been through; only 8 felt they always had the freedom to leave therapy when they were ready. We have seen how some people used the authority of the therapist to overcome their doubts and to justify avoiding contact with disbelievers. Indeed, 42 respondents reported that they were discouraged from talking to family members or friends who did not believe they were abused.

But what of the 17 respondents who felt that it was at least partially true that they had the freedom to leave (Q42) or the 16 who reported that it was their own discomfort that led them not to see family members who disagreed (Q32)? They, of course, were more likely to endorse the self-narrative account (i.e., 13 of the 18 endorsers) and they appear to have been at least partly trapped by the relief, sympathy, and understanding gained by the abuse narrative. In fact, one may conjecture that people may find it easier to retract when mind control rather than self-narrative is involved.

Finally, we have the factor of shame, and self-doubt, or rather the avoidance of the pain of shame and self-doubt that must occur when a people begin to consider that they have been misled about their own identity. Although they were not asked about these issues, several respondents spontaneously commented:

> "I don't know what to believe about anything anymore. I have lost my faith in my own rationality" (RP 36).

> "It is too scary to let go of 'victim' identity unless an alternative is offered" (RP 37).

"The overwhelming *shame* I have to live with for having 'sold my soul' and my accused perpetrator's reputation for the sense of belonging and security I got from my therapist ... the total sense of self-deprecation from realizing you've been duped" (RP 25).

It must require a good deal of courage to face the fact that one can be so misled. The most recent survey conducted by the FMS Foundation indicated that 25% of the children who succumbed to FMS have resumed contact with their families. However, only 7% have fully retracted (FMS Foundation, 1997). Most have not yet been able to discuss the painful self-deception that was involved.

The research reported in this chapter suggests that the narratives we may use to explain the development of FMS do not involve arbitrary attributions. Rather, they reflect different processes that are related to what happened in the course of psychotherapy. Because the accounts of respondents are retrospective, we cannot be sure of what actually occurred, but they are consistent and the processes make sense. In the case of mind control, the imagining that is believed in appears to stem initially from the therapist. It is the *therapist's* story to explain the client's pain and the therapist's will that imposes this reality. There were 30 respondents who indicated that the therapist was the main author of their own abuse narrative, and 28 respondents who reported that there was a struggle of wills and that they finally gave in to the therapist's idea.

In the case of self-narrative, the imagining and believing stem more from the client: 19 of the respondents stated that it was at least partly true that they were unhappy with themselves and wondered what might have happened to them as a child. They were more likely to report that the abuse narrative helped them to understand their unhappiness and provided them with a sense of relief and the opportunity for sympathy. Furthermore, they maintained control in the sense that they felt they had the freedom to leave therapy.

Both the mind-control and self-narrative accounts appear compatible with a role-enactment narrative, and they often were endorsed along with role enactment. However, those who endorsed the role-enactment account were more likely to have been part of a survivor group, to experience themselves as *choosing* to search for memories, and to receive attention for their memories and become fully absorbed in enacting the role. Thus, for the moment, such an account seems to have enough distinctiveness to be maintained in its own right, as another coherent narrative explanation for the development of FMS. Although only 6 respondents failed to endorse any of the accounts, it appears desirable to develop an account based on the mutuality that more typically characterizes the therapeutic relationship. If such a narrative were presented, it is possible that it might be endorsed by substantial numbers of FMS retractors.

CONCLUSION

FMS is clearly an excellent example of a believed-in imagining and one that has detrimental consequences. The cultural basis of the imagining seems clear. Just as other cultures have imagined ghosts, witches, and malevolent spirits, our own has imagined repressed memories. For many, repressed memories are a believed-in fact. There *is* evidence that some people can avoid thinking of troubling events, that others can dissociate feelings from their intellectual knowledge of troubling events, and that some people suffered such troubled childhoods that they lead extremely troubled lives and can remember very little about any aspect of their past. However, I know of *no* evidence that people may completely repress the memory of a traumatic childhood, lead relatively normal lives, and then recover the putative memories and suffer PTSD. This appears to be an imagining, what Loftus and Ketcham (1994) have termed the "myth" of repressed memory. It is a myth that has been narrated in books, movies, on TV, and in countless therapeutic sessions.

Given this mythic narrative, what are the conditions that could lead relatively normal individuals to come to believe that this imagining applied to themselves in spite of contradictory memories and in spite of loved ones' denials of the putative events? In all the cases we have examined, an authority figure on whom the person is dependent asserts that the narrative explains the person's problems or supports the validity of the narrative. However, the influence of this authority appears to be exercised in three different ways.

When the mind-control account applies, the narrative in which people become involved is really the authority's narrative, and its reality is maintained by the authority who uses his or her will to overcome people's resistance to accepting the narrative. In what we might call pure mind control, people become confused and lose confidence and the ability to make decisions and to narrate their own story. The authority discourages people from leaving the dependency relation and being exposed to other views of reality, and people may reject the narrative when the dependency relation is ended.

When the self-narrative account applies, people experience themselves as being in control and attempt to develop self-narratives that will explain problematic behavior. Although they are often encouraged by an authority figure and draw heavily on readily available material, they use their own imaginations to create narratives so that they experience them as their own stories. The story is functional in that it explains problematic (non-ideal) behavior, provides relief from the demand to be perfect, and helps people to attract sympathy for problems they are facing in actual life. Because the story is self-narrated, it may be more resistant to change and modified only when alternative explanations become available, there are changes in the person's life circumstances, and there is some way for the person to struggle over the shame that is inherent in having been involved in a false narrative.

When the role enactment account applies, people find themselves in groups or subcultures where the narrative of repressed memories is part of a social script that requires them to enact the role of a survivor and exhibit the behaviors believed to characterize the survivors of abuse. In exchange, they receive welcomed attention and may extend the role into the wider community so that they become an authority in their own right. Although people may be thrust into this role, under conditions of pure role enactment they experience themselves as trying on the role and choosing to search for memories. However, they become so involved in the role that their reality is affected as long as group membership is maintained and attention is secured.

FMS does not simply involve the development of false memories. It involves the development of a false identity, an identity based on the myth of repression, an identity that is imagined and then believed-in by the enactments described by Sarbin in the first chapter of this book and because of supporting social relationships. When people return from this excursion—those who do—they attempt to understand how they could have strayed so far. The particular narrative that best accounts for their experience—whether a narration of mind-control, of self-narration, or of role-enactment—appears to depend on what actually occurred in therapy, the degree to which the identity construction was imposed by a controlling therapist, self-created in the search for understanding and sympathy, or enacted in the context of a small group. Identity is always the product of collaboration, formed in social community. The problem with the identity inherent in FMS is not only that it involves false memories and accusations, or that it often involves an abuse of authority and collusions, but that it usually involves pseudo-communities that are isolated from the legitimate social communities of which the individual is truly a member.

REFERENCES

de Rivera, J. (1997a). The construction of false memory syndrome. *Psychological Inquiry, 8,* 271–292.

de Rivera, J. (1997b). Estimating the prevalence of false memory syndrome. *American Psychologist, 52,* 996–997.

FMS Foundation Newsletter. (1997, April). Memory and reality: Next steps (p. 1).

Goldstein E., & Farmer, K. (1993). *True stories of false memories.* Boca Raton, FL: SIRS Books.

Haney, C., Banks, C., & Zimbardo, P. (1973). Interpersonal dynamics in a simulated prison. *International Journal of Crimonology and Penology, 1,* 69–97.

Hassan, S. (1990). *Combating cult mind control.* Rochester, VT: Park Street Press.

Kihlstrom, J. F. (in press). Exhumed memory. In S. J. Lynn & N. P. Spanos (Eds.), *Truth in memory* (pp. 3–31). New York: Guilford Press.

Loftus, E., & Ketcham, K. (1994). *The myth of repressed memory: False memories.* New York: St. Martin's Press.

Lynn, S. J., & Kirsch, I. I. (1996). Alleged alien abductions: False memories, hypnosis, and fantasy proneness. *Psychological Inquiry, 7,* 151–155.

Pendergrast, M. (1996). *Victims of memory: Sex abuse accusations and shattered lives* (2nd ed.). Hinesburg, VT: Upper Access Books.

Sarbin, T. R. (1994). A narrative approach to "repressed memories." *Journal of Narrative and Personal History, 5,* 51–69.

IV

THE SOCIAL
SIGNIFICANCE OF
BELIEVED-IN IMAGININGS

11

SOCIAL CONSTRUCTION OF SATANIC RITUAL ABUSE AND THE CREATION OF FALSE MEMORIES

JEFFREY S. VICTOR

The idea that many people can believe in the existence of purely imaginary creatures, monsters, spirits, aliens, and dangerous human deviants and can swear that they remember seeing them, should come as no surprise to anyone. There is plenty of evidence. Historical and anthropological research offers abundant examples.

When thousands of people believe that they have memories of being tortured by secret Satan worshippers, such a belief does not arise from some esoteric mental functioning. It is a product of identifiable social processes that influence many people's beliefs. Most fundamentally, these social processes include the effects of authority on belief, and the consensual validation of reality within people's social networks and reference groups.

The past offers numerous examples of collective behavior during which widespread, fearful rumors and accusations about dangerous deviants resulted in false accusations of crime against innocent people. This form of collective behavior has been tagged by various labels: persecution, witch-hunt, scare, and panic. In some cases, the widely feared deviants are products of ethnic, racial, or religious stereotypes. In other cases, the invented deviants are creations of popular imagination. The classic example of this form of collective behavior is the European witch-hunt, during which thousands of people, mostly women believed to possess evil magical powers, were executed (Ben-Yehuda, 1981; Levack, 1987). Another example is the anti-Communist "Red Scare" in the United States in the 1950s, during which many thousands of Americans were labeled as "subversives" and lost their jobs (Caute, 1978). Such forms of collective behavior can be classified together and regarded as moral panics.

THE CHARACTERISTICS OF MORAL PANICS

Moral panics are a product of sociopolitical processes and not psychological characteristics of individuals, such as suggestibility, a disposition to fantasize, delusions, or personal anxieties. The sociopolitical concept of a moral panic differs significantly from psychiatric concepts, such as "mass hysteria" or "emotional contagion," which focus on emotionality and fight–flight behavior (labeled as irrational, because of the absence of a verifiable threat; critical reviews of these psychiatric concepts can be found in Bartholomew, 1990, 1994; Gehlen, 1997; and Stallings, 1994). In contrast, the concept of a moral panic focuses on cognition and communication behavior.

A moral panic is a societal response to beliefs about a threat from moral deviants. The term "moral panic" was coined by British sociologist Stanley Cohen in his book, *Folk Devils and Moral Panics: The Creation of Mods and Rockers*, a study of British public reaction to the deviant behavior of the "mods" and "rockers" youth. Cohen used the term to identify a form of collective behavior characterized by widely circulating rumor stories disseminated by the mass media, which exaggerated the threat posed by some newly identified type of moral deviant (Cohen, 1972). Cohen defined a moral panic as a form of collective behavior during which

> A condition, episode, person or group emerges to become defined as a threat to societal values and interests; its nature is presented in a stylized and stereotypical fashion by the mass media; the moral barricades are manned by editors, bishops, politicians and other right thinking people; socially accredited experts pronounce their diagnosis and solutions; ways of coping are evolved or (more often) resorted to; the condition then disappears, submerges or deteriorates. (Cohen, 1972, p. 9)

Cohen employed a societal reaction and labeling perspective on deviance, which was an early antecedent of current social constructionism.

Although the concept of a moral panic has been widely used by British sociologists, American sociologists regarded it as suffering from a lack of precise indicators and made little use of it. Recently, Goode and Ben-

Yehuda (1994, pp. 33–39) suggested five specific indicators of a moral panic, which are summarized as follows:

1. Volatility—the sudden eruption and subsiding of concern about a newly perceived threat to society from a category of people regarded as being moral deviants.
2. Hostility—the deviants are regarded with intense hostility as enemies of the basic values of the society and attributed stereotypes of "evil" behavior.
3. Measurable Concern—concern about the threat is measurable in concrete ways, such as attitude surveys.
4. Consensus—there is consensus in significant segments of the population that the threat is real and serious.
5. Disproportionality—the concern about the numbers of moral deviants and the extent of the harm that they do is much greater than can be verified by objective, empirical investigations of the harm. The numbers of deviants may be minimal or even nonexistent, and their harm may be very limited or even nonexistent, whereas the measurable concern is very great. (This last indicator is the key characteristic of a moral panic.)

In brief, a moral panic is a form of collective behavior characterized by suddenly increased concern and hostility in a significant segment of a society, in reaction to their belief about a threat from a category of moral deviants. Careful, empirical examination at a later time, however, reveals that the perceived threat was either greatly exaggerated or nonexistent. A moral panic often gives rise to social movements aimed at eliminating the threatening deviants and may generate moral crusades and political struggles over use of the law to suppress the dangerous deviants. Sometimes, local panics in response to threat rumors may also occur, but such dramatic events are not inevitable during moral panics. The essence of a moral panic is that significant segments of a society are reacting to a socially constructed threat from moral deviants. The main observable behavior during a moral panic is the communication of claims, accusations, and rumors. The 1950's anticommunist scare in the United States is a good example of this social phenomenon.

THE STUDY OF RUMORS AND CLAIMS ABOUT MORAL DEVIANTS

The particular type of rumor that is most commonly part of a moral panic is that of a contemporary legend (formerly called an urban legend). A contemporary legend is a variety of persistent rumor story, transmitted primarily in oral communication, and only secondarily through the mass media. The narrative communicates shared anxieties about a newly emergent, collectively perceived threat, conveyed in age-old recurring motifs and metaphors that usually embody a moral–political message (Victor, 1993b). Like an ordinary rumor, the story is told "as if" it were true and widely believed "as if" it is likely to be true. In contrast, contemporary legends tell stories that are more universal in significance and less relevant to specific people, locations, and events than are ordinary rumors.

A contemporary legend is a process of collective behavior, rather than a fixed and unchanging narrative. The collective behavior consists primarily of the collaborative creation and communication of rumor stories in ever-changing variations (Ellis, 1990). A contemporary legend is always emergent out of interaction and never finished. The story is constantly being reshaped, as people add parts, forget parts, and distort parts. Contemporary legends are often regarded as being merely amusing tales having little social consequence, like those about poisonous spiders found in bunches of bananas or fried rats served as chicken. However, some contemporary legends can have harmful consequences, such as false accusations of crime, the destruction of reputations and property, riots and even killings. Examples of dangerous contemporary legends include racist and anti-Semitic rumors, which are derived from age-old folklore themes. There are even anti-American contemporary legends that have resulted in violent attacks upon American tourists in Latin American countries (Lopez, 1994). Persistent rumors there claim that wealthy Americans pay for the kidnapping of poor children, who are then murdered for use of their body parts in medical operations in the United States (Campion-Vincent, 1990, 1997).

Claims making about moral deviants is a central phenomenon during moral panics. The content of claims about deviance include matters such as stereotypes of deviants and their behavior, typologies of variations among deviants, descriptions of the dangers and particular harms caused by deviants, and rationales for dealing with deviants. These claims construct the definitions (symbolic meanings) attributed to deviance. Current social constructionist research and analysis focus not on the behavior and people defined as deviant, but instead on the arguments of the claims makers, their vested interests, and their authority and power in a society (Best, 1989; Conrad & Schneider, 1992).[1]

---

[1]Criticism of social constructionism has emphasized that this perspective ignores the "objective" realities of deviant behavior, such as empirically verifiable physical, psychological, and interpersonal harms that may result from certain behaviors (Miller & Holstein, 1993). The criticism suggests that the social constructionist perspective regards claims making about deviance as if it comes into existence entirely unrelated to any objective empirical measures of harm done by deviant behavior in a society. In response, social constructionists argue that "contextual" social constructionist research does relate the claims defining deviance to empirical measures of those claims (Best, 1993). My analysis of SRA accusations follows the contextual form of social constructionism.

The claims made about satanic ritual abuse (hereafter abbreviated as SRA) have been studied by Hicks (1991), Jenkins (1992), Nathan and Snedeker (1995), and Victor (1993a, 1994, 1995, 1996). Most claims assert the existence of secret, criminal organizations, which commit horrible crimes against children, motivated by worship of Satan. Some claims assert the existence of an international conspiratorial network. Less extreme versions assert that the secret networks consist only of generational family clans. A common claim is that ritual torture and sexual abuse of children is done to "program" children to reverse good and evil. The supposed aim is to "brainwash" children into the ideology of Satan worship.

These claims assert the Satan-worshipping criminals sometimes kill and ritually sacrifice infants born to impregnated "breeders" and commit cannibalism with the body parts. Some claims even hold that satanic cults kidnap runaway youth for ritual sacrifice, commit random murders of indigent people, and engage in the child pornography business, forced prostitution, and drug dealing. Many claims makers assert that these purported criminals are able to maintain their secrecy and avoid detection because satanists have infiltrated all the institutions of society. The claims makers' usual tactic of deflecting potential skepticism is to argue that satanic cult crimes are so horrendous that most people are naturally skeptical. Some even attempt to equate skepticism about satanic cult crimes with skepticism about the Holocaust.

The authorities that have attributed credibility to SRA claims include some fundamentalist clergy, local law enforcement officials, members of anti-cult volunteer organizations, as well as some psychotherapists and social workers. Some psychotherapists and social workers communicated these assertions in speeches at professional conferences and training seminars, in interviews published in newspapers and popular magazines, on television talk shows, in professional journals, and in books. (A few examples of assertions about SRA can be found in the following articles and books: Cozolino, 1989, 1990; Feldman, 1993; Fewster, 1990; Friesen, 1991; Gould & Cozolino, 1992; Hill & Goodwin, 1989; Hudson, 1990, 1991; Kelley, 1988, 1989, 1990; Mayer, 1991; Noblitt & Perskin, 1995; Rockwell, 1994; C. Ross, 1995; Ryder, 1992; Sakheim & Devine, 1992; Shaffer & Cozolino, 1992; Sinason, 1994; Smith, 1993; Smith & Pazder, 1980; and Young, Sachs, Braun, & Watkins, 1991.) Survey research has found that only a small minority of psychotherapists and social workers report ever having encountered a patient suffering from SRA; and only a small number of these therapists account for the majority of SRA diagnoses (Bottoms, Shaver, & Goodman, 1996; Poole, Lindsay, Memon, & Bull, 1995). However, their unverified assertions about SRA in the mass media were crucial in influencing public opinion, and the opinion of other therapists, toward belief in the existence of SRA.

THE MORAL PANIC OVER SATANIC RITUAL CHILD ABUSE

Does the societal reaction to claims about satanic cult crime, including SRA, fit the defining criteria of a moral panic? The SRA phenomenon has certainly been quite volatile, as is characteristic of moral panics. Accounts appeared rather suddenly. The oldest know satanic cult "survivor" account was published in 1980 in the book, *Michelle Remembers*, written by the Canadian psychiatrist Lawrence Pazder, with his patient (and later wife), Michelle Smith. After that date, personal accounts of SRA survival, SRA accusations against parents, and local satanic cult rumors spread rapidly across the United States and Canada, and then to other, mainly English-speaking counties. (See Victor, in press, for information about the international transmission of SRA claims.) By the early 1990s, SRA accounts, accusations, and rumors had rapidly declined.

Indicators of the concern and hostility characteristic of moral panics can be found in claims about a national threat from dangerous satanic cult criminals, communicated in the mass media. Such claims were reported in many alarmist articles in local newspapers and in some national magazine articles, in sensational television talk-shows, and in a few pseudo-documentaries on television (Victor, 1993a). Indicators that SRA claims and accusations are regarded as being real and serious by sizable segments of the American population can be found in attitude surveys. A 1994 national survey reported in *Redbook* magazine, for example, showed that 70% of Americans "believe that at least some people who claim that they were abused by satanic cults as children, but repressed the memories for years, are telling the truth" (A. Ross, 1994). More survey evidence of widespread belief in the threat from dangerous satanic cults can be found in an opinion poll done in Texas, which showed that 80% of respondents believed that Satanism is an increasing problem in American society (reported in Crouch & Damphousse, 1992). Additional evidence can be found in several national surveys of American psychotherapists, social workers, and counselors (Andrews et al., 1995; Bottoms, Shaver, & Goodman, 1996; Poole, Lindsay, Memon, & Bull, 1995). These researchers found that a sizable proportion of mental health professionals, numbering in the thousands, attributed credibility to SRA accounts as being accurate memories.

Finally, disproportionality in reaction to SRA claims, characteristic of a moral panic, is affirmed by the fact that no law enforcement agency or scientific research study has found the kind of physical evidence needed to support SRA accounts. No one has turned up written or electronic communications, bank account records, meetings in process, members who can identify leaders, or any of the vast number of corpses of people who were supposedly murdered by satanic cults.

All that can be proven to exist that bears any resemblance to SRA claims are teenage juvenile delinquents and mentally disordered individual killers who call themselves satanists, but these deviants do not constitute an organization, a criminal network, or a religious cult. The public perceptions of these deviants have been distorted by the claims makers. The absence of scientific evidence to confirm claims about the existence of organized groups that torture and sexually abuse children during rituals justified by a Satan-worshipping ideology suggests that the reaction to the perceived threat is far in excess of the evidence of the threat.

Official government reports from several countries could show no evidence to support the previously noted claims about SRA. These reports include those from the Department of Health of the United Kingdom (La Fontaine, 1994); the Netherlands Ministry of Justice (1994); the Behavioral Science Unit of the FBI (Lanning, 1992); and government agencies in Michigan (Michigan State Police, 1990), Virginia (Virginia State Crime Commission Task Force, 1991), and Washington (Parr, 1996). In addition, in a national survey of psychotherapists (Bottoms et al., 1996), not a single SRA accusation was reported by the psychotherapists where there was reliable evidence to corroborate SRA accusations from either children or adults. In short, the reports of psychotherapists about their patients' SRA accusations provide no convincing external corroborating evidence for the existence of satanic cult criminals, either in organization or intergenerational family clans.

THE CAUSES OF MORAL PANICS

Three Theoretical Models

There are three theoretical models for analyzing the causes of moral panics: (1) the grass roots model, (2) the elite-engineered model, and (3) the interest group model (Goode & Ben-Yehuda, 1994). The grassroots model suggests that a moral panic arises spontaneously across a broad spectrum of a society's population. The concern and anger about the threat from perceived moral deviants is a response to persistent and widespread social stresses. Anxieties arising from these social stresses are not able to gain direct expression, but instead they are displaced and directed toward social deviants, who become regarded as the cause of concern.

Newly detected deviants essentially function as collective scapegoats for the anxieties transferred to them. A contemporary legend may function as a catalyst for a sudden outbreak of collective behavior, such as in an aggressive mob. The actions of special interest groups are not necessary to promote moral outrage directed at the newly perceived deviants. The mass media and social control authorities basically reflect public opinion about the reality of the threat. The key argument of the grass roots model is that these agencies cannot fabricate public concern where none previously existed.

An example of a grass roots moral panic occurred in France in 1968, when widespread rumors in several cities had Jewish clothing store owners being accused of kidnapping teenage girls in their stores and selling them into forced prostitution, controlled by international criminal syndicates (Morin, 1971). Mobs attacked Jewish-owned clothing stores, as well as stores wrongly reputed to be owned by Jews. The rumors were based on the centuries-old ethnic stereotype and accompanying folklore about Jews as kidnappers of Christian children.

The elite-engineered model suggests that moral panics are orchestrated by a powerful elite that controls the major institutions of a society. The elite deliberately promotes a campaign to generate and sustain public moral outrage about a threat from a target category of deviants. The actual intention of the campaign is to divert attention away from real problems in a society, the solution of which would threaten the economic and political interests of the elite. The elite fabricates a definition of the nature of the threat and uses it power and authority in the institutions of society, including the mass media, religion, and law enforcement, to shape public opinion. The threat from supposed dangerous deviants is invented, or at least exaggerated, by the elite, to serve its own vested interests. In medieval times, the hierarchy of the Catholic Church organized moral panics and persecutions directed at the Cathar heretics and later the Knights Templars. The Stalinist purges and persecution of millions of imaginary internal enemies of the Soviet state is another example.

The interest group model is the one that best explains the causes of the moral panic in response to beliefs about dangerous satanic cults. The interest group model suggests that moral panics are an unintended consequence of moral crusades launched by specific interest groups and their moral entrepreneurs who attempt to focus public attention on moral evils that they perceive to be threats to society. In modern times, many interest groups direct their efforts toward presenting special concerns in the mass media in order to influence public opinion, because they believe that their efforts serve a moral cause beneficial to the whole society. Nevertheless, their efforts also function to advance their own group's social influence, prestige, wealth, and ideological interests. As these interest groups become increasingly successful in influencing public opinion, they stimulate resistance and conflict from other competing interest groups. The interest group model suggests that a moral threat expressed in a preexisting contemporary legend may be consistent with the moral concerns of certain interest groups and can be employed by them as an instrument to influence public opinion.

False Accusations and the Social Construction of Imaginary Deviants

How is it possible that a moral panic could be caused by widespread accusations of crime, even when there is little evidence that the criminals even exist? The key insight is that accusations of crime are a claims-making activity. False accusations can construct imaginary deviants, especially when accusations are systematically legitimized by social control authorities. In order for a moral panic to take hold among a large number of people, it is necessary for some people to be publicly identified with the perceived threat, even if the accusations against them are false. It is necessary for a group that feels threatened to have visible scapegoats.

Criminologist Elliott Currie has shown how even when deviant acts are purely imaginary, as in the case of witchcraft, people can always be found and fitted into the stereotype of the deviants. Currie's (1986) study of the European witch-hunts suggests that a particular combination of four circumstances caused false accusations of witchcraft to be affirmed by authorities as evidence that some people were witches. One, there was widespread belief in and fear of secret, conspiratorial witches who supposedly practiced black magic to harm people. Two, in response, there gradually evolved a new occupation of experts specialized in detecting witches—the witchfinders. Three, the witchfinders used ambiguous tests ("spectral evidence") to detect witches, so that the accused were almost automatically found guilty and this confirmed their expertise and enhanced their authority. Four, in addition, the ideology of traditional Christian religion concerning Satan's corrupting influences fueled the Inquisition's search for any kind of potential heretic.

Klemke and Tiedeman (1990) studied a wide variety of false accusations of crimes, in order to identify the social conditions that increase the prevalence of false accusations. They found three social conditions associated with increases in false accusations. First, there is a widespread belief in the existence of a threat from new kinds of deviants. Second, there is competition over jurisdictions of authority between newer and more traditional social control authorities. As a result, the newer authorities attempt to justify and expand their newfound authority. Third, the search for deviants relies on faulty investigative instruments and tests, which are so oversimplified and ambiguous that many innocent people are falsely identified as the deviants.

In addition, I suggest a fourth social condition: the symbolic resonance of the perceived threat with a demonology (Victor, 1993a). This condition results in a distinctly moralistic perception of the deviants. The term *demonology* was coined by anthropologists. Stevens (1991) defined a demonology as "an ideology of evil, a elaborate body of belief about an evil force that is inexorably undermining society's most cherished values and institutions" (p. 21). A demonology is an explanation of the ultimate power that threatens to destroy the moral order of a society. It is the core conception of most moral belief systems, whether religious or secular, and functions to cognitively organize those belief systems.

THE CAUSES OF MORAL PANICS: THE CASE OF RITUAL CHILD ABUSE

The following interpretation of the causes of the moral panic over satanic cult ritual child abuse is offered as a case study of social dynamics of the interest group model of the causes of moral panics. It also illustrates how false accusations of deviance during moral panics can construct deviants from imaginary sources.

Widespread Beliefs About a Threat From New Forms of Deviance

Before a moral panic can begin, belief in a potential threat from moral deviants must spread widely in a society. How did the belief in child abuse by secret satanic cults spread through American society? Most past studies of moral panics suggest that belief in a threat from moral deviants is largely a product of mass media sensationalism (McRobbie & Thornton, 1995). This assumption is consistent with a grass roots model of a moral panic, but it may not be valid in the case of the satanic cult scare. Crouch and Damphousse (1992), for example, carried out a content analysis of eight major U.S. city newspapers to investigate their role in the scare. They concluded that the newspapers provided a forum for purported experts (local police, clergy, and psychotherapists) to identify the symptoms of satanic cult crime, but the newspapers did not function as autonomous moral entrepreneurs to inflame rumors about these crimes. They functioned essentially to disseminate the claims of authorities, who were presented as being so-called experts in detecting satanic cult crime.

In my own research I came to a similar conclusion about the role of the mass media. Although a few hosts of television talk shows and authors of true-crime books and Christian religious books acted as moral entrepreneurs, claims making from experts were rare in large city newspapers and largely absent on national network news (Victor, 1993a, pp. 253–255). Thus, belief in a threat from satanic cult crime spread widely only after the claims, accusations, and rumors were legitimized by certain authorities and interest groups.

Timing is also crucial to the emergence of a moral panic. The moral panic involving SRA begin in the 1980s, at a time when several similar panics involving the violent victimization of children had emerged. For example, there was already widespread belief that child sexual abuse was much more common than had previously been thought and that there were a great many deviants hidden in society who sexually abused children (Howitt, 1992). In the 1980s, there was also already a moral panic over crimes against children. Claims were being made that thousands of children were being kidnapped, sexually assaulted, and murdered (Best, 1990). As a result, the general public was more receptive to the self-appointed authorities who lent credibility to SRA stories.

The Expansion of Authority in Social Control

Authority plays a key role in defining forms of deviant behavior and in providing legitimacy for claims about new threats to society. Established institutional authorities do not easily regard new claims about threats to society as being credible. However, when new forms of authority begin to develop and to compete for power over a jurisdiction with previously established authorities, the newer authorities may be tempted to use a newly perceived threat to expand their power. In such conditions, the newer authorities are likely to overreach their expertise and attribute credibility to false accusations of victimization by a newly discovered threat. This is what I believe led to the legitimization of SRA accusations.

Sociologists specialized in the study of deviant behavior (i.e., behavior that is socially disapproved) believe that the most important contemporary social change affecting authority to define the meanings of deviance is the process of the "medicalization of social control" (Conrad, 1992; Conrad & Schneider, 1992). In the 20th century, the social authority to define and interpret deviant behavior and to make judgments about good and evil has gradually shifted from religious and political authorities to medical and mental health authorities. Increasingly, these authorities have tried to reframe the way in which deviant behavior is understood, so that deviance is seen through the lens of the medical model, as being a form of sickness. A good example is homosexual behavior, which was defined formerly as a sickness, but was redefined as a gender orientation in 1973 by the same authorities as a result of political pressure (Bayer, 1987). Authorities still commonly interpret the nature of alcohol abuse (Fingarette, 1988) and illegal drug use (Goode, 1993) as being forms of sickness. The metaphor of sickness has such a powerful influence on popular culture that rapists, serial murderers, child molesters, habitual gamblers, excessive dieters, and people who commit suicide are commonly defined as "sick" people.

One consequence of the medicalization of social control is that medical and mental health authorities have been drawn, however reluctantly, into the arenas of politics, law making, and legal judgments. Other authorities, such as legislators, police, judges, and juries, increasingly rely on their expertise. It is important, however, to recognize that the medicalization of social control is a product of American society's confidence in medical techniques to manage life's problems. It is not the result of any deliberate planning and certainly not any conspiracy on the part of medical and mental health authorities.

Pfohl (1977) provided an excellent social constructionist analysis of the political developments leading to the redefinition of violent physical aggression by parents against children, from a crime to a public health concern relabeled "child abuse" (see also Howitt, 1992). His analysis is particularly relevant for understanding the social construction of the label "ritual child abuse." Indications of severe physical trauma in a child in cases of a suspected crime were initially redefined as "symptoms" of the battered child "syndrome." Thereafter, medical and mental health experts, rather than police, became the authorities relied on to define the indicators of criminal behavior on the part of parents. Parents suspected of child abuse, rather than being treated as suspects of crime (and therefore, fully protected by civil liberties laws), were redefined as possibly "sick" personalities and redefined as "patients". Medical and mental health authorities were inevitably drawn, however reluctantly, into legal judgments of parents suspected of engaging in child abuse. Medical and mental health authorities lobbied government for new laws and more funds to deal with what they claimed was the discovery of the new and widespread public health problem of child abuse. The mass media sensationalized reports about a newly discovered epidemic of child abuse, even though there was no scientific evidence that violent physical assaults against children had increased over past decades.

We can understand the social construction of concept of SRA as similarly a product of the medicalization of social control. The concept is an extension of sensationalized concern about an epidemic of child abuse and, later, sexual child abuse. Initially, some mental health specialists who claimed to have developed new medical techniques capable of detecting illegal sexual contact between adults and children (sexual child abuse) believed that their clients' accounts of sexual victimization by secret satanic cults might be true. These mental health professionals included some psychotherapists specialized in the treatment of mental disorders characterized by dissociated memory processes, who claimed that these disorders were caused primarily by sexual activity forced upon a child by an adult. (Mulhern, 1991, 1994, provided a detailed history of the roles of these mental health professionals in the social construction of SRA.) These professionals also included some child protection social workers specialized in the detection and treatment of sexually victimized children (Nathan & Snedeker, 1995, provided a detailed study of the history of the role of these mental health professionals in the social construction of SRA.)

Psychotherapists specialized in the treatment of dissociative disorders and social workers specialized in the treatment of sexually victimized children were drawn into collaboration with each other. They shared a similar focus of professional interest in sexual child abuse, and they also shared a similar social situation. Both groups of specialists were struggling to gain greater recognition and respect within their larger community of professionals. The discovery of the SRA of children thrust these marginal specialists into the spotlight of mass media attention, even when they did not seek it. If this important discovery could be confirmed in the courts of law and science, these specialists could obtain well-deserved recognition and respect for their work.

At first, some of these mental health professionals publicized their discovery of SRA by communicating it to other professional specialists in conferences and training seminars. Their audiences included many diverse kinds of therapists and counselors, as well as interested police, clergy, nurses, medical doctors, and self-proclaimed victims of SRA. (See Mulhern, 1991, 1994, for sources of audiotapes of lectures from these conferences.) Some communicated the horrifying discovery of SRA to the general public in newspaper interviews, magazine articles, and (a few of them) on television talk shows. (See Victor, 1993a, for sources in newspaper and magazine articles and videotapes of television talk shows.) A few of these specialists published details of their claims about the link between SRA and multiple personality disorder in professional journal articles and books. (See, e.g., Cozolino, 1989, 1990; Feldman, 1993; Fewster, 1990; Friesen, 1991; Gould & Cozolino, 1992; Hill & Goodwin, 1989; Hudson, 1990, 1991; Kelley, 1988; 1989; 1990; Mayer, 1991; Noblitt & Perskin, 1995; Rockwell, 1994; C. Ross, 1995; Ryder, 1992; Sakheim & Devine, 1992; Shaffer & Cozolino, 1992; Sinason, 1994; Smith, 1993; Smith & Pazder, 1980; and Young, Sachs, Braun, & Watkins, 1991.) Never before had a new form of secretly organized criminal activity been discovered by mental health experts. In this way, they functioned as agents of social control more than as scientists or therapists.

These authorities played a key role in causing a moral panic over SRA. Some elements of the mass media quickly responded to bizarre accounts of SRA by self-proclaimed SRA survivors and used these experts to give credibility to the accounts as evidence that there existed hidden in American society secret networks of vicious criminals that threatened our children (Victor, 1993a). Television and radio talk shows, local newspapers and some national magazines used the dramatic claims of these mental health authorities to attract audiences. Some of these experts were invited to be professional advisors to social movement organizations concerned with sexual child abuse. Some of them helped to lobby state legislatures for new laws to protect children from criminal satanic cults (Victor, 1995). They were successful in obtaining laws in at least four states. The passage of special laws against SRA, then functioned to provide some political legitimacy to SRA accusations.

When interest groups expand their authority and power, they almost inevitably encounter opposing interest groups. The SRA claims of some therapists and child protection social workers aroused the concerns of many behavioral scientists, as well as psychotherapists whose therapy was grounded in behavioral and biomedical treatments. In response, these professionals organized themselves to influence professional and public opinion, framing the issue in a civil liberties context of false accusations and false memories (Beckett, 1996).

Faulty Techniques for Investigating Deviant Behavior

Widespread false accusations of deviance are produced when authorities rely on faulty techniques for distinguishing between true and false accusations. The main problem in investigations of accusations of sexual child abuse, including SRA accusations, is that reliable, scientific techniques have not yet been developed (Ofshe & Watters, 1994; Pendergrast, 1995; Wakefield & Underwager, 1994; Yapko, 1994—however, see Poole & Lamb, in press, for recommendations regarding more reliable techniques). The types of faulty investigative techniques used to detect SRA include those resulting in false confessions and false accusations, those resulting in false memories, and those employing unreliable indicators.

In past persecutions, it has been common for investigators to rely on manipulative or coercive interrogations to produce false confessions and false accusations. Confessions coerced with torture occurred during the European witch-hunts. However, voluntary false confessions of witchcraft also occurred. Frightened women sometimes voluntarily confessed to being witches and to having had intercourse with the Devil, thereby condemning themselves to death (Cohn, 1975; Jackson, 1995; Sebald, 1990).

Lloyd (1992) recently showed how commonly used conversational interaction patterns during interrogations between child protection workers and children that they suspect of being sexually abused can easily, although inadvertently, prompt a child's false confirmation of abuse because of the adult's authority and the child's resultant susceptibility to coercion. The elaborate accounts of some children of victimization by adults in satanic cults are probably the result of the same interrogation techniques. (See Nathan & Snedeker, 1995, for detailed evidence of this interpretation of children's SRA accounts.) Some cognitive psychologists have suggested that the memory recovery techniques employed by some therapists to uncover so-called repressed memories of childhood sexual abuse are the means by which false memories are elicited (Lindsay & Read, 1994; Loftus, 1993). The label "memory recovery" technique encompasses a very wide range of specific practices. A study by cognitive psychologists Lindsay and Read, (1994) related the scientific research on memory processes to the therapy processes employed to uncover so-called "repressed" memories and came to the conclusion that these techniques were those most likely to produce false memories. Some of the practices include hypnosis, guided imagery, and visualization exercises (suggesting to patients to imagine and visualize certain scenarios), stream-of-consciousness daily journal writing, interpreting dreams as messages from the unconscious, interpreting physical symptoms as "body memories," and interpreting unconscious memories in a patient's drawings or in the play activity of children. Bottoms et al. (1996) found that psychotherapists who claimed that their patients had memories of SRA were particularly likely to use these techniques. The problem is that these memory recovery techniques easily create behavior resulting from therapists' suggestions (Lindsay & Read, 1994).

Another faulty technique in the investigation of sexual child abuse includes checklists that contain highly ambiguous and broadly applicable "symptoms" in children's behavior. The work of Debbie Nathan, an investigative journalist, and Michael Snedeker, a lawyer who has defended several parents accused of SRA, is particularly informative in this regard. They have presented evidence to show that when child protection workers use these ambiguous checklists, inaccurate suspicions that a child has been sexually victimized are easily prompted. These suspicions then lead legal authorities to make false accusations. Ambiguous checklists of symptoms are also used by some psychotherapists to identify the presumed long-term effects of sexual child abuse on the behavior of adult clients. As was the case with spectral evidence during the witchcraft trials, when authorities rely on faulty indicators, the suspicions of respected authority also lead to the public's presumption of guilt.

Symbolic Resonance

What is the mechanism whereby shared moral beliefs in groups lead to the consensual validation of particular claims and accusations of deviance? The concepts of a master frame and framing processes have been used to study how the ideologies of social movements are linked to the cognitive schema of individual participants (Hunt, Benford, & Snow, 1994; Snow & Benford, 1992; Snow, Rochford, Worden, & Benford, 1986). A master frame functions to organize selective attention to particular problems, to attribute meaning to them, to articulate relevant events and experiences, to explain the underlying causes, and to propose solutions. A demonology cognitively functions like a master frame for interpreting possible threats to people's shared moral values. Claims about a threat from a form of deviance are viewed through the perceptual lens of a culturally shared demonology, especially when there is great ambiguity and little manifest evidence to verify the claims.

I use the concept "symbolic resonance" to indicate that certain claims about threats are symbolically consistent, or resonant, with a demonology and are more likely to be attributed credibility, whereas other claims are ignored and disregarded because they are inconsistent. The symbolic resonance of specific claims with the demonologies of specific groups enables the consensual validation of the reality of those claims within those groups.[2] The dissemination of fearful satanic cult claims and rumors spreads more rapidly through particular social networks in which people share moral beliefs, which, in turn, function as selective conduits for consensual validation (Victor, 1993a). More specifically, the symbolism in claims and rumors about SRA is consistent with the demonologies of three different moral belief systems: Christian traditionalist, radical feminist, and social conservative.

Proponents of Christian traditionalist demonology regard the ultimate cause of evil as being due to the activities or working of Satan. In this frame, satanists are seen as being actual agents of Satan, who are trying to spread immorality of all kinds in order to destroy the moral order of American society and hasten Satan's takeover of the world. The logic is that if good people are working for God, then evil people must be working for Satan. Satanic cult crime is seen simply as being one manifestation of the conspiratorial work of Satan and his earthly followers. Thus SRA is one more example of the growing moral corruption in American society by evil people who reject God and true Christianity (Jenkins, 1992; Jenkins & Maier-Katkin, 1992; Lippert, 1990; Victor, 1994).

There are different feminist ideologies. Some stress socioeconomic class inequality as the essential destructive force or "evil" in society. Other forms of feminism stress a demonology in which patriarchy (male power dominance) and its exploitation of women and children function as the essential destructive force in society. This "radical" (for lack of a better label) feminism frames SRA in terms of an analogy with the victimization of women by male sexual aggressions, as in cases of rape, incest, and sexual harassment. In this moral belief system, SRA is seen as one more example of the many kinds of hidden sexual exploitation of women and children by patriarchy (Nathan, 1991; Nathan & Snedeker, 1995; Victor, 1993a). Skepticism about accusations of SRA is regarded as being one more attempt by men to discredit women and children's testimony about their sexual victimization. The anomaly that many of the people accused of SRA are mothers or female child care workers is ignored or is attributed to male manipulations.

According to social-conservative views of demonology, "liberal permissiveness" is the underlying cause of most moral evils. In this frame,

---

[2]In other words, people who share a moral belief system are likely to selectively define certain purported threats and not others as ones to be taken seriously by society. This principle does not deny that moral beliefs are often used to justify group interests in wealth, power, or prestige. This principle also does not deny that many people's critical thinking ability leads them to be skeptical about claims that are consistent with their moral beliefs. However, it is quite another matter to be able to challenge the conformity pressures that enforce consensual beliefs within one's social networks.

"ritualistic" crime is seen as being caused by the hedonistic pursuit of pleasure and the increasing climate of moral permissiveness, which has its source in the so-called moral anarchy of the 1960s. Currently, for example, many psychotherapists identify themselves ideologically as being either "Christian therapists," or "feminist therapists" (Goleman, 1991). There are no survey data on the ideologies of psychotherapists who attribute credibility to their patients' accounts of SRA. However, several researchers have found anecdotal evidence that psychotherapists who make claims about SRA, or are involved in lawsuits concerning their patients' accounts of SRA, disproportionately profess these ideologies (Jenkins, 1992; Nathan, 1991; Nathan & Snedeker, 1995; Victor, 1994). Among police "Satan hunters," the social conservative and Christian fundamentalist ideologies are common (Hicks, 1991).

NEGOTIATING A SHARED DEFINITION OF REALITY IN PSYCHOTHERAPY

The social interaction between psychotherapists and their patients involves a mutual negotiation of a shared definition of the situation, as is true in any face-to-face interaction. Both therapist and patient play social roles and both struggle to negotiate expectations for the interaction. The joint concern that brings them together is the need for an explanation for the patient's emotional pain. On one hand, the therapist struggles to prove his or her competence in relieving emotional pain. On the other hand, the patient struggles with the dilemma of dependence on an authority figure who may or may not be worthy of his or her trust. The self-presentations and interpersonal strategies of both are always guided, in part, by these concerns.

Patients who present themselves to therapists as victims of SRA do so through the process of "ostension," a term coined by folklore scholars. The process of ostension involves appropriating a social script from a widely communicated folklore narrative, or rumor story or mass media report, and using it for one's behavior. The process is similar to the copycat appropriation of a script from a movie as a model for one's behavior. The ostension of social scripts from contemporary legends or mass media stories explains how similar satanic cult stories can be heard from people from distant locations, independent of each other. It explains why similar SRA accounts are heard from psychotherapy patients in different countries around the world.

Ostension can sometimes manifest itself as mass imitation. A recent example was the nationwide rash of copycat false reports of syringes and other dangerous objects found in Pepsi-Cola cans. The whole episode was a hoax. Journalists who investigated these incidents reported that, curiously, not even one claim was proven to be true (Toufexis, 1993). Yet, more than 50 false reports were made in at least 23 states. More than a dozen people were arrested for filing false reports, some of whom actually placed objects in Pepsi cans. Their motives varied from the desire to make money from personal injury suits to simple desires for a brief moment of fame via media attention. A forensic psychologist suggested another motive: "Just as some people induce signs of illness in themselves to enjoy the benefits of the patient's role, others fake tampering to enjoy the benefits—emotional support, nurturing—of the victim's role" (Toufexis, 1993, p. 41).

A recent example of ostension demonstrates that even false accusations of incest can be appropriated from social scripts in popular culture. About 50 parents of autistic children across the country were falsely accused of incest, and many of their children were taken away from them by child protection workers and police (Berger, 1994; Rimland, 1992). In these cases, the technique of "facilitated communication" (see chapter 9, this volume) was employed in the belief that autistic children could communicate by using a typewriter if an adult facilitator held their hands. However, later scientific testing proved that the children could not possibly have typed the words of accusation (Hostler, Allaire, & Christoph, 1993). Instead, the facilitators must have made the accusations of incest against the parents. The possible motives of the facilitators are entirely unclear. However, the accusations arose during a time when accusations of sexual child abuse were being sensationalized in the mass media. One may logically speculate that these facilitators appropriated the social script from popular culture that blamed parents for the afflictions of their children.

The SRA accounts offered by psychotherapy patients appear to be another case of ostension, given the lack of evidence for the existence of criminal satanic cults. There are several possible sociocultural explanations for the ways in which stories of satanism become incorporated into these accounts (Victor, 1996).[3] One link between an individual's sociocultural environment and their personal cognition exists in the function of social scripts, such as stories about satanic cult crime, as cognitive scripts (maps, schema) into which fragmentary emotional memories can be integrated and organized. These are four possible explanations for SRA stories:

1. SRA accounts may simply be fearful confabulated memories drawn from a mass media story or local rumor story about a horrific satanic cult crime.
2. SRA accounts may constitute confabulated memories of emo-

---

[3]Evidence of the ostension of SRA stories can be found in interviews with former patients who have retracted their previous "memories" of SRA (Goldstein & Farmer, 1992; Gondolf, 1992; Nelson & Simpson, 1994). Evidence can also be found in forensic psychology case studies, in which researchers have investigated the origins of some patients' SRA memories (Coleman, 1992; Ganaway, 1991; Rogers, 1992).

tional pain from parental neglect, separation from parents, or even conflict between parents—memories that are then distorted and embedded in the symbolism of a social script about satanic cult victimization of children.

3. SRA accounts may be confabulated memories of actual sexual victimization perpetrated during childhood by an adult, whether a stranger or parent, and then embedded in the symbolism of a social script about satanic cult victimization of children.

4. SRA accounts may be consciously fabricated from materials from the mass media and local rumor stories.

What possible incentive (or reward) could a psychotherapy patient possibly seek for telling bizarre, horrific tales, accusing their parents of crimes that did not actually occur? The reward arises from suggestion effects.[4] Initially, SRA accounts are offered to psychotherapists in a very tentative way. The stories are not told all in one piece at the beginning of therapy. If a patient perceives that he or she has received some degree of validation from the therapist for an account hinting at SRA victimization, then SRA stories are likely to be told more easily, frequently, and dramatically. If the therapist is publicly known to believe in SRA accounts, or if the therapist engages in suggestive questioning, a patient is even more likely to offer SRA accounts to please the therapist. The emotional satisfaction gained by a patient is the ability to please the therapist. Suggestion effects commonly occur in response to people in positions of authority, especially if the authority is a psychotherapist (Frank, 1973; Milgram, 1974; Spanos, 1996).

A related incentive for false testimonials of SRA is that these accounts enable patients to play a very dramatic victim role, much like playing the sick role. It enables patients to gain attention, care, and sympathy. (A sociological analysis of the mass adoption of the sick role in outbreaks of unusual collective behavior can be found in Gehlen, 1977. See also, Bartholomew, 1990 and 1994, for an up-to-date reinterpretation of "mass psychogenic illness" and "hysterical contagion", from a cross-cultural, an-

---

[4]Variations of this interaction effect are referred to as the placebo effect, experimenter effects, expectancy effects, the Hawthorne effect and demand characteristics. What essentially happens in suggestion effects is that a subject (or patient) responds to a question, experiment, or research study by giving the questioner what the subject perceives the questioner wants to find (Rosenthal, 1966). The underlying motivation of the subject is to please the authority figure and to "look good" in the light of assumed evaluation. Frank (1973) observed that "belief" is central to the effectiveness of psychotherapy, as much as it is to the effectiveness of the priest or minister. A psychotherapist's power to help a patient depends on the patient's expectations for the therapist. It is the patient's faith, trust, and confidence in a therapist that gives a therapist "power" to influence the patient. Even an empirically false explanation can have a placebo effect and reduce the anxiety generated by the patient's uncertainty over the origins of his or her emotional pain, at least temporarily (Frank, 1973). A mistaken explanation for emotional pain can be preferable for a confused person to the ambiguity of uncertainty.

thropological perspective.) In recent years, the victim role has been trans-formed into one of public heroism, as compared with private sorrow. Vast numbers of Americans are currently seeking to validate their victimization in one 12-step program or another, or one survivors group or another. Some of these groups promote the notion that many people's vaguely defined emotional turmoil is due to repressed memories of victimization by inces-tuous parents (or, perhaps, satanic cults). SRA support groups and even sympathetic friendship networks can function to reinforce false memories of victimization. The persistence of confidence in the accuracy of false memories is more likely if a person repeatedly rehearses the cognitive im-agery of those false memories and when that rehearsal is cued and sup-ported by other people (Lindsay & Read, 1994).

CONCLUSION

The basic thesis of this chapter is that collective belief in stories about imaginary dangerous deviants become false memories of victimization through the social processes of ostension and interpersonal influence. In a nutshell, social scripts from popular culture are adopted by individuals as cognitive schemas for organizing their fragments of memory. There are now many hundreds of people in the United States who have had false mem-ories of being victimized by their parents in satanic cult rituals.[5] Their accounts are offered by credulous psychotherapists as the primary evidence for the existence of SRA in the absence of any external corroborating evidence.

An understanding of the social processes that lead to the creation of false memories of SRA is useful for understanding the creation of other false memories, such as those of being abducted by aliens from UFOs, having encounters with Yeti and other fantastic creatures, and being sex-ually victimized as a child.

My perspective is one in which psychotherapy is invested in the larger sociocultural system, rather than being an isolated relationship that is somehow sheltered from the surrounding society. Accounts of SRA offered by patients emerge out of the reciprocal interaction between patient as help-seeker and therapist as helping authority. Both are influenced by social

[5]No national survey is available to provide accurate estimates of the numbers of psychotherapy patients who have accused their parents of SRA. However, a national survey of APA member clinical psychologists by Bottoms, Shaver, and Goodman (1996) found that the psychologists reported seeing 1228 cases of adult patients that they identified as being victims of ritual child abuse. In terms of criminal court cases, a legal survey done by the False Memory Syndrome Foundation of criminal cases involving allegations of child sexual abuse made by adults on the basis of recovered memories offers some useful data. A legal survey done in September, 1996, found that out of 78 criminal cases in the United States from 1989 through early 1996, 60% (47 cases) involved allegations of ritual abuse (FMSF, personal communication, September, 1996).

forces in the society in which they live. According to this perspective, SRA accounts are introduced into psychotherapy interaction from outside of therapy interaction. They arise neither from the personal experience of the patient, or from the deliberate, direct manipulations ("brainwashing") of the therapist. Nevertheless, a psychotherapist who is not attentive to potential suggestion effects and lends credibility to SRA accounts by validating them is the key authority responsible for facilitating the creation of false memories.

The social interaction between psychotherapist and patient, which results in a patient's belief that he or she has experienced SRA, is a microcosm of the social dynamics in the larger society. Authority figures interpret ambiguous accounts of experience and associated emotional expression and attribute meanings to them. If authority figures lend credibility to one particular interpretation, such as SRA, people who accept that authority as a source of their understanding reality easily come to believe that interpretation. Fortunately, in the larger society there are usually competing authorities and therefore competing versions of reality.

REFERENCES

Andrews, B., Morton, J., Berkerian, D., Brewin, C., Davies, G., & Mollon, P. (1995, May). The recovery of memories in clinical practice: Experiences and beliefs of British Psychological Society practitioners. *The Psychologist*, 209–214.

Bartholomew, R. E. (1990). Ethnocentricity and the social construction of 'mass hysteria'. *Culture, Medicine and Psychiatry*, 14, 455–495.

Bartholomew, R. E. (1994). Tarantism, dancing mania and demonopathy: the anthro-political aspects of 'mass psychogenic illness'. *Psychological Medicine*, 24, 281–306.

Bayer, R. (1987). *Homosexuality and American psychiatry*. Princeton, NJ: Princeton University Press.

Beckett, K. (1996). Culture and the politics of signification: The case of child sexual abuse. *Social Problems*, 43(1), 57–76.

Ben-Yehuda, N. (1981). The European witch craze of the 14th to 16th centuries: A sociologist's perspective. *American Journal of Sociology*, 86, 1–31.

Berger, J. (1994, February 12). Shattering the silence of autism. *New York Times*, pp. 21, 27.

Best, J. (1989). *Images and issues: Typifying contemporary social problems*. New York: Aldine de Gruyter.

Best, J. (1990). *Threatened children: Rhetoric and concern about child-victims*. Chicago: University of Chicago Press.

Best, J. (1993). But seriously, folks: The limitations of the strict constructionist interpretation of social problems. In G. Miller & J. A. Holstein (Eds.), *Constructionist controversies: Issues in social problems theory* (pp. 109–127). New York: Aldine de Gruyter.

Bottoms, B. L., Shaver, P. R., & Goodman, G. S. (1996). An analysis of ritualistic and religion-related child abuse allegations. *Law and Human Behavior, 20*(1), 1–34.

Campion-Vincent, V. (1990). The baby-parts story: A Latin American legend. *Western Folklore, 49,* 9–26.

Campion-Vincent, V. (1997). *La legend des vols d'organes* [The legend of organ stealing]. Paris: Les Belles Lettres.

Caute, D. (1978). *The great fear.* New York: Simon & Schuster.

Cohen, S. (1972). *Folk devils and moral panics: The creation of mods and rockers.* New York: St. Martin's Press.

Cohn, N. (1975). *Europe's inner demons.* New York: New American Library.

Coleman, L. (1992). Creating "memories" of sexual abuse. *Issues in Child Abuse Accusations, 4*(4), 169–176.

Conrad, P. (1992). Medicalization and social control. *Annual Review of Sociology, 18,* 209–232.

Conrad, P., & Schneider, J. W. (1992). *Deviance and medicalization: From badness to sickness.* Philadelphia: Temple University Press.

Cozolino, L. J. (1989). The ritual abuse of children: Implications for clinical practice and research. *Journal of Sex Research, 26*(1), 131–138.

Cozolino, L. J. (1990). Ritual child abuse, psychopathology, and evil. *Journal of Psychology and Theology, 18*(3), 218–227.

Crouch, B. M., & Damphousse, K. R. (1992). Newspapers and the antisatanism movement: A content analysis. *Sociological Spectrum, 12,* 1–20.

Currie, E. P. (1986). Crimes without criminals: Witchcraft and its control in Renaissance Europe. *Law and Society Review, 3*(1), 7–32.

Ellis, B. (1990). Introduction: Contemporary legends in emergence. *Western Folklore, 49*(1), 1–7.

Feldman, G. C. (1993). *Lessons in evil, lessons from the light.* New York: Crown.

Fewster, G. (Ed.). (1990). In the shadow of Satan [Special issue]. *Journal of Child and Youth Care, 100.*

Fingarette, H. (1988). *Heavy drinking: The myth of alcoholism as a disease.* Berkeley, CA: University of California Press.

Frank, J. D. (1973). *Persuasion and healing: A comparative study of psychotherapy* (Rev. ed.). Baltimore: Johns Hopkins University Press.

Friesen, J. G. (1991). *Uncovering the mystery of MPD.* San Bernardino, CA: Here's Life Publishers.

Ganaway, G. K. (1991, August). Alternative hypotheses regarding satanic ritual abuse memories. Paper presented at the meeting of the American Psychological Association.

Gehlen, F. L. (1977). Toward a revised theory of hysterical contagion. *Journal of Health and Social Behavior, 18*, 27–35.

Goldstein, E., & Farmer, K. (1992). *Confabulations*. Boca Raton, FL: Social Issues Resources Series.

Goleman, D. (1991, September 10). Therapists see religion as aid, not illusion. *New York Times, 10*, C1, C8.

Gondolf, L. P. (1992). Traumatic therapy. *Issues in Child Abuse Accusations, 4*(4), 239–245.

Goode, E. (1993). *Drugs in American society* (4th ed.). New York: McGraw-Hill.

Goode, E., & Ben-Yehuda, N. (1994). *Moral panics: The social construction of deviance*. Cambridge, MA: Blackwell.

Gould, C., & Cozolino, L. J. (1992). Ritual abuse, multiplicity, and mind control. *Journal of Psychology and Theology, 18*(3), 194–196.

Hicks, R. (1991). *In pursuit of Satan*. Buffalo: Prometheus Press.

Hill, S., & Goodwin, G. (1989). Satanism: Similarities between patient accounts and pre-inquisition historical sources. *Dissociation, 2*, 39–43.

Hostler, S. L., Allaire, J. H., & Christoph, R. A. (1993). Childhood sexual abuse reported by facilitated communication. *Pediatrics, 91*(6), 1190–1191.

Howitt, D. (1992). *Child abuse errors: When good intentions go wrong*. New Brunswick, NJ: Rutgers University Press.

Hudson, P. S. (1990). A survey of symptoms and allegations [Special issue]. *Journal of Child and Youth Care, 19*, 27–52.

Hudson, P. S. (1991). *Ritual child abuse: Discovery, diagnosis and treatment*. Sarasota, CA: R & E Publishers.

Hunt, S., Benford, R., & Snow, D. (1994). Identity fields: Framing processes and the social construction of movement identities. In E. Larana, H. Johnson, & J. Gusfield (Eds.), *New social movements: From ideology to identity* (pp. 183–208). Philadelphia: Temple University Press.

Jackson, L. (1995). Witches, wives and mothers: Witchcraft persecutions and women's confessions in seventeenth-century England. *Women's History Review, 4*(1), 63–83.

Jenkins, P. (1992). *Intimate enemies: Moral panics in contemporary Great Britain*. New York: Aldine de Gruyter.

Jenkins, P., & Maier-Katkin, D. (1992). Satanism: Myth and reality in a contemporary moral panic. *Crime, Law and Social Change, 17*, 53–75.

Kelley, S. J. (1988). Ritualistic abuse of children: Dynamics and impact. *Cultic Studies Journal, 5*(2), 228–236.

Kelley, S. J. (1989). Stress responses of children to sexual abuse and ritualistic abuse in day care centers. *Journal of Interpersonal Violence, 4*(4), 502–513.

Kelley, S. J. (1990). Parental stress response to sexual abuse and ritualistic abuse of children in day-care centers. *Nursing Research, 39*(1), 25–29.

Klemke, L. W., & Tiedeman, G. H. (1990). Toward an understanding of false accusations: The pure case of deviant labeling. In C. D. Bryant (Ed.), *Deviant behavior: Readings in the sociology of norm violations* (pp. 266–268). New York: Hemisphere.

La Fontaine, J. S. (1994). *The extent and nature of organized and ritual abuse: Research findings* (United Kingdom Department of Health Report). London: HMSO Publications.

Lanning, K. V. (1992). *Investigator's guide to allegations of "ritual" child abuse.* Quantico, VA: Federal Bureau of Investigation, National Center for the Analysis of Violent Crime.

Levack, B. (1987). *The witch-hunt in early modern Europe.* New York: Longman.

Lindsay, D. S., & Read, J. D. (1994). Incest resolution psychotherapy and memories of childhood sexual abuse: A cognitive perspective. *Applied Cognitive Psychology, 8,* 281–338.

Lippert, R. (1990). The social construction of satanism as a social problem in Canada. *Canadian Journal of Sociology, 15*(4), 417–439.

Lloyd, R. M. (1992). Negotiating child sexual abuse: The interactional character of investigative practices. *Social Problems, 39*(2), 109–124.

Loftus, E. F. (1993). The reality of repressed memories. *American Psychologist, 48*(5), 518–537.

Lopez, L. (1994). Dangerous rumors. *Time,* April 18.

Mayer, R. S. (1991). *Satan's children: Case studies in multiple personality.* New York: Putnam.

McRobbie, A., & Thornton, S. (1995). Rethinking "moral panic" for multi-mediated social worlds. *British Journal of Sociology, 46*(4), 1–17.

Michigan State Police. (1990). *Michigan state police occult survey.* East Lansing: Michigan State Police Investigative Services Unit.

Milgram, S. (1974). *Obedience to authority.* New York: Harper & Row.

Miller, G., & Holstein, J. A. (Eds.). (1993). *Constructionist controversies: Issues in social problems theory.* New York: Aldine de Gruyter.

Morin, E. (1971). *Rumour in Orleans.* New York: Random House.

Mulhern, S. (1991). Satanism and psychotherapy: A rumor in search of an inquisition. In J. T. Richardson, J. Best, & D. G. Bromley (Eds.), *The satanism scare* (pp. 145–172). New York: Aldine de Gruyter.

Mulhern, S. (1994). Satanism, ritual abuse, and multiple personality disorder: A sociohistorical perspective. *The International Journal of Clinical and Experimental Hypnosis, 42*(4), 265–288.

Nathan, D. (1991). Satanism and child molestation: Constructing the ritual abuse scare. In J. Richardson, J. Best, & D. Bromley (Eds.), *The satanism scare* (pp. 75–94). New York: Aldine de Gruyter.

Nathan, D., & Snedeker, M. (1995). *Satan's silence: Ritual abuse and the making of a modern American witch hunt.* New York: Basic Books.

Nelson, E. L., & Simpson, P. (1994). First glimpse: An initial examination of subjects who have rejected their recovered visualizations as false memories. *Issues in Child Abuse Accusations, 6,* 123–133.

Netherlands Ministry of Justice. (1994). *Report of the working group on ritual abuse* (J. W. Nienhuys, Trans.). Den Haag, The Netherlands: Direction of Constitutional and Criminal Law.

Noblitt, J. R., & Perskin, P. S. (1995). *Cult and ritual abuse.* Westport, CT: Praeger.

Ofshe, R., & Watters, E. (1994). *Making monsters: False memories, psychotherapy, and sexual hysteria.* New York: Scribners.

Parr, L. E. (1996). *Repressed memory claims in the crime victims compensation program.* Olympia, WA: Department of Labor and Industries.

Pendergrast, M. (1995). *Victims of memory: Incest accusations and shattered lives.* Hinesburg, VT: Upper Access Books.

Pfohl, S. J. (1977). The "discovery" of child abuse. *Social Problems, 24,* 310–323.

Poole, D., & Lamb, M. (in press). *Interviews of children: A guide for helping professionals.* Washington, DC: American Psychological Association.

Poole, D., Lindsay, D. S., Memon, A., & Bull, R. (1995). Psychotherapy and the recovery of memories of childhood sexual abuse: U.S. and British practitioners' opinions, practices, and experiences. *Journal of Consulting and Clinical Psychology, 63*(3), 426–437.

Richardson, J. T. (1991). Satanism in the courts: From murder to heavy metal. In J. Richardson, J. Best, and D. Bromley (Eds.), *The satanism scare* (pp. 205–220). New York: Aldine de Gruyter.

Rimland, B. (1992). Facilitated communication: Now the bad news. *The Autism Research Review International, 6*(1), 3.

Rockwell, R. B. (1994). One psychiatrist's view of satanic ritual abuse. *Journal of Psychohistory, 21,* 443–460.

Rogers, M. L. (1992, March). A case of alleged satanic ritual abuse. Paper presented at the meeting of the American Psychological Association, Chicago.

Rosenthal, R. (1966). *Experimenter effects in behavioral research.* New York: Appleton-Century-Crofts.

Ross, A. (1994, June). Blame it on the devil. *Redbook,* pp. 86–89, 110, 114, 118.

Ross, C. (1995). *Satanic ritual abuse: Principles of treatment.* Toronto: University of Toronto.

Ryder, D. (1992). *Breaking the circle of satanic ritual abuse.* Minneapolis: CompCare.

Sakheim, D. K., & Devine, S. E. (Eds.). (1992). *Out of darkness: Exploring satanism and ritual abuse.* New York: Lexington Books.

Sebald, H. (1990). Witches' confessions: Stereotypical structure and local color. *Southern Humanities Review, 24*(4), 301–319.

Shaffer, R. E., & Cozolino, L. J. (1992). Adults who report childhood ritualistic abuse. *Journal of Psychology and Theology, 18*(3), 188–193.

Sinason, V. (Ed.). (1994). *Treating survivors of satanic abuse.* New York: Routledge.

Smith, M. (1993). *Ritual abuse: What it is, why it happens, how to help.* New York: Harper-Collins.

Smith, M., & Pazder, L. (1980). *Michelle remembers.* New York: Congdon & Latte.

Snow, D. A., & Benford, R. (1992). Master frames and cycles of protest. In A. Morris & C. Mueller (Eds.), *Frontiers of social movement theory* (pp. 133–135). New Haven, CT: Yale University Press.

Snow, D. A., Rochford, E. B., Worden, S., & Benford, R. (1986). Frame alignment processes, micromobilization, and movement participation. *American Sociological Review, 51,* 464–481.

Spanos, N. (1996). *Multiple identities and false memories: A sociocognitive perspective.* Washington, DC: American Psychological Association.

Stallings, R. A. (1994). Collective behavior theory and the study of mass hysteria. In R. Dynes & K. Tierney (Eds.), *Disasters, collective behavior, and social organization* (pp. 207–228). Newark, DE: University of Delaware Press.

Stevens, P. (1991). The demonology of satanism: An anthropological view. In J. Richardson, J. Best, & D. Bromley (Eds.), *The satanism scare* (pp. 21–40). New York: Aldine de Gruyter.

Toufexis, A. (1993, June 28). A weird case, baby? *Time,* p. 41.

Victor, J. S. (1993a). *Satanic panic: The creation of a contemporary legend.* Chicago: Open Court.

Victor, J. S. (1993b). The sociology of contemporary legends: A review of the use of the concept by sociologists. *Contemporary Legend, 4,* 63–84.

Victor, J. S. (1994). Fundamentalist religion and the moral crusade against satanism: The social construction of deviance. *Deviant Behavior, 15,* 169–198.

Victor, J. S. (1995). Satanic panic update: The dangers of moral panics. *Skeptic, 3*(3), 44–51.

Victor, J. S. (1996). How should stories of satanic cults be understood? *Harvard Mental Health Letter, 12*(6), 8.

Victor, J. S. (in press). Moral panics and the social construction of deviant behavior: A theory and application to the case of ritual child abuse. *Sociological Perspectives.*

Virginia State Crime Commission Task Force. (1991). *Final report of the Task Force Studying Ritual Crime.* Richmond: Virginia State Crime Commission.

Wakefield, H., & Underwager, R. (1994). *Return of the furies: An investigation into recovered memory therapy.* Chicago: Open Court.

Yapko, M. (1994). *Suggestions of abuse: True and false memories of childhood sexual abuse.* New York: Simon & Schuster.

Young, W. C., Sachs, R. G., Braun, B. G., & Watkins, R. T. (1991). Patients reporting ritual abuse in childhood: A clinical syndrome. Report of 37 cases. *Child Abuse and Neglect, 15,* 181–189.

12

THE MYTHIC PROPERTIES OF POPULAR EXPLANATIONS

DONALD P. SPENCE

Popular explanations almost always begin life as partial descriptions that are buttressed by some of the facts and resonate with long-standing beliefs about the way the world works. Some of these explanations stay within the bounds of normal science, get reinforced by increasingly precise observations, and become part of an accepted textbook account. Another set—the alternative explanations that fall outside of normal science—are not reinforced by new data but survive because they offer a comprehensive, often mythic account of unexplained happenings.

Both types of explanations probably start out as believed-in imaginings that tend to go beyond the information given and substitute a persuasive narrative for a jumble of chaotic facts. If the explanation becomes part of normal science, it will gradually amend its account to make room for new observations and boundary conditions. But once a certain synthesis has been achieved, it quickly becomes the official version and crowds other factors out of the picture. Consider the fate of an established treatment in medicine. Even when the approved procedure does not seem to be reducing major symptoms or is apparently making things worse, the treatment story (and its underlying rationale) may seem so persuasive that the patient feels disloyal in merely voicing complaints. Something like this may have happened with the practice of blood letting in the 19th century. Consider how long this procedure persisted in normal medicine despite the many indications that it was doing more harm than good. The few times that blood letting helped to heal the patient were remembered and talked about; the many times that it proved of no benefit were forgotten. It is generally believed that prior to the turn of the century, almost everything that physicians did was of no significant use to the patient. But the doubtful state of the art of medicine mattered less than the fact that the patient was receiving the approved treatment (e.g., bleeding) and was therefore getting an equal chance with all other sufferers—in other words, the best available care. Because the patient was receiving mainstream treatment, he or she was protected from some dubious, alternative medicine that had no popular standing and was probably practiced by poorly trained quacks with dubious moral credentials.

Procedural errors continue to plague us throughout the 20th century. Meehl (1994) has told us that

> several thousand people are today totally blind because they developed the disease called retrolental fibroplasia as a result of being overoxygenated as premature newborns. For twenty years or so, obstetricians and pediatricians debated hotly the merits of this allegedly "prophylactic" procedure. It was only when an adequate statistical analysis of the material was conducted by disinterested parties that the question was finally resolved. (pp. 25–26)

Before this comprehensive analysis was carried out, both sides of the controversy invoked their clinical experience and, quite naturally, could always find evidence in their caseload to support their favored position. We can be sure that the story told by those who used too much oxygen did not focus on the risk of blindness but on the advantages that stem from high-tech medical care. Dangers of using midwives instead of fully trained physicians may also have been mentioned, if not emphasized, and frequent use of the word *science* was probably an important part of the explanation. The mere fact that the use of oxygen represented the latest and most advanced mode of treatment was almost certainly an important selling point, building as it did on the assumption that progress in medicine is linear and ever forward.

The history of retrolental fibroplasia brings into relief the important role of science and technology in supporting advances in modern medicine and how easily a story of progress and the latest science can screen out embarrassing facts. A frequent feature of the fashionable treatment story is its popularity; if it is the treatment of choice by highly regarded practitioners, then little more needs to be said. Fashion gets confused with adequacy; if something is practiced by a majority of doctors, then it must be the best medicine. But note that fashion can be highly localized. Surveys of approved treatments tend to show a highly geographic pattern, which suggests that word-of-mouth dominates. What is popular in a particular catchment area (e.g., routine tonsillectomies) may not extend to another if it is more than a certain distance away.

A fashionable treatment story is persuasive for several reasons. First off, it makes patients feel that their illness is understood and that their treatment, now in the hands of science (and therefore good medicine), will proceed along a predicted path and that the outcome is no longer in doubt. Popularity breeds contentment; if everyone else (or at least, a majority of everyone else) is getting the same care, then there is no reason to worry. The fashionable treatment story tends to normalize the patient's complaint and take away the uncertainty (and the lurking danger) that always accompanies the unknown. There is the implied promise that the physician can always benefit by the experience of colleagues and learn from their mistakes. Whether these mistakes are always reported, much less openly discussed, is another question.

We see that the fashionable treatment story helps to dissolve the patient's feeling of isolation and uncertainty. By contrast, a new and untried procedure, with relatively few supporters, may only add to the patient's feeling of isolation and may be rejected for this reason. It would seem that patients may be even more conservative than doctors, and their reluctance to risk alternative forms of treatment may explain why some procedures are used long after their faults are known, and why some new procedures not generally adopted until long after their benefits are realized.

This last outcome describes the treatment history of stomach ulcers in the 20th century. For the greater part of this period, it was thought that ulcers were caused by stress and that the only treatment was rest and relaxation. A bacterial cause was thought unlikely because any organism of that kind would be killed by stomach acids. In 1982, two Australian scientists, Drs. Barry Marshall and Robin Warren, discovered that 80% of their ulcer patients were found to house the bacteria Helicobacter pylori, and they proposed that this organism was the underlying cause of stomach ulcers. The theory was hotly contested even after Marshall and a colleague infected themselves with H. pylori and developed gastritis, an early sign of stomach ulcers. Resistance continued even after other groups found that the elimination of H. pylori by antibiotics could heal the patient's ulcer. Why the stubborn adherence to the conventional theory?

Hindsight would suggest that the reluctance to adopt the new formulation stemmed from the conventional wisdom that no bacteria could survive immersion in stomach acids. What was not realized was that H. pylori generated the enzyme urease, which neutralizes stomach acid and that the form and motor habits of the bacterial organism allows it to penetrate the stomach's protective mucous lining. Now that the organism was identified, it became possible to develop ways of measuring it (including a noninvasive breath test); once identified, it could be treated with the right choice of antibiotics. As the disappearance of H. pylori began to coincide with the disappearance of stomach ulcers, the standard explanation began to change, and the new story was gradually adopted.

TALL TALES

So far we have looked at the fashionable treatment story as it is created by the local authorities. In the hands of treating physicians, it becomes the accepted account of the illness and its removal. But when no accepted explanation is available, the victims quickly begin to formulate their own accounts and these narratives show several distinctive features.

The initial grassroots account makes an attempt to fit words to a new experience, frequently one never seen or heard before (think of the first out-of-body experience or the first report of spaceship abduction) and one that falls outside the belief structures of normal science. Conceptually opaque, it often defies explanation. Either the phenomena are too vague and fleeting to pin down with language or no words are available to capture their unique nature. The combination of these factors makes the victims tend to doubt their own observations, particularly if they disagree with one another, and leaves them unusually vulnerable to local authority. But the authorities, even though they may have more elegant language, may be personally unfamiliar with the target phenomenon.

The result is an information trade-off. Many of the early reports would seem to be ghost-written by local authorities (e.g., journalists, politicians, or knowledgeable professionals) who need to put the experience into words. The victim is more than happy to accept a partial account if it uses language that will make others listen because there is a strong need to be validated and understood. He or she may be willing to sacrifice certain details if no apt language is available. But once a general explanation has been established, this account of the target happening may be remembered in place of the original experience. The power of language is such that a well-crafted narrative can easily displace a more stumbling first-person account that is badly worded and therefore less persuasive.

Very quickly, an official narrative is established, which feeds on the details of the more sensational accounts; these become a kind of media virus that instantly infect all current explanations. The story with the most popular details becomes the one most likely to be believed because truth, under these rules, is governed by what everyone is saying and not by some basic understanding of how the world works.

The most popular grassroots explanation, as it gathers more and more persuasive details, rapidly assumes the form of a myth with its own power to persuade and hold its ground against all kinds of disconfirming evidence. The need for a single, comprehensive account stands out above all else. Early in the *Culture of Narcissism*, Christopher Lasch called our attention to the way in which unremitting self-awareness has become the bane of modern society. People long, he suggested, for the "suspension of self-consciousness." Modern man, "imprisoned in his pseudo-awareness of the self ... would gladly take refuge in an *idée fixe*, a neurotic compulsion, a 'magnificent obsession'—anything to get his mind off his own mind" (1978, pp. 96, 99). Could this be one of the reasons why people are eager to believe in the preposterous, even (or perhaps especially) in the face of no confirming evidence? An exotic and fantastic explanation (think of flying saucers and satanic ritual abuse) may help to counteract the hum-drum nature of daily existence and the constant boredom that roosts inside our own head. We may even prefer an exotic, grassroots account to the prosaic facts of real life; thus the early evidence of a true explanation is suppressed in favor of the more glamorous myth. Claims that the govern-ment is trying to "cover up" the true facts surrounding the UFO landing of 1947 may be seen as another attempt to celebrate the original story and thus keep the mythic and exotic explanation alive.

The mythic explanation, as it feeds on other popular accounts, tends to suppress complicating variations and replace them with a kind of uni-form simplicity. In a recent book by Christopher Bollas (1992) titled *Being a Character: Psychoanalysis and Self-Experience*, the author argued that op-timum mental health demands a tolerance for a variety of inner states. For many people, Bollas suggested, it is easier to do away with the necessary conflicting voices and settle on what he calls a fascistic state of mind— one voice, one thesis. Unanimity of this kind can be found, in extreme cases, by merging with another person; more common examples might in-clude such familiar states as being in love, being absorbed in a piece of work or a hobby, or belonging to a special interest group (stamp collecting or scuba diving). "Given the ordinary unbearableness of this complexity [of modern living]," Bollas wrote, "I think that the human individual partly regresses in order to survive, but this retreat has been so essential to human life that it has become an unanalyzed convention, part of the religion of everyday life." Could it be that believing in the most correct grassroots explanation provides another way to achieve this uniformity of mind?

A second feature of the popular explanation that is supplied by the victim and crafted in folk psychology is that it provides the sufferer with an all-consuming personal narrative—a new identity. If you are a victim of spaceship abduction or have recovered memories of early child abuse, a single story now dominates your life; your entire existence has been trans-formed and is now invested with a mission. Now that you have become a certain kind of victim, you are eligible to join a highly visible and readily defined group that we all have heard of and can relate to. The new identity, what is more, can never be challenged; more than that, it gives the holder a way of explaining his or her present status, view of life, continuing bad luck, and any number of other features that had formerly seemed baffling and beyond explanation. It may also give him or her a claim to a special kind of distinction; consider the fact that many victims of alien abductions say that they have been specially chosen to donate sperm or eggs to the visitors from outer space. Presumably they were not chosen at random.

We should not lose sight of the fact that the new "identity–explanation–narrative" is remarkably successful—almost invulnerable—as a piece of causal reasoning to explain present unhappiness. Tell someone that you were abused as a child and their attention is immediately captured. From that moment on, they are a slave to your story and will frequently reinforce your reasoning; whatever links you may wish to form between the early abuse and your present condition, their imagination will do your bidding. The more mysterious the initial cause of present unhappiness, the quicker our imagination sets to work spinning out its possible effect. (We may also be secretly congratulating ourselves that we are not in the victim's shoes and in our efforts to be charitable and sympathetic, we may grant them lapses in reasoning that we would probably not allow under other circumstances.)

Not only are the stories mysterious and compelling, they are also frequently impossible to argue with because acts of seduction or abduction, almost by definition, take place without witnesses. You may doubt some details of my claim, the survivor may reason, but doubting is all you can do because I was there and you were not. Thus the structure of the average report makes it certain that the survivor's authority can never be challenged. As a participant in some unusual scene from the distant past, he or she gains an authority and a power of persuasion that is simply not present in everyday life. It may be this feature in particular that makes these stories so inviting for those who feel they are never listened to or believed in. It may be that UFO survivors have replaced their day-to-day anonymity with a kind of out-of-this-world notoriety. And we can now see more clearly why reason and argument have so little impact on the details because one of the main reasons for telling an abduction story is to become an authority and, in so doing, become immune to revision, emendation, and second-guessing.

We have seen that the grassroots story tends to turn the victim into an authority: Because the story stands almost entirely on first-person testimony, it becomes very hard to validate. Here is another example of its fascistic nature. If you go to your physician with a symptom that you suspect indicates a stomach ulcer, he or she will listen, make a further examination, and possibly suggest some tests. The final diagnosis emerges as the outcome of the complete pattern of evidence, and, as each new piece is added, it reinforces the certainty in the outcome. What has begun as an hypothesis gradually turns into a certainty; with all the evidence in agreement, we can be reasonably confident of both diagnosis and treatment.

By contrast, the grassroots account cannot be confirmed in this piecemeal manner because it does not emerge from a fabric of interlocking observations, and because it is usually an amalgam of the sensational and the respectable. UFO abductions leave no visible scars; childhood sexual abuse tends to leave no physical traces. The survivor's narrative carries the full burden of the traumatic event. Not only, as we have seen, are there no witnesses but also it often happened so long ago that all physical signs have since disappeared. The physician is thus left with no bone scans to conduct, no blood samples to be evaluated; the survivor is left with only the one story to tell. Perhaps for this reason, each time the survivor tells the story it tends to acquire new features as he or she tries to make the story more persuasive and more complete.

Not only does the recognized expert—the physician or therapist—have no way of confirming the account but also because the grassroots story turns the survivor into an authority, the usual roles are reversed. The expert, who has lost most of his or her influence, now becomes the novice and has little to offer the patient except support and agreement. The stage is set for a disturbing unspoken pact with the following implicit message: If you agree with my story and don't cause too much trouble, I'll keep coming and pay your fees. But if you make trouble and ask embarrassing questions (or require uncomfortable tests, etc.), I'll seek help elsewhere. Once this contract has been established, the grassroots story has been accepted by both parties, and the way is open for supporting details to be uncovered. Doubtful memories can be brought to light and thereby reinforced, and, in the most extreme case, patient and therapist are competing to see who can add the latest twist to the explanatory narrative. As it becomes more embellished, it tends to dominate the discussion and even spread to other venues as this or that detail attracts attention and becomes embedded in new accounts.

MYTHIC CONTENT

It would seem that grassroots tales have certain formal features that distinguish them from the more evidential accounts that grow out of laboratory investigation. The grassroots account, first of all, tends to show a certain uniformity across different accounts, and the basic story line tends to assume a kind of mythic simplicity that leaves out complicating details, troubling subplots, and the variability always generated by individual differences. Second, it provides the teller with a new identity, often making the teller an instant authority and as a result, the traditional roles of patient and doctor tend to get reversed. Third, it gives the victim an explanation that cannot be challenged.

What can be said about the content of some of the more popular grassroots explanations? In a recent article about reports by UFO survivors, Newman and Baumeister (1996) have reminded us that in the average story, the victim is a helpless captive of a superior force. What is more, the stories are dominated by the loss of self. In any number of stories, the individual feels that after being abducted, he or she has lost a sense of individuality or uniqueness. It is tempting to argue that this theme of helplessness and loss of control may be a metaphor for our current social condition. It is common knowledge that established structures such as family, church, and profession are losing their influence; as a result, the nature of present life and future existence, particularly in this era of downsizing, becomes increasingly unpredictable. As new diseases emerge, or threaten to emerge, and as established drugs and other medical procedures seem to lose their effectiveness, our sense of mortality is significantly affected. Could it be that many of these fears are encapsulated in the current grassroots explanation for such things as UFO abductions and recovered memories of early child abuse?

There is an interesting difference between current UFO accounts and what was claimed in the 1950s and 1960s, and the change may give us another reason to see the current stories as metaphors for our current condition. Newman and Baumeister made clear how the earlier reports were more benevolent, all-knowing, and supportive. Even if many of these early victims were deliberate hoaxers, as the authors asserted, their stories can still be read as projections of the cultural and political conditions obtaining at the time. The Eisenhower and Kennedy years were marked by a strong sense of certainty about the future and the reassuring feeling that America was still the strongest nation on earth. The dollar was still strong, inflation had been kept in check, the population was still relatively small, and the established structures of church and family were still intact. As the political and cultural climate have changed in the intervening years, the abduction stories have become more ominous and more focused on helplessness and loss of identity.

Particularly striking is the way in which both sets of scenarios portray the victim as helpless and vulnerable to the influence of a superior being (parent or alien). Both flying saucer reports and recovered memories of early child abuse are dominated by a loss of choices; by a sense of powerlessness, immobility and indoctrination; and by a sense of inevitability and loss of control. If free will has become too much of a burden in modern life, it may be a relief to be turned into a prisoner (or a child) and reduced to obeying orders. A close study of the population that believes in recovered memories of early child abuse or UFO abduction might reveal that the people in that population have an unusually low tolerance for modern-day hassles and a predominant sense that the support system is often just out of reach.

By this way of thinking, victims' stories may provide the kind of escape from freedom that Erich Fromm (1941) identified in the Germany of the 1930s, and many features of his analysis of democracy and authoritarianism can be applied to our current situation. Fromm began by arguing (at a time when World War II had already begun) that "the crisis of democracy is not a peculiarly Italian or German problem, but one confronting every modern state" (p. 5). Is there, he wondered, "an instinctive wish for submission?" (p. 6). Fromm was one of the first social critics to identify the oppressive burden of freedom that often leads to what he called the "first mechanism of escape . . . the tendency to give up the independence of one's own individual self and to fuse one's self with somebody or something outside" (p. 141). He identified the unbearable feelings of aloneness and insignificance that could overpower contemporary people and argues that these could be overcome by an annihilation of the individual self in the course of becoming part of an external power—such as an institution or a nation. "One surrenders one's own self and renounces all strength and pride connected with it, one loses one's integrity as an individual and surrenders freedom; but one gains a new security and a new pride in the participation of the power in which one submerges" (p. 156).

BELIEVED-IN IMAGININGS

We have seen how certain kinds of grassroots explanations have the power to make us see the world differently and behave accordingly. What is sanctioned by the popular account gradually becomes the way things are. What is believed in can no longer be called imaginary but now becomes a piece of our everyday reality that may dictate who gets reimbursed for treatment, who gets trained in particular techniques, and who gets grant support for research.

Grassroots accounts, it would seem, tend to spring up when no competing explanation is available, and this rule appears to operate both inside and outside of normal science. Early explanations of ulcers and retrolental fibroplasia relied as much on popular folklore as on replicated science. What stands out are the features that many of these popular explanations have in common, and further detailed study of flawed explanations may sensitize us to their telltale clues and mythic features.

It would also appear that we cannot tolerate the absence of explanation: If the authorities have nothing to say about a newly appearing symptom or disease, the sufferers will quickly generate a useful account. When a background network of useful (and widely validated) observations is in short supply (and this is always the case in the early stages of a new public health danger), the grassroots account will show many of the features of established myths—simplified story line, little allowance for individual differences, and a comprehensive explanation that goes beyond the data given and resonates with an underlying cultural preoccupation. Consider how the right and left hemispheres of the brain were discussed by three different countries in the 19th century:

> In Germany, united for the first time under the Prussian bureaucracy, most scientists described the brain as a set of functionally distinct departments; English medical writers, confronted with the psychiatric consequences of a class-based society, worried how the rational cortex could control lower, more primitive elements of the central nervous system. It was only in France, especially in the uncertain early years of the Third Republic, that anti-Catholic liberal scientists were determined to show that civilization and rationality resided necessarily on the Left, while decadence and mysticism were on the Right. (Pauley, 1988, p. 422).

We have also seen that many of the more popular grassroots accounts seem to provide the holders of these accounts with another kind of escape from freedom—an alternative identity that is shared with millions and protects them from the burden of finding his or her own way in the world. If explanation is only part of their function, they we can understand why the appeal to better science will not put a stop to the wilder explanations because they are motivated by a need to establish a recognizable identity and thus escape from the anonymity of modern society.

We may also want to postulate some kind of balance between normal science and popular explanation. This kind of division of labor may parallel the balance between individual and federal forms of democracy. Grassroots explanations clearly belong to the people (although often ghost-written by the authorities) and represent the longstanding voice of American populism; normal science, in contrast, belongs to the establishment—the authorities—and is somewhat elitist and antipopular. As explanations become more rooted in the evidence (more "scientific"), they also begin to lose their mythic grandeur and as a corollary, their popular appeal. They necessarily become more complicated, surrounded by more qualifying conditions, and their language changes from mythic pronouncements, understood by all, to technical jargon that defies comprehension (consider quantum mechanics). As the explanation becomes more technical, it is less useful as an alternative identity, a liberating escape from freedom. As the story is taken away from the victims, more power flows into the hands of the authorities and the victim becomes more dependent on their technical wizardry.

Could it be that we are constantly seeking new signs and symptoms to support the kind of grassroots story that everyone can share and that as each explanation is normalized and turned into standard science, a new symptom springs up, crying out for explanation? This line of reasoning would suggest that at any one time, there needs to be a certain number of unexplained symptoms and their explanations circulating in the popular press which provide just enough mystery to baffle the authorities and keep some kind of power in the hands of the victim. We may find that the balance between explained and unexplained symptoms tends to remain constant and that the world need a certain level of wonderment on its horizon at any one time. Perhaps we should extend this rule to include accidents as well; by this way of thinking, the story of TWA Flight 800 is on a par with some stories of early child abuse. Popular grassroots accounts have developed to explain each of these mysteries and will probably remain current until each mystery is laid to rest or until a minimum number of mysteries have been generated. One mystery may substitute for another, and we might find that after the TWA crash in July of 1996, there was a significant decrease in the number of recovered memories of child abuse; in other words, the onset of a new mystery somehow preempted the appetite for the old (and somewhat timeworn) puzzlements. Or, applying the same line of reasoning, we might find that juries' verdicts in child abuse cases turned somewhat more negative, finding against the defendant, after the TWA disaster; in other words, they were less impressed by one mystery because another had come along to take its place.

If there is a constant need for a certain number of non-normal explanations, it may be related to the need to maintain a fixed level of awe and mystery in our everyday life. This description would apply to the conspiracy theories surrounding the TWA crash and the Oklahoma bombings and the satanic ritual and the multiple personality chapters of the child abuse stories. It may be the exotic elements in these explanations that last the longest because they supply a kind of cosmic mystery that is missing from most accounts in normal science. Some of this mystery was once supplied by standard religious traditions and practices; now that this part of our society is losing its importance, we may find more mystery in the way we talk about everyday life. But as normal science becomes more exotic (consider the 1997 Mars landing), the balance may shift again and some of our more mysterious grassroots explanations may start to disappear.

The point to keep in mind is that the universe of exotic explanations probably determines the fate of any one set of imaginings. Normal science teaches us that explanations stand or fall on the evidence but we are now beginning to learn that the fate of any one grassroots account may ride on the level of mystery in the cultural atmosphere. We may need to keep this level within certain fixed limits—neither too much nor too little. Grassroots explanations will flourish if there are no other mechanisms (e.g., established religious traditions) for supplying a certain level of awe and wonder; on the other hand, grassroots explanations may start to disappear if we are suddenly confronted by too many Oklahoma bombings. And time may take its toll. Faced by too many mysterious explanations, we may stop believing in those that have been with us for the longest because they are now out of fashion and have served their purpose.

In the final analysis, we need to remember that grassroots explanations are only data driven to a certain degree. We have seen that they do much more than merely explain; not only do they seem to provide a new identity to those in need but they may also be sensitive to how much mystery we need to incorporate in our daily life. Complete understanding can only come by studying the larger community of explanations. Membership in this community gives us a way of understanding why one set of imaginings will come into existence, flourish for a certain period, and then die out to be supplanted by a new set of beliefs. Careful study of this community will take some of the mystery out of the grassroots explanation and perhaps give us a better way of understanding their rise and fall. By coming to understand the role of mystery in our working lives, we may end up being less perplexed by the ever-emerging, sometimes baffling, always unexpected grassroots explanation, which, it seems certain, will always be with us.

REFERENCES

Bollas, C. (1992). *Being a character: Psychoanalysis and self experience.* New York: Hill and Wang.

Fromm, E. (1941). *Escape from freedom.* New York: Rinehart.

Lasch, C. (1978). *The culture of narcissism.* New York: Norton.

Meehl, P. E. (1994). Subjectivity in psychoanalytic inference. *Psychoanalysis and Contemporary Thought, 17,* 3–82.

Newman, L. S., & Baumeister, R. F. (1996). Toward an explanation of the UFO abduction phenomenon. *Psychological Inquiry, 7,* 99–126.

Pauley, P. (1988). Review of Anne Harrington's "Medicine, mind and the double brain." *Science, 239,* 422.

13

IMAGININGS OF PARENTHOOD: ARTIFICIAL INSEMINATION, EXPERTS, GENDER RELATIONS, AND PATERNITY

JILL G. MORAWSKI

Human reproduction is considered a natural act and scientific fact, yet even this apparently secure feature of the world can be altered by imaginings. Cases are not uncommon of women who believe they are pregnant (and who even display a growing abdomen) when they are not; there are women who think they are not pregnant, disregarding their changing body and ultimately seeking medical attention for stomach ailments when the problem is labor pain. Less definitive instances of imaginings about reproduction occur in men: men who think they are the father of a child when they are not, and those who believe they are not the father when they are. For women, the ultimate arrival or nonarrival of a child brings these imaginings to an end. For men, the only certain check against these imaginings is the recently developed technology of genetic screening.

For much of the 20th century, a medical procedure known as artificial insemination by donor sperm (AID) has incorporated some practices that have accented the ambiguity of paternity. These practices, I propose, have enabled infertile husbands whose wives underwent AID to have believed-in imaginings of fatherhood. My claim relies upon Sarbin's working definition of believed-in imaginings: "to believe in one's imaginings is to conduct oneself as if the imaginings had the credibility that is given to constructions that have their antecedents in publicly observed ecological events" (1983, p. 170).

The credible beliefs about reproduction normally are those derived from scientific knowledge; by contrast, believed-in imaginings about reproduction such as false pregnancy or polyspermy tend to draw upon claims about reality found in folk wisdom, science fiction, or personal fantasy (generally called delusions). The case of men who imagined themselves to be biological fathers of children produced through AID gained support not from these latter sources of knowledge but rather largely from the very authorities of science, namely members of the medical community. This case of believed-in imagining, then, lends a twist to our general presuppositions about the antithesis of scientific knowledge and imaginary beliefs. It also reveals how so-called facts of paternity arise and are modified through social and political negotiations, not simply through the findings of science. Changing notions of paternity that have arisen because of new reproductive technologies that are intimate changes in what we take to be fatherhood.

In this chapter I provide a historical review of practices associated with artificial insemination to provide evidence of two particular underappreciated features of believed-in imaginings. First, the subject of AID illustrates how individuals can and do occupy places between imagined and publicly consensual beliefs, an in-between zone of action that needs to be further explored. Second, the case of AID indicates that gender can be a crucial component of believed-in imaginings. In his definitional essay, Sarbin stated that there are two kinds of conditions that influence a person to "participate in the imagined formation of a new identity": situational "cognitive strain" and biographical experiences that promote "the acquisition of skill in shifting from one perspective to another" (1983, pp. 182–183). The imaginal role of biological father that was available to some AID fathers undoubtedly was facilitated by these two conditions. But it was bolstered also by gender, specifically by the social fact that paternity is chosen (or decreed) and is not a simple, natural given.

In order to assess the special circumstances of men whose wives have borne children by means of AID, it is necessary first to comprehend the historical context of reproductive knowledge in the modern world. With that background, I proceed to describe the medical practices surrounding AID and especially the conditions that have enabled men's believed-in imaginings about paternity. In the conclusion I return to consider both the status of scientific authority, the ambiguous zone between belief and the imaginary, and the implications of gender.

THE ROLE OF SPERM IN ARTIFICIAL INSEMINATION

In the genetics-obsessed construal of human nature that is coming to figure so centrally in our contemplations, especially with promises of genetic control (Keller, 1992; Nelkin & Lindee, 1995), we forget the recency of our knowledge about genes and reproduction. As Jennifer Terry described the present, "We are now living in the age of the magical sign of the gene" (1997, p. 281). Prior to the mid-19th century, there existed multiple theories about generation.[1] By the 1840s the scientific community concurred that sperm and egg both contributed to reproduction, although the nature of that contribution was not clear until the acceptance of Weismann's theory of heredity in the early 20th century, a theory that also displaced assertions that the sperm dissolved in the egg or that egg and sperm fused into a new form (see Cole, 1930; Farley, 1982).[2] Despite the recency of knowledge about reproduction, and the oscillations of diverse and sometimes contradictory scientific ideas, paternity has been long established as a social fact. Modern science was unnecessary to the acknowledgment that the male seed, spermatozoa as we now call it, is alienable from its possessor. Given the alienability of a man from his reproductive material, paternity, until very recent times, was deduced, claimed, and believed on social terms. As Mary O'Brien noted: "It is hard to grasp, given the immense and visible parcel in which man-made history has packaged the idea of paternity, that paternity is in fact an abstract idea. It rests very specifically on theory, not unified immediately with practice" (1981, pp. 29–30). Paternity, through custom and law, has existed through a set of rules or what O'Brien called "relations of trust" between men and women and among men (1981, pp. 53–54).[3]

Finally, part of the history of human reproduction entails efforts to modify, enhance, or otherwise control generation. Regarding the engineering of insemination, there is a formal account of this history, told and retold by scientists and historians alike. In the first reported successful human artificial insemination—conception realized through means other than coitus—a husband's sperm was artificially inseminated by the British physician John Hunter in the late 18th century, and the first such operation

---

[1]For example, the "ovists" claimed that the egg gives rise to the offspring; men were thought to be incidental to reproduction, and some scientists conjectured that sperm were parasites or that seminal fluid simply was a stimulant for egg development. By contrast, "spermists" hypothesized that sperm is constitutive of the developing fetus, and some of them claimed to have observed the fully formed human in a sperm.

[2]Even in the face of this new knowledge about reproduction, scientists as eminent as Jacques Loeb experimented with "artificial parthenogenesis" in the early 20th century, attempting to generate life without the contribution of sperm (Pauly, 1987). Recent scientific reports of cloning in mammals also intimate the dispensability of sperm, yet most popular accounts pass over this feature of cloning technology.

[3]Roof (1996) has argued, using Lacanian theory, that reproductive technologies undermine the established connections between the symbolic laws and the law, thus freeing women from that symbolic ordering of human relations.

in the United States was performed by Dr. Marion Sims in the 1860s. The first recorded case of artificial insemination (conducted by a professional) with donor sperm occurred in 1884 but was not publicly reported until 25 years later (Hard, 1909). Consistent with the abstract and socially determined yet ambiguous nature of paternity, this case provoked speculations about the donor. Fifty-five years after the account was published (the account was written not by the performing physician but by a man who was a medical student studying under that physician at the time), an article in a prestigious medical journal claimed that the author of the 1909 account, that is, the medical student was himself the donor (Gregoire & Mayer, 1965).[4]

By the 1930s artificial insemination was described in medical textbooks and journal articles, in which physicians routinely reported their technical innovations and success rates.[5] The procedure ultimately gained acceptance: A 1941 survey of the practices of 7,642 U.S. physicians reported 9,489 successful inseminations of which 3,649 used donor sperm (Seymour & Koerner, 1941). In 1987 the Congress's Office of Technology Assessment (1988) conducted a similar survey of 1,558 physicians and 30 commercial sperm banks: These data show a 300% increase in the five years between 1982 and 1987.[6] Within this century, AID has become an established practice available to couples in which the man has impaired fertility and to women who seek conception without a male partner.

HISTORICAL CONCERNS ABOUT ARTIFICIAL INSEMINATION

From the earliest reports, the medical community's interest in AID extended beyond diagnosis and technique: articles were devoted to moral, legal, aesthetic, social, and psychological aspects of the procedure. In the early years, the propriety of a stranger (physician) introducing an alien substance (donor sperm) into a female patient's body was controversial, leading a few physicians to develop procedures that circumvented these so-called aesthetic problems (Davis, 1923). Most of their attention, however, fixed on legalities, notably the questions of whether or not AID constituted adultery, whether or not the resultant child was a legitimate offspring of the husband, and whether or not physicians performing the operation were legally liable for the consequences of that medical act. Prior to World War II almost as much space in medical articles was devoted to these legalities

---

[4]Hard (1909) reported that at the time of insemination, neither husband nor wife were informed that donor semen was used. The physician later told the husband.

[5]Although commercially produced and marketed devices, "impregnators," were available to the general populace as early as the 1870s (Marsh & Ronner, 1996), the growing professional literature indicated a trend toward the medicalization of artificial insemination.

[6]The OTA sample alone indicated that 172,000 women underwent artificial insemination in a 12th-month period (1986–1987) resulting in 75,000 births (30,000 of which were AID).

as to scientific analyses and techniques. Medical advocates writing between 1930 and 1970s characterized AID as a means toward a healthy marriage, a women's realization of her biological drive, and a man's experience of fatherhood.

Empirical studies of AID couples corroborated these benefits. The psychological complications resulting from AID were scrutinized. Regarding the wife, it was observed that disgust and guilt may be experienced, and even a sense of having committed adultery. Some physicians suggested a medical corrective to these psychological reactions: injection of donor sperm into the seminal vesicle of the husband who would soon after engage in coitus with his wife. By so inseminating the husband, "the source of the spermatozoa may be revealed or not, at the discretion of the husband, although in studies of our cases, the written consent of both husband and wife has always been obtained" (Stepita, 1933, p. 450).

Regarding the husband, the psychological reactions were held to consist of two sorts, those related to his sterility and those directly connected with AID. It was believed that sterile men experienced guilt—for being the cause of the couple's infertility—as well as feelings of inadequacy and inferiority. The latter feelings derived not only from a failure to beget a child (a desire acknowledged as less powerful than women's drive toward maternity), but feelings of inadequacy also were accentuated by the cultural association of virility with fertility. By the 1940s these psychological conjectures were codified in the psychoanalytic writings of Helene Deutsch (1945; see also Schellen, 1957).[7] Although some physicians warned that AID should not be undertaken in cases where the husband's interest was an attempt to escape the self-accusations of inferiority, many writers promoted AID as being therapeutic for sterile men. Not only would AID enhance his wife's "admiration for his broadmindedness," claimed Drs. Seymour and Koerner in 1936, but the husband "sublimates his feelings and raises the child even more carefully than he would raise his own" (pp. 1532–1533).

Psychological matters seemed to haunt these authors, for in most of their writings, even the ostensibly technical ones, they also enumerated (through anecdote or guarded speculation) mental entanglements that potentially could result from AID. Do not use the husband's brother as a donor, cautioned some physicians, for although brothers maximize genetic similarities, their participation invites a myriad catastrophes: transference of the wife's affections to the brother; transference of the brother's affections to the wife; marital breakup of the brother and his wife; the brother's later decision to sue for custody of the child; and the disastrous effects of the child's eventually learning the facts of his or her paternity, an inevi-

---

[7]These writings are most explicit in describing the fragility of men. As Daniels (1997) has suggested, that fragility is a curious blend of virility—strength and power—and vulnerability—in this case, the vulnerability of both body and masculine psyche.

tability given the number of people who would know about the insemination (Seymour & Koerner, 1936).

Worries about psychic well-being commingled with legal and moral concerns. What if someone tricked the physician or spouse about the source of sperm? What if the husband subsequently denied legitimacy of the child? What if the donor, should anonymity not be maintained, blackmailed the parents or was charged for support? What if the wife disclosed the events? Even authors who did not explicitly address such horrors frequently recounted stories that intimated the duplicitous possibilities attending artificial insemination. The fraudulent dramas that were invoked include an often-cited account of stealing sperm from Arab's stallions in the 14th century; wives who tried to received AID without the husband's knowledge; a druggist who filled a prescription capsule with sperm; and doctors who conducted AID without the knowledge of husband or wife (Davis, 1924; Rohleder, 1934).

Throughout these psychological machinations, the well-being of the child received rather sparse consideration.[8] Writers simply asserted that the child would suffer if he or she discovered the nature of his or her creation. With such knowledge, wrote Seymour and Koerner, "The damage to its psychologic make up would be disastrous. An inferiority complex would be set up with a root that psychoanalysis could not destroy and the child's maladjustment to society would result" (1936, p. 1533). Seymour and Koerner's was the first coherent prognosis about the AID child's mental status, and it provided a theory justification for establishing regular guidelines for physicians' delivery of artificial insemination. Although their recommended guidelines were intended to furnish legal safeguards to physicians, they also purportedly served to eliminate or minimize psychic damage. The proposed regulations ensured secrecy about the procedure and likewise protected against the underside of secrecy—the mistrust of all parties that can materialize once the fact of a secret is known (Bok, 1979). The guidelines were designed in anticipation of the most nefarious possibilities. For instance, husband and wife were to be fingerprinted to enable later determination that the sterile man presenting in the office was, indeed, the husband and not another sterile man. To preclude the donor from engaging in blackmail, it was recommended either that wife and donor be hospitalized during the procedure or that the donor deliver his specimen to an address other than the location where the insemination would transpire.

To guarantee legitimacy, Seymour and Koerner (1936) recommended that an obstetrician other than the physician who performed the insemination be used for delivery of the child so that the second doctor could "in all good faith" (p. 1533) name the couple on the birth certificate. They

---

[8]Foremost of the worries about psychological consequences were those concerning the husband. Concerns about the wife—that she could not contain the secret or that she would experience a sense of adultery—were voiced, but rarely were therapeutic interventions proposed.

also suggested that the donor's blood type match the husband's because "There have been recent cases in the New York courts in which an effort has been made to prove the paternity of the child through determination of peculiarities of hereditary characteristics shown by blood grouping" (1936, p. 1533).

Seymour and Koerner's proposal heightened public awareness of AID, mostly through positive sensationalism, and it also marked the codification of concerns about AID into a protocol that was to blur legal, moral, psychological, and professional interests. Over the next 30 years, AID procedures incorporated various safeguards against these anticipated complications. Many of the practices upheld the professed necessity for the secrecy of paternity. In keeping that secret, a secret believed to be essential for the psychic state of the child as well as the father and mother, practitioners opened the way for those families to *imagine* paternity rather than *remember* a particular course of events. Physicians thus helped maintain and steady the family narrative.

PRESCRIPTIONS FOR KEEPING ARTIFICIAL INSEMINATION SECRET

How was the secret of paternity maintained through the medical implementation of AID? In Seymour and Koerner's protocol, attempts to maintain secrecy by hiding facts either from the husband or wife were condemned, yet other means to protect the secret were introduced. In theirs and related articles (Jackson, Bloom, Parkes, Blacker, & Binney, 1957; Russell, 1950; Seymour & Koerner, 1936; Weisman, 1942), a number of precautionary measures for secrecy were devised:

1. Assume anonymity of both donor and couple to protect against spread of information about the insemination.
2. Have the baby delivered by a different obstetrician-gynecologist who does not know that AID was performed and who will sign the birth certificate with the husband named as father.
3. Warn the couple not to tell anyone of the facts of paternity.
4. Encourage the husband not to undergo formal adoption of a child (which would ensure that the child be a legal heir), because the adoption process would make the AID public knowledge.
5. Match all possible physical characteristics of the husband and the donor, including blood type, to eliminate later scientific determination of paternity or the child's learning of paternity through science education in school.

6. Prohibit use of relatives as donors to reduce the number of people knowing about the insemination.

These six safeguards functioned to mitigate against potential legal consequences (Israel, 1941) as well as protect the central secret. The necessity of secrecy was echoed in legal reviews of AID. In a legal article criticizing the idea that AID babies be adopted by the husbands, J. C. Schock (1942) argued that "the very life-blood of artificial insemination is secrecy" (p. 274) and that adoption procedures would make the secret part of the public record. Public knowledge would make these children bear the scar of being "half-bastards" (p. 272). Schock's interest was in the children: "These are the normal, healthy children whose fathers were test tubes and whose mothers were experimental laboratories, but who are nevertheless human beings undistinguishable and unmarked" (p. 272). He desired most that "the child, to his own belief and to that of his family's friends, is the offspring of his mother's husband" (p. 274) and, therefore, his inquiry sought grounds for the legal protection of the secret.

By the 1940s other experts, most of whom were physicians, both expanded the grounds for secrecy and created additional strategies to ensure it. Nondisclosure was not just a prophylactic for healthy child development or a legal defense, it also served the husband and the couple. Secrecy could abet forgetting and foster the idea that the child was the husband's. "The process should be kept as secret as possible," wrote Dr. R. T. Seashore in 1938, "in order that the couple may more readily forget the artificial character of the conception" (p. 643). In "A Physician's Credo for Artificial Insemination," Dr. Alan Guttmacher's "Rule Four" was

> forget signed papers. If the patients are carefully selected, contracts and arguments are unnecessary, and simply act as permanent reminder for something which should be forgotten as quickly and completely as possible. In the ideal case, by the time the patient reaches the term, the woman, the husband, and the doctor have to think twice to remember that the pregnancy is physically not the husband's for psychically it has become his. (1942, p. 358).

Guttmacher's interests were simultaneously psychological and legal (to prevent the child from becoming a "legal bastard"). Above all, Guttmacher found AID to be "one of the most satisfying of all medical experiences. It would require a petrified heart not to warm to the scene of the sterile father doting on his two children who, according to the neighbors, resemble him very closely" (p. 359).

Whether directly stated or implied in specific techniques, the husband's psychology was of serious concern, and it prompted development of additional technical maneuvers. Two of the techniques involved simulating the conceptive act: (a) the aforementioned method of injecting donor sperm into the husband's seminal vesicles thus enabling the husband to deliver the sperm via intercourse, and (b) enlisting the husband's assistance in the procedure, usually by giving him the inseminating syringe, making him the "physiologic 'messenger boy'" (Folsome, 1943, p. 923).[9] Other maneuvers functioned, quite literally, to scramble the facts of paternity. Some physicians recommended that following an insemination, husbands engage in coitus with their wives.

Eventually this act of genetic confusion was medicalized when it was suggested that husband and donor sperm be mixed and the wife inseminated with the composite. Perhaps, wrote Dr. David Cristol, the "reluctant partner might more enthusiastically enter into the agreement for artificial insemination if he realizes that with the mixing of his semen with that of a normal donor, there will be at least a mathematical possibility that he may contribute to the genetic background of his child" (1948, p. 1258).

Mixing the donor's and the husband's semen offered something other than a low-odds lottery ticket: It obscured knowledge about paternity. Drs. Robert Rutherford and A. Lawrence Banks advocated mixing as a routine practice, noting that "our action cannot be defended either scientifically or emotionally" (1954, p. 274). Their own account reveals the limits of trust and belief: "She is told that this will be mixed with the donor specimen, and it is. In other words, theoretically, the husband might be the father of the child. We accept the indictment of confused thinking here" (p. 274).

These practitioners were not poor statistical reasoners; they knew it was unlikely that the husband's sperm would fertilize the wife's egg. One group candidly suggested that mixing semen when the father had oligozoospermia might relieve the husband's "emotional tension" (Jackson et al., 1957, p. 206), and Dr. Guttmacher and his colleagues characterized mixing as "a psychotherapeutic aid to the couple" (Guttmacher, Haman, & MacLeod, 1950, pp. 266–267). Another physician depicted this "pooling" procedure as a desirable form of confusion, for "it would be highly improbable to know whose sperm was responsible, particularly if the donor's physical characteristics closely resemble the husband's" (Russell, 1950, p. 461).

The first set of guidelines for attaining secrecy were aimed (at least in part) at obfuscating public knowing, but the latter strategies were devised to alter private knowing. Practitioners saw AID as being psychologically beneficial—as preserving families, reducing the chance of divorce, and simply making two people happier in this life. By the 1960s writers also were claiming that one distinct advantage of AID over adoption was its possibility for secrecy (Dienes, 1968, p. 269). Among its benefits, secrecy

[9]The first of these techniques proved to be unsuccessful. The second, allowing the husband to assist in the procedure, eventually was abandoned as physicians sought a more professional atmosphere for reproductive health care. However, in the 1960s and 1970s, alternative approaches to medicine advanced the idea of self-insemination without supervision.

enabled the couple to suppress, even repress, the facts of conception. For the husband especially, rethinking parenthood in this way posed a challenge. In an article on the role of the husband, Dr. Fred Simmons (1957) reported success among husbands, citing their frequent requests for additional children through AID:

> The husband is able to consider the child his for he requests in writing that the doctor make it possible for his wife to have a child by insemination and by the time the child arrives, the husband says to himself: "I asked for this child and it is mine." (p. 548)

Simmons used "*the patient's* own words" to verify this outcome by reprinting a letter in which a husband writes that AID "has permitted both of us to experience fully the bringing of a child into the world" (1957, p. 549). Other physicians supplied similar case reports. In one instance of AID and mixing, used to produce two sons, "Each parent is convinced that the children are their own, and the donor concept has dropped out of their thinking entirely" (Rutherford & Banks, 1954, p. 278). In another case, one where the husband was azoospermic, the couple elected AID over adoption because they preferred "a child born by the wife, presumably of the husband's" (Rutherford & Banks, 1954, p. 278). Still other accounts hinted at the complexities of such beliefs, describing the psychological events in "as if" terms. Thus, Walter Williams' 1964 textbook survey of sterility recounts the "almost universal elation" of the husband: "In my experience the husband cherishes the child just as much as if he were the biological father, and sometimes even more, since his happiness is in reality just as much at stake as that of the wife" (1964, p. 259).

Not all experts embraced this positive psychology of AID, nor did all physicians condone secrecy even when they did endorse the procedure. In the 1960s several writers employed psychoanalytic theory to explain the perils of artificial insemination (Gerstel, 1963; Sants, 1964), and one even argued that artificial insemination toyed dangerously with the incest taboo (Rubin, 1965). A number of experts were impressed with Helene Deutsch's psychology of male sterility and artificial insemination, a model that suggested that only some men could overcome ego concerns and adapt to the procedure (Lamson, Pinard, & Meaker, 1951). These critics, however, remained in the minority, and it was not until the early 1980s that reproductive experts systematically questioned the practices of secrecy employed in AID.

Even in the late 1970s many involved professionals advocated secrecy on psychological grounds. More than one writer defended the confusion of paternity by mentioning that paternity, after all, cannot be absolutely known by anyone, even the physician. They also noted the remote possibility that a sterile husband could produce a viable sperm (Beck, 1976) and that "unknown paternity" is a common feature of the general population (Curie-Cohen, Luttrell, & Shapiro, 1979, p. 589).[10] At the same time, however, these and other writers were beginning to suggest that AID children, for medical and psychological reasons, should have access to records of their paternity (Curie-Cohen et al., 1979, p. 589). A few studies indicated that the husband's psychological adjustment was not complete, and their guilt lingered: The husband's regard for "the semen of the donor as a mere fertilizing agent whose product in conception imparted nothing alien to the marriage" was interpreted not as a healthy belief but as a "narcissistic" attitude (David & Avidan, 1976, p. 531).

Challenged in the psychoanalytic writings almost two decades earlier, confidence in the robustness of husbands' psychological adaptability eventually began to falter. What had been taken as an achievable shift in attitudes and beliefs began to be discussed as a protracted, difficult, and risky process (Christie, 1980; Matthews, 1980). This fissure in confidence, and the subsequent reappraisal of secrecy-maintaining strategies, was widened beyond repair with 1981 publication of *The Artificial Family* by R. Snowden and G. D. Mitchell, two British family policy experts. Arriving at a moment of heightened concern about family life, the very pairing of the words *family* with *artificial* evoked distaste. Snowden and Mitchell's analysis of AID was a detailed one. Dismissing earlier published papers as mainly "opinion and conjecture," they predicted that personal disasters would ensue if husband and wife were to retain any negative emotions (p. 44). More important, they challenged the conventions of secrecy as being dangerous and imperfect deception: "The high professional status of the A.I.D. practitioner and the deep desire of couples to appear normal constitute a powerful combination encouraging wishful thinking and self-deception. Nevertheless, it is sometimes not at all easy to keep such a secret from the child" (1981, p. 84).

To their critique of secrecy they appended self-statements of children who, upon learning about their conceptive origins, were hurt by the secret. The Snowden and Mitchell report echoed one husband's recently published autobiographical account: *Blizzard and the Holy Ghost* (Blizzard, 1977) poignantly recalls the psychological demons that haunted his own experience with AID. And Blizzard was a physician himself.[11] At the end of the decade another trade text, *Lethal Secrets: The Shocking Consequences and Unsolved Problems of Artificial Insemination* (Baran & Pannor, 1989), again sporting an alarmist title, denounced the secrecy of AID and produced an alternative set of recommendations for psychological well-being. In claiming the child's right to know, the authors asserted that the parents "must accept the importance of the donor father as the genetic father of

---

[10]Although entrenched in the rhetoric of population studies and reproductive medicine, the authors of these articles admitted the universal problem of ascertaining paternity.
[11]Blizzard's autobiography, in its very raw reporting, details his experiences of failed manhood (inferiority), thoughts of AID as adultery, and suspicions about the attending physicians.

their child" and "support their child's desire to meet his genetic father at an appropriate age" (p. 169). Once secrecy was discarded, AID was thought to be comparable to adoption and was accorded the same psychological explanations and prescriptions.[12]

Without the secrecy surrounding AID, imagining paternity and the paternal role was no longer possible, and *father* began to become plural: one could speak of genetic, social, and adoptive fathers, stepfathers, and so on. Secrecy and the believed-in imaginings that secrecy enabled and even encouraged, were challenged neither by experts on reproduction, nor by physicians performing AID, nor by recipients. It was primarily the policy makers, psychotherapists, ethicists, and feminist scholars who were investigating both matters of identity and the apparent risks of new reproductive technologies, who found AID, by then an established procedure, to be an institution requiring reform.

SCIENCE, GENDER, AND IMAGININGS OF PATERNITY

The scientific community proclaimed the impossibility of the husband being the real father, or genetic father, of children produced by AID. How, then, could experts promote and, along with recipients, collude in, disguising the facts of paternity? How could all of the participants attempt to imagine a paternity that was refuted by publicly shared scientific knowledge? The conditions for such believing were, at least momentarily, right. There existed, as Sarbin suggested in the case of believed-in imaginings, a big, gnawing personal problem—sterility—that could be resolved through such imaginings. The multiple implications of sterility, both material and emotional, certainly induced a cognitive strain in the husbands.

Another condition proposed by Sarbin—men's skill at shifting perspectives—also existed, albeit perhaps not precisely the kind of skill to which Sarbin referred. The claiming of paternity is a *gender-based* social skill, one embedded in longstanding social relations and institutions; it is but one of many skills essential to "doing gender" in our culture (West & Zimmerman, 1987). Although this particular skill attaches to repeated acts of doing gender, it has its basis in the raw fact of sexual difference, the alienability of reproductive material from the body of the male human. Claiming paternity connects the male body with the symbolic order of families; such acts both constitute gender and reaffirm it. However well-instituted in culture, the gender-based practice of claiming paternity has

---

[12]It was long held that adopted children should learn about their adoptive status, although there was no consensus about how and when they should be told. By the 1960s, psychological experts had confirmed the importance of such telling through studies of "genealogical bewilderment," a term referring to the negative psychological consequence of not knowing facts about one's origins.

240   *JILL G. MORAWSKI*

its underside: a fear of being deceived about paternity. With the ever-potential possibility of deception it is understandable that so many of the medical accounts (cited earlier in the chapter) of AID included anecdotes of fraud and duplicity (women who sought AID surreptitiously, doctors who used their own sperm, soldiers who stole sperm from the horses of their enemies, druggists who smuggled sperm in prescriptions, doctors who informed neither husband nor wife of AID, women who claimed to have been artificially inseminated but who actually became pregnant through adulterous acts, and so on). The social customs of ascribing paternity, once shored up by elaborate laws, lost some of their steady foundation with the advent of insemination technologies.

Cognitive pressures and the agility of the male gender role alone were not enough to displace the beliefs of (and in) science in the 20th century. Scientific experts, namely physicians practicing what was to become reproductive medicine, constructed a social atmosphere—lending to it their authority and consent—in which fearful and distressed couples could live more harmoniously. They did so by guarding the secrets of paternity, enabling and even insisting on such secrets, and sometimes disrupting the few acts that seemed to garner factual evidence of fatherhood. These obstetrician-gynecologists were part of the professionalization of everyday life, the increased dependence of individuals on expert classes (Bledstein, 1976). The greater physicians' technical skills (improved instruments, fertility drugs to improve chances of fertilization, calculation of the menstrual cycle, microscopic analyses of semen, etc.), the more influence they gained with infertile couples. And if these experts on reproduction were making child "bombs" against God, as one religious critic wrote in the aftermath of the atomic bomb (Doyle, 1953), then they also must be seen as earnestly fulfilling their professional aim to better the physical and emotional well-being of their patients—to give them the children they so desired in order to be normal members of what was increasingly depicted as a family-centered culture. These experts, then, deployed their technical and social powers to smooth the tremendous awkwardness of a medical technology—a social-psychological entanglement they had to face directly in their offices. They did so as they struggled to provide their patients with what they wanted, a goal that coincidentally accorded these doctors remuneration and further secured their professional status. Both doctor and patient benefited from the construction of an alternative understanding of paternity.[13]

Through an extended processes of eliminating, negotiating, and refin-

---

[13]Not only did physicians articulate certain notions of paternity, but a certain paternalism pervaded these physicians' reports. Although a fatherly attitude was not uncommon among doctors during this historical period, its performance in reproductive medicine sometimes caused a self-consciousness about the duplication of fathering. Such anxious self-awareness was most apparent in occasional suspicions that the donor sperm actually was that of the physician.

ing their participation in acts of artificial insemination, physicians created what Laqueur has called a ritual of "de-paternalizing sperm" in which the doctor has "performed his or her priestly function, de-blessed the sperm, and gotten rid of its 'paternity'" (1990, p. 217). Physicians held the authority to enact such transformations, and their particular techniques for doing are what I have described in detail. These rituals of transfiguring the meaning of fatherhood illustrate Laqueur's claim that the "facts" of motherhood and fatherhood "are not 'given' but come into being as science progresses and as the adversaries in political struggles select what they need from the vast, ever-growing storehouse of knowledge" (1990, p. 207).

Just how men believed they were the biological fathers of children produced by AID—sporadically, partially, totally, or fervently—we cannot ascertain without speaking with them. Even then, we still probably would be uncertain of the authenticity of their imaginings. The professional literature, both the proactive and the critical, indicates that there were occasions when these men believed themselves to be biological fathers. At the least, these men lived in a social–psychological zone where they had access to two relatively coherent worlds of belief—the scientific and the imagined. William James, who called these different realities "sub-worlds," proposed that most individuals have access to more than one of these realities, which appear "to most men's minds in no very definitely conceived relation to each other, and our attention, when it turns to one, is apt to drop the others for the time being out of its account" (1890, p. 293). The more our belief corresponds with the senses, or has corporeity, the more it is real and "passes from fairy-land to mother-earth" (p. 305). Passion and will also play a large part in maintaining these subworlds of belief for "we need only in cold blood ACT as if the thing in question were real, and keep acting as if it were real, and it will infallibly end up growing into such a connection with our life that it will become real" (James, 1890, p. 321).

So concludes James's chapter on "The Perception of Reality" in which he reconsiders distinctions between real and imagined, knowledge and belief, science and common sense. I end with James's theory not simply because it supports the hypothesis that these men could believe the imaginary as well as the broader thesis that there is a large habitable space between public or scientific knowledge and fanciful or delusional imagining. His theory also can be understood as symptom, perhaps a prophetic one, of the historical making and remaking of reality. If in his extensive contemplations James gave us a complex of realities, then our psychologies since his have striven to tidy the mental mess that he depicted, ever seeking exact cognitive rules for appropriate and inappropriate beliefs. However, as we redraw cognitive maps, charting new territory and renaming old land, so the rest of the world is being reinvented.

Physicians and psychological workers, coming to the assistance of

AID couples, worked within a newly emerging reproductive world in which reality was being transformed—a world where the real and the imaginary were in flux. The new technologies of reproduction were coupled with social technologies, in this case the practices of medical experts, to generate new versions of fatherhood. That world-making required more than the template of one mother, one father, and a certain social fact of paternity. What was to be taken as a "real" father was renegotiated; no longer could some biological "fact" of paternity be taken as an indisputable mark of fatherhood.

Today's mental health workers portray a world in which multiple fathers and sometimes multiple mothers exist, and one in which gender roles are often askew. Relations of trust, to use O'Brien's term, no longer center around a single social fact of paternity or neatly demarcated gender relations. Rational belief now consists in nothing less than a child's acknowledgment of the reality of multiple parents and, conversely, in parents acknowledging their child as simultaneously theirs and not theirs. Even genes, the ultimate data of science, are taking form in scientific discourse as mere copies, simulacra of the real thing amenable to editing and simulation (Rabinow, 1992). The simple social fact of paternity, and men's role in maintaining and enacting it, lived its final moments with the advent of AID. Today's "genetic dad," currently deemed important for a child's sense of identity and a definitive check against the possibility of a "social dad's" flight of fantasy, tomorrow may be nothing more than technical information, a prior signifier. Tomorrow undoubtedly will bring other systems of beliefs upon which to build and sustain our desires for kinship and authenticity.

REFERENCES

Baran, A., & Pannor, R. (1989). *Lethal secrets: The shocking consequences and unsolved problems of artificial insemination.* New York: Warner Books.

Beck, W. W. (1976). A critical look at the legal, ethical, and technical aspects of artificial insemination. *Fertility and Sterility, 24,* 1–8.

Bledstein, B. J. (1976). *The culture of professionalism: The middle class and the development of higher education in America.* New York: Norton.

Blizzard, J. (1977). *Blizzard and the holy ghost.* London: Peter Owen.

Bok, S. (1979). *Lying: Moral choice in public and private life.* New York: Vintage Books.

Christie, G. L. (1980). The psychological and social management of the infertile couple. In R. J. Pepperell, B. Hudson, & C. Wood (Eds.), *The infertile couple* (pp. 229–247). New York: Churchill Livingstone.

Cole, F. J. (1930). *Early theories of sexual generation.* Oxford, England: Clarendon Press.

Cristol, D. (1948). Observations on the mixture of semens: Preliminary report. *The Journal of Urology, 59,* 1253.

Curie-Cohen, M., Luttrell, L., & Shapiro, S. (1979). Current practice of artificial insemination by donors in the United States. *New England Journal of Medicine, 300*(11), 585–590.

Daniels, C. R. (1997). Between fathers and fetuses: The social construction of male reproduction and the politics of fetal harm. *Signs: Journal of Women in Culture and Society, 22*(3), 579–616.

David, A., & Avidan, D. (1976). Artificial insemination donor: Clinical and psychologic aspects. *Fertility and Sterility, 27*(5), 528–532.

Davis, F. P. (1923). *Impotency, sterility, and artificial impregnation.* St. Louis: C. V. Mosby.

Deutsch, H. (1945). *The psychology of women* (Vol. 2). New York: Grune & Stratton.

Dienes, C. T. (1968). Artificial impregnation: Essays in tubal insemination. *Transactions of the American Gynocological Society for the Year, 45,* 141–156.

Doyle, J. B. (1953). The bomb, the baby and the pope. *The Linacre Quarterly, 20,* 10–14.

Farley, J. (1982). *Gametes and spores.* Baltimore: Johns Hopkins University Press.

Folsome, C. E. (1943). The status of artificial insemination: A critical review. *American Journal of Obstetrics and Gynecology, 45*(6), 915–927.

Gerstel, G. (1963). A psychoanalytic view of artificial donor insemination. *American Journal of Psychotherapy, 17*(1), 64–77.

Gregoire, A. T., & Mayer, R. C. (1965). The impregnators. *Fertility and Sterility, 16*(1), 130–134.

Guttmacher, A. F. (1942). A physician's credo for artificial insemination. *Western Journal of Surgery, Obstetrics and Gynecology, 50,* 357–359.

Guttmacher, A. F., Haman, J. O., & MacLeod, J. (1950). The use of donors for artificial insemination: A survey of current practices. *Fertility and Sterility, 1*(3), 264–270.

Hard, A. D. (1909). Artificial impregnation. *The Medical World, 27,* 163–64.

Israel, L. (1941). The scope of artificial impregnation in the barren marriage. *The American Journal of the Medical Sciences, 202,* 92–98.

Jackson, M. H., Bloom, P., Parkes, A. S., Blacker, C. P., & Binney, C. (1957). Artificial insemination (Donor). *The Eugenics Review, 48,* 203–211.

James, W. (1890). *The principles of psychology* (Vol. 2). New York: Holt.

Keller, E. F. (1992). Nature, nurture and the human genome project. In D. J. Kelves & L. Hood (Eds.), *The code of codes: Scientific and social issues in the human genome project* (pp. 281–299). Cambridge, MA: Harvard University Press.

Lamson, H. D., Pinard, W. J., & Meaker, S. R. (1951). Sociologic and psychological aspects of artificial insemination with donor semen. *Journal of the American Medical Association, 145*(14), 1062–1064.

Laqueur, T. (1990). *Making sex: Body and gender from the Greeks to Freud*. Cambridge, MA: Harvard University Press.

Marsh, M., & Ronner, W. (1996). *The empty cradle: Infertility in America from colonial times to the present*. Baltimore: Johns Hopkins University Press.

Matthews, C. D. (1980). Artificial insemination—Donor and husband. In R. J. Pepperell, B. Hudson, & C. Woods (Eds.), *The infertile couple* (pp. 182–208). Edinburgh, Scotland: Churchill Livingstone.

Nelkin, D., & Lindee, M. S. (1995). *The DNA mystique*. New York: Freeman.

O'Brien, M. (1981). *The politics of reproduction*. Boston: Routledge & Kegan Paul.

Office of Technology Assessment. (1988). *Artificial insemination: Practice in the United States: Summary of a 1987 survey—Background paper* (OTA Publication No. OTA-BP-BA-48). Washington, DC: U.S. Government Printing Office.

Pauly, P. (1987). *Controlling life*. New York: Oxford University Press.

Rabinow, P. (1992). Artificiality and enlightenment: From sociobiology to biosociality. In J. Crary & S. Kwinter (Eds.), *Incorporations* (pp. 234–252). New York: Zone.

Rohleder, H. (1934). *Test tube babies: A history of the artificial impregnation of human beings*. New York: Panurge Press.

Roof, J. (1996). *Reproductions of reproduction: Imaging symbolic change*. New York: Routledge.

Rubin, B. (1965). Psychological aspects of human artificial insemination. *Archives of General Psychiatry, 13*(1), 121–132.

Russell, M. (1950). Artificial insemination: A plea for standardization of donors. *Journal of the American Medical Association, 144*(6), 461.

Rutherford, R. N., & Banks, A. L. (1954). Semiadoption technics and results. *Fertility and Sterility, 5*(3), 271–281.

Sants, H. J. (1964). Genealogical bewilderment in children with substitute parents. *British Journal of Medical Psychology, 137*(2), 133–141.

Sarbin, T. (1983). The quixotic principle: A Belletristic approach to the psychological study of imaginings and believings. In V. L. Allen & K. E. Scheibe (Eds.), *The social context of conduct: Psychological writings of Theodore Sarbin* (pp. 169–186). New York: Praeger.

Schellen, A. M. C. M. (1957). *Artificial insemination in the human*. Amsterdam: Elsevier.

Schock, J. C. (1942). The legal status of the semi-adopted. *Dickinson Law Review, 46*, 271–280.

Seashore, R. T. (1938). Artificial impregnation. *Minnesota Medicine, 21*, 641–644.

Seymour, F. I., & Koerner, A. (1936). Medicolegal aspects of artificial insemination. *Journal of the American Medical Association, 107*(19), 1531–1534.

Seymour, F. I., & Koerner, A. (1941). Artificial insemination: Present status in the United States as shown by a recent survey. *Journal of the American Medical Association, 116*(25), 2747–2749.

Simmons, F. A. (1957). Role of the husband in therapeutic donor insemination. *Fertility and Sterility*, 8(6), 547–550.

Snowden, R., & Mitchell, G. D. (1981). *The artificial family: A consideration of artificial insemination by donor.* Concord, MA: Allen & Unwin.

Stepita, C. T. (1933). Physiologic artificial insemination. *The American Journal of Surgery, 21,* 450–451.

Terry, T. (1997). The seductive power of science in the making of deviant subjectivity. In V. A. Rosario (Ed.), *Science and homosexualitites* (pp. 271–297). New York: Routledge.

Weisman, A. I. (1942). The selection of donors for use in artificial insemination. *Western Journal of Surgery, Obstetrics, and Gynecology, 50,* 142–144.

West, C., & Zimmerman, D. H. (1987). Doing gender. *Gender and Society,* 1(2), 125–151.

Williams, W. W. (1964). *Sterility: The diagnostic survey of the infertile couple.* Springfield, MA: author

14

WOMEN'S STORIES OF HIDDEN SELVES AND SECRET KNOWLEDGE: A PSYCHOANALYTIC FEMINIST ANALYSIS

JANICE HAAKEN

The scientific–academic mind and the feminine–mystical mind shy from each other's facts, just as they fly from each other's temper and spirit.

William James, 1890

In 1909, almost a century ago, psychologists gathered at Clark University to make sense of fanciful tales, many of which were produced by women. Joining scientific inquiry and clinical practice, these early pioneers of the psyche hoped to unravel the mysteries of hypnotic states, hysteria, and mediumship. Women participated in the drama as subjects and patients, whereas men were cast as experts in decoding female communications from "beyond the normal."

Indeed, it was a teenage girl, a self-described medium, who captured center stage at this historically momentous meeting between Freud and his American colleagues. During his only trip to the United States, Freud met at Clark with other luminaries in the field of psychology. G. Stanley Hall, president of Clark University, was among those in attendance. Hall later

Portions of this chapter were adapted from Haaken, Janice, *Pillar of salt: Gender, memory, and the perils of looking back*. Copyright 1998 by Janice Haaken. Reprinted with permission of Rutgers University Press.

recounted a dramatic moment when he came to believe that the true psychological basis of mediumship was revealed. After months of interviewing the girl, Hall described his embarrassment as Freud uncovered the romantic motive behind the fanciful inventions of this young medium: "Now the whole situation stood forth in a new light. An erotic motive, of which there had hitherto been no hint, appears to have been the dominant one throughout" (1918–1919, p. 153).

In ferreting out the real motive—a girlish infatuation—Freud triumphed over the medium. As Hall pointed out, mediumship permits women to violate strict moral codes while disavowing such transgressive impulses. Even as he was persuaded by Freud's interpretation, Hall, having spent a great deal of time with the young woman, offered his own insights on mediumship, which in many respects were more incisive than those of Freud. Prior to what many of those assembled believed to be Freud's interpretive victory, Hall had portrayed this adolescent girl as socially isolated and as philosophically inclined. Her mediumship enunciated a world she envisioned but could not directly inhabit, and it enlarged her ego by "widening experience" (p. 153). She and her mother, who were shunned in their small town because of the mother's "estrangement" from her husband, formed an enclosed and enchanted world of their own, centered on exploring the girl's "budding" spiritual gifts. Hall summarized the conditions that had been so conducive to her nascent mediumship: "Rich fantasy, stimulated by the warmest maternal sympathy, favored the highest flights of fantasy, and the world of imagination grew inversely and more or less as a surrogate of the normal expansion of interests which were lacking in the environment" (1918–1919, p. 147).

Does one interpretation of the story serve as well as another? From the perspective of a psychology of women, demystifying mediumship, whether rooted in erotic motives or in compensatory fantasy, is both a step forward and a step backward. On the one hand, as turn-of-the-century psychologists began to stress the "double consciousness" of female mediums, the various personages that occupied them during a trance state could be recognized as latent aspects of women themselves, including culturally repressed capacities and desires. On the other hand, the clinical investigation of mediumship stripped the medium of her magnificent social power, as the tricks of her trade were exposed. Once mediumship was clinically interpreted as a *disguise*, an operation of the ego itself, interest in the phenomenon declined, leaving these female performers without an audience. As Hall confessed in his "obituary" on mediumship, "The next generation will be hardly able to believe that prominent men in this (generation) wasted their energies in chasing such a will-of-the-wisp as the veracity of messages or the reality of a post-mortem existence" (1918–1919, p. 154).

How, then, should we listen to women's communications from "beyond the normal?" If the aim of science is to demystify, how should one interpret such awesome accounts without dismissing them or stripping them of their vital meaning? And furthermore, how does the increasing participation of women, as translators or interpreters on the scene, make a difference?

The short answer to this latter question is that it both does and does not matter. It matters in the sense that women bring particular experiences and concerns to the enterprise of science that have been habitually repressed in male-dominated discourses. But this history of marginalization does not insulate women, as scientists or practitioners, from the problematic aspects of their own authority. Defending the testimony of patients under the banner of "believing the victim" may be used defensively by women practitioners, just as it may by men, particularly in obscuring their own influence over the past that is recovered in treatment (Haaken, 1995, 1996; Loftus & Ketcham, 1994; Ofshe & Watters, 1994).

In this chapter I present a framework for rethinking "hysterical" storytelling—specifically clinical narratives that center on the uncovering of an imagined domain of concealed knowledge. This framework draws on intersubjective, interpersonal currents in contemporary psychoanalytic theory. My use of the psychoanalytic tradition is based on a critical and cultural reading of theory, specifically through the lens of feminist analysis (see Benjamin, 1988; Flax, 1990; Gallop, 1982). Hysterical storytelling, from this perspective, emerges out of an interactive field, one in which participants co-construct the emotionally gripping drama that unfolds.

The term *hysteria* often implies a derisive, dismissive, and sexist stance toward the tales that are told. My use of this term carries quite a different meaning. As a cultural idiom, hysteria suggests the dominance of emotion over reason, a situation in which emotional arousal overrides the capacity to think rationally. Hysterics, it is commonly thought, are suspect storytellers who generate more heat than light. But we may also understand hysteria as a battle for recognition and as a revolt against conventional discourse (see Showalter, 1985). Hysterical storytelling may be understood as signifying a crisis in normal discursive practices—and an employment of emotion, the body, and the imagination to tell a new story.

The idea of a hidden reality operating below the threshold of normal perception has a problematic social history, even as it has been employed progressively. In narratives that unfold around a shadowy underworld of unseen forces, this same underworld may come to serve as a screen upon which various anxieties and fantasies are projected. Witch-hunts typically organize around this idea of concealed, malevolent powers of influence whose magnitude justifies extraordinary methods of containment.

In theorizing about believed-in imaginings, I argue that the idea of hidden knowledge has been employed in both rational and irrational ways in women's storytelling practices. Because women have themselves been hidden from history in patriarchal societies, with their narratives concealed behind dominant cultural scripts, women may enlist the idea of the hidden self to subvert men's power. At the same time, the position of cultural invisibility makes women's psychic spaces and ambiguous emotional conditions vulnerable to the projected anxieties and fantasies of authority figures on the scene.

The clinical concept of multiple personality disorder, which gained wide currency in the mental health field during the 1980s, is presented here as a modern variant of hysterical storytelling. I argue that multiplicity, as a clinical construction of fluctuating mental states, simultaneously reveals and conceals the dilemmas of many women. As a contemporary example of hysterical storytelling, multiplicity serves multiple psychological social functions for practitioners and patients alike, functions that bridge the imaginary and the real.

PSYCHOANALYSIS, WOMEN, AND THE DYNAMIC UNCONSCIOUS

As a psychology of secrets—a theory of hidden knowledge revealed through narratives—psychoanalysis creates a more hospitable stage and a more receptive audience for women's storytelling than does the highly operationalized world of scientific psychology. In contradistinction to much of cognitive psychology, which stresses the encoding and retrieval of memory, psychoanalysis asserts a narrative coherence to mental life. From a psychoanalytic perspective, repression is not understood simply as interference in the mental retrieval of information, but rather, it signifies human conflict concerning self-knowledge. A central question underlying clinical discourse on the unconscious involves whether or not the unconscious "tells a story," that is, whether or not intelligible patterns of meaning may be deciphered from processes of mind operating outside of conscious awareness (see Schacter, 1996; Spence, 1982). Used heuristically and in a less reified way than it has been used in the recovered memory debate, the idea of repression sensitizes us to the drama of consciousness and to the painful aspects of relational knowledge.

Hypnosis played a key role in the emergence of the concept of the dynamic unconscious, although schools of thought carried this concept in divergent directions. Before they parted company over their own bitter disputes, Freud, Breuer, and Janet shared, in the early 1890s, a common set of ideas concerning hypnosis and hysteria. Drawing on Charcot's concept of dynamic amnesia, they used hypnosis to recover a forgotten past and to therapeutically alter the course of that same past's effects on the mind.

In his autobiography, Freud (1935/1995) noted the unsettling emotional power of the therapeutic journey. He described his own response to a hypnotized patient, an experience that was decisive in his abandonment of hypnosis as a therapeutic technique.

> As she woke up on one occasion, she threw her arms around my neck. The unexpected entrance of a servant relieved us from a painful discussion, but from that time onwards there was a tacit understanding between us that the hypnotic treatment should be discontinued. I was modest enough not to attribute the event to my irresistible personal attraction, and I felt that I had now grasped the nature of the mysterious element that was at work behind hypnotism. (p. 27)

And what was this mysterious element, this sexually arousing aspect of hypnosis that perpetually haunted its practitioners? Freud's brief intrigue with hypnosis, a procedure he claimed to have never been particularly good at, ended in what he felt to be a resolution of the mystery. For Freud, hypnosis directly accessed a deep psychic reservoir of repressed sexuality and infantile yearnings. He substituted free association for hypnosis as a tool for accessing unconscious processes. Because hypnosis was so laden with seductive meanings and bypassed the patient's voluntary control over revealed material, Freud came to the conclusion that it was counter-therapeutic and highly "suggestive" (p. 20).

Yet a central theme in the contemporary controversy over recovered memory is the revelatory power of the trance, the potential of hypnotic states to reveal formerly concealed truths (see Yapko, 1994). Feminists have made various uses historically of the concepts of hypnotic states, concealed selves, and hidden knowledge. Over the past decade, therapeutic claims concerning extraordinary revelations—such as psychic phenomena, past-life regression, and alien abductions—have been woven through many of the clinical narratives on recovered memory. For critics of recovered memories of childhood sexual abuse, these highly implausible assertions underscore the antiscientific deluded thinking that has come to dominate some quarters of the mental health profession (see Loftus & Ketcham, 1994; Ofshe & Watters, 1994; Pendergrast, 1994).

Focusing on these extreme claims, however, obscures a deeper source of tension between scientific explorations of mind on the one hand, and the lived experience of women on the other. As I suggested previously, there *is* a certain affinity between feminism and beliefs in "occult" psychological processes, because women have themselves been hidden from history, operating behind a screen, as it were, of masculinist assumptions and fantasies (see Butler, 1990; Herman, 1992; Penley, 1989). Indeed, any project of progressive social change requires a capacity to transcend mundane reality, to probe for deeper meanings, and to uncover hidden potentialities. At the same time, it is important to recognize how the idea of a hidden reality so readily becomes the basis of a paranoid psychology, a theme I revisit.

We can see how a feminist analysis would take aim at the male hypnotist, stripping him of his real and imagined powers and exposing the stage work behind the act. But we are on more uncertain ground when approaching the hypnotic as a feminine craft, particularly given the history of prejudices and paranoia toward women's so-called occult powers. By stepping back from the heat surrounding hypnosis and other suggestive procedures commonly employed in uncovering forgotten memories, we may be better able to establish a new point of entry into the dilemmas of women as storytellers, particularly in their efforts to break out of the binding constraints of conventional tales.

NINETEENTH-CENTURY HYPNOTIC ENCOUNTERS

The preoccupations of late 19th century psychologists followed in the wake of tumultuous social changes—industrialism, religious revivalism, and urbanization—that reworked the cultural landscape, even as they excited the human imagination. The awakened passions of 19th century people moved in a conservative direction for some and in a reformist or radical direction for others. But there was a commonality in outlook in many areas of inquiry, a mutual embracing of the idea of *latent possibilities* within the mind, which could be realized through a mystical transformative experience. This historical convergence of influences is also described as critical to the birth of the modern psychological subject (see Ellenberger, 1970). The idea of selfhood was intimately tied to the idea of inner transformation, brought about through accessing the mind's hidden potential. In 19th century religious revivalism in the United States, inner promptings could be embraced and received as gifts of the spirit, shedding their former chains in more Calvinistic expressions of Christianity.

This cluster of attitudes based on experiential receptivity to spiritual states and altered consciousness came to define the "secular soul," those latent aspects of mind investigated by late 19th-century psychologists (Hacking, 1995; Hawthorn, 1983; Kenny, 1986). Mediumship entranced psychologists, particularly in the United States, as hypnotic states began to be understood as a two-way affair. As the medium entered the trance state, so, too, did her audience. The mid-19th century may be described as the golden era of mediumship, as women assumed unprecedented authority on the public stage, making use of a spiritual idiom of ecstasy to mobilize a following (Braude, 1989; Owen, 1990). Female mediums migrated across the unstable, American political landscape, gaining enthusiastic adherents to spiritualism (Oppenheim, 1985).

Clinical Encounters

As women employed hypnosis to enchant audiences on both sides of the Atlantic, assuming a spiritualized authority through the trance state, physicians engaged in their own spell-binding performances. Jean-Martin Charcot, the charismatic lecturer and administrator of the Salpetriere hospital in France, created a new discourse of mind by demonstrating the essentially *psychological* basis of the bodily contortions and mysterious anaesthesias that were the hallmark of the late 19th-century hysteric. Charcot's famous Tuesday morning lecture series, in which he used hypnosis to induce symptoms in his favorite women patients before audiences of rapt observers, is now legendary. Charcot is often described as a skilled diagnostician, whose careful, detailed descriptions and riveting demonstrations of hysterical symptoms boldly introduced the dispassionate gaze of science into the unsettling mysteries of this predominantly female condition (see de Marneffe, 1996; Showalter, 1985, 1997).

Like the medieval clerics searching for the mark of the devil on the bodies of accused witches, the new medical priesthood was mesmerized by its own subjects. In mapping the stages and zones of hysterical conditions, Charcot was able to express conventional concerns within an emotionally detached, medicalized discourse. Through his demonstrations of hysterical fits, Charcot imported into the clinical field myriad Victorian sentiments and anxieties over female sexuality.

Just as the sight of a lady's ankle could arouse titillating speculation on the part of Victorians, the veil of hysterical neurosis became a screen upon which men's longings and fears could be projected. For some observers, the sexual arousal associated with the hypnotic state was linked with what was believed to be a tendency for women to make false sexual allegations, particularly directed toward the hypnotist. The aroused female participant, overcome by the effects of the treatment, could easily *confuse* the situation, particularly when an active imagination combined forces with a state of bodily excitation (see Laurence & Campbell, 1988).

We can readily imagine how the bodily articulated displays of turn-of-the-century hysterics aroused rapt interest on the part of staid medical observers, who were schooled in the dispassionate rigor of scientific investigation. There is an unmistakably voyeuristic subtext to these clinical encounters. But how do we understand the social psychology of hysterical displays in the contemporary period? Victorianism has certainly faded, although erotic motives may continue to operate in contemporary therapeutic encounters. Yet the choreography of hysterical suffering is not under the absolute direction of whatever authorities are at hand, but these authorities often do find some responsiveness in the mental states and experiences of the patient, particularly, we may suspect, in the contemporary era when women are more active protagonists in cultural storytelling.

In discussing the reemergence of multiplicity in the 1980s, as a modern variant of women's hysteria, I explore the social symbolic, interactive field in which it took hold. Two primary questions are pursued. First, why did so many women in the 1980s embrace multiple personality disorder as an explanation for their suffering? Second, why did MPD come to mesmerize vast numbers of clinicians in the 1980s? Even the most inflated estimates of the incidence of this disorder place it at one percent of the population (Ross, 1989), raising the puzzling question of why it came to capture the psychiatric "gaze."

THE CONTEMPORARY MULTIPLE PERSONALITY MOVEMENT

After the flurry of intense psychiatric interest in "double personality" at the turn of the century, MPD lapsed into obscurity until its robust revival in the 1980s. The resurrection of multiplicity from its turn-of-the-century grave was achieved, according to philosopher Ian Hacking (1995), primarily through the anima of the contemporary child abuse movement. Hacking argued that throughout its labile history, the condition of multiplicity has always required a cultural "host." In other words, it emerges through a more dominant societal concern. In the 19th century, that host was cultural anxiety over the incursions of science into the religious realm; in the late 20th century, it was cultural concern over child sexual abuse.

Hacking's notion of multiplicity in search of a host anthropomorphizes multiplicity, however, in implying that it stands ready and waiting in the wings of the cultural stage, emerging at opportune moments. We may want to reverse Hacking's formulation, while retaining his insight, by exploring how the suffering of *women* often requires a "host" for its entry into public consciousness. In this context, MPD may be understood as a predominantly feminine "idiom of distress," one which, like mediumship in the late 19th century, simultaneously expresses and mystifies the sources of women's misery (see Kenny, 1986). Furthermore, the near unanimous belief in the trauma field that child sexual abuse is the primary cause of MPD may itself be an attempt to "locate" and concretize the more diffuse concerns of women.

Sexual conflicts infiltrate women's storytelling practices in complicated ways. One of the most deeply rooted divisions in cultural consciousness centers on the Madonna/whore dichotomy—irreconcilable images of maternal purity and sexual defilement. Throughout the history of multiplicity, a dominant "good girl" personality—chaste, inhibited, and moralistic—has contended with a subsidiary "bad girl" personality, sexually adventurous and intent on destroying her timid "host" and on wreaking havoc on the latter's domesticated world (see Hacking, 1995; Kluft, 1993; Ross, 1989). In the contemporary period, this "double personality" has proliferated into a phenomenal array of alters. Most women experience such conflicts and disjunctures in their phenomenological world without recourse to multiplicity, even though the gulf between good girl/bad girl self-representations is a predominate theme in the psychology of women (Maglin & Perry, 1996; Nathanson, 1991). In the classical understanding of neurotic conditions such as hysteria, the anguished divisions between various self and self-other representations emerge as a source of conflict and anxiety while retaining a basic psychological coherence and stability over time.

The multiple emerged as psychiatric heroine in the 1980s, displacing the impotent hysteric, the people-pleasing co-dependent, and the manipulative borderline personality of times past. And the multiple achieved this exalted status in mental health culture because her condition spoke of broader motifs in women's lives. In the contemporary period, there is an awakening of the feminine imagination and a refusal to be silenced, but these assertions of self remain a chaotic, unrealized potential for many women. Alternative selves and avenues of self-expression have opened up on the cultural horizon; nonetheless, they often prove to be illusory. Like late 19th-century hysterics and double personalities, the modern multiple registers unrealized potential in the realm of the imaginary. A cast of characters is created of "alters" at one end of the dissociative continuum and various "ego states" at the other. Multiplicity may very well describe this state of emotional and imagistic flooding, this groundless place between the refusal of old constraints and the discovery of new possibilities for self and identity.

Different historical periods may create a tendency toward particular defenses and disorders, and historical factors may influence how therapists shape and interpret clinical material. Women have made significant advances into public life that permit new sublimatory possibilities and avenues of identity formation. It may be that disorganizing experiences associated with childhood abuse or environmental deficits are more effectively contained or dissociated through multiple identity states than was possible for women in the past. The multiple's vast cast of alters, whose function it is to "hold" trauma memories, suggests an emergent sense of women's entitlement on the one hand, and fragmentation and helplessness on the other. Unlike the monotheism of Western psychologies, which assert the underlying unity of the self, the MPD movement evokes a more "pagan" psychology, with its little selves vying for control over consciousness.

The MPD movement also enacts broader cultural anxieties over sexuality and women's rebellion, translating it through the moral authority of the sexual abuse recovery movement. Multiplicity may emerge, as many practitioners claim, out of the desperate, creative efforts of girls who are attempting to escape the trauma of sexual invasions. But the chronic demands and neglects that girls and women endure in daily life, as well as the stunted opportunities, may also be experienced as a form of captivity, and these more mundane forms of bondage are more difficult to dramatize and less arousing of psychiatric intrigue.

THE CRISIS OF THE THERAPEUTIC IN CONTEMPORARY MENTAL HEALTH CULTURE

In a sense, MPD emerged as the alter of psychiatry—its own soul—returned from its turn-of-the-century grave to awaken and haunt a profession that was already in a state of crisis. For unlike the profusion of diagnostic categories that have proliferated over the past few decades, MPD—as the glorious blossom of the trauma tree—resists normal psychiatric intervention. Indeed, the *DSM* symptom profile has an unusual criterion: "The patient has long been diagnosed with many other psychiatric disorders. The average number of years a multiple spent in the mental health system prior to diagnosis is almost seven" (Herman, 1992, p. 157).

The MPD patient, in other words, is a kind of feminine Munchausen (that other psychiatric wanderer in search of a cure). Her journey tells an embarrassing story of therapeutic employment of various diagnoses and treatments, with the patient's condition worsening. Indeed, part of the folk wisdom of MPD speaks to an acquired knowledge of psychiatric stigmatization. One patient described the reconfiguration of her illness in the late 1980s as follows: "When you are a schizophrenic, nobody cares what your voices are saying. When you get labeled MPD, everybody gets very nosy and wants to know everything they are saying and how many of them are saying it" (cited in Randal, 1994, p. 9).

In reaction to contemporary psychiatry's focus on symptom management and behavioral control, MPD specialists assert the communicative meaning of psychic disturbances. Psychoanalytic clinicians most certainly would agree, as I suggested earlier, that symptoms may tell an unconscious story and that the clinical project is one of deciphering disguised communications within the configuration of symptoms. But there is a mystical aura surrounding MPD, with its dramatic appearances and disappearances of concealed persona.

Just as Protestantism grew in part out of a deep crisis within the Catholic church, the MPD movement is also partially a reaction to very real problems in how psychiatry operates as a "normalizing" discipline, that is, as an adjudicator of the boundary between normalcy and madness. One of these problems involves the increased bureaucratic control of diagnostic categories and mental health practices that is driven by the insurance industry (Kirk & Kutchins, 1992). Of the many hundreds of categories currently available, MPD has the glorious distinction of often parading as many other disorders. Braun, a leading writer in the MPD field, noted that "every diagnosis in the *Diagnostic and Statistical Manual of Mental Disorders* (1980) has at one time or another been applied to MPD" (1986, p. xv). Even more elastic and chameleon-like than hysteria, MPD is described as being easily confused with manic depression, the schizophrenias, histrionic disorders, and various psychosomatic disorders and neurological conditions. Whereas skeptics argue that MPD is "really" one of these other conditions, defenders assert that these other conditions are "really" MPD (see Aldridge-Morris, 1989).

Without dismissing the importance of differential diagnosis, we may recognize a curious agreement in these two positions concerning the refractoriness of MPD to normal psychiatric classification. Out of her very fragmentation, the multiple encompasses the mutating state of psychiatric nosologies. The multiple's search for unity in psychiatric heterogeneity may be fascinating for clinicians because she embodies the wandering soul of psychiatry itself. In attempting to recuperate this "soul," MPD specialists also strive to reduce the emotional distance between healer and sufferer. The folklore of MPD within the professions includes the caveat that multiplicity cannot be revealed or treated quickly—it takes considerable time with the patient—and that it requires new standards of care. In the professional literature, there are caveats concerning overinvolvement and excessive fascination with multiples. Yet even widely respected clinicians such as Putnam and Kluft have stressed the importance of more frequent and longer sessions—for example, 90 minutes over the standard 50-minute hour.

It is true that patients often are shunted into pragmatic treatment regimes that minimize or deny the scope of clinical concerns. Even in outpatient settings, evaluation, diagnosis, and prescription of medication often take less than an hour. Like attacks against the Church's selling of Indulgences during the Reformation, the MPD movement's attack on quickly dispensed treatments reverberates with deeper grievances. Central to these grievances is the sense among many therapists of diminished professional autonomy and of intensified pressure to produce symptom relief.

By uncoupling this severe dissociative condition from the legacy of schizophrenia and the psychoses, MPD is a means of reviving interest in madness, in recouping the ground lost to biological psychiatry, and of resisting interventions that have as their principle aim the elimination of abnormal symptoms. Throughout the 1980s, inpatient units specializing in dissociative disorders sprang up throughout the country, on the basis of the principle that medication was largely ineffective in the treatment of trauma-related conditions. In resisting the tide of psychopharmaceutical control over the field, programs specializing in dissociative disorders relegitimized psychotherapeutic inquiry into madness.

THE MOTHER OF ALL MULTIPLES: SYBIL

In the contemporary MPD movement, Cornelia Wilbur, a psychiatrist and psychoanalyst, is recognized as the leading theorist in the study of multiplicity in the immediate postwar period. Along with Kluft, Braun, Allison, and others, Wilbur promoted interest in MPD through an "oral tradition" within psychiatry (Ross, 1989). Although these psychiatrists presented workshops at American Psychiatric Association meetings, their work was marginal to the field until interest in dissociation and multiplicity reached a fever pitch in the 1980s.

The case of Sybil, the basis of a book published in 1973 and a film released in 1976, also initiated a new genre of psychiatric docudrama—books collaboratively written or jointly authored by women patients and their therapists. The book and the film that portrayed Sybil's case were significant in bridging clinical discourse and popular culture, and in granting women patients a historically unprecedented role in conarrating the clinical encounter. By the late 1980s, this genre—including titles such as *When Rabbit Howls*, *The Flock*, and *The Magic Daughter*—had displaced the preexisting female genre of codependence literature on many bookstore shelves throughout the country.

Sybil as Cultural Text

Wilbur treated Sybil over an 11-year period—from 1954 to 1965—and invited Flora Schreiber, a professional writer, to chronicle the development of the treatment. Before taking on the project, however, Schreiber wanted to be assured of a cure. She agreed in 1962 after being told by Wilbur that a happy ending was in sight, thus ensuring the book's place within the tradition of American success stories and marketable stories of overcoming unhappiness.

The book, *Sybil* (Schreiber, 1973), charts the troubled waters of a female identity in flux. Unlike the 1950s case popularized in the 1957 film *The Three Faces of Eve*, Sybil displayed a plethora of alters—17 by the end of treatment—portending a trend that accelerated into the dizzying cast of alters that became commonplace by the 1980s. The uniqueness of the case at the time is also founded on Sybil's "being the only multiple personality to have crossed the borders of sexual difference to develop personalities of the opposite sex" (Schreiber, 1973, p. 291). Since *Sybil*, male alters have become commonplace. The case also is considered to be historically significant because it raised public awareness of early child abuse, particularly of sexual abuse. Unlike the many cases of sexual abuse that emerged in the clinical literature in the decades to follow, in which the perpetrator was typically a father figure, Sybil was presented as the victim of a sexually sadistic, psychotic mother.

The case was historically significant for other reasons as well. As an explicitly feminine narrative, Sybil's story represents a modern mother–daughter clinical dialogue that grew out of the transformative events of the postwar era. Sybil's own dissociative episodes unfold like an epoch saga of American history. An identity forged in the confining security of small town America is shattered as the Great Depression and World War II mark her passage to the cosmopolitan world of New York City. The book opens with flashbacks to the summer of 1945, during Sybil's adolescence, with her quiet "war of nerves"—an inexplicable nervousness—festering like a silent, feminine counterpart to the cataclysmic events being played out on the world stage.

Although much of the history that emerges in the course of treatment is undoubtedly based on actual events in Sybil's life, it is still important to recognize what was at stake for Wilbur in unearthing traumatic memory. It is not a matter of whether or not Sybil was telling the truth about the past. Understanding the new history Sybil found—the clinically recovered trauma memories and various alter personalities—requires that we consider the powerful context in which this clinical subject came to life (see Borch-Jacobsen, 1997).

The Presenting Picture

As Sybil crossed the threshold into adulthood, she became entranced by trains, by their power to carry her away. At 22 years of age, when she entered treatment with Wilbur, she was unable to emotionally separate from what she experienced as the suffocating control of her mother. Unlike the hysterics and multiples of the turn-of-the-century, whose symptoms commonly included paralysis, Sybil caught glimmers of freedom on the horizon and frequently found herself lost in strange places. She was a woman of the night, finding herself in seedy hotels, without place or identity.

In taking on the case, Wilbur apparently became increasingly obsessed with her mysterious patient, a condition among therapists that has become as much a standard feature of MPD as have the patients' amnesic states. For Wilbur, this absorbing preoccupation was tied to the power of a pioneering discovery. Beyond the sense of intrigue associated with fugue states, akin to a good detective story, the citizens of the postwar era were enthralled with the general possibility of medical breakthroughs—through the redemptive power of science.

Sybil's problems initially took the form of a lack of interest in sex or marriage—a putative sign of "feminine maladjustment"—and difficulties in fulfilling her considerable intellectual promise. The trouble centered on inexplicable fits of rage. During a chemistry class at Columbia University, Sybil had abruptly smashed some glassware, under the control of what we later learn to be one of her rebellious alters. Something was clearly wrong. We are informed in the book's introduction, however, that Sybil's madness was not schizophrenia—that dreaded disorder that overtakes its victims early in adulthood. We are told that Sybil was possessed with "Grande Hysterie"—a condition that has a long history as a mysterious disturbance of women.

Postwar Psychiatry

Wilbur's formulation of this case unfolded over a period of time when the psychiatric understanding and treatment of schizophrenia were undergoing revolutionary change. With the development of the major tranquilizers in the 1950s, schizophrenia no longer meant an inevitable, downward spiral into mental deterioration and institutionalization. But this same chemical breakthrough transformed treatment regimes governing mental illness (including psychoanalytic treatment of the severely mentally ill). It is within this context of transformations within psychiatry, specifically the shift toward drug management of psychiatric patients, that the Sybil case became a new chapter—a kind of apocrypha—in postwar psychiatry. Wilbur was staking new ground within the lost terrain of psychiatry, and this venture required that she establish the essential differences between Grand Hysteria and its ominous look-alike, schizophrenia. Just as Freud minimized the extent of illness among his early patients in advancing the effectiveness of the "talking cure," Wilbur continued to insist that Sybil was "not crazy," even as her condition steadily worsened.

A seemingly devoted and caring therapist, Wilbur was also apparently driven by her own determination to cure Sybil through excavating trauma memories. Unlike the schizophrenic, whose loss of contact with reality and tortured hallucinatory visions compromises his or her capacity to speak coherently about the past, Wilbur believed Sybil's symptoms to be a rational response to an irrational situation. The essential wisdom and sanity of the patient's mental strategy for survival separated her from the psychotic. And this required Wilbur to establish a corollary set of early experiences that would logically explain and provide sufficient cause for the severe, debilitating symptoms that plagued her young patient in the present.

Female Autonomy

Breakthrough discoveries often involve heightening, even grossly exaggerating, distinctions between the old findings and the new ones. For Wilbur, the secondary personalities of *earlier* multiples in psychiatric history "exhibited very little independence in voluntarily moving about in a social world—working, acting, and playing. Clearly, this was not true of Sybil.

Her alternating personalities were obviously autonomous" (Schreiber, 1973, p. 109). This theme of feminine autonomy is important in several respects. First, the emphasis on the *autonomy* of the personalities countered the conventional psychiatric view that MPD is merely a hysterical elaboration of different sides of the self. Women who are in a state of role conflict or who are caught between the demands of a strict upbringing and rebellious impulses may enact the conflict through alternating states of mind. The presence of amnesia or partial amnesia of at least one personality or alter for the others is central clinically. But Wilbur's own engrossing engagement in the drama may have contributed to the patient's experience of *distinctive* states. Like Morton Prince, whose pioneering work on multiplicity made psychiatric history during the early years of the century, Wilbur engaged in dialogue with various alters, treating them as though they were separate people.

Wilbur's claim of autonomous personalities worked to counter the inevitable suspicion that therapy may have induced these dissociative states. The question of therapeutic influence, looming on the horizon since MPD's psychiatric birth in the late 19th century, has always been threatening to the profession because it undermines the ideal of scientific objectivity that is assumed to be foundational in any applied science. But if the alter personalities are understood to *resist* discovery, Wilbur could be reassured that they were discovered rather than created. Indeed, the MPD literature tends to stress the alters' reluctance to manifest themselves. It is as though both patient and therapist are drawn, unwillingly, into a drama the magnitude of which overtakes them as an irresistible force.

There is yet another aspect to this claim of autonomous personalities, once again related to the cultural and historical contours of MPD. The postwar multiples are, like so many of their contemporary female therapists, struggling to achieve a level of independence that had not been conceivable during earlier eras. Whereas the turn-of-the-century raft of cases may have similarly followed in the wake of profound cultural changes, including the emergence of new claims for women's rights, the post-World War II era signaled a turning point, accompanied by large-scale anxieties on the one hand and rising expectations on the other.

Sybil is the prototypical postwar daughter. A child of rural parents and a bitterly unhappy mother, she moved to the city in search of a more promising life. She rejected marriage and family, and was unable to separate from the inexorable pull of her strict religious upbringing. The "independence" of the various alters—their assertions of will and rebellious actions—stood in stark contrast to the dependent, cowering Sybil who failed to recognize her own strivings in this otherness within her. Wilbur did have a keen sensitivity to the profound social constraints on women's lives, and she aligned herself with those "personalities" within Sybil fighting for freedom. At the same time, Wilbur apparently failed to recognize that she, as a woman in battle with her own profession, may have been midwife to these autonomous, glorious selves that inhabited her prized patient.

The New Mother

Sybil—this postwar daughter full of creativity, intelligence, and ambition—was in need of a new mother. And here, too, one may speculate that the world of this powerful new mother drew some of its majestic power from the ashes of the old mother. In other words, the idealization of this therapeutic relationship is achieved through the de-idealization and de-valuation of the original mother–daughter tie. The trauma scenes that unfolded over the 11 years of treatment became increasingly graphic and horrific, shifting from conventional losses—the death of a beloved grandmother, the emotional breakdown and withdrawal of a psychotic mother, the rigidity of a strict religious family—to chilling scenes of sadistic torture. Under the unwavering belief that her patient would get well only if the original trauma was excavated and released, Wilbur pressed on for the pernicious source of her patient's deteriorating condition. To my mind, srikingly absent in Sybil, as well as in Wilbur's own published accounts, is any reflection on the pitfalls of this aggressive search for trauma memory.

As a rebel against the orthodox practices of psychoanalysis—particularly against the practice of maintaining emotional distance or "abstinence" toward patients—Wilbur became the apotheosis of the "good mother." She purchased clothing for Sybil, and they went on long drives together in the country. They even lived together for a period of time. By the close of Sybil, we learn that after treatment ended, Wilbur has loaned Sybil money for a down payment on a house and that they continue to spend time together, including weekends in the country (Schreiber, 1973, 442–444).

The Sybil narrative reveals an eerie parallel between the sadomasochistic memories of childhood torture and the ritualized encounters of therapy itself. Wilbur moved from conventional therapeutic listening to hypnosis, and then to the use of sodium Pentothal as she became more worried about the worsening condition of her patient. Wilbur came to Sybil's apartment regularly to administer Pentothal intravenously. Even though she had earlier emphasized the value of "straight psychoanalysis" for Sybil, Wilbur reasoned that her patient's deteriorating mental health required more aggressive methods (Schreiber 1973, p. 355).

Although "Pentothal brought to the surface the deeply buried, debilitating hatred of her mother" (p. 357), Sybil also became highly addicted to the treatment. The drug provided a euphoric release from the unending nightmare that had become her waking state of mind. But Wilbur's frequent visits to her apartment also brought additional comfort:

> Feeling more alive, more interested, Sybil redecorated the apartment, made it more attractive for her doctor-guest. The jab in the vein, the occasional inability to find a new vein after months had passed and so many veins had been pressed into service, the not-infrequent-swelling of the injected part of the anatomy, the feeling of chill that sometimes ran through the patient . . . this physical discomfiture was there. None of it mattered, however, in the light of the bright new day sodium Pentothal had brought. (Schreiber, 1973, p. 357)

These treatments may have been associated, for Sybil, with a regressive return to the womb of the good mother. But countervailing this, these treatments seemed to have had the character of a sadistic, sexual encounter. Just as the memories of being essentially raped by her mother with an enema bag included the rationalization that "this is for your own good," the intravenous administration of Pentothal may have been justified as "for your own good." The memories of early sexual torture at the hands of her mother may have been stimulated by the introduction of hypnosis and, later, Pentothal, and could very well have symbolically communicated distress over the invasiveness of the treatment itself.

Pornographic Encounters

As new personalities and trauma memories emerged, the material became more sadistic and sexual, and this trajectory has its parallel in the movement of therapy. Sybil produced new memories of her mother that featured "horsey games," involving mutual masturbation with young girls in the woods outside of her home town: "Finger moving. Palms stroking. Bodies gyrating. Ecstatic expressions. Everybody seemed to be holding somebody. Her mother was holding Hilda. Her mother's hands were at Hilda's crotch" (Schreiber, 1973, p. 206).

This pornographic material involving "secret rituals," sexual games, and "atrocities" foreshadowed the satanic ritual abuse theme that emerged in the trauma stories of multiples in the 1980s. And it also signifies a continuing blindness to how the therapeutic relationship casts its own indelible shadow on the past that is recovered. Wilbur's fixation on finding the "taproot" of Sybil's dissociations seems to have blinded her to her own demand for a performance. The talk of "secret rituals" of childhood finds a peculiar echo in the search and seizure rituals of treatment itself. The scenes that emerged during these therapy sessions are unspeakably chilling. And we have no way of knowing the degree to which they represent fact or fantasy. Making sense of this material, however, does require that we attend to how it was obtained.

It is inescapably ironic that Joanne Woodward, who played the role of patient in *The Three Faces of Eve*, released in 1957, is cast as Dr. Wilbur in the film version of *Sybil*, the next generation's multiple story. Wilbur has cast off the traditional role restraints of the dowdy Eve White, emerging with resplendent powers as a modern maternal authority. In one final scene, Wilbur and Sybil, played by Sally Fields, are picnicking in a bucolic setting. With birds chirping in the background, Sybil reveals the deeply buried trauma memory that has imprisoned her since childhood. The scene begins with Wilbur and Sybil sitting at the base of a forked tree, shaped like massive, open legs. The imagery strongly evokes childbirth, with Wilbur holding the daughter she has given psychological birth to, and Sybil expelling, like afterbirth, the final memory of her traumatizing mother.

The entire *mise en scene* may be understood as a cultural fantasy—a collective, female fantasy—of the new mother and the new daughter, the wish for unity free of the pain of conflict and disappointment. In representing this fantasy of a more whole, intact maternal other, *Sybil* hypnotizes us, suspending critical awareness of the costs of such fantasies, including those borne by the mother who is left behind. Whereas many women do struggle to work their way through the effects of destructive mothers, the film *Sybil*, like much of the trauma therapy movement, disavows both the daughter's own aggression toward the mother and the possibility of unholy alliances among women in overthrowing pernicious legacies.

Psychiatric Noir: Saints and Sinners

There is a *noir* element to the psychiatric discourse on MPD, that bears striking resemblance to the "woman of the night" in this film genre. Like the detective who moves between the masculine, rational world of the day and the feminine, irrational world of the night, modern MPD therapists are arbiters of the changing boundaries of gendered identity. In the noir convention, the detective is voyeuristically captured by the fantasy of a concealed, nocturnal world where female powers operate. Feminist film critics have argued that man's pursuit of the woman of the night, whom he ultimately brings under control, mobilizes collective anxieties over a maleness readily overwhelmed by a culturally emergent female authority (see Hirsch, 1981; Kaplan, 1980). Not reducible to actual men and women, these masculine and feminine positions in the narrative are unstable, fluctuating identifications and fantasies for both sexes.

Similarly, MPD is "a pathology of hiddenness" (Kluft, 1993, p. 25), requiring intensive efforts on the part of the therapist to ferret out the layers of concealed alters. Clinicians focus on missing time or gaps in the life narrative. Their reports of patients' histories are filled with intrigue— with mysterious clothing and meetings with strangers. The multiple is the woman with a secret life, the woman who finds herself in unexpected places, arousing suspicion in others. In the clinical reports of male and female clinicians alike, there is a highly paranoid aspect to this psychiatric probing. For women therapists, the sexual and aggressive aspects of this anxiety-ridden, voyeuristic gaze are more readily concealed within a protective, maternalized authority.

The female MPD patient expresses, through this new mythology that is permitted her, a creativity and rebelliousness much less evident in clinical portraits of the past. The clinical discourse of MPD permits women to express socially prohibited feelings—murderous rage, lesbian fantasies, grandiosity. This clinical permissiveness does have its cost: The patient must produce the requisite trauma memories that anchor and redeem the clinical project. And as both patient and therapist search in the remote areas of the psyche for a hidden memory of sexual abuse, both are spared the difficulty of confronting the intrusive invasions more immediately at hand.

CONCLUSION

I began with the problem of hysterical storytelling, and the question of how the presence of women, as translators on the scene, may mediate the interpretations of women's communications from "beyond the normal." We can see how women, whether as patients or practitioners, may make use of the idea of the hidden self because women, themselves, have been hidden from history. Yet the vital project of uncovering concealed knowledge and capacities—including exposing the fathers' dirty secrets— confronts the lingering problem of the hypnotic aspects of the therapeutic encounter. Authority figures, whether men or women, may intervene in the ambiguous disturbances of patients, still more typically women, making use of them in giving expression to their own preoccupations and anxieties.

One picture that I have assembled centers on multiplicity as a vehicle for rebellion within the mental health professions and for the struggle to recapture its own soul. Women patients with histories of various injuries and deprivations, including those inflicted by psychiatric authorities, find common cause with rebels in the mental health system who themselves feel fragmented and under siege.

But there is a companion story, in the affinity between multiplicity— as a modern variant of hysteria—and contemporary dilemmas of women. The MPD diagnosis permits the expression of aggressive and sexual "personalities" of women within a trauma–dissociation model that locates the meaning of these powerful enactments in discrete events of the past. Women can more freely express promiscuous, vengeful, and infantile selves because these selves are clinically constructed as visitations of the traumatic past. The feminine imagination is unleashed, evoking a rapt audience in the person of the therapist, but this permissive stance toward feminine transgressions is channeled into a search for sadistic sexual scenes.

On a cultural level, a number of forces may be operative that contribute to both this emerging clinical expression of women's conflict and the therapeutic construction of these conflicts. The 1950s era of *The Three Faces of Eve*—the woman caught between the stifling safety of the home and the wild abandon of the streets—has given way to more complex feminine narratives, a wider street of dreams than was formerly imaginable. Although the worlds of women are undoubtedly larger and freer than in the past, many women continue to find themselves harnessed with domestic responsibilities, trapped in lower-status occupations, and no longer having the steam engine of an activist women's movement to help them barge through the barriers.

Because defenders of MPD are so clearly mesmerized by the *productivity* of the multiple's imagination, many critics respond phobically, dismissing its rich significance. Yet between the poles of exalting and degrading the MPD narrative, we must recognize the painful dilemmas women continue to face in making integrative use of the rich potentiality of their inner worlds. There continues to be less recognition and less "holding" of female potentiality, both within families and within the larger society. If MPD treatment takes this potentiality down the dead-end street of a paranoid psychiatry, this may be attractive to many women because the present alternatives are so often stuntingly limited.

REFERENCES

Aldridge-Morris, R. (1989). *Multiple personality: An exercise in deception*. Hillsdale, NJ: Erlbaum.

Benjamin, J. (1988). *The bonds of love: Psychoanalysis, feminism, and the problem of domination*. New York: Pantheon Books.

Borch-Jacobsen, M. (1997, April). Sybil—The making of a disease: An interview with Dr. Herbert Spiegel. *The New York Review*, 24, 60–64.

Braude, A. (1989). *Radical spirits: Spiritualism and women's rights in nineteenth century America*. Boston: Beacon Press.

Braun, B. G. (1986). (Ed.). *Treatment of multiple personality disorder*. Washington, DC: American Psychiatric Press.

Brennan, T. (Ed.). (1989). *Between psychoanalysis and feminism*. New York: Routledge.

Butler, J. (1990). *Gender trouble: Feminism and the subversion of identity*. New York: Routledge.

de Marneffe, D. (1996). Looking and listening: The construction of clinical knowledge in Charcot and Freud. In B. Laslett, S. Kohlstedt, H. Longino, & E.

Hammonds (Eds.), *Gender and scientific authority*. Chicago: University of Chicago Press.

Ellenberger, H. (1970). *The discovery of the unconscious: The history and evolution of dynamic psychiatry*. New York: Basic Books.

Flax, J. (1990). *Thinking fragments: Psychoanalysis, feminism, and postmodernism in the contemporary West*. Los Angeles: University of California Press.

Freud, S. (1995). *An autobiographical study*. London: Hogarth Press. (Original work published 1935)

Gallop, J. (1982). *The daughter's seduction: Feminism and psychoanalysis*. Ithaca, NY: Cornell University Press.

Haaken, J. (1995). The debate over recovered memory: A feminist–psychoanalytic perspective. *Psychiatry: Journal of Biological and Interpersonal Processes, 58,* 189–198.

Haaken, J. (1996). The recovery of memory, fantasy, and desire: Feminist approaches to sexual abuse and psychic trauma. *Journal of Women in Culture and Society, 21,* 1068–1093.

Hacking, I. (1995). *Rewriting the soul: Multiple personality and the science of memory*. Princeton, NJ: Princeton University Press.

Hall, G. S. (1918–1919). A medium in the bud. *American Journal of Psychology, 29–30,* 144–158.

Hawthorn, J. (1983). *Multiple personality and the disintegration of literary character*. New York: St. Martin's Press.

Herman, J. L. (1992). *Trauma and recovery*. New York: Basic Books.

Hirsch, F. (1981). *Film noir: The dark side of the screen*. New York: Da Capo Press.

James, W. (1961). In G. Murphy & R. O. Ballou (Eds.), *William James on psychical research* (p. 27). London: Chatto & Windus. (Original work published 1890)

Kaplan, A. (Ed.). (1980). *Women in film noir*. London: British Film Institute.

Kenny, M. (1986). *The passion of Ansel Bourne*. Washington, DC: Smithsonian.

Kirk, S., & Kutchins, H. (1992). *The selling of DSM: The rhetoric of science in psychiatry*. New York: Aldine de Gruyter.

Kluft, R. (1993). Multiple personality disorder. In D. Spiegal (Ed.), *Dissociative disorders: A clinical review*. Lutherville, MD: Sidram Press.

Laurence, J., & Campbell, P. (1988). *Hypnosis, will, and memory: A psycho-legal history*. New York: Guilford Press.

Loftus, E., & Ketcham, K. (1994). *The myth of repressed memory*. New York: St. Martin's Press.

Maglin, N. B., & Perry, D. (Eds.). (1996). *Bad girls/good girls: Women, sex, and power in the nineties*. New Brunswick, NJ: Rutgers University Press.

Nathanson, C. (1991). *Dangerous passage*. Philadelphia: Temple University Press.

Ofshe, R., & Watters, E. (1994). *Making monsters: False memories, psychotherapy, and sexual hysteria*. New York: Scribner.

Oppenheim, J. (1985). *The other world: Spiritualism and psychical research in England 1850–1914*. New York: Cambridge University Press.

Owen, A. (1990). *The darkened room: Women, power, and spiritualism in late Victorian England*. Philadelphia: University of Pennsylvania Press.

Pendergrast, M. (1994). *Victims of memory: Incest accusations and shattered lives*. New York: Upper Access.

Penley, C. (1989). *The future of an illusion: Film, feminism, and psychoanalysis*. Minneapolis: University of Minnesota.

Randal, J. (1994). The legacy of abuse: How it contributes to illness. *Substance Abuse and Mental Health Services Administration News, 11*, 8–11.

Ross, C. (1989). *Multiple personality disorder: Diagnosis, clinical features, and treatment*. New York: Wiley.

Schacter, D. (1996). *Searching for memory: The brain, the mind, and the past*. New York: Basic Books.

Schreiber, F. (1973). *Sybil*. New York: Warner Books.

Showalter, E. (1985). *The female malady: Women, madness, and English culture, 1830–1980*. New York: Pantheon.

Showalter, E. (1997). *Hystories: Hysterical epidemics and modern culture*. New York: Columbia University Press.

Spence, D. (1982). *Narrative truth and historical truth*. New York: Norton.

Yapko, M. (1994). *Suggestions of abuse: True and false memories of childhood sexual trauma*. New York: Simon & Schuster.

15

THE PROOF IS IN THE PASSION: EMOTION AS AN INDEX OF VERIDICAL MEMORY

MICHAEL KENNY

The habit of feeling pleasure or pain at mere representations is not far removed from the same feeling about realities.

Aristotle, 1988

At the root of the false memory controversy is the commonly held notion that images and emotions associated with seemingly forgotten traumatic events may be recovered in something like their original form (Loftus & Ketcham, 1994; Spanos, 1996; Yapko, 1994). One influential but questionable version of this idea, which dates back at least to Breuer and Freud's 1895 *Studies on Hysteria*, holds that traumatic memories are encoded in the brain differently than are those of ordinary things (Terr, 1994; van der Kolk, 1994). It is maintained that, unlike ordinary memories, these recollections, still cathected with all the passion aroused by the original events, lie beneath the surface of consciousness, but they leak through in the camouflaged form of dreams, flashbacks, neurotic symptoms and déjà vu experiences; under special conditions full awareness of the original situation may be restored, accompanied by powerful emotional effects. The overwhelming subjective power of such abreactive displays, coupled with

I would like to thank Karen Frances for first calling the "alexithymia" concept to my attention. Special thanks also to Joe de Rivera for inviting me to the conference on "believed-in imaginings" at Clark University where I delivered a first run of the present chapter.

269

their dramatic impact on others, generate an aura of authenticity around what is being remembered. But what exactly do such displays prove?

In this chapter I consider restored emotion as a species of believed-in imagining. My approach is dramaturgical, an apt choice given that the Greek-derived concept of "catharsis" is itself rooted in dramatic theory. As always, my perceptions in this matter are steered by anthropological work demonstrating how powerful emotion may be evoked in ritual contexts, such as the ritual of spirit possession (Kenny, 1981). When seen as ritual, psychotherapies that encourage or expect emotional catharsis obviously have the same suggestive potential as do the possession dramas witnessed by anthropologists in the field. In such dramas the "performers" assume alter-identities attributable to spirit intrusion, and they display a full panoply of personality traits culturally associated with the spirits possessing them. Expectations about the possibility of such happenings contain implicit theories about the mind, its operations, and the metaphysical relation of humanity to the world at large. It is the interplay between theory, expectation, performance, and experience that concerns me here.

After some observations in the next section on the performative aspects of emotion, I give two examples of how the performance aspect of emotion has become intertwined with underlying psychological propositions about the nature of memory. The first example is Dr. John Mack's by now well-known study of people claiming to have been abducted by extraterrestrial aliens, a study in which Mack consistently argued that the truth of abduction memories is validated by the intense emotional displays accompanying their recovery. In my second example, I explore the theoretical assumptions that underwrite Mack's widely shared approach to emotion and memory through a discussion of the evolving psychiatric concept of *alexithymia* (a lack of words for feelings) and its relation to modern traumatology. I focus particularly on the work of the well-known trauma researcher, Bessel van der Kolk, who, like Mack, was very much concerned with the narrative reconstruction of voiceless traumatic experience. Alexithymia is a cutting-edge concept of "knowledge" concerning the relation between trauma and memory, because new expectations now taking shape may well end up being translated into clinical practice, thus affecting doctor–patient interactions, the construction of theory-driven meaning in clinical settings, post hoc validation of the theory itself, and, possibly, even the emergence of a new diagnostic category within North American psychiatry—a new believed-in relationship among cognition, emotion, and self-experience.

THE PERFORMATIVE ASPECTS OF EMOTION

That "mere representations"—believed-in imaginings—can stir powerful and visceral emotions hardly needs saying. Imagining a dramatic episode approaches the effects of witnessing it on the stage or being a part of it oneself; the emotions conventionally associated with experiencing real-world situations can reappear with surprising force and range in fantasy: anger, fear, grief, joy, desire, and more subtle affections as well. As Darwin observed in *The Expression of the Emotions in Man and Animals*,

> Anger and joy are from the first exciting emotions, and they naturally lead, more especially the former, to energetic movements, which react on the heart and this again on the brain. A physician once remarked to me as a proof of the exciting nature of anger, that a man when excessively jaded will sometimes invent imaginary offenses and put himself into a passion, unconsciously for the sake of reinvigorating himself. (1965, pp. 79–80)

I suspect that most people do something of the sort from time to time and would regard the inability to do so as a failing. Of course, what is to be imagined is never an emotion itself but is the situation (e.g., an imaginary offense, a romantic encounter) to which a given emotion is an appropriate response. Constructs such as anger and the rest of what we usually think of as emotions are dependent on context and can scarcely be conceived without one. As philosophers have pointed out, it would seem unusual—and certainly in defiance of common usage—for someone to say, "I'm angry, but I don't know at what." Emotions may be in the body or mind, but they are also a constitutive part of the social world.

However, although we must be angry, fearful, etcetera, in relation to *something*, the "true" source of our passion may remain obscure. Suspicions that our emotions are not directed at their true objects arise when they are poorly matched to circumstances: there is too much passion, too little, or the wrong kind. In extreme cases, a mismatch between emotions and circumstances can indicate a psychotic disorder, a radical loosening of the usually integral bond between cognition and emotion. As Bleuler said in his classical description of schizophrenia, "Schizophrenics can write whole autobiographies without manifesting the least bit of emotion. They will describe their suffering and their actions as if it were a theme in physics" (1950, p. 41). Along similar lines, in *An Anthropologist on Mars*, Sacks told the strange story of an autistic professor of veterinary medicine who had to learn socially appropriate emotional responses by observing normal human beings as though they were members of an alien species that she was obliged to imitate in order to live with (Sacks, 1995, pp. 244–296).

An unfeeling demeanor arouses hostility or suspicion, because no one can tell what, if anything, is going on inside. I think of Albert Camus's antihero in *The Stranger*, who went to the guillotine because he was not seen to weep at his mother's funeral. A similar fate awaited the convicted Oklahoma City bomber, Timothy McVeigh, who was closely watched by the media and jury for any sign of emotion as his putative atrocities were described in court. Having shown little reaction, it might be concluded that McVeigh is a stoic, an excellent actor, or a psychopathic zealot—"like the emotionless androids depicted in science fiction, unable to imagine what real humans experience" (Hare, 1993, p. 44).

Whereas psychopaths supposedly are *unable* to feel empathy for others because of some constitutional flaw, alexithymics—rather sad people who seem unable to fully partake in life—are believed to have a capacity for feeling but for whatever reason are unable to verbalize it and instead experience their affective lives in terms of somaticized physical illness. Emotion, and capacity for emotion, define the limits of our humanity. Ideas about this capacity are inextricably mixed with deeply rooted cultural presuppositions about normality and pathology, free will and determinism, and the limits of legal culpability.

It is widely supposed that some cases of mismatch between emotion and context arise because passion is not necessarily a response to present circumstances but instead is modeled on things that happened long ago, things long forgotten that became dispositional templates shaping future character. It is said that the past infests the present, in extreme cases bringing about the symptoms of "delayed" post-traumatic stress disorder (PTSD). These symptoms may include emotional deadening or overreaction to stimuli that resemble in some way the original traumatic experience—for example, a backfiring car responded to as though it were an enemy shell, any closed space experienced as though it were the elevator in which one was raped.

Like some varieties of schizophrenia, but by a different neurophysiological route, PTSD is held to disrupt the bond between cognition and emotion or, to put it differently, the relation between verbally discursive memory and inarticulate embodied feeling. If this kind of "feeling" is in fact inarticulate, how are the words to be found for it, and what are the consequences of finding it? How do we know what we really feel? Why should finding words for such feelings bring relief? Whatever the answer, the psychoanalytic tradition lives on in the common presumption that finding words will somehow help, especially words adding up to a coherent story that articulates one's emotional experience in a comprehensible life history.

The education in the feelings has long been seen as a necessary part of education in general. The epigram for this chapter, in fact, is drawn from Aristotle's *The Politics*; it originally appeared in the course of an argument supporting the value of music in cultivating good citizenship. According to Aristotle, artistic performances that arouse empathy, and stimulate proper responses to good and evil, are of great aid in helping these sentiments become second nature (1988, p. 191). Emotions are not cathartically purged "but transmuted and integrated into a new level of response and understanding" (Simon, 1978, p. 144). From this point of view, *"emotions are judgments*, not blind or irrational forces that victimize us" (Solomon, 1976, p. 15). In her study of anger, Tavris (1982) observed that "anger, like love, is a moral emotion" (1982, p. 23)—not a spontaneous instinctive reaction but a complex (although not necessarily conscious) social act involving concepts of natural justice, honor, and shame as well as a fair share of dramatic skill. Sarbin made a similar point: "The uncritical acceptance of the concept of passions and its implied mechanistic causality has frustrated attempts to connect "emotions" with the language of everyday life as represented by dramatists, novelists and poets" (1986, p. 85). The upshot of such arguments is that emotion—whatever else it may or may not be in neuropsychological terms—is also a form of symbolic communication imbued with cultural values keyed to the libretto of ongoing social life.

But, as I have said, problems arise when there is an existential disjunction between reason and passion, such that the latter appears as an alien force or is somehow poorly matched to circumstances. Aristotle, who was both physician and dramatic theorist, recognized this too, and his statements about it—or rather, interpretations of his statements—echo down to us in the form of widely shared propositions about memory, emotivity, and cathartic healing. Interpretations of Aristotle's theory of art take two rather different directions, each of which can seemingly be supported from his writings. One position is the one just mentioned, that catharsis entails not the purging of sentiment, but its cultivation. The alternative interpretation focuses on the purging or at least equilibration of emotion and can be summed up as follows: People differ in innate temperament; some are more susceptible to certain emotions, some less; those with an unhealthy surfeit of passion may be helped, via a kind of homeopathic therapy, with a dose of that which normally ignites the selfsame passion—thus bringing about purgation and healing, a restoration of proper balance in the soul (Aristotle, 1988, p. 195). This type of medical reasoning led 19th-century classicists to the model of catharsis that informs present-day understandings about the dynamics of the emotions and the nature of traumatic memory (Kenny, 1997); it led down another rather different path to the Nietzscheian theory of tragedy. I would suggest that it is actually the *first* Aristotelian model—catharsis as education, articulation—that is most applicable to the types of ends sought by our latter-day traumatologists.

Breuer and Freud were influenced by a cultural controversy set in motion by the philologist (and Martha Freud's paternal uncle) Jacob Bernays, who had written on the medico-religious implications of the Greek catharsis concept. Aristotle's observations in *The Politics* concerning pity and fear refer back to what he said about tragedy in the *The Poetics*—namely that tragedy brings about catharsis through the arousal of these same emotions (Aristotle, 1988). The audience empathically participates in the drama, finding a kind of pleasure or relief in bearing witness even to the awful fates of Oedipus, Orestes, and Antigone. In Aristotle's aesthetics one comes away from a good play not just entertained, but better for it. One's own life appears in a different light when compared to individuals forced by fate into the toughest of all choices.

How the Greeks actually conceived of the nature of these feelings was and remains a subject of vigorous debate among scholars (not least about whether "purgation" is the most apt translation of "catharsis"). However, here I am primarily interested in the dramatic evocation of emotion as an index to the truth of believed-in imaginings about past events—a subject entangled with the cultural history of drama and abreactive psychotherapies. And so I turn to consider the nature of the highly evocative displays elicited among putative alien abductees.

EMOTIONAL INTENSITY AND ALIEN ABDUCTION STORIES

If a play did not grab us on some level, we would not think very highly of it, and we would perhaps attribute our lack of responsiveness to bad writing or lousy acting. In real life we might be puzzled by a chronicle of horror recited, like Bleuler's schizophrenics, in an apparently unemotional monotone. Emotion is convincing. It helped to convince John Mack—professor of psychiatry at Harvard and author of a Pulitzer Prize-winning biography of T. E. Lawrence—that the stories he was being told about abduction by extraterrestrials recounted actual events. Not only that, emotion helped convince the abductees themselves.

The theory that led to these revelations is of a familiar and really rather simple type. Mack is psychoanalytically oriented. He has allowed that the physical evidence for abductions is equivocal but that psychological evidence has its own validity: "a *correct psychodynamic formulation* [italics added] explains past memories and current behaviors and predicts future behaviors" (Mack, 1994, p. 425). Mack became convinced that there was more to abduction accounts than psychopathology or overactive imagination by "the consistency of the stories told by individuals who had not been in communication with each other" (p. 1). The "intensity of the energies and emotions involved as abductees relive their experiences" (p. 3) under hypnosis lent added credibility, whereas the personal transformations initiated by these experiences—particularly a heightened ecological concern—had common features that were taken to express a common underlying purpose on the part of our interdimensional visitors (p. 389).

Mack contended that past memories, current actions (particularly the display of strong emotion), and future behaviors were therefore commensurate with the abduction hypothesis. Whatever the status of the objective physical evidence, Mack concluded that the phenomenon as a whole points toward the spiritual evolution of humanity, a fusion of human and alien consciousness accompanied by a paradigm shift (his term) away from the western mechanistic world view and toward an expanded epistemology that requires "the legitimization of neglected aspects of ourselves as instruments of knowing" (p. 387). Mack (1994) stated:

> The alien abduction phenomenon appears to have something to teach us about the redemptive and transformational role of emotion in human life. The terror, rage, grief, and, on a few occasions, joy expressed during my sessions with experiencers are among the most powerful I have ever witnessed. For me and other who have attended the sessions, as well as for the abductees themselves, it is this intensity of *recovered emotion* [italics added] that lends inescapable authenticity to the phenomenon. (p. 400)

Mack's own criterion for including a particular story was "whether what has been reported was felt to be real by the experiencer and was communicated sincerely and with powerful affect appropriate to what is being reported" (p. 16). One patient, recalling an alien object being inserted in her vagina, "sobbed and panted, at times crying hysterically or expressing rage" (p. 152). Another, regressed hypnotically to age 6, recounted his experiences while "grimacing, frowning, eyebrows furrowing, teeth clenching; body twitching, tensing, head shaking, face contorting, expression changing every second or two" (p. 215). Each episode in his abduction story was punctuated by a minor convulsion—like one of Charcot's hysterical crises—as he went on to the next scene. Mack summarized,

> When the experiences are recalled consciously, or during hypnotic sessions, the abductees go through an emotional *reliving* of great intensity and power. Otherwise quite controlled individuals may writhe, perspire, and scream with fear and rage, or cry with appropriate sadness, as they remember their abduction experiences. This emotional expression appears altogether authentic to those who are unfamiliar with the abduction phenomenon and witness it for the first time. (1994, pp. 391–392)

Most of Mack's patients had forgotten their experiences and only slowly came to the conclusion that something unusual had happened to them that needed explaining. One, for example, had been engaged in meditation and began to have unsettling auto-hypnotic flashbacks that led him to make contact with a UFO informational network. By that route he came to Mack, who would characterize him as a bit of a lost soul.

In the course of the "relaxation" session (or "regression" or "hypnosis"—Mack seems to have used the terms interchangeably), the patient began to recover material so extraordinary that at first he did not believe it himself. He asked the doctor, "Am I bullshitting you?" Mack responded with psychoanalytic neutrality, "I don't know. Are you?" Forced to examine his own impressions, the patient concluded that the memories were genuine because they kept returning, saying that "the sincerity of myself says it's not coming from just, it's not I'm just making this up" (p. 44). He did not think it could have come from some external source, say a *Twilight Zone* plot. Over time this sense of reality grew stronger.

Another patient, although she had cultivated an interest in the paranormal since childhood, nonetheless had similar doubts. While being treated with massage for a pain at the base of her skull, she began to have experiences of "small beings" communicating with her telepathically, and she also found herself making automatic drawings of aliens with big eyes. Her contact with Mack was preceded by a serious illness of uncertain nature accompanied by progressive estrangement from her husband and eventual divorce. Like the patient described earlier, she at first could not believe, although she was "reassured to learn that other abductees had been struggling with the same philosophical questions" (p. 206). As Mack recounted,

> [Her] wish to be hypnotized grew out of her desire to "know what's true. . . I don't want to know a story that I make up or anybody else makes up," she said. "I really want to know! I really want to know! It's the only thing that's important." [She] wants to be responsible for her experiences. "To tell you the honest truth," she said, "I don't know if I believe myself. . . . There's a part of me that really, really does. But there's a part of me that doesn't, and that part feels like it's destroying me." (p. 197)

Other patients were convinced of the reality of their abduction experiences by the emotions themselves:

> As more and more details of her troubling experiences were relived with intense emotions, [she] clung to her doubts as to their actuality. . . . Most instrumental in [her] emerging acknowledgment of the personal truth of what she had undergone was her sense of herself as a person not given to the expression of strong feelings without a solid basis in actual experience. (p. 164–165)

> He felt "a little incredulous" to discover that he was living "a double existence" [as a symbiotic half human, half alien entity], but the emotional power of the session, together with the objective clarity, convinced him of the authenticity of what he had just been through. (p. 177)

Clear enough. But what about Mack's view on the *process* that allowed these memories and their associated emotions to reemerge after years in the dark? As with PTSD, there may be a perceptual "trigger"—"something seen or heard which may bear only a minimal relationship to the actual abduction" (Mack, 1994, p. 10, cf. pp. 15–16)—that opens up a chain of associations leading backward to memories of the abduction experience. This does not explain their original relegation to the unconscious. Mack considered traumatic "dissociation" to be a possible psychical mechanism, even though he observed that this does not tell us anything about the nature of the trauma itself. For example, he stated that not a single case of abduction that he studied revealed a history of childhood sexual abuse, but that the opposite had "frequently occurred." Given the enthusiasm of the aliens for proctological intrusion, this was evidently an important issue.

If abductee amnesia is due to "dissociation" or "repression," just how does that work? The traditional answer would be that repression keeps painful material out of consciousness in defense of the ego. A more recent alternative would have it that dissociation is an automatic process brought about by the effects of trauma on the neural circuits that normally link emotion and discursive memory; recollections of highly emotive traumatic events are separately stored and generate the pathological symptoms of PTSD when they spill over into everyday life. However, abductees themselves maintain that their amnesia has an alien rather than an endopsychic origin, "the result of an outside turning or switching off of memory by something the aliens themselves do" (p. 9, cf. p. 399). If so, the abductees are in no way responsible for any of this themselves, a view that Dr. Mack apparently accepted. He noted that these extraordinary long-buried memories proved remarkably easy to access:

> The inducement of a nonordinary state [relaxation, regression, hypnosis], seems to be highly effective in bringing abductees' walled off experiences into consciousness and in discharging their traumatic impact. (p. 9)

> But we have little understanding of how this repressing force works, or, for that matter, why an altered state of consciousness, facilitated in a caring, protective setting, is so effective in recovering abduction memories. (p. 399)

It seemed to Mack and his patients as if the aliens set it all up so that memories would return when needed—a thesis consistent with the claim that a spiritual transformation was underway, instigated by aliens, mediated by pain, and culminated in growth. Cathartic expression of emotion—"fully experiencing the terror and rage" (p. 33)—led to the integration of dissociated material into the life story of the abductee, material that powerfully affected the body as it entered consciousness in communicable form. In this context emotion was therefore "redemptive and transformational" (p. 190), part of "a process of information reception, storage, recovery, and integration of great purpose and potential power" (p. 38).

The religious imagery is unmistakable, as is the evocation of what is familiar to anthropologists as a rite of passage, whereby—in a ritual punctuated by pain and fear—a person is moved from one stage of life to another. I think that many therapists working in this area would also accept such a view. Seen in this light, emotion most certainly *is* transformational. But is it *recovered* emotion?

• This capacity of hypnosis to evoke dramatically appropriate affect is well known to researchers in this field (and to stage hypnotists), although Mack himself seems to have been surprised by it. That hypnosis is capable of reviving memory is itself a widely shared cultural assumption. One investigator, referring to emotional phenomena elicited during age regression, observed that "when hypnotized subjects themselves cannot be certain whether their hypnotically elicited recollections are fact or fantasy, it behooves the investigator to be cautious" (Perry, 1988, p. 150; see also Spanos, 1996). If emotion is largely evaluative, contextual, and performative in nature, then how, in the kind of case at issue here, is one to separate method acting from the supposedly real thing—an outpouring of fossilized passion?

From an anthropological point of view it does not much matter: The therapeutic evocation of emotion is part of a ritual process in the present, however it may relate to the past. Perhaps it usually does not matter much to psychotherapists, either, insofar as their practical goal is not that of establishing the abstract truth of memory but rather of helping their clients transcend present distress. One takes psychic reality as it comes; if that reality includes some seemingly bizarre material, then so be it. However, if one is evaluating the objective reality of alien abduction, recovered memories of childhood sexual abuse, or the ontological status of dissociative identity disorder, then truth claims matter a great deal.

THEORETICAL ASSUMPTIONS ABOUT EMOTION AND MEMORY

The Need for Emotional Expression

Truth claims such as those made by Mack's patients hinge on the credibility of theories and clinical observations pertaining to the relation between amnesia and traumatic stress. The theoretical assumptions underlying this relationship are somewhat commonsensical, an indication of how deeply these notions are embedded in the general culture. The widely accepted North American theory about emotion and healing is based on propositions like the following (drawn from Lutz, 1988; Tavris, 1982):

- Emotion and reason are in a state of chronic tension (Freud likened the ego's attempt to master the id with a rider trying to stay atop an unruly horse).
- Unexpressed emotion is dangerous (it is responsible for neuroses and psychosomatic illnesses. Dammed up affect must go

somewhere; if it does not go out into the world, it goes into the body and causes physical disease, somatization, and the conversion symptoms of classical hysteria).

- Expressing one's feelings is the key to good mental and physical health (therefore we should learn how to become more expressive).

- If dysphoric feelings are linked to memories that have been ignored, repressed, or dissociated, then these memories must be reclaimed and incorporated into one's explicit life story (such that horse and rider become one—integrated).

The same set of initial assumptions about emotion and memory can lead to a variety of outcomes when put into clinical practice: alien abduction, multiple personality, satanic ritual abuse, past life regression, as well as the more mundane therapeutic outcomes that are usually sought (see Hacking, 1995; Kenny, 1981; Showalter, 1997). When put into practice, a theory such as the one outlined here is quite capable of leading one to find affective phenomena that validate one's expectations. And it may be especially easy to find such phenomena with people who have had prior involvement with various forms of occultism.

Multiple personality exemplifies the social construction of emotional memory (and recall that some of Mack's patients considered themselves to be human–alien symbiotes). In cases of MPD, traumatic emotion is usually in the keeping of an alter personality whose existence is unknown to the "normal" waking self, but who emerges dramatically under hypnosis to reveal unpleasant secrets about the past: "abreactions convince the therapist of the reality of the childhood abuse. There is just no way that clinical abreactions by multiples are faked. They are dissociative recreations of the original trauma and are important healing rituals" (Ross, 1989, p. 248). Putnam (1989) described such abreactions as follows:

> For MPD patients, the recovery of hidden memories is usually traumatic. In many instances, the act of remembering will produce a florid abreaction. . . . The therapist and patient must learn to induce, control, and process these experiences if the patient is to derive therapeutic benefits from abreactive episodes. . . . The therapist should make every effort to help the patient recover, re-experience, and reintegrate split-off affects and somatic sensations, as these are probably the most potent sources of everday discomfort and dissociative behavior. (pp. 230, 237, 247–248)

Many of those who therapeutically utilize cathartic or abreactive techniques are united, whatever their theoretical differences otherwise, by the belief that strong emotion is a definite sign of progress and even an essential part of the cure, part of "detoxifying and metabolizing traumatic memories" (Kluft, 1996, p. 103). Much of the literature on recovered memories of childhood sexual abuse focuses on the necessity for expression of the emotions (rage, fear, grief) associated with the original trauma that have been dissociated since then. As I have said elsewhere, these abreactive techniques are sometimes modeled on procedures first developed to deal with grief and mourning, classic rites of passage greatly influenced by the thanatologist, Elisabeth Kübler-Ross (Herman, 1992; Kenny, 1997).

Demonstrative abreaction radiates authenticity as well as therapeutic efficacy. No doubt it also helps to bring patients around, in much the same way as emotion helped convince Mack's patients that something had genuinely happened to them and that they were moving onto a new plane of being. And again the question must be asked: Are these emotions the product of forgotten trauma or a histrionic enactment of the survivor role? There seems no ready way to tell, even when the traumatic experiences themselves are fully authenticated.

Linguistic Expression of Emotion

Various pathologies are attributed to dammed up feelings, and therapy is aimed at breaching whatever dam is holding them back. These endeavors tend not to be based on a simple purgation model but on a more subtle and complex theory summed up by the concept of "integration." The goal is assimilation of dissociated pathogenic affect into consciousness, not purging it out of the system altogether. To that end words must be found for what was hitherto inarticulate and incomprehensible suffering; once again the way in which this is done opens up theory-driven possibilities for the creation of believed-in imaginings that are validated by the emergence of strong emotion.

The relation of emotion to language is an interesting topic, well worked over by the linguistic philosophers. How do we know when we feel this or that; by what marks are feelings known? Identifying and labeling an emotion is a rather different matter than identifying a table or chair by pointing at it and uttering a word in the same way as Adam and Eve named the animals. One answer might be that emotions can only be known post hoc; we encounter a situation and find out how to label our reaction by noting the diacritical physical changes taking place in our bodies. A more plausible account would have it that emotion is an integral part of the initial judgment, a passionate judgment whose physical echoes slowly fade away, leaving behind the mistaken impression that the judgment was a bodily phenomenon all along (i.e., it was a causal force). The conceptual distinction between *emotion* (a meaningful judgment) and *feeling* (an obscure bodily sensation) seems very fuzzy, but it is still commonly drawn and just as commonly effaced. Deterministic illusions can also arise out of ignorance. People make most judgments without knowing that we are doing so; things just come naturally. Here it can make sense to talk about nonconscious or unconscious emotion and about the educative value of psychoanalysis (and anthropology) in bringing implicit knowledge to conscious awareness: "the expansion of the consciously acknowledged self" (Krystal, 1995, p. 83).

The problem of emotion and language stands out in peculiar relief in research on the increasingly popular psychiatric notion of *alexithymia*—a term coined by psychiatrist Peter Sifneos to denote "lack of words for feeling." This neologism filled the need for a term for what seemed to be common among some patients suffering from psychosomatic disorders such as ulcers and colitis: They had great difficulty discussing their affective life and admitting that there was anything worth discussing. In other words, they may have had feelings but not emotions per se. If, as it is widely believed, verbalizing feelings cancels out the pathogenic effects of leaving them unknown and unsaid, then the therapeutic trick is to transform the former into the latter.

Alexithymics have been described as "emotional illiterates" (Lesser, 1981, p. 532; Sifneos, 1996, p. 138). They seem dull, have an impoverished capacity for fantasy, and are not easily reached by therapists who try to get them to talk about emotions they do not seem to have (but that the therapist surmises must be there anyway or else they would not be sick). "Alexithymic individuals show a striking difficulty in recognizing and describing their own feelings, and they have difficulty discriminating between emotional states and bodily sensations" (Taylor, 1984, p. 726). Catharsis shows promise in such cases, because acting out may prove more effective than speaking out (Sifneos, 1973, p. 261). Lesser (1981) described one group of alexithymics as follows: "Because they lacked the ability to discharge tension through verbal, gestural or symbolic means, these patients got 'stuck with their tension,' with somatic channels as the only means available for discharge of this tension" (p. 532).

So why is expressing emotion problematic for alexithymics? The problem is riddled with difficulties. The standards for proper emotional expressiveness vary with class, gender, and ethnicity. For example, ethnic Chinese people and many Latin Americans downplay emotional self-reference and tend to somatize when in difficulty; there may be significant differences between women and men within one cultural tradition; emotion vocabularies may be more or less elaborated in given languages; and so forth. The literature contains two rather different although not necessarily mutually exclusive ways of interpreting alexithymia: psychodynamic and neuropsychological (assuming, which not everyone does, that alexithymia is a discriminable phenomenon in the first place, that is empirically separable from symptoms associated with the affective disorders "or general clinical distress" (Rief, Heuser, & Fichter, 1996).

Theoretical work on alexithymia tends to elide research on other disorders in which the capacity for feeling is either diminished or distorted, notably psychopathy and PTSD. Current writings on psychopathy tend toward the view that the incapacity of psychopaths to feel strongly and to empathically identify with others is the expression of a hard-wired, and possibly genetic, neurobiological deficit. Psychotherapy has little effect on those who not only do not feel, but *cannot* feel as others do. Psychopaths are hyper-rationalists who must be convinced that better behavior is in their own best interest. They may have words for feeling, but they are empty and manipulative words:

> Psychopaths seem to suffer a kind of emotional poverty that limits the range and depth of their feelings. While at times they appear cold and unemotional, they are prone to dramatic, shallow, and short-lived displays of feeling. Careful observers are left with the impression that they are play-acting and that little is going on below the surface. Sometimes they claim to experience strong emotions but are unable to describe the subtleties of various affective states. (Hare, 1993, p. 52)

Whereas psychopaths supposedly have an innate affective deficit, it is thought that alexithymics *can* feel, but have failed to develop their potential for affective expression or have lost that capacity as a result of trauma. The concept has found a particularly evocative application with respect to people who went emotionally dead after their experience in the Nazi concentration camps.

Theoretical work on alexithymia connects with that on PTSD. The criteria for PTSD cited in the fourth edition of the *Diagnostic and Statistical Manual of Mental Disorders* (*DSM-IV*) include various forms of reliving the trauma *and* various forms of affective blunting or avoidance, such as "markedly diminished interest or participation in significant activities, feeling of detachment or estrangement from others, restricted range of affect" as well as inability to remember aspects of the trauma (American Psychiatric Association, 1994, p. 428) It was this blunting of affect coupled with a proclivity for psychosomatic illness that impressed psychiatrists working with Holocaust survivors in the 1950s and that now supports a retroactive diagnosis of PTSD (which first appeared under that name in the *DSM-III* in 1980).

The therapeutic goal with alexithymics and PTSD patients is to get them back on line emotionally. If forgotten, repressed, or dissociated traumatic memories are at the root of the problem, then the solution is recovery of such memories and fusion with the illness-producing emotions that they unconsciously generate. But for this to occur, a conceptual or narrative scaffolding is needed to which the feelings and emotions can be attached. When traumatic etiology is suspected, but troubling emotions and behaviors are the only thing directly known in a clinical sense, then these intrusive symptoms may well be taken to refer back to the hidden events that gave rise to them; however, the reference is veiled and the code must be deciphered, an approach that has led to the recovered memory controversy with its exotic penumbra of abduction stories and their like.

This code-breaking exercise should be tailor made to the individual. It is recognized that not everyone responds in the same way to otherwise similar situations. Responses involve the meaning of the trauma in relation to the constitution of the person who endured it, and the threat to psychophysical integrity that the trauma subjectively entails. In practice what tends to emerge is eclectic psychoanalysis that is shrouded in a fog of neurobiological speculation. On the one side we have the trappings of hard science, and on the other an emphasis on the highly variable subjective meaning of trauma. If *subjective meaning* is the fundamental criterion for traumatic experience, then the concept of trauma itself becomes increasingly nebulous.

The unvarnished psychoanalytic tradition is most evident in the work of Krystal who, with Niederland (1964), was in on the beginning of modern traumatology through his work with Holocaust survivors, work that led to Krystal's editorship of the seminal book *Massive Psychic Trauma* (1968). For Krystal, the alexithymic characteristics of trauma victims were explained by regression to an infantile condition in which the distinctions between cognition, feeling, and emotion are blurred (Krystal, 1988). He observed that there was a "progressive constriction of cognitive processes, including memory and problem solving, until a mere vestige of self-observing ego is preserved" (Krystal, 1995, p. 81).

The overall consequence is that a greater and greater range of experience—intrusive memories, dreams, and emotions—come to be feared as ego-alien and avoided by whatever means possible—dissociation, avoidance, denial—with psychosomatic illness as a consequence. Like many other workers in this field, Krystal has expressed the opinion that reclaiming such material is part of a process akin to mourning, a process he called "*mastering* the loss" (Krystal, 1988, p. 229). Caruth (1995) described the process as learning how to "own" the experience, "integrating" it "both for the sake of testimony and for the sake of cure" (p. 153). Krystal and others have attributed traumatically induced alexithymia to fear of being overwhelmed by one's own memories. The therapeutic literature therefore stresses the necessity for a "controlled re-experiencing of the trauma," accompanied by a nonthreatening modicum of cathartic emotional release, what one clinician specializing in DID called "fractionated abreaction" (Kluft, 1996, p. 107; cf. Kenny, 1997).

The use of religiously loaded terms such as *owning* and *testimony* evokes the moral passion inherent in contemporary traumatology. The traditional goal of psychoanalysis—expanding the scope of the ego at the expense of the id—has become fused to the political goal of expanding collective awareness of trauma at the expense of societal denial. That in turn leads to paradigmatic turf wars within psychiatry (Kenny, 1995). Will alexithymia end up being "owned" by the trauma theorists?

ALEXITHYMIA AND TRAUMATOLOGY INTERTWINED

An association between alexithymia and psychic trauma is well established in professional writings, although it is also acknowledged that some alexithymic characteristics may arise from innate factors and others from anomalies in psychological development (Taylor, 1994; Taylor, Bagby, & Parker, 1991; van der Kolk & McFarlane, 1996). It seems that everyone in psychiatry now reads Thomas Kuhn and have rather ironically (given what Kuhn has said about textbooks) come to treat *The Structure of Scientific Revolutions* (1962) itself as a textbook on the social process through which vague pre-paradigmatic generalizations get elevated into commonly shared understandings about how the world actually works (Kenny, 1995). So it is with alexithymia, which some researchers see as a construct on the verge of breaking out of its pre-paradigmatic phase into professional acceptance as the foundation of psychosomatic medicine (Taylor, Bagby, & Parker, 1991).

Alexithymia is not currently recognized in the *DSM-IV*, although I predict that it will be included in future editions. There is even a proposed new meta-category, "disorders of emotional regulation," that may subsume it, and there are a number of disorders or syndromes currently classified under other headings (Taylor, 1994, p. 63). If alexithymia does become officially recognized, the question then becomes that of etiology, a vexed issue within North American psychiatry because of the professedly atheoretical and descriptive nature of the *DSM* nosology. This is a domain where psychoanalysis, neurobiology, and politics cross paths—with interesting implications for the future of the catharsis concept and abreactive therapies. During what has been called the pre-paradigmatic phase of alexithymia in the early 1980s, one pair of authors, citing no less an authority than Sarbin, observed that "the metaphor of one generation becomes the myth of the next" (Lesser & Lesser, 1983, p. 1307) and warned that giving a name to alexithymia may tend to reify a concept that has no clear referent. Whether that will be its fate remains to be seen, but it can at least be said that alexithymia is now well on the way to becoming part of the standard discourse of psychiatry.

The well-known trauma researcher van der Kolk has observed that "an experience does not really exist until it can be named and placed into larger categories," thus providing the kind of conceptual scaffolding needed for the articulation of nameless feeling (van der Kolk & McFarlane, 1996, p. 4). A merging of the concepts of PTSD and alexithymia could well result in a broadening of the scope of putative effects of trauma through the attribution of alexithymic characteristics to a traumatic etiology. As I have mentioned elsewhere (Kenny, 1995, 1996), there has been a tendency among certain trauma researchers and clinicians, as well as specialists in the dissociative disorders, to extend the reach of the trauma paradigm to embrace an increasing variety of neuroses and personality problems.

Van der Kolk has been quite clear about this agenda (one shared with kindred spirits such as Judith Herman). As he said in his recent edited book *Traumatic Stress* (1996)—dedicated, as it happens, to Nelson Mandela—the aim is to give psychiatry back its "soul," to reclaim this branch of medicine from the myopic reductionists and trivializers by showing how the study of trauma brings unity to a subject in sad theoretical disarray, of which the *DSM's* etiologically agnostic classification of mental disorders is but one very important sign. Large numbers of symptoms and syndromes currently assigned to a variety of *DSM* categories (the somatoform, dissociative, anxiety, and personality disorders) may be brought under PTSD's tent. Because, according to van der Kolk, trauma is the single greatest cause of mental disorder and much other suffering besides, it is also the most worthy of medical and political attention. Not only this, the diagnosis "validates" the suffering of many who heretofore had no labels for their experience (van der Kolk & McFarlane, 1996, p. 5).

He has maintained that one reason for this widespread ignorance about trauma is that its effects resemble so many other things, whereas, in fact, somatization, dissociation, and "affect dysregulation" may well be tied together by psychological trauma as "the common etiological factor" (van der Kolk, 1996; see also Herman, 1992 who has proposed rehabilitating the "garbage-can" borderline personality disorder diagnosis by redefining it as a variant of PTSD; see also Kenny, 1996). Particular responses to trauma are complex, but the PTSD conceptualization is comparatively simple: the unity underlying superficial diversity (van der Kolk & McFarlane, 1996, p. 16). These are hegemonic claims, and alexithymia is already half caught in the net.

Now, if psychological trauma actually does underlie many otherwise heterogeneous psychiatric symptoms, then the process leading from trauma to such an extraordinarily wide range of illness outcomes becomes a matter of very great interest indeed. Van der Kolk has focused on dissociation. It is a rather slippery concept, not easy to pin down, but in the present context it signifies an inability to integrate traumatic memories into explicit recollection of one's personal past. Instead these memories persist in an intrusive "timeless" and speechless ego-alien form: *"The very nature of a traumatic memory is to be dissociated"* (van der Kolk, 1996, p. 289, italics added), precisely what is supposed to have happened with Mack's patients, perhaps with alien help.

> Because people with PTSD have a fundamental impairment in the
> capacity to integrate traumatic experiences with other life events, their

traumatic memories are often not coherent stories; they tend to consist of intense emotions or somatosensory impressions, which occur when the victims are aroused or exposed to reminders of the trauma. (van der Kolk & McFarlane, 1996, p. 9)

Avoidance of such emotions is at the root of alexithymia, because these sensations arouse people's fear of being traumatized all over again. Seen from a psychodynamic point of view, such people may find it best to retreat from feeling itself. It may prove difficult or impossible to help some alexithymic survivors integrate affect-laden memories into their conscious life stories (Krystal, 1995); all that can be hoped for is showing them how to recognize and cope with the warning signs that dissociated material impelling their behavior (van der Kolk et al., 1996, pp. 90–91). In other cases integration of this material most definitely *is* prescribed, which means that "traumatic experiences need to be located in time and place and differentiated from current reality" (van der Kolk, 1994, p. 261). These "unassimilated scraps of overwhelming experiences . . . need to be integrated with existing mental schemes, and be transformed into narrative language" (van der Kolk & van der Hart, 1995, p. 176).

This entails the construction of a coherent story into which these experiences can be placed, thus bringing the unfinished past to closure (see Waitzkin & Magana, 1997). But need the story also be true? Autobiographies, we have learned, are not necessarily true or false, but rather are literary constructions, narrative forms that retroactively interpret the pattern and meaning of one's life. For that reason, "the stories that people tell about their traumas are as vulnerable to distortion as people's stories about anything else" (van der Kolk, 1996, p. 297; see also Freeman, 1993).

On the one hand, van der Kolk et al. (1996) recognized that narrative truth may differ from historical truth. On the other hand, they claimed that traumatic memories are absolutely veridical because of the unusual circumstances in which they were laid down: a special stress-induced form of mnemonic encoding involving disruption of neural circuits between the brain structures usually involved in declarative memory (the loop between thalamus, amygdala, hippocampus, and prefrontal cortex; van der Kolk, 1994, 1996, p. 282). This notion seems widely accepted among those in tune with the political and social implications of establishing a scientific basis for veridical traumatic memory; a search for such validation is, in fact, the foremost trench line in the defense of recovered memory therapy. As the editor of one recent collection on the subject declared, "the images of traumatic reenactment remain absolutely accurate and precise" but "they are largely inaccessible to conscious recall and control" (Caruth, 1995, p. 151). However, anthropologist Alan Young's study of a U.S. Veterans Administration PTSD clinic outlined in detail the social process through which such memories become *acknowledged as truth* and assigned etiological significance through retrospective reconstruction of a life-story consistent with the trauma hypothesis (Young, 1996).

So, if all goes well, unconscious although veridical memories of horrifying events will eventually find their niche in fully conscious autobiographical narratives emergent from the therapeutic process. This is meaning-centered therapy. "Although the reality of extraordinary events is at the core of PTSD, the meaning that victims attach to these events is as fundamental as the trauma itself" (van der Kolk & McFarlane, 1996, p. 6). Therefore "the exploration of personal meaning of the trauma is critical; since patients cannot undo their past, giving it meaning is a central goal of therapy" (p. 19). Obviously that is impossible if the victim is unaware of having been traumatized in the first place; in these instances, memory recovery is a necessary first step. The animals must be named before they can be tamed, and at this point treatment of PTSD and alexithymia may well amount to much the same thing: Whereas before I just had a chronic through obscure pain in the guts, now I know I am angry or afraid, but at what, of what . . .? As van der Kolk et al. (1996) put it, "Enhanced capacity to name and manage intense affective and somatic reactions often is a necessary prerequisite for the exploration of the traumatic past. Exploration of the past might, in turn, be a necessary prerequisite for the resolution of the trauma" (p. 91). However,

> Merely uncovering memories is not enough; they need to be modified and transformed (i.e., placed in their proper context and reconstructed in a personally meaningful way). Thus, in therapy, memory paradoxically needs to become an act of *creation* rather than the static recording of events. Like memories of ordinary events, the memory of the trauma needs to become merely a (often distorted) part of a patient's personal past (van der Kolk & McFarlane, 1996, p. 19).

Memory of the trauma will remain an alien pathogenic force "until a person learns to remember simultaneously the affect and cognition associated with the trauma through access to language" (van der Kolk & van der Hart, 1995, p. 167). Unless traumatic experience is organized on a linguistic level it will return "as somatic sensations, behavioral reenactments, nightmares, and flashbacks" (p. 172). Until this is done, "the traumatic experience/memory is, in a sense, timeless. It is not transformed into a story, placed in time, with a beginning, a middle and an end (which is characteristic of narrative memory)" (p. 177).

Van der Kolk described the practical therapeutic process in his account of a woman who putatively survived the disastrous 1942 Coconut Grove fire in Boston, only to have memories of it return in 1984. In the course of therapy, heterogeneous symptoms, some of them seemingly psychotic in nature, were interpreted and said to be resolved through articulation to the famous story of the fire (van der Kolk, 1987). However, it is not clear from the case account that the woman was even verifiably involved in the fire, or instead had found an autobiographical place for it post hoc. As van der Kolk himself said elsewhere, it is not so much the raw trauma that matters, but how much of the survivor's life comes to revolve around memory of it afterwards (van der Kolk & McFarlane, 1996).

Could not the fire-related memories just as well have found a place in some other story, as long as the coherence criterion was met? As Spence said, "the search after meaning is especially insidious because it always succeeds" (1982, p. 108). To be sure, not just any story will do; I doubt, for example, if the patient in this case would have found an abduction narrative acceptable, but another might well have served. I do not think that such people should be regarded merely as the passive dupes of ignorant or manipulative Svengali-style therapists; they will always be bringing *something* of themselves to the therapeutic encounter, something that allows a given interpretation to catch hold. Nevertheless, the Coconut Grove fire story and alien abduction narratives have much in common in that the personal histories of those involved have come to revolve around these putative events, which—given the nature of the recovery process— can be seen as believed-in imaginings with uncertain truth value. However it is accomplished, once emotion and memory actually fuse, they supposedly become part of an integral unalienated life. That is spiritual growth: painful, necessary—*and* creative.

CONCLUSION

Van der Kolk's observations about dramatic plot construction are straight out of Aristotle's *Poetics*. Likewise, the ancient concept of catharsis turns out to occupy an intriguing place in the theory that healing can be brought about through narrative autobiographical reconstruction, the creation of a personal myth. Such an idea is not far from the thoughts of van der Kolk and his colleagues themselves, and very close indeed to Mack, who invoked actual myths that seemingly justify the premise that alien contact reaches far back into the human past. Myths are needed: "Individuals and societies without coherent myths about having successfully transcended adversity lack the identity necessary to serve as a guide on how to structure responses to current challenges" (McFarlane & van der Kolk, 1996, p. 29). To have a coherent future-directed life, one must have a coherent life story, a plot line rather than a meaningless jumble. This is why giving a name to one's affliction (PTSD, borderline personality disorder, trauma-induced ADHD, etc.) is so important at the onset of the process (Kenny, 1996; Ziporyn, 1992).

"People seem to be unable to accept experiences that have no meaning; they will try to make sense of what they are feeling. Once people become conscious of intrusive elements of the trauma, they are likely to try to fill in the blanks and complete the picture" (van der Kolk, 1996, pp. 296–297). Helping them do so—establishing a presence where once there was an absence—thus becomes an important therapeutic goal. Along the pilgrimage route toward this goal there will be the usual ritual phases of the rite of passage, in which the emergence of strong emotion is a dependable and necessary element pointing toward realization, integration, and transcendence. Emotion and narrative truth are thus closely linked (Sarbin, 1986).

Van der Kolk and others in the trauma field have come to the conclusion that archaic traumatic memories will and must be activated in the transference relationship with the therapist: "the trauma, almost inevitably, will be revived in the therapeutic relationship. . . . The taming and utilization of these transference expressions of the trauma to integrate past horror with current experience is one of the great challenges in the therapy of traumatized patients" (van der Kolk & van der Hart, 1995, p. 179; see also Davies, 1996). Because traumatic memories are necessarily veridical, so, according to this theory, the emotions must also be veridical or at least the patterns of emotional interaction that accompany them. But I ask the question one last time: Are they?

Catharsis, like the ecstasies associated with sudden religious conversion, can be seen as an important phase in the creation of a new social identity. Yet the area is full of obscurities: On the one hand there is real suffering and the avoidance of things we would rather not know. On the other hand is the search for causes of this suffering that are compatible with the orientation of specific researchers and their clients, the general state of psychological knowledge, and the social–political concerns of the time. Whether catharsis is therapeutic in itself beyond the immediacy of the moment is an open question; one must judge this in terms of the long-term psychological *and* social effects.

I have shown that strong emotion validates abduction narratives and MPD, and that a theory of catharsis, which originated with Aristotle, was refracted through Breuer and Freud and further developed by a host of latter-day traumatologists, can lead down a number of more or less exotic and questionable paths. But I do not want to throw out the baby with the bath water. Speaking as an anthropologist, the ritual process model of emotional expression and cathartic release has great appeal. Aristotle knew that participating in or witnessing a well-constructed drama can have a personally transforming quality and even civic value; one can say the same thing for psychotherapy if conceived of in dramatic terms. Aristotle may or may not have conceived of catharsis as purgation; more likely he thought of it as articulation and balance. In his thoughts on Greek tragedy, Nietzsche held that in any event purgation is the *wrong* interpretation of ritual drama, that its original function was "*not* so as to get rid of pity and terror, not so as to purify oneself of a dangerous emotion through its vehement discharge—it was thus Aristotle misunderstood it—but, beyond pity and terror, to *realize in oneself* the eternal joy of becoming" (Nietzsche, 1992, p. 51).

I have discussed the relation between emotion and becoming, emotion as part of a creative ritual process expressive of cultural assumptions about the relation between feeling, rationality, and history. I have illustrated that the same essential theory can have a number of practical expressions. That cathartic emotional release can have therapeutic value seems beyond question, but there can also be unintended and unpleasant side-effects if emotion is naively taken to be a sign of the objective truth of memory.

REFERENCES

American Psychiatric Association. (1994). *Diagnostic and statistical manual of mental disorders* (4th ed.). Washington DC: American Psychiatric Press.

Aristotle. (1988). *The politics.* Cambridge, England: Cambridge University Press.

Bleuler, E. (1950). *Dementia praecox or the group of schizophrenias* (J. Zinkin, Trans.). New York: International Universities Press.

Breuer, J., & Freud, S. (1955). Studies on hysteria. In *The standard edition of the complete psychological works of Sigmund Freud* (Vol. 2). London: Hogarth Press. (Originally published in 1895)

Caruth, C. (1995). Recapturing the past: Introduction. In C. Caruth (Ed.), *Trauma: Explorations in memory* (pp. 151–157). Baltimore: Johns Hopkins University Press.

Darwin, C. (1965). *The expression of the emotions in man and animals.* Chicago: University of Chicago Press.

Davies, J. M. (1996). Dissociation, repression and reality testing in the countertransference: The controversy over memory and false memory in the psychoanalytic treatment of adult survivors of childhood sexual abuse. *Psychoanalytic Dialogues, 6,* 189–218.

Freeman, M. (1993). *Rewriting the self: History, memory, narrative.* London: Routledge.

Hacking, I. (1995). *Rewriting the soul: Multiple personality and the sciences of memory.* Princeton, NJ: Princeton University Press.

Hare, R. D. (1993). *Without conscience: The disturbing world of the psychopaths among us.* New York: Pocket Books.

Herman, J. (1992). *Trauma and recovery.* New York: Basic Books.

Kenny, M. G. (1981). Multiple personality and spirit possession. *Psychiatry, 44,* 337–358.

Kenny, M. G. (1986). *The passion of Ansel Bourne: Multiple personality in American culture.* Washington, DC: Smithsonian Institution Press.

Kenny, M. G. (1995). The recovered memory controversy: An anthropologist's view. *The Journal of Psychiatry and the Law, 23,* 437–460.

Kenny, M. G. (1996). Trauma, time, illness, and culture: An anthropological approach to traumatic memory. In P. Antze & M. Lambek (Eds.), *Tense past: Cultural essays in trauma and memory* (pp. 151–171). New York: Routledge.

Kenny, M. G. (1997). Trauma, memory, and catharsis: Anthropological observations on a folk-psychological construct. In S. Lindsay & J. D. Read (Eds.), *Recollections of trauma: Scientific research and clinical practice* (pp. 475–481). New York: Plenum Press.

Kluft, R. P. (1996). Treating the traumatic memories of patients with dissociative identity disorder. *American Journal of Psychiatry, 153*(7), 103–110.

Krystal, H. (Ed.). (1968). *Massive psychic trauma.* New York: International Universities Press.

Krystal, H. (1988). *Integration and self-healing: Affect, trauma, alexithymia.* Hillsdale, NJ: The Analytic Press.

Krystal, H. (1995). Trauma and aging: A thirty-year follow-up. In C. Caruth (Ed.), *Trauma: Explorations in memory* (pp. 76–99). Baltimore: Johns Hopkins University Press.

Kuhn, T. (1962). *The structure of scientific revolutions.* Chicago: University of Chicago Press.

Lesser, I. M. (1981). A review of the alexithymia concept. *Psychosomatic Medicine, 43*(6), 531–543.

Lesser, I. M., & Lesser, B. Z. (1983). Alexithymia: Examining the development of a psychological concept. *American Journal of Psychiatry, 140,* 1305–1308.

Loftus, E., & Ketcham, K. (1994). *The myth of repressed memory: False memories and allegations of sexual abuse.* New York: St. Martin's Press.

Lutz, C. A. (1988). *Unnatural emotions: Everyday sentiments on a Micronesian atoll and their challenge to Western theory.* Chicago: University of Chicago Press.

Mack, J. E. (1994). *Abduction: Human encounters with aliens* (2nd ed.). New York: Ballantine.

McFarlane, A., & van der Kolk, B. A. (1996). Trauma and its challenge to society. In B. A. van der Kolk, A. C. McFarlane, & L. Weisaeth (Eds.), *Traumatic stress: The effects of overwhelming experience on mind, body, and society* (pp. 24–46). New York: Guilford Press.

Niederland, W. G. (1964). Psychiatric disorders among persecution victims. *Journal of Nervous and Mental Disease, 139,* 458–474.

Nietzsche, F. (1992). *Ecce homo* (R. J. Hollingdale, Trans.). London: Penguin Books.

Perry, C. W. (1988). Hypnotic age regression techniques in the elicitation of memories: Applied uses and abuses. In H. M. Pettinati (Ed.), *Hypnosis and memory* (pp. 128–154). New York: Guilford Press.

Putnam, F. W. (1989). *Diagnosis and treatment of multiple personality disorder*. New York: Guilford Press.

Rief, W., Heuser, J., & Fichter, M. (1996). What does the Toronto alexithymia scale (TAS-R) measure? *Journal of Clinical Psychology, 52*(4), 423–429.

Ross, C. A. (1989). *Multiple personality disorder: Diagnosis, clinical features, and treatment*. New York: Wiley.

Sacks, O. (1995). An anthropologist on Mars. In O. Sacks, *An anthropologist on Mars: Seven paradoxical tales*. Toronto: Vintage Canada.

Sarbin, T. R. (1986). Emotion and act: Roles and rhetoric. In R. Harré (Ed.), (pp. 83–97). Oxford, England: Basil Blackwell.

Showalter, E. (1997). *Hystories: Hysterical epidemics and modern media*. New York: Columbia University Press.

Sifneos, P. E. (1973). The prevalence of "alexithymic" characteristics in psychosomatic patients. *Psychotherapy and Psychosomatics, 22*, 255–262.

Sifneos, P. E. (1996). Alexithymia: Past and present. *American Journal of Psychiatry, 7*(2), 137–142.

Simon, B. (1978). *Mind and madness in ancient Greece: The classical roots of modern psychiatry*. Ithaca, NY: Cornell University Press.

Solomon, R. C. (1976). *The passions*. Garden City, NY: Anchor Press.

Spanos, N. P. (1996). *Multiple identities and false memories: A sociocognitive perspective*. Washington, DC: American Psychological Association.

Spence, D. P. (1982). *Narrative truth and historical truth: Meaning and interpretation in psychoanalysis*. New York: Norton.

Tavris, C. (1982). *Anger, the misunderstood emotion*. New York: Simon & Schuster.

Taylor, G. J. (1984). Alexithymia: Concept, measurement, and implications for treatment. *American Journal of Psychiatry, 141*(6), 725–732.

Taylor, G. J. (1994). The alexithymia construct: Conceptualization, validation, and relationship with basic dimensions of personality. *New Trends in Experimental and Clinical Psychiatry, 10*(2), 61–74.

Taylor, G. J., Bagby, R. M., & Parker, J. D. A. (1991). The alexithymia construct: A potential paradigm for psychosomatic medicine. *Psychosomatics, 32*(2), 153–164.

Terr, L. (1994). *Unchained memories: True stories of traumatic memories lost and found*. New York: Basic Books.

van der Kolk, B. A. (1987). *Psychological trauma*. Washington, DC: American Psychiatric Press.

van der Kolk, B. A. (1994). The body keeps the score: Memory and the evolving psychobiology of posttraumatic stress. *Harvard Review of Psychiatry, 1*, 254–265.

van der Kolk, B. A. (1996). Trauma and memory. In B. A. van der Kolk, A. C.

McFarlane, & L. Weisaeth (Eds.), *Traumatic stress: The effects of overwhelming experience on mind, body, and society* (pp. 279–302). New York: Guilford Press.

van der Kolk, B. A., & McFarlane, A. C. (1996). The black hole of trauma. In B. A. van der Kolk, A. C. McFarlane, & L. Weisaeth (Eds.), *Traumatic stress: The effects of overwhelming experience on mind, body, and society* (pp. 3–23). New York: Guilford Press.

van der Kolk, B. A., Pelcovitz, D., Roth, S., Mandel, F. S., McFarlane, A., & Herman, J. L. (1996). Dissociation, somatization, and affect dysregulation: The complexity of adaptation to trauma. *American Journal of Psychiatry, 153*(7), 83–93.

van der Kolk, B. A., & van der Hart, O. (1995). The intrusive past: The flexibility of memory and the engraving of trauma. In C. Caruth (Ed.), *Trauma: Explorations in memory* (pp. 158–182). Baltimore: Johns Hopkins University Press.

Waitzkin, H., & Magana, H. (1997). The black box in somatization: Unexplained physical symptoms, culture, and narratives of trauma. *Social Science and Medicine, 45*(6), 811–825.

Yapko, M. (1994). *Suggestions of abuse: True and false memories of childhood sexual trauma.* New York: Simon & Schuster.

Young, A. (1996). *The harmony of illusions: Inventing post-traumatic stress disorder.* Princeton, NJ: Princeton University Press.

Ziporyn, T. (1992). *Nameless diseases.* New Brunswick, NJ: Rutgers University Press.

V

CONTRASTING
AGREEMENTS

16

THE POETIC CONSTRUCTION OF REALITY AND OTHER EXPLANATORY CATEGORIES

THEODORE R. SARBIN

In this commentary, I try to illuminate and clarify three constructions used in the preceding chapters: truth, emotion, and reality. Several of the contributors employed these constructions to spell out the social psychological and epistemic processes involved in assigning to imaginings the properties of belief. My comments are intended to reduce the penumbra of ambiguity that surrounds each of these constructions. In so doing, I hope to show that the negotiation of truth, the shaping of reality, and the complex actions we call emotions can be regarded as poetic constructions. I use *poetic* in its original sense of making, fashioning, and configuring in the context of telling stories.

The preceding chapters have provided data and argument to support the notion that under some conditions, imaginings are assigned a degree of credibility ordinarily reserved for the perception of objects and events

My thanks to Sanford Berger, Ralph Carney, James Mancuso, and Karl Scheibe for discussions that were most helpful in the preparation of this essay.

in the real world. It is important to emphasize that we, the contributors to this book, intended our use of the term believed-in imaginings to serve as a relatively neutral descriptor. Such a neutral term allows us to separate the moral judgments that may be assigned to the articulation of any particular believed-in imagining from the study of the social psychological and epistemic processes involved in belief. That is to say, the frameworks of social and cognitive psychology are well suited for understanding how believings are formed and negotiated. However, the declaration that a particular believed-in imagining is good or bad, appropriate or inappropriate, warranted or unwarranted, wicked or benign, cannot be understood outside the framework of moral judgment and behavior. Thus, Clark's discussion of the magical powers attributed by children to their transitional objects (chapter 5), Victor's descriptions of people who claim satanic ritual abuse (chapter 11), de Rivera's observations of people who made accusations of abuse and later recanted (chapter 10)—these and other believed-in imaginings—can be described without employing the implicit moral verdicts contained in the medically inspired vocabulary of hallucination and delusion.

In chapter 2, Wiener asserts that classifying the conduct of Joan of Arc as believed-in imaginings distorts the narrative. Although I agree with his premise that any description has implicit rhetorical and judgmental properties, I respectfully disagree with his contention that my assignment of Joan's claims to the category "believed-in imaginings" is unwarranted. He suggests that we accept at face value her declaration that she heard the voices of long-dead saints. If we followed this advice, we would be implicitly concurring with the ontological basis of her claims. I prefer the position taken by scholars of history: holding in abeyance the truth value of her claims and instead finding a more neutral way to describe her claimed conversations with supernatural beings. From our contemporary perspective, identifying her claims as believed-in imaginings places no value judgment on her claims or her actions.

A HISTORY OF TRUTH

The story of Joan of Arc reminds us that it is a common human practice to "make" truths. Under the political control of the English military, the ecclesiastical court, with its coercive and legitimate power, made the decision as to what was true and what was false and she was excommunicated. No longer under the protection of the Church, the English put her to death. At a later time, the Church, with its charismatic and legitimate power, repudiated the truths made by the first court. Joan's claims were thus assigned truth value, and 500 years later she was elevated to sainthood. A modern-day psychiatrist might enunciate still another truth by reframing Joan's claims with the aid of recent editions of the *Diagnostic and Statistical Manual* of the American Psychiatric Association. Needless to add, the practice of diagnosing her claims as delusional or hallucinatory removes them from the wider domain of political and religious history and places them in the narrower domain of Kraepelinian psychiatry.

Without accepting or rejecting her ontological premise, I would treat Joan of Arc's believings as arising from the same propensities and skills that characterize all members of the human species. My analysis identifies believings as human actions, not cranial objects, that arise from multiple sources: from commerce with the empirical world through induction, and from imaginings. The actor constructs his or her beliefs from either or both sources: the empirical world and the world of imagination. These worlds provide the inputs for storied accounts that through discourse with self and others may be expressed as propositions that serve as guides to action. It is important to add that the shaping factors for many imaginings are in stories related by authority figures: not only parents, teachers, and religious leaders, but also journalists and television talk show hosts, books, tabloids, and other print media.

A discourse on the concept of truth is especially pertinent to the claims of people who, during participation in psychotherapy, claim truth for their rememberings of abuse that purportedly occurred decades earlier. The alleged perpetrator of the abuse denies the allegations and claims truth for the denial. The same conflict of truths applies to people who claim having been victims of satanic ritual abuse in the face of overwhelming evidence that such victimization did not occur. The literature on multiple personality is replete with truth conflicts—the so-called multiple and his or her therapist make the claim of multiplicity as denoting a truth; the critics offer a contrary truth claim. This all-too-common state of affairs invites a discussion of how to resolve contrary claims to truth.

Concern with the notion of truth has a long and controversial history. At the heart of the controversy are contrary major premises: Some argue from the premise that an absolute truth exists to be discovered by science or by revelation; others argue that truth is constructed through discourse. Etymology is sometimes helpful in deciphering the meanings of currently used words. The word *truth* appears to have been derived from the root for *trust*. It is related to *troth*, which carries the connotation of fidelity. When John Doe makes a claim, then, his discourse partner might covertly inject the query, "Are his statements true?" A constructed affirmative answer would then provide a basis for trust.

Those who hold to the absolutist conception appeal to "facts" as the basis for discovery of truth. In ordinary discourse, facts are differentiated from fiction. Both *fact* and *fiction* are, however, etymologically distant cousins. *Fact* derives from *facere*, to make or to do, *fiction* from *fingere*, to invent or to make. A moment's reflection will lead to the conclusion that both facts and fictions are constructed in discourse. In general, that which we call facts are subject to, and sometimes derived from, empirical tests. Fictions, of course, are not subject to test. One could test the fact that the earth is round, but no test exists to establish the truth value of the adventures of Alice in Wonderland.

The history of truth making in jurisprudence and in science provides support for the constructed and discursive nature of truth. That truth is made rather than discovered is supported by examining the history of jurisprudential testing for truth. In the Middle Ages, truth was established by employing institutional devices such as the ordeal, the oath, and the judicially sponsored duel (Lea, 1866/1974). The torture of the ordeal was considered to be an efficient means of discovering truth. In the context of early church practices, the authorities operated on the basis that God was omniscient and omnipresent and would not intervene in the ordeal if the accused was testifying falsely. In the same religious context, swearing an oath was a means of warranting the truth of a claimant. Because a plaintiff and a defendant might both take the oath, the institution of compurgation or co-swearing came into being. The litigant might bring in a dozen or more compurgators (often kinfolk) who would take the oath. The compurgators did not testify as witnesses to the events under litigation. This institution continued because of the belief that oaths were solemn covenants between the compurgator and the Deity. When two persons were in conflict over the truth of a claim, the judicial (usually ecclesiastical) authority could issue an order that a wager of arms be conducted. For centuries, judicial-sponsored duels provided a means of establishing a litigant's claim to truth.

From our present perspective, hardly anyone would question the conclusion that these early jurisprudential procedures were the instruments for *making* rather than discovering truths. We still employ the oath despite the observation that perjury is the most common (if unpunished) crime (Misner, 1988). However, in modern jurisprudence claims to truth must be supported by evidence rather than the purported intervention of the Deity. The judge and the jury are the contemporary truth makers, the employment of complex rules of evidence providing some, but not complete, assurance of fairness.

As in jurisprudence, history records the evolution of truth making in science. Beginning in the 18th century, the practice of science was conducted not by identified scientists but by gentlemen (Shapin, 1994). To be a gentleman meant honoring the virtue of truth telling with its implication of trustworthiness. Furthermore, the findings of gentlemanly scientists were communicated, not to the uneducated public, but to a relatively small core set of other gentlemen experimenters. Because they followed the implied rules of truth making, such as spelling out the experimental procedures and identifying the logical steps in reaching a conclusion, they were regarded as legitimate authorities by members of their core set. The gentlemanly tradition contained the rule that a proposition regarded as true at Time$_1$ would be rejected or modified as the result of evidence introduced at Time$_2$. The discourses, in the main, had to do with the phenomena of chemistry and physics, such as the reciprocal relation of volume, pressure, and temperature of gases. To a great extent the gentlemanly traditions prevail in scientific discourse, now augmented by the institution of peer review. As in earlier times, the core set of serious scientists engaged in any particular research forum is relatively small.

However, the gentlemanly tradition and the concern with the virtue of trustworthiness has all but disappeared from claims advanced about phenomena such as multiple personality, satanic ritual abuse, abduction by extraterrestrial aliens, and other instances of what we have called believed-in imaginings. In an age dominated by mass media, the core set of interested parties is no longer a small number of like-minded scientists committed to the virtue of trust and to the rules of evidence to support their claims. Rather a person may write about a single case and become an instant expert in the eyes of a public that follows the practice of believing any story unless an effort is made to disbelieve (as outlined by Gerrig and Pillow in chapter 6). Haaken (chapter 14) has commented on the therapeutic encounters of the psychiatrist and a young client, the notes of the encounters serving as the basis for the popular book, *Sybil*. This book appears to have been the impetus for an epidemic of multiple personality diagnoses (Hacking, 1992).

Now appealing to the masses as a core set are instant experts who appear on television talk shows, whose ideas are published in tabloids and newsletters, and who, failing to subscribe to the rules of gentlemanly inquiry, make extravagant truth claims. Most of the consumers are not qualified to pass judgment on the merits of the claims of these journalistic and television experts. Some of those who adopt the status of authority may have credentials, such as MD or PhD, but, unlike the heirs of the practitioners of gentlemanly discourse, they assign no credibility to contrary conclusions drawn from experiments conducted within the constraints of science, such as those reported by Loftus (1997); Kihlstrom (1996); Spanos (1996); and Lynn, Pintar, Stafford, Marmelstein, and Lock (chapter 7, this volume).

In both jurisprudence and science, we have come a long way on the road from the ordeal to gentlemanly inquiry conducted according to rules for supporting truth claims. The conclusion to this brief historical survey is that truths are created out of narrative discourses. Claimants to multiple personalities, to memories of events that may not have happened, to space travel in alien spaceships, and even to the existence of Santa Claus and his reindeer, assign truth value to their claims. To understand such claims to truth in the face of contrary evidence and gentlemanly argument invites inquiry into the narrative contexts of the claimants. Such an inquiry leads to the hypothesis that the act of assigning belief to one's imaginings flows from reasons influenced by one's self-narrative.

EMOTION

The concept of emotion was used by Gerrig and Pillow (chapter 6) and by Vinden (chapter 4), who employed the term in a general way to suggest that the fear inspired by an imagined event perdures and contributes to the decision to avoid a similar event. Interested in how people "transport" themselves from the world of art (books or movies), Gerrig and Pillow point to the persisting effects of reading the story of a man poisoned by drinking a Coca-Cola that had been laced with cyanide. They invoke the notion of the stimulus to action being the "feeling" (presumably the physiological accompaniment of action) and add the opaque term "cognitive effects."

Would it not be more parsimonious to recognize that the reader had been provided with narrative resources to emplot an imagined story rather than positing the residual effects of "emotion" as a cranial or visceral object? To the extent that the actor continues to be involved in the imaginatively created plots, he or she will make behavioral choices influenced by belief. Although the actor's preferred soda is Coca-Cola, the cyanide narrative leads him to ask for Seven-Up. In addition to the narrative emplotted from inputs provided by the art form, the actor constructs a parallel story: to present oneself to others as a rational being, that is, not to be seen as believing in, and acting on, his or her art-inspired imaginings. The actor could *publicly* express belief in such a parallel story ("I can differentiate between real danger and imagined danger") but *privately* hold the belief in the potential danger of drinking the soda.

The causal attribution of the complex conduct of believing to vaguely defined or undefined emotion fails to make intelligible the transformation of imaginings to believings. As Averill (1974) has so convincingly demonstrated, the word *emotion* is most often located in a semantic space labeled "psychophysiological symbolism." Often used interchangeably with *feeling*, the term *emotion* has evolved into a marker for sensed events within the body. To conclude a causal connection between bodily perturbations and the formation of believings is at best an oversimplification. More useful is the concept "emotional life," a derivative of one's ongoing life narrative. Common emotion terms, such as anger, love, grief, and jealousy, are names for cultural narratives rather than bodily perturbations.

I have elsewhere reported the results of an informal study, which support the distinction between "emotion" and "emotional life" (Sarbin, 1995). In the course of ordinary social conversation, I would ask my informant (most often a psychologist) to define *emotion*. In over 80 cases, with hardly an exception, the informants provided definitions that would qualify as instances of psychophysiological symbolism. Most of the definitions were constructed around bodily "feelings."

After the informant indicated that he or she was satisfied with the definition, I asked the informant to give an example of emotion. The exemplifications of *emotion* rendered by the informants were remote from the definitions that had been uttered only a few minutes before. The exemplifications made no mention of bodily states. They were presented as narratives with multiple actors, told with a beginning, a middle, and an ending. In all cases, the stories hinged on the protagonist (usually the self) relating emotional experiences such as "anger," "jealousy," and "fear" to some moral conflict and its resolution. Thus, reframing Gerrig and Pillow's "emotion" to "emotional life" would direct us to examine the person's involvements in cultural or idiosyncratic stories. Instead of focusing on bodily perturbations, the behavior analyst interested in the study of believed-in imaginings would entertain hypotheses drawn from the person's current life narrative.

REALITY

Any discussion of imagining must include the connections, if any, between what is imagined and what is real. In Western ontologies, the construction that is set off as the opposite of imagining is reality. "Real" is an attribution and can be applied not only to mundane objects but to abstractions (e.g., country, *Vaterland*, soul). The person can place a high value on such abstractions and declare, for example, belief in souls and their peregrinations. In the Western intellectual tradition, the world of things is separate from the world of imagination, the former being more privileged as the basis for reality. Note the relative prestige value of *Naturwissenschaften* over *Geisteswissenschaften* in providing inputs for the construction of reality.

In chapter 1, I discuss briefly Cohen's argument that the words *real* and *reality*, have no place in rational argument. They are "excluder" words; they convey not what something is, but rather what something is not, and then only if the discourse partner knows the context in which this vocabulary is employed. Austin, the philosopher of ordinary language, spoke directly to the issue:

A "real duck" differs from the simple "a duck" only that it is used to exclude various ways of not being a real duck—but a dummy, a toy, a picture, a decoy, etc.; and moreover I don't know *just* how to take the assertion that it's a real duck unless I know *just* what . . . the speaker has it in mind to exclude. This, of course, is why the attempt to find a characteristic common to all things that . . . could be called "real" is doomed to failure. (Austin, 1962, p. 70)

In the present context, we could ask what is excluded when a person uses the word *reality*. The answers are not clear cut. Vinden (chapter 4) describes the behavior of people in an exotic culture who assign truth value to the assertion that a dangerous pig is really a malevolent person. As seen in chapter 17, de Rivera favors the argument that there must be some ultimate reality, and Scheibe (chapter 3) devotes his essay to the "question of authenticity—how objects and experiences are taken as real or not real." It is often overlooked that the term *reality* is derived from the Latin *res*, meaning things. In common parlance, if an entity has "thing character," it qualifies as real. Thing character is tested by ponderability, having shape, color, and other physical attributes. As I said earlier, in the Western intellectual tradition, the world of things is more privileged in constructing reality claims. However, as Vinden (chapter 4) writes, some non-Western cultures do not draw a hard and fast line between such worlds. Perceptions, imaginings, and rememberings are equally privileged as sources of reality construction. Even in the Western world in earlier times, authorities such as St. Augustine regarded the world of corporeal objects as a less adequate resource for reality construction than intellectual and spiritual worlds.

In chapter 17, de Rivera offers a description of reality as "brought into presence." If taken literally, one would be adopting the spiritualist position (like the account of Bishop Pike in chapter 1) and act as if a nonvisible spectral ghost-like entity is present. I find the evidence for spiritualism noncompelling. Observations of the conduct of children telling ghost stories better reflects the metaphor of "brought into presence." The ghosts are imaginatively constructed, and the children's security-seeking conduct implies that they assign high negative value to the imagined ghosts.

"Bringing into presence" is a useful metaphor. The reader of Tolkien's stories, such as *The Hobbit* (1937) that is peopled by elves, leprechauns, trolls, dragons, and other mythical creatures, becomes involved in the fanciful stories with their detailed descriptions of landscapes, flora and fauna, and other details that provide the basis for verisimilitude. The reader is "brought into presence" through the artistry of the author and bookmaker. "Bringing into presence" requires no spiritualist component. It is an apt alternate metaphor for the process that Gerrig (1993) described as "being transported." The fictional story has the potential of transporting the reader from his workaday world into the world of the book. Both metaphors, "bringing into presence" and "transporting" reflect the creative exercise of the imagination.

To argue that *reality* does have functional meaning requires that one brackets the objects of analysis as if he or she were a realist. In everyday life, even the most ardent constructionist engages in such bracketing. Vinden's observations of esoteric cultures in which perceptions, imaginings, and believings appeared to be undifferentiated did not constrain her from writing ethnographic reports using English syntax and categories common to ethnographers and developmental psychologists. To take the position that the world is socially constructed is not to say that nothing exists out there. We can assume that something is out there. How we construe that something and what we call it are the products of construction and negotiation.

In what ways are perception of the physical world and imagining alike and in what ways are they different? Under some stimulus conditions, a perception may be taken for an imagining, and vice versa. Perky (1910) demonstrated this for visual perception. The numerous demonstrations of sensory suggestibility make clear that perceptions and imaginings can be confused. Ordinarily, perceptions can be differentiated from imaginings under conditions of low personal involvement and low stimulus ambiguity in that there can be immediate feedback. I can engage in reality testing of my wall by trying to walk through it. Empirical reality testing is neither possible nor appropriate for imaginings inasmuch as imaginings are comprised of hypothetical instantiations of *absent* objects or events.

When "recovered memory" clients come to believe that they participated in satanic rituals, they place a high value on their stories, which provide them with narrative substance to maintain or enhance their failing identities. In the context of the therapeutic milieu in which client and therapist were conjointly trying to make sense of conflict, contradiction, frustration, failure, and so on, the claims to having participated in satanic rituals provided some coherence to the self-narrative. From knowledge acquired from other sources (e. g., Lanning, 1992), we know that the satanic story is not authentic, it is fictional.

We can grant a world made up of natural objects, such as trees and mountains, and human artifacts, such as trains and totem poles. This would be a transcultural world. There are also transcendental worlds created by human beings, and these worlds are different cross-culturally and even between individuals. For many people in the world, even today, the devil is as real as the kitchen stove.

Historical sources make the case that the devil is a construction initially created as a means of social control. From my perspective, the devil is an imagining. Like the believer, most of us have the skill to imagine the devil. Our imaginings are influenced by storybook pictures, by religious stories, even by movies. Most of us attach no special value to imaginings of the devil, regarding this construction as belonging to a class of imaginatively inspired theological forms. Thus we regard the devil and the kitchen stove as belonging to different ecological classes: The devil is a member of the class of fictional or imagined objects, the stove is a member of the class of human-made artifacts. In ordinary language, the stove is real in that it is ponderable and has shape, color, and function. For the believer, the devil is as real as the stove, even in the absence of tests for ponderability, shape, and so on, the attribution of reality flowing from convincing stories told with the imprimatur of authority.

Some of the contributors in this volume (e.g., Wiener and Vinden) have questioned the necessity of the believed-in imagining conception. Lest we become entangled in efforts to establish absolutist and final meanings for our terms, it is instructive to remind ourselves of the phenomena that stimulated the organization of this book. Consider this reference case: A man renders an account that he had been abducted by extraterrestrial creatures, transported in a circular aircraft to a place in intergalactic space, subjected to numerous indignities, and deposited by his abductors in his back yard, all within a period of 60 minutes. Rational arguments offered by scientists and theologians fail to convince him that his narrative is fictional. Assuming that the man is not intentionally deceiving his audience, we can reasonably infer that the imagined narrative is a segment of his reality. The process of believing in the extraterrestrial story is no different from "bringing into presence" or "transporting" (discussed before) when becoming involved in imaginative tales, such as *The Lord of the Rings*, *The Wind in the Willows*, *The Wizard of Oz*, and *Alice in Wonderland*.

What makes this reference case interesting is the observation that the claimant and the counterclaimant do not employ the same rules for establishing truth, and they subscribe to different views of reality. The counterclaimant cites time–space restrictions and the absence of credible corroboration. The counterclaimant can also point to the ready availability of extraterrestrial stories in the public media and in the movies as the prime source of the claimant's narrative.

As ambiguous as it is, human beings (at least in the Western world) need an ontological construction such as "reality" against which to assess fiction or imaginings. But we cannot get away from the premise that reality is a social construction, a premise so well articulated by Berger and Luckman (1966). Having said this, it would be fatuous, for example, to say that the brick wall is only a social construction. One quickly learns that you cannot walk through brick walls. However, the meanings we assign are social constructions: Is the brick wall a form of protection, or is it a prison?

The 18th-century philosopher, Jeremy Bentham, wrote: "To language, then—to language alone—it is that fictitious entities owe their existence, their impossible, yet indispensable existence" (1827/1931, p. 21). I would extend Bentham's assertion and substitute *narrative* for *language*. "Fictitious entities" are the characters and their supporting environmental features in stories told and stories read. The contributions of Lynn et al. (chapter 7), Morawski (chapter 13), Kenny (chapter 15) and Victor (chapter 11) make the case clearly for looking upon believed-in imaginings as being guided by narrative plots.

A final word. The stories of interest to students of believed-in imaginings are often filled with terror. The accounts of unconfirmed cannibalism, incest, rape, infanticide, and so on, have their progenitors in the sagas, legends, and folktales of historically distant cultures. For as long as human beings have been able to exercise the imagination, that is, to tell stories, they have molded imaginings that have the power to fascinate, to enthrall, and to terrify. These imaginings may be as real as the demons, dragons, gods, fairies, and elves that filled the universe when civilizations were young.

REFERENCES

Austin, J. L. (1962). *Sense and sensibilia*. London: Oxford University Press.

Averill, J. (1974). An analysis of psychophysiological symbolism and its influence on theories of emotion. *Journal for the Theory of Social Behavior, 4,* 147–190.

Bentham, J. (1932). *Bentham's theory of fictions*. London: Kegan Paul, Trench, & Trubner. (Original work published 1827)

Berger, P. L., & Luckman, T. (1966). *The social construction of reality*. New York: Anchor Books.

Gerrig, R. (1993). *Experiencing narrative worlds*. New Haven, CT: Yale University Press.

Hacking, I. (1992). Multiple personality and its hosts. *History of the Human Sciences, 5,* 3–31.

Kihlstrom, J. F. (1996). The trauma memory argument and recovered memory therapy. In K. Pezdek, & W. P. Banks (Eds.), *The recovered memory/false memory debate* (pp. 297–311). San Diego: Academic Press.

Lanning, K. V. (1992). *Investigator's guide to allegations of "ritual" child abuse* (2nd ed.) Washington, DC: National Center for Missing and Exploited Children.

Lea, H. C. (1974). *The duel and the oath*. Philadelphia: University of Pennsylvania Press. (Original work published 1866)

Loftus, E. F. (1997). Creating false memories. *Scientific American, 277,* 70–75.

Misner, G. (1988, April). *Perjury: The most common crime*. Paper presented at the convention of the Academy of Criminal Justice Sciences, San Francisco, CA.

Perky, C. W. (1910). An experimental study of imagination. *American Journal of Psychology, 21,* 422–452.

Sarbin, T. R. (1995). Emotional life, rhetoric, and roles. *Journal of Narrative and Personal History, 5,* 213–220.

Shapin, S. (1994). *A social history of truth*. Chicago: University of Chicago Press.

Spanos, N. (1996). *Multiple identities and false memories*. Washington, DC: American Psychological Association.

Tolkien, J. R. R. (1937). *The hobbit*. Boston: Houghton Mifflin.

17

EVALUATING BELIEVED-IN IMAGININGS

JOSEPH DE RIVERA

The concept of believed-in imaginings is intended to be nonperjorative, a nonpathological way of describing how any person may come to believe things that others (often at different times or in different circumstances) may regard as untrue, even ridiculous or bizarre. However, because what is imagined is often contrasted with what is actual, to call something a believed-in imagining may itself be taken as a devaluation as though a believed-in imagining is something that is not real. Because of this dichotomy between the imagined and the actual, the concept of believed-in imagining may be attacked either for saying too little or for implying too much. On the one hand, Wiener (chapter 2) appears to be saying that *all* narratives are believed-in imaginings or, at least, that there is no way to distinguish a believed-in imagining from a believed-in actuality. On the other hand, Vinden (chapter 4) appears to argue that the concept reduces all believing to imagining and to impoverish reality by implying that pragmatic actuality is all that exists.

In this chapter, I address these concerns. First, I take the empirical, secular, perspective of social science on believed-in imaginings, the perspective that Sarbin (chapter 1) takes and address Wiener's (chapter 2) critique from this perspective. Second, I examine the "a-rational" perspective implicit in Vinden's (chapter 4) plea for some reality that is not socially constructed. This examination leads me to look at the concept of reality, Scheibe's (chapter 3) attempt to go beyond pragmatic tests of what is real by using the concept of dynamic authenticity, and the nature of the emotion that is implied in authenticity. Finally, returning to the nature of reality, I draw on the work of a contemporary philosopher to propose a way of evaluating the reality captured by believed-in imaginings.

AN EMPIRICAL PERSPECTIVE

The concept of believed-in imaginings is designed to describe how people in our culture can come to honestly believe—take as real—things that have no factual support and to describe how they can sometimes become entrapped in what are illusions, at least to those committed to a rational perspective. The experimental studies reported in this volume—those by Kirsch (chapter 9); Mazzoni and Loftus (chapter 8); and Lynn, Pintar, Stafford, Marmelstein, and Lock (chapter 7)—establish that people can be led to hold beliefs that are clearly counterfactual.

Of course, when we do not have experimentally controlled variables, there will always be some disagreement about whether a belief is an imagining; Wiener (chapter 2) argues that, in the absence of experimental controls, we can never be sure whether or not a given belief is an imagining. Certainly, we cannot rely on popular vote. There are thousands of people who believe in facilitated communication, the repression of memories of satanic cults, and alien abductions. Wiener appears to argue that one belief is as likely to be as veridical as another, but, at least insofar as a belief makes a general claim about empirical reality, this position seems impossible to defend. To illustrate his position, Wiener charges Sarbin with using words that bias the listener's judgment, and he replaces these words with more "neutral" words that make the beliefs seem more credible. However, as Wiener himself expounds, words are never neutral. Rather, their use must be defended, and, if we are using them to refer to empirical reality, they cannot be used as arbitrarily as Wiener imagines. I would argue that in the examples given by Sarbin, Sarbin's words rather than Wiener's are justified by the empirical facts. If the accuracy of word use is in question, third-party judges can examine the evidence and collect more if it is necessary.

To the extent that people claim that phenomena are matters of fact, their claims must be subject to empirical tests, the presence or absence of evidence, and the critique of logic and common sense. If people who use pragmatic reasoning and are open to evidence are not convinced of the existence of a phenomenon that claims empirical support, we may presume the phenomenon is a believed-in imagining. There may be initial doubts, but putative phenomena such as facilitated communication, satanic ritual abuse, and the recovery of repressed traumatic memories, like cold fusion, are being increasingly dismissed as illusory.

Thus, from a rational perspective, the concept of believed-in imaginings appears to be a useful tool for understanding how people may come to have counterfactual beliefs. There are, however, many beliefs that do not claim pragmatic existence. Joan of Arc did not suppose that other people could hear the voices she heard and took to be divinely inspired. Wiener raises the question of whether her belief was a believed-in imagining. Was she delusional, following the will of God, or a witch?

AN A-RATIONAL PERSPECTIVE

It must be admitted that the rational world view emphasized by our culture is not the only possible world view. Whenever we attempt to understand other cultures (including preenlightenment European culture), we find ourselves dealing with world views that do not prioritize rationality and personal agency. In order to make sense of another culture from our own rational perspective we speak of their "beliefs." Even when we try to craft a historical narrative that captures the point of view of other people, we find ourselves distancing from them by using the concept of belief and, essentially, using the concept of believed-in imagining.

For example, rather than dealing with the external causes of the Santal rebellion of 1855 (as a traditional British historian of India might), Guha (1988) attempted to make the insurgent peasant's consciousness (their will and reason) the subject of a historical narrative about the rebellion. However, the peasent leaders denied their subjecthood or agency! They stated that their God (Thakur) made an appearance, issued a divine command to fight, and assured them that British bullets would not harm his devotees. They stated that it was Thakur and not themselves who were fighting.

In his critique of Guha's account, Chakrabarty (1997) noted that there is no way for Guha to "give us a narrative strategy that is rationally-defensible in the modern understanding of what constitutes public life. The Santal's own understanding does not directly serve the cause of democracy or citizenship or socialism. It needs to be reinterpreted" (p. 23). In the narrative of the rebels, the rebellion was not secular. What we might call the supernatural was part of the Santal's public life. However, Chakrabarty observed, "the professional historian must tell a narrative . . . in which the idea of historical evidence, like evidence allowed in a court of law, cannot admit of the supernatural except as part of the nonrational (i.e., somebody's belief system)" (p. 23).

Chakrabarty appreciated the value of rational historical narratives and noted that our own culture's secularizing enables us to construct the social sciences and is tied to the way in which our society searches for justice. However, he was also sensitive to the fact that there are other modes of public being in the world. "The supernatural can inhabit the world in these other modes and not always as a problem or result of belief; the supernatural or the divine can be brought into presence by our practice" (1997, p. 30).

Of course from a pragmatic standpoint this is no different from how Sarbin articulates believed-in imaginings. That is, if we act as if something is present and become fully involved in the enactment, then the believed-in imagining will be instantiated—that is, taken as real. However, from a nonpragmatic standpoint, "brought into presence" does not simply mean taken as real (which implies that which is illusory); rather, it asserts a spiritual reality or a spiritual dimension to reality.

Vinden (chapter 4) makes the important point that many cultures do not have a sharp boundary between the material or natural world and the immaterial or supernatural world. Rather than divide the world into separate spheres, these realities are seen as interpenetrating. Magic or miracles exist; they are just as real as the facts and explanations of the material world. In fact, whereas we may refer magic and miracles to a supernatural dimension of being, Werner (1948) pointed out that in children, and for peoples who believe in magic, there is no complete differentiation among magic, religious activity, and nature. He established the existence of "primitive" organizations of thought in which behavior is relatively undifferentiated, less articulate and definite, and more rigid and labile. In such primitive thinking, everything exists in action, and objects are understood as animate in the same way as we may perceive a landscape as being sad or cheerful. Likewise, the difference between subjective and objective is not as clearly defined, so that dreams and wishes may be treated as being intimately connected with reality.

Objects are primarily understood through motor and affective attitudes. Whereas adults in our culture tend to make distinctions among perceiving, imagining, feeling, thinking, moving, and so on, primitive thought tends to unify these events and often not distinguish subject and object. Thus, "things" do not exist in their own right but exist as "signal-things." A dog is not an objective structure with parts but something that bites or that one pets. Motor and affective elements are merged in the perception of things such that the objects of perception have dynamic powers and magical properties. This is inherent in primitive perception. The world perceived by primitive people is filled with what we might categorize as magical entities that reflect fears and desires. When a traditional Papuan rubs his back and leg against rocks to obtain strength and durability, or when one burns a lock of someone's hair to injure an enemy, the person is not making magic by analogy or imagining an as-if behavior. In primitive thought modes, the person is actually bringing the strength or harm into being through the magical activity.

Werner noted

> the basic tendencies of magic behavior proceed out of a kind of thinking which, although deviating from the western man's point of view, is quite intelligible and in no sense is of mysterious import to the native himself. . . . It is natural that things should be mutable in essence. . . . Only in higher civilization, where material and supernatural events are completely separated and where magic does not pervade the whole culture, is it possible for the specifically mystical experience to develop. (1948, p. 352)

As was noted by Vinden (chapter 4), even those of us who live in highly civilized cultures may be able to engage in primitive thinking when our emotions are engaged, as when we hesitate to drink from a water bottle on which we have pasted a cyanide label. Let the reader observe the defenses enacted if he or she burns out the eyes of a loved one's face from a photograph.

Our own culture, or at least a dominant segment of its people, has rejected a good deal of the interpenetration of supernatural and natural worlds in favor of rational explanations. Science and rational thought have extended the realm of our control over much of the material world so that we have less use for magic and dismiss many beliefs as superstitions. Although some flirt with ghosts, angels, and other spiritual beings, they are likely to regard them as figurative or metaphorical rather than taking them seriously. For most, such immaterial beings are not-believed-in imaginings.

We have learned that there are many things in the world that do not exist. At least we *think* we have learned that. A skeptic might suggest that our hold on rationality is quite tentative, and that past beliefs have merely been replaced by beliefs in the influence of repressed memories, UFOs, and, of course, Satan (or his demonic material counterparts in the form of communists, terrorists, homosexuals, sex-abusers, etc.). Also, although it is clear that many academics view religious beliefs as opiates, the majority of people subscribe to some sort of belief in God and spiritual reality, although this tends to be underutilized and quite removed from their belief in science and the material world.

In fact, it may be argued that Western society's emphasis on rationality and personal agency is actually a consequence of its adoption of the Judaic–Christian narrative of creation. In this narrative the world is regarded as created by God, and, hence, is worthy of our attention, and individuals are regarded as created in God's image.

Hillman (1975) for example, pointed out that our modern world view confines subjectivity and agency to human people. He stated,

> The Christian idea of person as the true focus of the divine and the only carrier of soul is basic to this world view. . . . We do not believe that imaginary people could possibly *be as they present themselves*, as valid psychological subjects with will and feelings like ours but not reducible to ours. (pp. 1–2)

He argued that we should stop insisting that our egos are the only things that really exist. Rather, ghosts, angels, gods, and mental illness are a part of our psyche, and we should grant them agency and would do well to let them be and deal with them.

Thus, Hillman argued that what most in our culture take to be real —an empirical world of fact in which only people (and not gods, angels, and demons) are agents—is itself a believed-in imagining. Applying Sarbin's reasoning to ourselves, we might argue that empirical reality alone is real because of our complete involvement in such a world. And we are left with Vinden's plea for some reality apart from believed-in imaginings.

REALITY AND AUTHENTICITY

Sarbin (chapter 1), citing Cohen, argues that to say something is real is a rhetorical claim (i.e., that one's belief has credibility) rather than a descriptive term. For Sarbin the claim that a believed-in imagining is real masks the process that is involved. It would be more useful to speak of the extent to which one is involved in as-if behavior. The higher the degree of involvement, the more the actor will interpret the imaginings as veridical perceptions, will drop as-if qualifiers, and claim "reality" for what is imagined (see also the "perception of reality" offered by Morawski in chapter 13).

In one sense this is clearly so. In fact, Sarbin's analysis also pertains to observers of as-if behavior. A number of years ago I was working with a graduate student on the experience of realness. She witnessed a group of three children who were having a "parade" in front of a house with their saucepans and other accouterments. At first she was somewhat embarrassed for the children because they were taking their parade so seriously. However, her perception soon changed and her embarrassment ceased. The children were so involved in their imagining that she decided they had created a real parade.

In another sense, however, the relegation of reality to involvement seems to miss some important nonempirical referents of the term *real*. Sarbin assumes that imaginative constructions—"poetic narratives"—have no connection with a reality apart from themselves. From his perspective any claims about reality must simply reflect the degree to which the person is involved in the poetry of the narrative. This, however, reduces realness to mere pragmatic reality. To portray all believed-in imaginings as equally illusory implies that all poetic narratives are not real in spite of the fact that some aspects of reality—emotional experience, for example—are better captured by poetry than by prose. And certainly if art criticism has any merit and is not simply a matter of taste, works of art can be objectively judged as capturing some aspect of outer or inner reality. For example, there is agreement between discerning viewers who know a medium as to whether aspects of a work are contrived or reflect spontaneity and the personality of the artist. Good works of art are highly personal. Whereas people expect scientists to come up with the same observations of an event, we expect artists to come up with different renditions of the same referent. As Macmurray (1961/1979) stated,

> If two painters were to produce identical representations of the same scene, the genuineness of the work of the one or of the other or of both would at once be questionable. Either one would be a copy of the other one or both mere mechanical reproductions of the scene, using the same technique but devoid of genuine emotional reflection. (p. 18)

This facet of reality appears to be what Scheibe is referencing when he speaks of dynamic authenticity.

Scheibe (chapter 3) argues that tests of authenticity, which involve matching against a standard, have limited usefulness. In part they are limited because we are often biased by our beliefs and, in part, because we can never reproduce the historical context in which events occur. Whereas some inauthenticity may be revealed by pragmatic tests (e.g., a counterfeit coin or bill), the inauthenticity of much of modern life is revealed by its dramatic poverty. Scheibe clearly values the aliveness present in good drama. Although he does not directly address the question of why reproductions are of less value than originals, we might conjecture that he would say that reproductions are less authentic because the spontaneous emotion that led to the original creation is absent in the reproduction. Perhaps this is the reason why Scheibe appears to argue that emotion is what gives the mark of authenticity to an event. It is inherent in good drama. And in the event he relates—the ceremony of initiation into adulthood—it seems clear that emotion is an integral part of the ceremony. Ceremonies and rituals that *work*—so that a person really becomes an adult, or married, or dead—must involve emotion in order to succeed in transforming social reality (see Denison, 1928, p. 15).

However, Scheibe suggests that all emotion that is felt rather than feigned is real emotion. Of course, in one sense he is certainly correct. We can distinguish between *acting* as if one has an emotion and *feeling* the emotion. However, the extent to which an emotion is felt may simply reflect the depth of the person's involvement in a believed-in imagining that is illusory. Kenny (chapter 15) shows how it is a mistake to use emotion as an index of veridicality. When Scheibe argues that all felt emotion is real, this relegates emotion and feeling to the realm of subjectivity. Yet there are strong grounds for arguing that emotions have a cognitive dimension, that they are about the reality we perceive. From this perspective emotions may be as true and valid, or as false and mistaken, as our perceptions of reality. Just as a perception may prove to be an illusion, an emotion may be illusory even though it is strongly felt.

I am not speaking here of what we might call emotional mistakes. These are simply due to misinterpretations of objective reality as when a person who is hurt or angry at not being invited to a party discovers that he or she actually was invited, or when a slight was perceived but not intended. Rather I am referring to mistaken emotion. For example, Merleau-Ponty (1962, pp. 378–383) distinguished between illusory or imaginary feelings and actual feelings by referring to Scheler's distinction between the outer fringes and the core of the self. Thus, he spoke of feelings that are simply reflective of one's current situation (pleased at receiving a present, sad because one is at a funeral) as opposed to being moved at the core of one's being. The adolescent in love is familiar with narratives such as that of Romeo and Juliet and infuses the feelings of these narratives into his or her own life. However, this is largely sentimental fantasy and until a "personal and authentic feeling" occurs, the person has no way of discovering the illusory, literary element in the love. Thus, the person loses reality in the emotional narrative as an actor does in the part he or she plays. For Merleau-Ponty, one only gradually makes his or her own reality by acts of love or hatred that are directed toward real others.

THE NATURE OF EMOTION

Sarbin (chapter 16) argues that our emotional life is an aspect of our narratives and a result of how events effect the identity claims we make in these narratives. Although there is much to be said for this view, it seems important to note that there are two other important aspects of emotion. First, there are times when emotions appear to be an impetus for narratives. This occurs for some people much of the time and for many people some of the time. There are some whose fear leads them to anticipate danger in any unknown situation or whose anger leads them to repeatedly create hostile encounters. I remember one incident when my own anger created a narrative. I was meditating in a large group of people and became angry when I noticed that someone had turned up the heat in the meditation hall. The pleasant coolness of the hall was spoiled by someone who preferred heat and unilaterally inflicted it upon us. As I observed my anger grow, I noticed that it was making me hot; as it passed, I grew cooler. Finally, I realized that no one had turned up the heat in the hall. The heat I had attributed to some inconsiderate moron had been the heat of my own anger. Although that anger may have sprung from some unconscious narrative, it clearly formed the basis for the spinning of a believed-in imagining.

Second, even when emotion is a response to events that are shaped by a narrative, the emotion itself is not simply a reaction to those events or a narrative plot. Although I agree with Sarbin that it is not useful to regard emotions as bodily perturbations or states, I would also not reduce them to narrative plots. Narrative plots include stories of revenge or romantic love, and include anger or love, but they are not the emotions of anger and love per se. Rather, anger, love, and other emotions are aspects of the relationship between the actor and others involved in the narrative. They are "choices" or "judgments" that reveal the value of the object of the emotion and, accordingly, transform the embodied stance or "attitude" of the actor (see de Rivera, 1977; Solomon, 1984).

Macmurray (1932/1992), like Merleau-Ponty, distinguished between real and unreal feelings. For Macmurray, feelings grasp the value of things or people. When feeling ceases to be directed toward the person or thing with which it is connected, it becomes unreal. A bad temper may lead to unreal anger in that the person at whom we were angry only occasioned our outburst of anger. The anger was not really directed at the other. We may be in love with the feeling of love rather than the person whom we supposedly love, or we may refuse to admit that we are jealous when we really are.

Often, in fact, we are more concerned with enjoying our feelings than with enjoying the person or object we are engaged with. According to Winston (1996), viewers who prefer popular art (large-eyed children, idealized maidens, scenes of country life) are seeking the warm pleasant feelings produced by the image rather than feeling the dynamic tonal properties of high art images. They are being sentimental rather than experiencing a work of art per se. Speaking of reading a sensationalized story, Macmurray noted that "the feelings are unreal feelings, not because they are not felt, of course, (they are apt to be very intense), but because they are not grasping the real value of the story" (1932/1992, p. 102). To say that felt emotion is necessarily real is to say that emotions are merely subjective and, because values are intimately connected with emotions, that values are subjective. I want to argue that although emotions are always *personal*, and although they *may* be subjective, they ideally are objective in the sense that they reveal what is objectively valuable for the person and, hence, are tied to personal reality.

When Scheibe reports that farm life was real for him and movies an escape, but that he now sees people for whom movies are real, is he merely making a value-free observation, or does he want to argue that farm life is objectively more real? If the latter, is this simply because there are more constraints, more pragmatic matters that must be dealt with, or is it somehow more authentic? Certainly farm life brings us to our senses, demands we use our bodies, forces us to deal with the properties of things that we cannot control. This does not seem to merely invoke pragmatic tests, but authentic emotions. Let us contrast this, not with the life of mind, for this is authentic when one's ideas are one's own, but with the TV life that many are living today.

Many people become involved in TV soap operas and have "parasocial" interactions with the characters in the program, feeling comfortable with them, missing them, sending them baby presents, and so on. A recent study concluded, "While they are a functional alternative for those who seek but cannot handle real relationships, they are even more attractive for others who are not interested in real relationships in the first place" (Vorderer, 1996, p. 122). Is the love that motivates people to send presents to a baby born in a soap opera as real as the love that motivates people to help a neighbor's baby or to sponsor a child in a developing country, or is the former emotion unauthentic and the TV narrative unreal?

REALITY

What do we mean by "real"? Macmurray (1992) argued that something that is real is not necessarily something that exists in a pragmatic sense, but something that is significant, has consequences, and provides meaning to our lives. In one sense, Sarbin does not disagree with this, for he equates believing and hence organismic involvement with the value that a narrative has for the person. However, for Sarbin the reality of a believed-in imagining is simply a function of this involvement, an index to it. To the extent that we are dealing with narratives, at least with nonrational narratives, one person's reality is another's fantasy, and all involve illusion. At least, there is no way of distinguishing between them without the possibility of empirical tests. By contrast, for Macmurray, a believed-in imagining may be real or illusory: One acts as if a friend is faithful, and the friend may prove to be faithful or false.

For Macmurray, the rational includes science, pragmatic tests, and historical narratives, but it is not limited to that domain. It also includes art criticism, for an artistic object may or may not express spontaneity and capture the form of an object as it is uniquely experienced by the individual artist; it includes religous thought; and it includes feelings, which may or may not be in touch with external reality. Furthermore, whereas rocks, plants, and animals cannot be unreal, people can be. People are not always themselves. They may engage in unreal thinking by thinking about matters that have no significance, or by dealing with generalities for which no examples can be provided, or by divorcing their thought from its application to their lives. They may engage in unreal feeling. They may be engaged in self-deception (Shapiro, 1996). We are often called upon to confirm or disconfirm another's emotions and identity. If we fail to confirm genuine feelings we cause pain, whereas if we confirm unreal ones, we support pretenses and reinforce self-delusion. If we confirm another's pretensions in exchange for their confirming our own, we become engaged in what Keen (1937/1975) terms a collusion, and we become locked into static identities that ignore contrary evidence. To the extent that a person's thinking or feeling is unreal, the person will be unreal. If a person has no real feelings, he or she must rely on external authority. Feeling divorced from thought becomes sentimental and at the mercy of tradition, feeling what one is supposed to feel, or feeling what is stimulated rather than one's own feelings. To be real is to be oneself, and that can only occur when one's actions are directed to the world.

If reality simply depends on the degree of our involvement, then valuing is a subjective phenomena in that there are no values apart from the narrative. One poetic narrative is as good as another as long as one is sufficiently involved. Yet this does not ring true. When Jesus becomes so involved in the narrative told by Isaiah that he offers himself as the sacrificial lamb for his people, we personally may or may not become involved in the narrative, accept his sacrifice, and take him as the Messiah, but we all recognize a significant narrative, a narrative having some sort of authenticity, of touching some sort of reality. Jesus cannot be dismissed as delusional in the way we may dismiss a contemporary who claims that he is Jesus (see Schweitzer, 1968/1975).

Is Wiener correct that the dismissal of a contemporary who claims to be Jesus is solely a function of our not giving credence to the narrative? Or is the narrative less compelling because it is less in touch with what is objectively valuable, with what is personally real? Just as we can be mistaken about empirical reality, we can be mistaken about interpersonal reality, we may trust in someone who betrays us, and we may live in the illusion that we are hated when we are actually loved. Likewise, we may live in the illusion that there is a meaning we can give our lives or in the delusion that there is no such meaning. There is an ultimate Reality. We simply cannot be sure what it is.

DISTINGUISHING REALITY FROM ILLUSION

The chapters in the book have attempted to clarify the psychological and social antecedents of believed-in imaginings. However, we may also inquire into how we might evaluate believed-in imaginings. One possibility is suggested by Macmurray's work (1961/1979). For Macmurray, as for Sarbin, the person is an agent, an actor, who is necessarily involved in social relationships. However, rather than grounding the analysis of these relationships in narratives, Macmurray grounded narratives in the motivational underpinnings of personal relationships. He asserted that there are always two central motivations present: a caring for the other and a concern for the self. At any moment, one of these motivations will be dominant. When caring for the other dominates a person's activity, the ego recedes, the person is available for mutuality, and there is a working relationship between imagined ideals and perceptions of the actual. People can trust one another and be themselves in friendship, and then they can struggle to unite the ideal and the actual. However, whenever people are hurt—either apparently or actually abandoned, betrayed, or injured—their concern for themselves becomes dominant, the ego becomes defensive, and the ideal world of imagination is split off from action in the perceived world. The dualistic thinking with which we are plagued—the separation of mind from body, feeling from reason, ideals from pragmatism, the self as presented from the self as felt—are symptoms of this splitting. Unity is achieved only when the person manages to restore the dominance of caring.

As long as concern for the self and the split between imagining and perceiving continues, people will either be "good," submitting to authority, conforming to custom, and identifying themselves with the social roles in whatever drama is being played out in their society, or they will be "self-serving," seeking power to protect the interests of the self. In the former case, they will use imaginings to create a fantasy life, and this ideal realm, divorced from the actual world, will be what is real for them. In the latter case, the imagination will simply be used to gain power, ideals will be viewed as unrealistic, and only pragmatic concerns will appear real. Because both cases are based on a concern for the self, one may conjecture that the underlying fear will be reflected in fearful narratives. When unity is restored by the person caring for what is other than him- or herself, the imagination will be used to create, and works will be spontaneous rather than contrived, friendships genuine, actions authentic, the person real.

We may use Macmurray's reasoning to evaluate the reality of any narrative. Let us consider those discussed by Wiener. In the case of a narrative based on a recovered memory of childhood sexual abuse, we may ask whether the narrative restores the client's ability to care for others and, hence, unifies the self, or whether it produces more self-concern and fragments the self. We know that when abuse has actually occurred, communication about that abuse is restorative in the manner outlined by Pennebaker (1993). By contrast, the narratives that are based on the idea of repressed or disassociative memories of traumatic abuse appear to have led clients to become more fearful and to lose their ability to love and to work.

An example is provided by the State of Washington's Victim Compensation Program (Loftus, 1977). In 1991, an amendment to the Crime Victims Act allowed individuals to request compensation if they suffered from the return of repressed memories. In the succeeding years, 325 people were awarded compensation. In 1996, a sample of 30 of these cases was selected for review. In 26 cases the first memory surfaced during therapy. Before the repressed abuse narratives were related (29 of these involved satanic ritual abuse), 3 people had attempted or thought of suicide, 2 had been hospitalized, and 1 had engaged in self-mutilation. At the time of the study—after the narrative and therapy—20 were suicidal, 11 had been hospitalized, and 8 had mutilated themselves. Before the narratives, 25 had been employed, and 23 were married. After the narratives, only 3 were employed, 11 of the 23 who had been married were separated or divorced, and all were estranged from their families of origin. This suggests that such narratives are illusory rather than real.

In the case of the Heaven's Gate deaths, we may note that the narrative of joining a space ship was not used to gain strength for a project in this life. Rather, it appears to be a use of imagining to compensate for unsatisfactory life experiences. The leader had been badly betrayed by a colleague, and we may conjecture that he became self-concerned and was unable to restore the dominance of his ability to care. It is also apparent that many of the members were disillusioned and found no meaning in living in this world. They were unable to care for things outside themselves. The notes that were left indicate that the "the essential rituals for . . . transmutation" (as Wiener puts it) were motivated by self-concern rather than by caring for others.

In the case of the retired postal worker who reported conversations with saints, we do not have enough details to engage in a motivational analysis. We would want to know what the voices said. Did they encourage him to act with charity to others, and did he do so, or did the voices simply relieve loneliness and secure needed attention? We are more fortunate in having these details about Joan of Arc.

In the case of Joan of Arc there are conflicting believed-in imaginings. Factually, we know that Joan, a peasant girl, reported that she heard the voices of various saints who, when she was 16, exhorted her to aid the Dauphin of France to recapture the throne of France from the English. There was a prophecy that France would be redeemed by a virgin from Lorraine, and she gradually succeeded in enlisting some supporters and eventually convincing the Dauphin himself that she was divinely inspired. She then persuaded the court to allow her to play a leading role in an expedition to relieve the siege of Orleans. Inspired by her presence, the French defeated the English in a series of important battles, and the Dauphin was (reluctantly) crowned as she had prophesized. In a later battle she was captured and turned over to a pro-English ecclesiastical court. She was tried for witchcraft and heresy (her claim that she was directly inspired by God was perceived to subvert the authority of the church hierarchy). Imprisoned and shackled, alone (save for the constant presence of five British soldiers who sometimes attempted to rape her), and without any legal assistance, she fought off her persecutors throughout a lengthy trial. However, after a verdict of guilty separated her from the church and made death inevitable, she recanted her belief, was condemned to life imprisonment, and was led back to her cell. She then retracted her abjuration and was burned at the stake. Just before her death, she prayed for the forgiveness of all those involved in her death. Her calm presence and last words so moved those assembled that a British soldier gave her a crucifix, many in the hostile audience became convinced of her innocence, and the executioner confessed that he had burned a saint. A latter, pro-French, court declared her innocent, and after 500 years she was canonized (Sackville-West, 1936).

These are the empirical events. What are we to make of the narratives? Many of the British believed she was a witch and that it was the use of witchcraft that allowed her to overcome their troops. She, and her French supporters, believed she was divinely inspired. How may we ourselves evaluate these conflicting narratives? Clearly, Joan was completely involved in her narrative, convinced others as to her claims, and altered the history of France. However, this says nothing about the objective reality of her narrative. However, when we examine the motivations underlying the two narratives, the differences seem clear.

The narrative of witchcraft was fear-based, as was the first court's desire to maintain the hierarchical authority of the church, and Joan's brief recanting of her belief. By contrast, Joan's narrative involved caring for her country, and the details of her life reveal concern for the soldiers she was with, and sympathy for the English troops (whose deaths she clearly mourned). Although it might be supposed that she wanted attention and that her ego was enlarged by her narrative, the evidence suggests that she simply wanted to fulfill the mission she was given by her voices. Finally, she died as she had lived, with the sort of purity and unity that impressed all those who knew her. Thus, an analysis in terms of motives supports her narrative as having the more reality.

It may, of course, be objected that such a judgment simply reflects Christian values of love, and it is true that analysis in terms of love for others and fear for oneself is fully compatible with the Christian narrative presented in the Gospels. However, I would argue that the analysis is compatible with all religious traditions. Elsewhere (de Rivera, 1989), I have attempted to show that although different societies differ in the defenses that they use, they agree as to valuing the unity that is achieved when ego concerns are subordinated to caring for what is other than the self.

Religion itself, of course, can be subjected to this analysis. After observing that all religion is concerned with overcoming fear, Macmurray (1979) noted that one can distinguish real from illusory religion by the way fear is overcome: "The maxim of illusory religion runs: 'fear not; trust in God and he will see that none of the things you fear will happen to you'; that of real religion, on the contrary, is 'fear not; the things that you are afraid of are quite likely to happen to you, but they are nothing to be afraid of'" (p. 171). That is, illusory religion is defensive, seeks security, and is grounded in the fear of life, whereas real religion is heterocentric, for the sake of something other than the ego. For Macmurray, religion is empirical in its search for reality, and philosophy should be a natural theology. Religious doctrines, like scientific theories, require constant revision and verification. However, although this verification must include pragmatic concerns, it must also go beyond them. Consequently, verification can only be by the commitment of people to the way of life prescribed by the religious doctrine in question.

Narratives that involve the denial of empirical facts, whether that involves the denial of sexual abuse within families or churches, the denial of poorly conducted psychotherapy, the denial of the effects of poverty within the United States, or the denial of the disappearance of people in Argentina, are narratives that are defensive, believed-in imaginings that are dominated by fear. However, there are also narratives that go beyond empirical fact, believed-in imaginings, that are dominated by love, compassion, and faith in the reality what we can never completely grasp. Such narratives minimize our defenses and our pain, help us live openly, help us care for one another.

REFERENCES

Chakrabarty, D. (1997). Minority histories subaltern pasts. *Humanities Research. 1,* 17–32.

Denison, J. H. (1928). *Emotion as the basis of civilization.* New York: Scribner.

de Rivera, J. (1977). *Structural theory of the emotions.* New York: International University Press.

de Rivera, J. (1989). Love, fear, and justice: Transforming selves for the new world. *Social Justice Research, 3,* 387–426.

Guha, R. (1988). The prose of counterinsurgency. In R. Guha & G. Chakravorty Spivak, (Eds.), *Selected subaltern studies* (pp. 46–47). New York: Harper & Row.

Hillman, J. (1975). *Re-visioning psychology.* New York: Harper & Row.

Keen, E. (1937). *A primer in phenomenological psychology.* New York: Holt, Rinehart & Winston.

Loftus, E. (1977). Repressed memory accusations: Devastated families and devastated patients. *Applied Cognitive Psychology, 11,* 25–30.

Macmurray, J. (1979). *Persons in relations*. Atlantic Highlands, NJ: Humanities Press. (Original work published 1961)

Macmurray, J. (1992). *Freedom in the modern world*. Atlantic Highlands, NJ: Humanities Press. (Original work published 1932)

Merleau-Ponty, M. (1962). *Phenomenology of perception*. London: Routledge & Kegan Paul.

Pennebaker, J. W. (1993). Putting stress into words: Health, linguistic, and therapeutic implications. *Behavior Research and Therapy, 31*, 539–548.

Sackville-West, V. (1936). *Saint Joan of Arc*. Garden City, NY: Doubleday.

Schweitzer, A. (1968). *The quest of the historical Jesus*. New York: Macmillan. (Original work published 1906)

Schweitzer, A. (1975). *The psychiatric study of Jesus*. Gloucester, MA: Beacon Press. (Original work published 1913)

Shapiro, D. (1996). On the psychology of self-deception. *Social Research, 63*, 786–800.

Solomon, R. C. (1984). Emotions and Choice. In C. Calhoun & R. C. Solomon (Eds.), *What is an emotion?* (pp. 305–358). New York: Oxford University Press.

Vorderer, P. (1996). Positive emotions in aesthetic appreciation. *Proceedings of the Conference of the International Society for Research on Emotions, 14*, 121–123.

Werner, H. (1948). *Comparative psychology of mental development*. New York: International Universities Press.

Winston, A. S. (1996). Positive emotions and popular art. *Proceedings of the Conference of the International Society for Research on Emotions, 14*, 124–126.

AUTHOR INDEX

Numbers in italics indicate names that appear in the reference list.

Gerrig, R. J., 102, 103, 104, 109, 110, 117, 118, 304, 307
Gerstel, G., 238, 244
Gilbert, D. T., 103, 104, 117, 118
Go, S., 99
Goldstein, E., 174, 187, 208, 213
Goleman, D., 207, 213
Gollwitzer, P. M., 162, 163, 167
Gondolf, L. P., 208, 213
Good, B., 96, 97, 99
Goode, E., 190, 195, 199, 211
Goodman, G. S., 130, 142, 195, 196, 210, 212
Goodwin, G., 195, 203, 213
Gorassini, D. R., 161, 168
Gould, C., 195, 203, 213
Graham, S. M., 167
Green, J., 137, 142
Green, J. P., 139, 141
Greene, S. B., 109, 118
Gregoire, A. T., 232, 244
Guha, R., 311, 323
Gur, E., 99
Guttmacher, A. F., 236, 237, 244

Haaken, J., 249, 267
Hacking, I., 66, 68, 252, 254, 267, 279, 290, 301, 307
Hall, G. S., 247, 248, 267
Haman, J. O., 237, 244
Haney, C., 171, 187
Hard, A. D., 232, 244
Hare, R. D., 272, 282, 290
Harmer, S., 111, 118
Harris, P. L., 108, 111, 115, 118, 119
Hassan, S., 171, 187
Hawthorn, J., 252, 267
Heelas, P., 76, 77, 84
Herman, J., 280, 285, 290
Herman, J. L., 251, 256, 267, 293
Hertzig, M., 94, 99
Heuser, J., 281, 292
Hicks, R., 195, 207, 213
Hilgard, E. R., 159, 164, 167
Hill, S., 195, 203, 213
Hillman, J., 314, 323
Hirsch, F., 264, 267
Hirt, E., 130, 131, 139
Hodgins, D. C., 168
Holbreich, M., 99
Holstein, J. A., 194, 214

Hoover, R. W., 55, 68
Hopkins, B., 126, 139
Horovitz, R., 136, 139
Hostler, S. L., 208, 213
Howitt, D., 201, 202, 213
Hubbard, M., 106, 118
Hudson, P. S., 195, 203, 213
Hume, D., 24, 29
Hunt, S., 205, 213
Hunter, I., 27, 30
Hyland, M. E., 166, 167

Israel, L., 236, 244

Jackson, L., 204, 213
Jackson, M. H., 235, 237, 244
Jacobs, D. M., 126, 139
Jacobson, J. W., 164, 167
James, W., 27, 30, 50, 54, 58, 68, 159, 167, 242, 244, 247, 267
Jenkins, P., 195, 206, 207, 213
Jensen, R., 58, 68
Jesus Seminar, the, 55, 68
Jhally, S., 61, 68
Johnson, B. T., 104, 118
Johnson, P., 97, 99
Juhasz, J. B., 15, 30

Kahneman, D., 115, 118
Kaplan, A., 264, 267
Katz, S., 84
Kavanaugh, R. D., 108, 118
Keen, E., 319, 323
Keller, E. F., 231, 244
Kelley, S. J., 195, 203, 213
Kellner, H., 43, 45
Kenny, M., 252, 254, 267
Kenny, M. G., 270, 273, 279, 280, 283, 284, 285, 288, 290, 291
Ketcham, K., 186, 187, 249, 251, 267, 269, 291
Khalsa, S., 132, 140
Kihlstrom, J. F., 159, 167, 169, 187, 301, 307
Kirk, S., 256, 267
Kirsch, I., 157, 158, 159, 160, 161, 164, 166, 167, 170, 188

Michigan State Police, 197, *214*
Milgram, S., 209, *214*
Miller, A., 60, 68
Miller, G., 194, *214*
Miller, J., 77, 78, 85
Millman, L., 75, *84*
Mimura, G., 94, 99
Misner, G., 300, *307*
Misuraca, A., 94, 99
Mitchell, G. D., 239, *246*
Mollon, P., *211*
Morin, E., 198, *214*
Morrison, M., 99
Morton, J., *211*
Mulhern, S., 202, 203, *214*
Mulick, J. A., 164, *167*
Murphy, D., 96, 98
Myers, B., 132, 133, 134, 135, 136, *141,*
    142, 143

Nankin, H. R., *246*
Nash, M. R., 134, 137, *141, 142,* 165,
    167
Nathan, D., 195, 202, 204, 206, 207, *214*
Nathanson, C., 255, *267*
Needham, R., 23, *30*
Neill, A., 105, *118*
Neisser, U., 134, *143*
Nelkin, D., 231
Nelson, E. L., 208, *214*
Nemeroff, C., 75, *84*
Netherlands Ministry of Justice, *215*
Newman, L., 128, 130, *142*
Newman, L. S., 224, *228*
Niederauer, K. L., *167*
Niederland, W. G., 283, *291*
Nietzsche, F., 290, *291*
Nilkin, D., *245*
Nisbett, R. E., 160, *168*
Noblitt, J. R., 195, 203, *215*
Norman, D. A., 160, 166, *168*

O'Brien, M., 231, *245*
O'Connor, K. J., 88, 99
Office of Technology Assessment, 232,
    245
Ofshe, R., 60, 68, 204, *215,* 249, 251,
    267
Ogden, R. M., 160, *168*

Oppenheim, J., 252, *268*
Orne, M. T., 55, 57, 68, 128, *142*
Ortega y Gassett, J., 59, 68
Owen, A., 252, *268*

Pannor, R., 239, *243*
Parker, J. D. A., 284, *292*
Parkes, A. S., 235, *244*
Parr, L. E., 197, *215*
Pasketitz, D. A., 55, 68
Pauley, P., 226, *228*
Pauly, P., 231, *245*
Payne, D., 133, 134, 135, 136, *140*
Pazder, L., 130, *143,* 195, 203, *216*
Pelcovitz, D., *293*
Pendergrast, M., 170, *188,* 204, *215,* 251,
    268
Penley, C., 251, *268*
Pennebaker, J. W., 320, *324*
Perky, C. W., 305, *307*
Perry, C. W., 278, *291*
Perry, D., 255, *267*
Perskin, P. S., 195, 203, *215*
Person, E. S., 155, *156*
Peterson, S. B., 109, *118*
Petty, R. E., 104, *118*
Pezzo, M., 128, 129, *142*
Pfohl, S. J., 202, *215*
Phelps, K. E., 112, *119*
Pike, J. A., 27, *30*
Pinard, W. J., 238, *244*
Pintar, J., 128, 137, 138, *142*
Poole, D., 195, 196, *215*
Potts, G. R., 109, *118*
Potts, R., 97, 98, 99
Powers, R., 102, *118*
Prentice, D. A., 103, 104, 110, *117, 118*
Psychology Today, 156, 156
Punnett, A., 94, 99
Putnam, F. W., 146, *156,* 279, *292*

Qin, J., 130, 131, *142*
Quindlen, A., 132, *142*

Rabinow, P., 243, *245*
Radford, C., 105, *118*
Radtke, H. L., *168*
Randal, J., 256, *268*

SUBJECT INDEX

control over imagining, 101–102
distinguishing reality from imagination, 74–76, 107–111
imaginal coping. See Imaginal coping in children
imagination and behavior, 111–117
investigation of satanic ritual abuse, 204–205
representational abuse, 108–109
ritual imaginings, 87
theory of mind, 73–74
transitional object relations, 88–89
See also Development

Cloning, 51–52

Cognitive functioning
actor's perception of volition, 160–161
in age of replication, 49–51
coping strategies, 96
function, 166
hypothesis-making, 19–20
as if thinking, 20
involvement in narration, 22–24, 29
memory effects, 115
mind control account of false memory syndrome, 171, 186
nature of consciousness, 166
primitive perception of reality, 312–313
transition to belief from imagining, 22–23
transition to belief from unbelief, 22, 155–156
willing construction/suspension of disbelief, 102–106

Compartmentalization, 109–110

Constructionism, 17

Contemporary legends, 193–194

Control
escape from freedom, 225
features of UFO abduction stories, 224–225
manipulation of moral panics, 198, 201–204
mind-control account of false memory, 171, 186
over imagining, 101–102
therapy experiences of people with false memory syndrome, 173–177

Cool, Nadean, 126

Coping strategies
imagining as, 6

social interaction in, 96
See also Imaginal coping in children

Cultural beliefs, 3
about emotion, 278–279
about paternity, 240–241
alien abduction, 128
biases, 32–35, 37, 41–42
child abuse, 202
continuity, 60
as derived from film, 53–54
distinguishing reality from imagining, 6
imagined dangers, 8–9
implausible, 123
influence of, 32–35
need for wonder, 244–246
perception of reality, 76–79, 311–314
psychopathology, 131
repressed memory, 185–186
reproduction and parentage, 9–10
satanic ritual abuse, 130–131
status of women, 10
theory of mind, 73–74
as transitional space, 89
truth making and, 298–299

Cycle of meaning, 65, 66–67

Dangers and threats, imagined, 307
construction of moral deviants, 199–200
cultural beliefs, 8–9
demonology, 199–200
moral panic, 192–195
pseudomemories induced by dream interpretation, 152–154
satanic ritual abuse, 200–201
symbolic resonance, 205–207

Deception, 75

Deconstructionism, 82, 83–84

Decoupling of representations, 108

Defensive process, dissociative identity disorder as, 7

Demonology, 199–200
symbolic resonance, 205–207

Determinism, 166

Development, 5–6
adult phenomenon, 106
children's festivals, 87
earliest memory, 134
interest in novelty, 63
muting speech, 21
skill in imagining, 20–21, 102

Development (*continued*)
   use of props in imaginative acts, 108
   See also Children
Diabetes, 88, 90, 92, 93, 95
Disbelief
   degree of self-involvement and, 104
   developmental perspective, 106
   emotional consequences, 104–105
   willing construction/suspension of,
      102–106, 116–117
Disciplinary matrix, 34
Disney parks, 52
Dissociative identity disorder, 65–66,
    125–126
   abreaction in, 279–280
   autonomy of personalities in, 260–261
   clinical popularity, 254
   diagnostic categorization, 140–141
   diagnostic conceptualization, 256–257
   film depictions, 258
   hysterical storytelling and, 250, 254
   legitimization of psychiatry in, 256–
      257
   pathogenesis, 7, 10
   as pathology of hiddenness, 264–265
   satanic ritual abuse and, 130–131
   social construction of emotional mem-
      ory, 279
   social construction of personal narra-
      tive, 138–139
   sociocultural context, 10, 254, 255–
      256
   spectrum of pathology, 138
   in *Sybil* (book/film), 258–264
   therapeutic narrative, 10
   therapeutically-induced, 139–141, 261,
      262–263
   treatment, 257, 262–263
   as women's pathology, 254–256, 264–
      266
Doubt, 50–51
Drama, 63–64
Dramatic frame, 5
   compartmentalization of fictional infor-
      mation, 109–110
   for emotional experience, 59–60
   for evaluation of authenticity, 47
   experience of past events, 49–50, 60–
      61
   lack of context in television experi-
      ence, 61–62
Dream interpretation

false childhood beliefs induced by,
    148–152
influencing belief through, 7
mechanism of pseudomemory induc-
    tion, 154–155
pseudomemories of danger induced by,
    152–154
pseudomemory induced by, 145–147,
    148–152, 156, 205

Easter Bunny, 87
Eidetic imagery, 42
Emotional expression
   abreaction in dissociative identity dis-
      order, 279–280
   in alexithymia, 281–282
   clinical significance, 10
   hysteria, 249
   language and, 280–284
   need for, 278–280
   in psychopathy, 282
   sociocultural differences, 281
   therapeutic goals, 280
   UFO abduction experience, 275
Encoding, memory, 269–270, 286–287
Ephemera, 58–61
Errors of memory, 132
Escape from freedom, 225, 226
Expectancies, 160
   response set theory, 161
Expert witnesses, 301
Eyewitness testimony, 55

Facilitated communication, 7, 164–165,
    208
Facts, 299–300
Faith, 22
   poetic, 102–103
   transitional phenomenon, 89
False memory syndrome
   abuse experiences of people with, 182–
      183
   causal attributions of people with,
      172–173, 180–182, 183
   common features, 169–170, 183–185
   etiology, 8
   false identity construction in, 187
   mind-control account, 171
   models for development of, 170–171,
      185–187

prevalence, 170
role enactment account, 172
self-narrative account, 172
therapy experience of people with, 173–180
Feminist thought
concept of hidden knowledge, 249–250
demonology in, 206
explanatory models of mediumship, 248–249
implications of hypnotic pseudo-memory, 251–252
significance of multiple personality, 10, 254–256, 264–266
Fictional accounts
acceptance of, 304
catharsis as education, 273–274
construction, 299–300
emotional response, 270–271, 317–318
Flagging of representations, 108–109
Flashbacks, 42–43

Gender differences, 230
Guided imagery, 145, 205

Hallucination, 16, 39–40
Heaven's Gate deaths, 16–17, 29, 40–41, 47, 321
Helicobacter pylori, 219–220
Hidden knowledge, 249–250
History, 32
artificial reproduction concerns, 232–235
artificial reproduction technology, 231–232
collective imaginings, 191–192
conceptualizations of reality, 78–79
experience of past events, 49–50, 60–61
imaginal coping in children, 88
truth making in, 298–302
Hume, David, 24–25
Hypnotherapy
as believed-in imagining, 164
Charcot's demonstrations, 253
client beliefs, 160–161
Freud and, 250–251

intensity of emotion in, 278
pseudomemory induced in. *See* Hypnotic pseudomemory
psychoanalytic theory, 250
Hypnotic pseudomemory, 6–7, 126, 145, 204–205
age regression, 134
alien abduction, 128–129
early investigations in, 253
implications for women, 251–252
mechanism, 133–137
risk of, 133–137
satanic ritual abuse, 131
Hypothesis-making, 19–20, 132
Hypothetical instantiation, 17, 19–21
Hysteria, 249
Victorian era theorizing, 253
Hysterical storytelling
multiplicity and, 250, 254
sociocultural context, 249–250

Identity
authentification of self, 65–67
in development of false memory syndrome, 187
features of UFO abduction stories, 224–225
as social category, 65, 66
social construction, 137–141
social processes in multiple personality enactment, 10
status of implausible narratives, 127
surrender of self to external power, 225
survivor as authority, 221–222, 223
victim, 9, 209–211, 221–222
Ideology, demonology in, 206–207
Idiot savant, 42
Illusion, 319–323
Imagery, 19
Imaginal coping in children
accomodation of, in biomedical approach, 96–98
administering disliked treatment to others, 92
with chronic illness, 87–88
examples of, 90–92
kept secret by child, 92
nature of, 88–90
obstacles to, 92–94
peer interaction in illness camps, 94–96

Malls, 52–53
Media
    in satanic ritual abuse beliefs, 200, 203
    talk shows, 62
    television, 61–62
Medical care
    acceptance of fashionable treatments,
        217–220
    accomodation of child's imaginal cop-
        ing, 96–98
    camp settings for children, 94
    medicalization of social control, 201–
        202
    security in transitional objects of, 88–
        92, 97–98
    See also Imaginal coping in children
Memory/memory processes
    alexithymia and, 270
    amnesia of UFO abductees, 277
    belief and, 109–110
    compartmentalization of fictional infor-
        mation, 109–110
    construction of rememberings, 28,
        132–133
    differential encoding of trauma, 269–
        270, 286–287
    earliest memories, 134
    effects on cognition, 115
    flashbacks, 42–43
    historical continuity and, 60
    photographic memory, 42–43
    recovery techniques, 133, 134, 135
    suggestibility, 132–133
    therapeutic mechanism for recovering,
        287–288
    validated by emotion, 270
    See also Hypnotic pseudomemory
Mental health profession
    construction of satanic ritual abuse be-
        liefs, 202–204
    in creation of collective beliefs, 8–9
    medicalization of social control, 201–
        202
Meta-narrative
    postmodern views, 80–81
    role of, 6, 82
Mind's eye, 18
Moral panics, 8–9
    construction of moral deviants, 199–
        200
    indicators of, 193
    as political manipulation, 198, 202

satanic ritual abuse, 196–197, 200–
    207
    as social control, 201–204
    sociopolitical model, 192
    theoretical models, 197–198
    timing in development of, 200–201
Motivation
    automatic movements and, 160
    to confirm unprovable claims in ther-
        apy, 223
    for constructing irrational accounts, 9
    for trust, 50–51
Movies, 53–54, 317–318
    emotional response, 102, 105–106
Multiple personalities. See Dissociative
    identity disorder
Muting speech, 21
Mystery, need for, 226–228
Myth
    attractive features, 220–221
    concept of repressed memory as, 185–
        186
    features of popular beliefs, 223–225,
        226
    in perpetuating popular explanations,
        217

Naming process, 75
Narrative construction
    alexithymia treatment, 286
    believed-in imagining as, 5
    degree of self-involvement, 22–24
    denial in, 323
    development of false memory syn-
        drome, 172, 186
    development of popular explanations,
        219–223
    distinguishing reality from imagining
        in, 5
    dramatic frame, 5
    emotional life in, 316–317
    healthful, 323
    hysterical storytelling, 249
    as if thinking in, 20–21
    imagining as, 4–5, 19
    memory and, 132–133
    need for, 9
    poetic nature, 10–11, 19
    process research, 6–8
    in psychoanalysis, 249–250
    psychological function, 15

Reality
  authenticity and, 314–316
  child's understanding of, 74–76
  conceptual significance, 24, 306
  cultural conceptualizations, 311–314
  culturally-mediated, 76–79
  distinguishing from illusion, 319–323
  distinguishing from imagining, 5, 73
  functional meaning, 303–305
  historical conceptualizations, 80–81
  language and, 34
  learning to distinguish, 6
  misinterpretations of, 316
  motion pictures and, 53–54, 317–318
  naming process and, 75
  perceptions of paternity, 242–243
  of poetic narratives, 314–315
  postmodern conceptualizations, 81–84
  shared conceptualization, 82–83
  shared imaginal experience, 90
  social construction, 306, 318–319
  sub-worlds of belief, 242
  thing character as quality of, 304
  Western intellectual tradition, 303
Recanting memory, 126
Red scare, 192
Religion/spirituality, 6, 11
  children's festivals, 87
  concept of belief, 22
  concept of reality, 24
  context of early psychological theoriz-
    ing, 6
  degree of self-involvement, 26–27
  evaluating illusory beliefs, 322–323
  fear and, 322–323
  language of belief, 39–40
  in perception of reality, 311–313
  supernatural beliefs, 78–79
  Western, 78–79
Replication
  boredom and, 63–64
  commercial application, 52–53
  experience of ephemera, 58–61
  human cloning, 51–52
  of knowledge and research, 57–58
  in modern era, 48
  psychological issues, 49–51
  television experience, 61–62
Representational abuse, 108, 110–111
Repressed memory
  as cultural myth, 185–186
  popular beliefs about, 131

Repression, 16, 35–36, 38
  psychoanalytic theory, 250
Reproductive processes
  concept of paternity, 231, 241–243
  cultural beliefs, 9–10, 240–241
  historical understanding, 231
  types of believed-in imaginings, 229–
    230
  See also Artificial insemination
Repudiating memory, 38
  frequency, 184
  therapy experiences of people with
    false memory syndrome,
    173–180
Response set theory, 161–164
Restlessness, 63–64
Ritual imaginings, 87
  emotion in, 315–316
  evocation of emotion in, 270
  in therapeutic process, 270
  See also Satanic ritual abuse
Role-taking, 20–21
  alien abduction, 128–129
  degree of self-involvement, 25–26
  development of false memory syn-
    drome, 172, 179–180,
    186–187
  loop of identity, 65–66
  survivor role, 172
  victim identity, 209–210, 221–222
Rumors, 191–192

Santa Claus, 87
Satanic ritual abuse, 123, 125–126
  common features of claims, 195
  conditions for collective believing, 8–
    9
  evidence for, 196–197
  investigative techniques, 204–205
  media dissemination, 200, 203
  mental health profession in beliefs of,
    202–204
  moral panic, 196–197, 200–207
  narrative construction, 130–131
  ostension processes, 208–209
  psychotherapist perceptions, 195
  public perception, 196
  social processes in belief in, 202–204,
    210–211
  symbolic resonance, 206–207

acceptance of implausible narratives, 125–126, 127
genesis of false memory syndrome, 184
mind-control account of false memory syndrome, 171
motivation to confirm unprovable claims, 223
trauma memory recovery, 289
Therapeutic technique
alexithymia, 282–283
catharsis, 273, 279–280, 288, 289, 290
construction of implausible narratives, 127, 137
expected evocation of strong emotion, 270
experiences of people with false memory syndrome, 173–180
genesis of dissociative identity disorder in, 7, 126, 139–141, 261, 262–263
genesis of satanic ritual abuse beliefs, 207–211
investigation of child sexual abuse, 204–205
memory recovery, 133, 134, 135, 287–288
pseudomemory construction, 6–7, 8, 16, 35–39, 132–133, 145
See also Hypnotic pseudomemory; specific technique
Three Faces of Eve, The, 258, 264, 266
Transference, 289
Transitional objects, 6, 89
in child medical care, 89–92, 97–98
confiscation of, 92–94
detachment process, 94
secret, 92
Transitional space, 88
child's experience of, 88–89
defined, 88
Transmigration, 111, 112–113

Treatment narratives, 9
Trust
mind-control account of false memory, 171
motivation for, 50–51
transitional phenomenon, 89
Truth
etymology, 299
expert testimony, 301
historical conceptualizations, 298–302
narrative vs. historical, 286–287

UFO abduction, 123, 124
cultural beliefs, 128
development of belief in, 170
emotional intensity of accounts, 274–278
features of narratives, 224
frequency of accounts, 128
memory recovery, 276–277
narrative construction, 128–130, 137
victim amnesia, 277
Ulcer, 237–238
Unconscious, response set theory, 161–162
Urban legend. See Contemporary legends

Victim
constructed identity, 9
power issues in popular beliefs, 223
as rewarding role, 209–210, 221–222
survivor as authority, 221–222, 223
Visualization, 18–19, 205

Wilbur, Cornelia, 258–264
Witch hunts/witchcraft, 76–77, 79, 191–192, 199, 204, 322
World view. See Meta-narrative

ABOUT THE EDITORS

Joseph de Rivera, PhD, received his doctorate from Stanford in 1961. He is Professor of Psychology at Clark University and is well known both for his investigations of emotional experience and his work on the psychological aspects of peace and justice. His seminal work on emotions was first reported in *A Structural Theory of the Emotions*, followed by *Field Theory as Human Science, Conceptual Encounter*, and numerous chapters, journal articles, and an issue of the *American Behavioral Scientist* devoted to the qualitative analysis of emotional experience. His work in political psychology includes *The Psychological Dimension of Foreign Policy* and edited issues on peace and justice in the *Journal of Social Issues* and *Social Justice Research*. He is currently integrating these different lines of inquiry by investigating the emotional climate of different neighborhoods, cities, and nations, observing how different believed-in imaginings (such as the nation-state) affect emotional climates, and how these climates affect the way in which conflict is managed.

Theodore R. Sarbin, PhD, is Emeritus Professor of Psychology and Criminology at the University of California, Santa Cruz and, since 1987, is Senior Research Psychologist at the Defense Personnel Security Research Center. He earned his doctorate at Ohio State University in 1941. He has been the recipient of a number of awards and fellowships, among them, the Fulbright award at Oxford University, the Guggenheim fellowship, the Center of the Humanities fellowship at Wesleyan University, and recently, the Henry A. Murray Award from the Society for Personality and Social Psychology. His publication list includes almost 250 papers, reviews, and books dealing with clinical inference, emotional life, role theory, hypnosis, metaphor, social identity, espionage, schizophrenia, imagination, and critiques of psychiatric nosological systems. His current work addresses some of the problems in narrative psychology raised in his book *Narrative Psychology: The Storied Nature of Human Conduct*.

DATE DUE

GAYLORD			PRINTED IN U.S.A.